DOCUMENTS ON THE HOLOCAUST

Selected Sources on the Destruction
of the Jews of Germany and Austria,
Poland, and the Soviet Union

EIGHTH EDITION

EDITED BY

Yitzhak Arad, Israel Gutman, and Abraham Margaliot

TRANSLATIONS BY

Lea Ben Dor

INTRODUCTION TO THE BISON BOOKS EDITION BY

Steven T. Katz

Published by the University of Nebraska Press,
Lincoln and London, and

Yad Vashem

Jerusalem

Published by the University of Nebraska Press, Lincoln and London, and Yad Vashem, The Holocaust Martyrs' and Heroes' Remembrance Authority Jerusalem.
Copyright © Yad Vashem 1981, 1987, 1988, 1990, 1993, 1996
Introduction to the Bison Books Edition and Updated Selected Bibliography © 1999 by the University of Nebraska Press
All rights reserved
Manufactured in the United States of America

∞

First Bison Books printing: 1999

Library of Congress Cataloging-in-Publication Data
Documents on the Holocaust: selected sources on the destruction of the Jews of Germany and Austria, Poland, and the Soviet Union / edited by Yitzhak Arad, Israel Gutman, and Abraham Margaliot; translated by Lea Ben Dor; with new introduction by Steven T. Katz.
p.   cm.
Originally published: Jerusalem: Yad Vashem in cooperation with the Anti-Defamation League and Ktav Publishing House.
Includes bibliographical references (p.   ) and indexes.
ISBN 0-8032-1050-7 (cl: alk. paper)
ISBN 0-8032-5937-9 (pa: alk. paper)
1. Holocaust, Jewish (1939–1945) Sources.   2. Jews—Germany—History—1933–1945 Sources.   3. Germany—Ethnic relations Sources.   I. Arad, Yitzhak, 1926–   .   II. Gutman, Israel.   III. Margaliot, Abraham, 1920–
.
D804.19.D63   1999
940.53'18—dc21
99-32577   CIP

Yad Vashem ISBN 965-308-078-4

INTRODUCTION TO THE BISON BOOKS EDITION
Steven T. Katz

The history of the Holocaust is encoded in a long and massive series of documents of many sorts from many sources. From Hitler's first writings on "The Jewish Question" at the end of World War I to his "Last Will and Testament" at the end of World War II, a trail of written materials tells the tale of the intended murder of all of European Jewry. Neither this trail nor its tale are easy to organize and reconstruct due to the sheer quantity of relevant sources, finally numbering in the tens of thousands of documents, totaling millions of pages in many languages, and overwhelming for all but the most expert scholar. Yet, to arrive at authentic knowledge of the series of events that we call the Holocaust, knowledge of this body of evidence in some comprehensible and manageable form is essential. Thus the intention behind this collection of primary materials.

The material included here is of several different sorts. The largest segments is drawn from various types of official Nazi, German, and related documents. These include early Nazi party programs from the Weimar era of the 1920s, before the Nazis ascended to power; the first anti-Jewish laws promulgated between 1933 and 1935 by the Third Reich after it came to power in January 1933; the immensely repercussive Nuremberg Racial Laws of 1935; Hitler's official speeches on various occasions; laws promulgated after the *Anschluss*, the takeover of Austria in 1938; material relating to *Kristallnacht*, the pogrom in Germany on November 9–10, 1938; orders of deportation for German and Austrian Jews; instructions for Nazi operations in Poland; a host of sources relating to the establishment and maintenance of the Polish ghettos; the protocols of the Wansee Conference of January 20, 1942, at which the "Final Solution" was planned; material relating to the Death Camps, which is not plentiful given the desire to keep their existence secret; and military and political sources related to the invasion of Russia in 1941, the creation and maintenance of ghettos in conquered Soviet territory (especially in the Baltic states), and the operations of the *Einsatzgruppen*, the special Nazi murder squads created as part of the battle plan for the invasion of Russia. Here, through these various documents formulated in an essentially impersonal bureaucratic style, one gains an insight into the official Nazi program of genocide.

One feature of this style requires particular notice. While carrying out the genocidal elimination of the Jewish people the Third Reich sought in its public discourse to *minimize* its actions, to deflect attention from its monumental criminality, and if possible, to keep as much of the "Final Solution"— itself a form of linguistic evasion—as secret as it could. Therefore, it regularly uses language formulated to reveal only the barest outline of its real intentions, to hide its deepest secrets rather than to expose them, and insofar as it is able, never to discuss in public the actual murder of the Jewish people. This intentionally ambiguous linguistic usage was most notable where references to mass death were at issue. That is, Jews were not usually referred to as being killed or murdered but rather were subject to *Saüberung*, cleansing; *Grossaüberungsaktionen*, a major cleaning action; *Ausschaltung*, elimination; *Aussiedlung*, resettlement; *Exekutivmassnahme*, executive measure(s); *Behandlung*, treatment; *Sonderbehandlung*, special treatment, or were *entsprechend behandelt*, treated appropriately.

There are also private German and related sources. These include extracts from Hitler's *Mein Kampf* published in 1923 and his "Secret Book" of 1926; extracts from Josef Goebbels diaries (Goebbels was Hitler's close, longtime confidant and Minister of Propaganda in the Third Reich); private notes on the extermination of Jews at Belzec by a Nazi official; selections from the personal memoir of Rudolf Höss, commandant of Auschwitz, written while in captivity in 1945–1946; and non-Jewish eyewitness testimony on the murder of Jews. This mixed collection of materials includes many different sorts of voices with differing perspectives and agendas, not the least of which are "justifications" by individual actors of their personal behavior or of the larger anti-Jewish campaign. All these sources must, therefore, be critically analyzed and evaluated accordingly.

The second large bloc of material, itself divided into official and private, is drawn from Jewish sources. These represent the all-too-often neglected response of the victims. Yet their response to the events in which they found themselves trapped are essential to an understanding of the Holocaust in its totality. Among the official documents that begin to emerge after the Nazi takeover and the initiation of their anti-Jewish campaign one can find, for example, Jewish communal requests for assistance; public proclamations by the German *Reichsvertretung*, formed as a centralized Jewish leadership organization in 1933, and its Austrian counterpart created in July 1939; special prayers for Yom Kippur, the Day of Atonement; documents of the *Judenräte*, the Jewish Councils created to oversee—under Nazi control—the ghettos of Eastern Europe; documents related to the activity of the American Joint Distribution Committee in Poland; and material produced by and relating to the Jewish Underground and resistance movements in Eastern Europe. Given the too little valued nature of Jewish resistance this latter batch of sources is to be noted in particular.

These public materials are supplemented by important private Jewish sources. Among these are early German-Jewish responses to Nazi anti-Jewish legislation, calls for help in transferring Jews and Jewish property to Palestine, observations on Jewish deportations from Germany and Austria to Poland, reports on the condition of those individuals now made refugees, reflections on the end of the Zionist Youth Movement in Germany, diaries from a variety of ghettos, informal records of Jewish Underground meetings, diaries of Jewish partisans, and a "protocol" by Jewish escapees from the Ninth Fort in Latvia written on December 26, 1943, detailing the exhumation and burning of twelve thousand bodies in order to conceal the mass-murder that these corpses represented.

What especially needs to be understood about the Jewish sources, both official and private, is the extraordinary circumstances under which they were produced. This material was composed by a people caught in an unprecedented situation who despite their precarious circumstances—defined by their constant fear of arrest or reprisal—were committed to record for posterity the crimes committed against them and others. So, for example, the official material generated by the *Judenräte*, the Jewish Councils, is an invaluable source. Produced with care and always with an acute consciousness that continued personal and communal existence hung by a thread, this catalogue of rules, decrees, food requisitions and reports, health statistics, documents and registers on forced ghetto labor, efforts at mitigation, responses to all sorts of circumstances and crises, and numbers on live births (few) and deaths (many) tells us about the public face of ghetto life in a unique way. Yet, at the same time, the ever dangerous situation in which the members of the Jewish Councils found themselves caused nearly every document to be composed with a distinctive sensibility and therefore to take on a special character. Even the most seemingly innocuous official text must be read both for what it says and what it does not say, for what it reveals and what it does not reveal. Thus, while the official records of the *Judenräte* tell us much of importance, they do not tell us directly about Nazi crimes, and they self-consciously avoid many crucial things about the inner life of the Jewish community. For example, they are silent on the fundamental matter of Jewish resistance, and they do not report the "spoken" but unrecorded inner dialogue that occurred in the Councils, full as it was of conflict, dread, and uncertainty, lest such potentially damaging material fall into Nazi hands.

The private Jewish material, which is more diverse in form and outlook, is also of great importance and likewise requires a sensitive reader. It represents individual and collective efforts—the latter most famously represented by the *Oneg Shabbat* group in the Warsaw Ghetto organized in 1940 by Emanuel Ringelblum, with imitators in most of the large ghettos—to document, at great personal risk, what was happening to the Jews of Europe. Every aspect of life in the ghetto, personal and communal, legal and economic, social and cultural, religious and educational, was recorded for posterity. This precious documentation, reflecting a wide variety of individual voices and literary styles, was carefully hidden away or buried or passed to those outside the ghetto for preservation until the war's end. And as hoped, much of this legacy was recovered after 1945.

Before leaving this discussion of Jewish writings there is one further source of major significance not represented in this collection to which I would like to call attention and which I would urge students and teachers to consult. This is the remarkable documentary testimony left by the *Sonderkommandos* who worked in the Death Camps. The *Sonderkommandos* were young Jewish men kept alive for a brief period to do the work of the Death Camps, especially of the gas chambers and crematoria. Knowing that they would soon die—these individuals were rotated regularly, the existing group being killed and replaced by another—some of these men took it upon themselves to record what they saw and knew of these infernal factories of death.[1] This material was secretly hidden away for a better time when the world would finally want to know what had occurred in this time and place.

Finally, there is a small selection of private and official testimony by non-German and non-Jewish bystanders and witnesses. So we have material from the non-Jewish Polish underground, diary entries from Poles who witnessed the treatment of the Jews in their midst, testimony from the Nuremberg trials, Lithuanian testimony regarding the Kovno Ghetto, and Russian reports on the massacre of Jews in various locations. Thus, taken altogether the selections in the present volume make up a rich mosaic of material on the three key Holocaust categories of murderers, victims, and bystander/witnesses.

Despite the richness of the material included in this collection the sources do not cover the nearly continent-wide scope of the Nazi murder-machine. Rather, they concentrate on four major geographical-political areas at the very center of events, Germany, Austria, Poland and the Soviet Union. Germany and Austria are important as the national homelands in which Nazism first emerged, took root, and flourished until the end of World War II. After 1933 Germany was responsible for the political and military actions that demanded and made possible the annihilation of six million Jews and millions of others. Poland—the conquered home of 3.3 million indigenous Jews—became the site of the first large Jewish ghettos and, beginning in late 1941, was chosen to become the location of six infamous death camps. At these six camps—Auschwitz, Treblinka, Sobibor, Chelmno [Kulmhof], Maidanek [Lublin], and Belzec—the "Final Solution" to the "Jewish Problem" was largely worked out. Lastly the Soviet Union is included—involving the *Reichskommisariat Ostland* (Lithuania, Latvia, Estonia and parts of Byelorussia), the *Reichskommissariat Ukraine*, and the rest of the captured sections of the Soviet Union—because the conquered territory of the Soviet Union was home to four to five million Jews whose organized murder between 1941 and 1944 was an essential aspect of the Nazi program of annhilation.[2] The mass-killing of Russian Jews was distinguished by the operation of the *Einsatzgruppen* who, in contradiction to the plan and operation of the Death Camps, killed Jews wherever they encountered them throughout the territory that comprised the western edge of the Soviet Union. Of the six million Jews killed during the war up to one and a half million were killed in Russia by *Einsatzgruppen*.

Given the just cited statistics on the number of Jews in Poland and the Soviet Union the obvious needs to be emphasized: the center of Jewish life—and of death—was located in these two major geographical areas. Western scholarship on World War II and on the Holocaust tends, for understandable reasons of language and context, to concentrate on events in Germany and other western countries overrun by the Third Reich. However, the epicenter of the military conflict and the destruction of European Jewry was in Eastern Europe. Students of these events therefore need to arrange (or rearrange) their conceptual map of the war and of the Holocaust accordingly. Moreover, it appears from the documents we possess, and the relevant chronology of events, that it was the preparation for war in Eastern Europe in the winter and spring of 1941—called by the Nazis "Operation Barbarossa"—and the invasion of Russia in June 1941 (and subsequent) that led to the fateful decision to carry out the annihilation of Russian Jewry and, either at the same time or in close proximity, to the decision to murder all European Jews. It was the fighting in Russia that unleashed total war, war fought without any ethical or other constraints, including the intended extermination of Russian and European Jewry.

Unfortunately, it is not possible to establish the exact date on which these genocidal decisions were made as the orders concerning them were considered so secret that they were conveyed orally, as indicated by *Einsatzgruppen* commanders at their Nuremberg trials. This particular lacunae notwithstanding, the well kept records of the *Einsatzgruppen*, who reported regularly to their superiors in the *Reichssicherheits-hauptant*—the main Office for Security of the Reich, headed by Reinhard Heydrich under the direct authority of Heinrich Himmler, *Reichsführer-SS*—in Berlin, leave no doubt as to their deadly activities. So, for example, in document 189 of this volume, the "Operations and Situation Report No. 6" sent by the *Einsatzgruppen* of the Security Police and SD in the U.S.S.R. (for the period October 1–31, 1941) reads: "In Kiev 33,771 Jews were executed on September 29th and 30th. . . . In Schitomir 3,145 Jews had to be shot. . . . In Cherson 410 Jews were executed." In this manner the weekly and monthly tolls of the victims continued to be tallied and relayed to Berlin throughout the second half of 1941, all of 1942, and early 1943.

The documents reproduced in this collection reflect editorial selectivity and require further interpretation. The latter is necessary because, while the material included in this anthology is from unimpeachable sources— the selections from personal documents raise questions of perspective, not authenticity—it still needs to be placed within a larger interpretive frame of reference. That is, it must be situated within the context of Nazi anti-Jewish policy, which in turn needs to be located within the overall narrative of Hitler's career and the history of the Third Reich. But these are not simple things to do because the Third Reich and the Holocaust have given rise to an enormous amount of scholarly literature containing widely disparate accounts and explanations, not so much regarding what happened but rather why and how things happened.

An extended analysis of the various competing theories of the Nazi

State and Hitler is beyond the scope of this introduction, but readers need, at a minimum, to be reminded of these methodological issues to begin to understand that in working through the present collection of materials they should also, simultaneously, try to organize an understanding of the Third Reich. To start to do so, one needs to ask some central questions. Was the Nazi State monolithic or pluralistic? Was it riddled (as the so-called "functionalist" account argues) with different factions, diverse interests, competing powers, alternative social, economic and political agendas? Or did it operate (as the so-called "intentionalist" view contends) in harmony according to a fixed centralized plan initiated by Hitler and communicated downwards throughout the entire political and military apparatus of the Nazi state? Or, in practice, was it some combination of both contingencies and design? What sort of a leader was Hitler? Was he a strong personality who organized, in particular, the annihilation of the Jews, or was he a weak and uncertain individual who, at least in part, was more follower than leader? Was the Holocaust a central aspect of the overarching Nazi program or a marginal part of it? How important was racial theory in the Nazi worldview? How did its importance dictate Nazi policy towards Jews and other non-Aryan groups caught up in the Nazi empire? Was the murder of the Jews unique, or was it just a significant, but not singular, aspect of a more general policy of racial oppression and mass murder?

These questions are large but unavoidable for those who would understand the history of the Third Reich, the general history of World War II, and the particular history of the Holocaust. Let the serious work of scholarly inquiry begin.

NOTES

1. See the English translation of five of these documents, most originally written in Yiddish (one in French), provided in Jadwiga Bezwínska, ed., *Amidst a Nightmare of Crime: Manuscripts of Members of Sonderkommando* (Oswiecim [Auschwitz], 1973).

2. The Jewish population of the entire Soviet Union was between five and six million. Of this population four to five million lived in the area conquered by the German army. Of these, approximately one and a half million were able to flee into the interior of Russia and so avoid the Nazi death trap. Of the remaining two and a half million, up to one and a half million, or sixty percent, were murdered by the *Einsatzgruppen*.

CONTENTS

PART TWO : POLAND

Introduction   167
Yisrael Gutman

PART THREE : SOVIET UNION

Introduction

Yitzhak Arad

FOREWORD

In this volume we have presented a comprehensive collection of essential documents for students and laymen interested in the history of the Holocaust. The collection reflects both the major trends and developments in Nazi ideology and policy towards the Jews and the behavior and reaction of the Jews in the face of the Nazi challenge in the following countries: Germany, Austria, Poland, the Baltic countries, and the areas of the Soviet Union occupied by the Germans in World War II.

The documents that have been chosen are concerned primarily with the following topics: the crystallization of the principles of Nazi anti-Semitism, the policies of the Third Reich towards the Jews, the period of segregation and enclosed ghettos, and the stages through which the "final solution" was implemented, on the one hand, and the Jewish public activities, the struggle for life, and the organization of the Underground and Jewish self-defense on the other. In addition to the German documents, a large part of which has been published in the past, the book includes many documents of Jewish origin, of which only a small amount was published previously. The documents derive from a variety of sources — German, Jewish and others — and appear here in chronological order and in accordance with the events they concern.

The book is divided into three sections:
1. *Germany and Austria* (according to the borders established after World War I).
2. *Poland* (in the borders that existed between the two world wars, excluding the eastern areas annexed by the Soviet Union during the war, but including the Bialystok District).

3. *The Baltic Countries* and areas of the *Soviet Union* occupied by Nazi Germany.

In each section the documents are presented consecutively, from the beginning of Nazi rule or occupation, but within its separate geographical-political area. At the same time some documents are also included whose application is not limited to any specific geographical-political unit, but concerned the Jews in all the areas under the rule or influence of the Nazi Third Reich. Thus, for example, the protocol of the Wannsee Conference is included in the section about Poland, although, of course, the decisions taken at the conference sealed the fate of all the Jews in all areas where the Germans were able to apprehend them.

Special care was taken to include in this collection only documents whose source and authenticity was not in doubt, and, except for a few, all were produced at the height of the period itself.

It must be noted here that the Nazis were particularly concerned to execute the murders in secret and not to leave traces in writing of the destruction process. Official documents make no reference in plain language to the extermination or its various stages, using accepted code phrases instead. Thus, for instance, the general plan for the destruction of the Jews of Europe was referred to as the "final solution (*Endlösung*) of the Jewish question."

We have tried to keep the translation as faithful as possible to the original. Each section in this volume is preceded by a short introduction. These introductions are not intended to take the place of a historical review; their purpose is to assist the reader in identifying the main events and viewing the documents against the background of these events and developments.

We tried not to burden the text with many notes. The documents themselves are accompanied by a small number of necessary explanations of the material and of expressions in use at the time.

A selected number of photocopies of original documents is

2

included, and a detailed index of names of persons, places, organizations and institutions, accompanied by explanations, complements the volume.

Most of the documents are reproduced in their entirety. Deletions have been indicated in the customary fashion. Words that appear here in italics were emphasized in the original. Most documents appear under a title chosen by the editorial board, and these titles are marked in larger type than the titles that existed in the original.

Proper use of these documents entails a broadening of the reader's knowledge of the subject through the study of research and background material on the Holocaust period.

The Editors

Part One

Germany and Austria

INTRODUCTION

The selection of documents in this section covers Germany and Austria and consists of two parts :

a) *Basic elements* of *National-Socialist anti-Semitism* that were formulated during the period of the Weimar Republic:

b) *Policy lines* of the *Third Reich* toward the Jews of Germany and Austria, as well as the *Jewish response* to this policy during the years 1933-1945.

The first part includes the 1920 Party Program (Document 1), which was in fact never changed. By comparison with its concentrated and relatively moderate formulations, the tone of Adolf Hitler in *Mein Kampf* (Document 4) is conspicuous for its incitement and violence. The passages from that book reveal of what its author accused the Jews, how he envisioned them, and how he described their position among the nations. The phrases and ideas coined in *Mein Kampf* became the iron, immutable basis of anti-Semitic demagoguery. They were brought to their conclusion in *Hitler's Secret Book* (Document 5), which was published after the war. This is the background to the extremist· proposals for the solution to the Jewish question that were raised at that time (Document 2).

For many years the National-Socialist Party was no more than a minority group within the anti-Semitic camp in Germany, and its rise was beset by failures (Document 6). Its leaders were required to demonstrate the party's merits over those of the other racialist factions, and to justify their demand for the leadership of the right-wing nationalist front (Document 3). The party's strength increased as a result of the severe economic crisis and the millions of unemployed. The outcome of the elections to the Reichstag in 1930 verify that the party became a decisive factor on the political scene from that date (Document 6). The passages from the original sources that set out the principles of the racialist doctrine referred to above make it possible to see — and even enforce the view — that they were at the root of the brutal policies adopted, in due course, by the German rulers and which emerge from the subsequent documents in the book.

There are five groups of documents in the second part of this section.

The *first group* deals with the events of the years 1933-34, the beginning of Adolf Hitler's rule. In these two years Hitler took action against the Jews in various ways: by means of threats and denigration (Document 22), by excluding them from their means of livelihood (Documents 2, 8, 22), and by the introduction of legislation to remove them from positions of influence in German public life (Documents 10, 22). But at the same time there were signs that radical anti-Semitism was being braked. The Ministry of Economics objected to the removal of Jews from economic activity (Documents 12, 30), and other state authorities sought to prevent violent persecution (Document 13).

The revolution in government came as a shock to the German Jews, and many of them no longer knew what to do (Document 16). The extreme assimilationist organizations tried to preserve their members' status as German citizens (Document 23), hoping that Hindenburg (Document 9) would help them, as loyal patriots, to protect their rights. The large Jewish organizations increased their mutual cooperation and joined forces in a Central Committee of German Jews for Relief and Reconstruction (Document 15). The Committee set up projects for mutual aid and vocational training and carried out other constructive tasks made necessary by the distress of the period. A *Reichsvertretung der deutschen Juden* was also set up (Document 21), which was to establish a unified policy on behalf of all parts of the community. The central institutions planned systematic educational work (Document 24) and, together

8

with the local communities, broadened the scope of the Jewish school network and of the Jewish adult education centers (Documents 17, 18). Aid was also extended to the Jewish theater and other branches of the arts (Document 25, 26). An emigration organization was set up by the *Hilfsverein der deutschen Juden* (Documents 27, 28), with the help of the Central Committee of German Jews for Relief and Reconstruction (Document 15). The Zionist institutions took care of emigration to Eretz Israel and assisted with the transfer of the emigrants' property through Ha'avara (Documents 19, 20). At the same time, through their journal, the *Jüdische Rundschau,* they endeavored to instill in the Jews a feeling of pride in their Jewishness (Document 14). There were some groups, such as the organization of independent Orthodox Communities, that protested to Hitler with regard to the persecution and oppression (Document 22).

After the year 1934 had brought with it a comparative let-up, the racial policies again became more oppressive in 1935, as can be seen from the *second group* of documents. A wave of attacks was directed against Jewish-owned businesses, despite the attempt of the Minister of Economics to stop it (Document 30); Jews were not permitted to join the ranks of the German Army, which was being rebuilt (Document 29); and the Nuremberg Laws (Documents 32-34) put an end to the "emancipation" of the Jews and their place in German social life. Differences of opinion among the German leadership concerning the Jewish question (Document 31) did not affect the general policy, which called for their total social segregation. For foreign consumption spokesmen of the regime, including Hitler himself, declared that the Nuremberg Laws made co-existence possible between the Germans and the Jews by creating separate living space for them (Documents 36, 37). Such re-assuring declarations made it more difficult for the Jewish public leadership to understand correctly the gravity of the position and to prepare for a future shrouded in mist (Document 38). Nevertheless, amongst themselves they expressed their feeling of anger at this racial oppression (Document 39).

9

In the course of these switches between pressure and the easing of government policy, the treatment of Jews improved somewhat in the years 1936-37. But the period 1938-39 brought bitter blows, violent attacks and unbridled hatred, as is recorded in the *third group* of documents.

In the spring of 1938 the legal position of the Jewish communities, which up to then formed the backbone of the life of the Jewish population, was reduced; organizations legally recognized as public bodies became private associations (Document 42). The process of excluding the Jews from the means of earning a living was also speeded up, until they were totally removed from their sources of livelihood (Documents 51, 52). The failure of the Evian Conference (Document 45), evidence of the indifference of the nations of the world to the fate of the Jews, served as a signal for Germany that she had nothing to fear from international pressure in aid of the victims. In the rioting on *Kristallnacht* (Document 49), in November 1938, tens of Jews were murdered, 26,000 of them were imprisoned in detention camps, and synagogues all over Germany were set on fire. The German government was now seeking a comprehensive solution to the Jewish question (Documents 51, 54); it began to uproot the Jews completely from German life and enforced a mass migration across Germany's borders (Documents 51, 54, 57). The German leaders' eyes were on the property of the Jews. They ordered the property to be registered and imposed an "Expiation Fine" of one billion German marks on the Jews (Document 53). Göring and Hitler threatened that they would settle accounts thoroughly (Document 51) and would exterminate the Jewish race in Europe (Document 59) if another war broke out.

At the end of October 1938, the first deportation was carried out; it was known as the Zbaszyn deportation and involved persons holding Polish citizenship (Document 55). The Jewish world rose to the aid of the deportees and helped them to the best of their ability (Document 56). Administrative pressure on the Jews increased continuously. In July 1939 the German Authorities set up a *Reichsvereinigung der Juden in Deutschland* (Document 62), a compulsory institution subject to German orders.

The *fourth group* of documents deals with the situation of the German Jews during World War II, when additional restrictions and bans were imposed on them. Jews were subject to forced labor, there was a general impoverishment of the Jewish population, and the first deportations of Jews from the Reich to the East (Document 65) and to occupied France began. The Jewish leadership tried to ensure the continued operation of schools and synagogues, of the vocational training farms and the Jewish theater, of social services and the last of the youth movements (Document 69). Despite the danger involved, rabbis continued to concern themselves with the maintenance of a religious way of life and the observance of the commandments (Document 70). But the machinery of destruction ground on without halt. In October 1941 the Gestapo prohibited the emigration of Jews from Germany (Document 68). At the same time mass deportations were begun across the border and these spread fear and despair among the remaining Jews. The number of suicides increased among those who sought to escape the fate of the deportees (Document 66). The end of German Jewry was near.

The *fifth group* of documents covers the Jews of Austria from the time of the *Anschluss* with Germany on March 13, 1938. As soon as the German troops entered Austria, a wave of anti-Semitic violence flooded its cities. Vienna became the scene of assaults on Jews and arbitrary arrests, their homes and stores were broken into and their property robbed. From the earliest days of the *Anschluss* the protection of the law had been withdrawn from the Jews of Austria, and they were placed under the direct jurisdiction of the heads of the SS and the Gestapo (Document 41). These did everything in their power to break the spirit of the Jewish population and to undermine their means of livelihood (Document 43). Eichmann, who came to Vienna as the Commander of the SD in the Danube Sector, found himself in charge of Jewish affairs in

Austria. He introduced close control over the entire lives of the Jews and imposed his will on all their institutions. He sought to turn their leadership into instruments to help him evacuate the Jews from Austria, and ordered the Jewish Community in Vienna to set up a special emigration department that would operate under his orders (Document 44). The whole range of Jewish organizations in Austria was changed completely so as to serve the needs of the forced emigration. In August 1938 a Central Office for Jewish Emigration was set up by order of the Government (Document 47). Under Eichmann's direction the "Office" automatically processed the various technical and financial arrangements connected with emigration. At times this operation became a means of despoiling the emigrating Jews of their property, as well as an organization that dispatched Jews to ghettos and camps in Eastern Europe. The Vienna office also served as a model for similar organizations that were to be established later in Berlin and Prague for the uprooting of the Jews. But even before the operation in Vienna got under way on a large scale and in an organized manner, a first experiment was made in mass expulsions from Vienna, in October 1938 (Document 48), about a month before *Kristallnacht*. As a result of the disturbances that took place at that time, the Austrian authorities considered the liquidation of Jewish businesses and enterprises and the confiscation of Jewish property (Document 51).

In order to maintain the life of the community, which had suffered as a result of the *Kristallnacht* riots, the Jewish leadership tried to obtain permission for the holding of public prayers (Document 60). In the atmosphere of depression and fear of that time, the Jewish schools played an important part in strengthening the powers of resistance in Jewish youth (Document 67). Eichmann personally intervened in order to prevent the loss of the Vienna Jewish Community's status as a legally recognized public body, as had happened in Germany in March 1938 (Document 42). He did this in order to ensure that Jewish relief organizations in England and the United States would continue to transfer funds to the Austrian Jews, enabling them to emigrate (Document 61). The cessation of this aid would have seriously jeopardized the possibility of emigration from Austria.

In the autumn of 1939 planning began for the transfer of the Austrian Jews to the Lublin District in Poland (Nisko transports). The deportations were organized by Eichmann in cooperation with the heads of the local Gestapo (Document 64). A second wave of deportations, to central Poland (Kielce District), in February and March 1941 was stopped because of the preparations for the invasion of Russia. The systematic deportations began in the middle of October 1941. The deportees were sent to Lodz, Riga, Minsk, the Lublin District and to Theresienstadt. Some were shot immediately on arrival at the first destination. Others were transferred to death camps. From the summer of 1942 a large proportion of the deportees was sent to Theresienstadt. Jewish officials were told by Eichmann that a permanent settlement for Jews would be established there, with equipment for public health care, hospitals and other necessary services (Document 71). The Germans presented Theresienstadt to the world as a "model ghetto." They concealed the fact that from there the roads led straight to the ovens of Auschwitz.

Abraham Margaliot

1

THE PROGRAM OF THE NATIONAL-SOCIALIST (NAZI) GERMAN WORKERS' PARTY

The Program of the German Workers' Party is a program for our time. The leadership rejects the establishment of new aims after those set out in the Program have been achieved, for the sole purpose of making it possible for the Party to continue to exist as the result of the artificially stimulated dissatisfaction of the masses.

1. We demand the uniting of all Germans within one Greater Germany, on the basis of the right to self-determination of nations.

2. We demand equal rights for the German people (*Volk*) with respect to other nations, and the annulment of the peace treaty of Versailles and St. Germain.

3. We demand land and soil (Colonies) to feed our People and settle our excess population.

4. Only Nationals (*Volksgenossen*) can be Citizens of the State. Only persons of German blood can be Nationals, regardless of religious affiliation. No Jew can therefore be a German National.

5. Any person who is not a Citizen will be able to live in Germany only as a guest and must be subject to legislation for Aliens.

6. Only a Citizen is entitled to decide the leadership and laws of the State. We therefore demand that only Citizens may hold public office, regardless of whether it is a national, state or local office.

We oppose the corrupting parliamentary custom of making party considerations, and not character and ability, the criterion for appointments to official positions.

7. We demand that the State make it its duty to provide opportunities of employment first of all for its own Citizens. If it is not possible to maintain the entire population of the State, then foreign nationals (non-Citizens) are to be expelled from the Reich.

8. Any further immigration of non-Germans is to be prevented. We demand that all non-Germans who entered Germany after August 2, 1914, be forced to leave the Reich without delay.

9. All German Citizens must have equal rights and duties.

10. It must be the first duty of every Citizen to carry out intellectual or physical work. Individual activity must not be harmful to the public interest and must be pursued within the framework of the community and for the general good.

We therefore demand :

11. The abolition of all income obtained without labor or effort.

Breaking the Servitude of Interest.

12. In view of the tremendous sacrifices in property and blood demanded of the Nation by every war, personal gain from the war must be termed a crime against the Nation. We therefore demand the total confiscation of all war profits.

13. We demand the nationalization of all enterprises (already) converted into corporations (trusts).

14. We demand profit-sharing in large enterprises.

15. We demand the large-scale development of old-age pension schemes.

16. We demand the creation and maintenance of a sound middle class; the immediate communalization of the large department stores, which are to be leased at low rates to small tradesmen. We demand the most careful consideration for the owners of small businesses in orders placed by national, state, or community authorities.

17. We demand land reform in accordance with our national needs and a law for expropriation without compensation of land for public purposes. Abolition of ground rent and prevention of all speculation in land.

18. We demand ruthless battle against those who harm the common good by their activities. Persons committing base crimes against the People, usurers, profiteers, etc., are to be punished by death without regard to religion or race.

19. We demand the replacement of Roman Law, which serves a materialistic World Order, by German Law.

20. In order to make higher education — and thereby entry into leading positions — available to every able and industrious German, the State must provide a thorough restructuring of our entire public educational system. The courses of study at all educational institutions are to be adjusted to meet the requirements of practical life. Understanding of the concept of the State must be achieved through the schools (teaching of civics) at the earliest age at which it can be grasped. We demand the education at the public expense of specially gifted children of poor parents, without regard to the latters' position or occupation.

21. The State must raise the level of national health by means of mother-and-child care, the banning of juvenile labor, achievement of physical fitness through legislation for compulsory gymnastics and sports, and maximum support for all organizations providing physical training for young people.

22. We demand the abolition of hireling troops and the creation of a national army.

23. We demand laws to fight against *deliberate* political lies and their dissemination by the press. In order to make it possible to create a German press, we demand :

a) all editors and editorial employees of newspapers appearing in the German language must be German by race;

b) non-German newspapers require express permission from the State for their publication. They may not be printed in the German language;

c) any financial participation in a German newspaper or influence on such a paper is to be forbidden by law to non-Germans and the penalty for any breach of this law will be the closing of the newspaper in question, as well as the immediate expulsion from the Reich of the non-Germans involved. Newspapers which violate the public interest are to be banned. We demand laws against trends in art and literature which have a destructive effect on our national life, and the suppression of performances that offend against the above requirements.

24. We demand freedom for all religious denominations, provided that they do not endanger the existence of the State or offend the concepts of decency and morality of the Germanic race. The Party as such stands for positive Christianity, without associating itself with any particular denomination. It fights against the Jewish-materialistic spirit *within* and *around* us, and is convinced that a permanent revival of our Nation can be achieved only from *within,* on the basis of :

Public Interest before Private Interest.

25. To carry out all the above we demand : the creation of a strong central authority in the Reich. Unquestioned authority by the political central Parliament over the entire Reich and over its organizations in general. The establishment of trade and professional organizations to enforce the Reich basic laws in the individual states.

The Party leadership promises to take an uncompromising stand, at the cost of their own lives if need be, on the enforcement of the above points.

Munich, February 24, 1920.

Das Programm der NSDAP ("The Program of the National-Socialist German Workers Party"), Berlin [1933].

2

ANTI-JEWISH PLANS OF THE NAZIS PUBLISHED BEFORE THEIR RISE TO POWER

Do a Proper Job on the Jews!

There are various views on the ultimate aim and task of the German-National (*deutsch-völkisch*) movement regarding the Jews. One believes that so-called explanatory work is all that is needed; the next only wants to "eliminate" the Jewish spirit from the "cultural" field; a third only from the economy, and a fourth has other aims again, and all the opinions become confused ... Quite apart from this we consider that it is much more urgent and necessary that the local groups should seek to operate first of all on their home ground and to sweep away *Ostjuden** and Jewish vermin in general with an iron broom...

The *Ostjuden* must be got rid of without delay, and ruthless measures must be taken immediately against all other Jews. Such measures might be, for instance, the introduction of lists of Jews in every city or community, the immediate removal of Jews from all Government employment, newspaper offices, theaters, cinemas, etc.; in short, the Jew must be deprived of all possibilities to continue to make his disastrous influence felt. In order that the unemployed Semites cannot secretly undermine us and agitate against us, they should be placed in collecting camps...

Völkischer Beobachter, No. 20/34, March 10, 1920.

* *Ostjuden* — the reference is to Jews who migrated from Eastern Europe, particularly Poland, to Germany. Anti-Semitic propaganda in the period of the German Empire and the Weimar Republic was directed mainly against these Jews.

3

THE NATIONAL-SOCIALIST PARTY AND THE GERMAN NATIONAL (CONSERVATIVE) PARTY, ESSAY BY HITLER, 1922

Nothing is more liable to render the entire German-National (*deutsch-völkisch*) movement, if not actually barren from the outset, then yet ineffective in its results, than the total lack of understanding of the fact that every idea is without value so long as its aim is not translated into action, but remains forever thought alone.

And, in the same way, no danger that is motivated by deliberate evil can ever be conquered through the mere recognition of its harmful nature or motivating power, but only through the deliberate confrontation with another power. In the whole of Russia there may today remain no more than 600,000 persons among its 150 million who are not horrified by the Jewish dictatorship of blood and its satanic infamy. Nevertheless, millions of helpless people suffer under the 600,000 destroyers, because the conviction of the latter expresses itself in bloody terror, but among the millions it is no more than impotent wishing — perhaps despite their better knowledge...

...And the German-National movement may well be the only one to realize that the whole internal structure of our state is not Germanic, but rather Semitic, that all our actions, even our thinking, are today no longer German but Jewish.

The movement may bewail a hundred times that our people are being destroyed by the poison of a mammonism that is so alien to its inner feeling; it may discern that class struggle and party disputes will rob us of the last remnant of resistance; it may foresee with prophetic spirit that we too shall sink into the blood-swamp of Bolshevism, and may prove a thousand times that the ultimate cause of all this misery, that the ultimate germ of this disease of the race is the Jew — the German-National movement may recognize this, but it will not be able to help and cannot do so, until it leaves the field of theoretical knowledge and replaces it with the decision to transform understanding into political power : to replace long-suffering scholarly study with the willingness to apply the organization of power... And yet only this is the real cause of the disintegration of our people. This cursed splitting of the nation into two classes that today oppose each other as enemies to the death is our worst misfortune, and it alone is the reason why there is no hope for a better future for our nation.

For this reason only that movement which removes Germany's greatest national misfortune will be able to call itself National.

The movement which will no longer be proletarian and may no longer be bourgeois, but will be simply German.

The movement which unites those that strengthen this Germanism (*Deutschtum*) day by day, not only in words but in all the thousandfold deeds of human activity...

In them lies the eternal fountain of the strength of our people. In them lies the future of our race. Whoever divides them strikes at Germany. Whoever unites them is National.

Finally, only that movement is National which does not bind this strength in order to lame it, but binds it in order to cast it as a solid block into the battle for victory for our own race.

And this battle will not be fought by majorities and parliamentary groups, but by the only form of majority that has shaped the fates of nations and states on this earth as long as it has existed. The majority of power and of the greater will and the strength to apply this power without consideration for mere numbers. To be German-National means not to dream today but to be a revolutionary; it means not to make do with academic knowledge; it means to have the passionate will to let deed some day follow on word.

Hundreds of thousands already know today what we need. But millions long for salvation. The first deed must today be to create an organization, from house to house, that will weld together the hundreds of thousands of the determined in order to fulfil the profound longings and hopes of the best of our people.

21

To liberate our race from inside, to free it from its chains on the outside...

H. A. Jacobsen and W. Jochmann, eds., *Ausgewählte Dokumente zur Geschichte des Nationalsozialismus* ("Selected Documents in the History of National-Socialism"), 1933-1945, I, Bielfeld, 1961.

4

EXTRACTS FROM MEIN KAMPF BY HITLER

... The Jewish doctrine of Marxism rejects the aristocratic principle of Nature and replaces the eternal privilege of power and strength by the mass of numbers and their dead weight. Thus it denies the value of personality in man, contests the significance of nationality and race, and thereby withdraws from humanity the premise of its existence and its culture. As a foundation of the universe, this doctrine would bring about the end of any order intellectually conceivable to man. And as, in this greatest of all recognizable organisms, the result of an application of such a law could only be chaos, on earth it could only be destruction for the inhabitants of this planet.

If, with the help of his Marxist creed, the Jew is victorious over the other peoples of the world, his crown will be the funeral wreath of humanity and this planet will, as it did thousands of years ago, move through the ether devoid of men.

Eternal Nature inexorably avenges the infringement of her commands.

Hence today I believe that I am acting in accordance with the will of the Almighty Creator : *by defending myself against the Jew, I am fighting for the work of the Lord* [p. 60].

... To what an extent the whole existence of this people

is based on a continuous lie is shown incomparably by the *Protocols of the Elders of Zion*, so infinitely hated by the Jews. They are based on a forgery, the *Frankfurter Zeitung* moans and screams once every week : the best proof that they are authentic... For once this book has become the common property of a people, the Jewish menace may be considered as broken [p. 279].

...His unfailing instinct in such things scents the original soul (*die ursprüngliche Seele*) in everyone, and his hostility is assured to anyone who is not spirit of his spirit. Since the Jew is not the attacked but the attacker, not only anyone who attacks passes as his enemy, but also anyone who resists him. But the means with which he seeks to break such reckless but upright souls is not honest warfare, but lies and slander.

Here he stops at nothing, and in his vileness he becomes so gigantic that no one need be surprised if among our people the personification of the devil as the symbol of all evil assumes the living shape of the Jew.

The ignorance of the broad masses about the inner nature of the Jew, the lack of instinct and narrow-mindedness of our upper classes, make the people an easy victim for this Jewish campaign of lies.

While from innate cowardice the upper classes turn away from a man whom the Jew attacks with lies and slander, the broad masses from stupidity or simplicity believe everything. The state authorities either cloak themselves in silence or, what usually happens, in order to put an end to the Jewish press campaign, they persecute the unjustly attacked, which, in the eyes of such an official ass, passes as the preservation of state authority and the safeguarding of law and order.

Slowly fear and the Marxist weapon of Jewry descend like a nightmare on the mind and soul of decent people.

They begin to tremble before the terrible enemy and thus have become his final victim.

The Jew's domination in the state seems so assured that now not only can he call himself a Jew again, but he ruthlessly

23

admits his ultimate national and political designs. A section of his race openly owns itself to be a foreign people, yet even here they lie. For while the Zionists try to make the rest of the world believe that the national consciousness of the Jew finds its satisfaction in the creation of a Palestinian state, the Jews again slyly dupe the dumb *Goyim*. It doesn't even enter their heads to build up a Jewish state in Palestine for the purpose of living there; all they want is a central organization for their international world swindle, endowed with its own sovereign rights and removed from the intervention of other states: a haven for convicted scoundrels and a university for budding crooks.

It is a sign of their rising confidence and sense of security that at a time when one section is still playing the German, Frenchman, or Englishman, the other with open effrontery comes out as the Jewish race.

How close they see approaching victory can be seen by the hideous aspect which their relations with the members of other peoples takes on.

With satanic joy in his face, the black-haired Jewish youth lurks in wait for the unsuspecting girl whom he defiles with his blood, thus stealing her from her people. With every means he tries to destroy the racial foundations of the people he has set out to subjugate. Just as he himself systematically ruins women and girls, he does not shrink back from pulling down the blood barriers for others, even on a large scale. It was and it is Jews who bring the Negroes into the Rhineland, always with the same secret thought and clear aim of ruining the hated white race by the necessarily resulting bastardization, throwing it down from its cultural and political height, and himself rising to be its master.

For a racially pure people which is conscious of its blood can never be enslaved by the Jew. In this world he will forever be master over bastards and bastards alone.

And so he tries systematically to lower the racial level by a continuous poisoning of individuals.

24

And in politics he begins to replace the idea of democracy by the dictatorship of the proletariat.

In the organized mass of Marxism he has found the weapon which lets him dispense with democracy and in its stead allows him to subjugate and govern the peoples with a dictatorial and brutal fist.

He works systematically for revolutionization in a two-fold sense : economic and political.

Around peoples who offer too violent a resistance to attack from within he weaves a net of enemies, thanks to his international influence, incites them to war, and finally, if necessary, plants a flag of revolution on the very battlefields.

In economics he undermines the states until the social enterprises which have become unprofitable are taken from the state and subjected to his financial control.

In the political field he refuses the state the means for its self-preservation, destroys the foundations of all national self-maintenance and defense, destroys faith in the leadership, scoffs at its history and past, and drags everything that is truly great into the gutter.

Culturally, he contaminates art, literature, the theater, makes a mockery of natural feeling, overthrows all concepts of beauty and sublimity, of the noble and the good, and instead drags men down into the sphere of his own base nature.

Religion is ridiculed, ethics and morality represented as outmoded, until the last props of a nation in its struggle for existence in this world have fallen.

Now begins the great last revolution. In gaining political power the Jew casts off the few cloaks that he still wears. The democratic people's Jew becomes the blood-Jew and tyrant over peoples. In a few years he tries to exterminate the national intelligentsia and by robbing the peoples of their natural intellectual leadership makes them ripe for the slave's lot of permanent subjugation.

The most frightful example of this kind is offered by Russia, where he killed or starved about thirty million people with

25

positively fanatical savagery, in part amid inhuman tortures, in order to give a gang of Jewish journalists and stock exchange bandits domination over a great people.

The end is not only the end of the freedom of the peoples oppressed by the Jew, but also the end of this parasite upon the nations. After the death of his victim, the vampire sooner or later dies too [pp. 293-296].

A. Hitler, *Mein Kampf* ("My Struggle"), Houghton Mifflin, New York: Hutchinson Publ. Ltd., London, 1969.

5

EXTRACTS FROM HITLERS ZWEITES BUCH

... Jewry is a people with a racial core that is not wholly unitary. Nevertheless as a people it has special intrinsic characteristics which separate it from all other peoples living on the globe. Jewry is not a religious community but the religious bond between Jews rather is in reality the momentary governmental system of the Jewish people. The Jew has never had a territorially bounded state of his own in the manner of Aryan states. Nevertheless his religious community is a real state since it guarantees the preservation, the increase and the future of the Jewish people. But this is solely the task of the state. That the Jewish state is subject to no territorial limitation, as is the case with Aryan states, is connected with the character of the Jewish people which is lacking in the productive forces for the construction and preservation of its own territorial state.

Just as every people as a basic tendency of all its earthly actions possesses a powerful urge for self-preservation as its driving force, likewise is it exactly so with Jewry too. Only here, in accord with their basically different dispositions, the struggle for existence of Aryan peoples and Jewry is also different in its forms. The foundation of the Aryan struggle for life is the soil, which he cultivates and which provides the general basis for an economy satisfying primarily its own needs within its own orbit through the productive forces of its own people.

Because of the lack of productive capacities of its own the Jewish people cannot carry out the construction of a state, viewed in a territorial sense, but as a support of its own existence it needs the work and creative activities of other nations. Thus the existence of the Jew himself becomes a parasitical one within the lives of other peoples. Hence the ultimate goal of the Jewish struggle for existence is the enslavement of productively active peoples. In order to achieve this goal, which in reality has represented Jewry's struggle for existence at all times, the Jew makes use of all weapons that are in keeping with the whole complex of his character.

Therefore in domestic politics within the individual nations he fights first for equal rights and later for super-rights. The characteristics of cunning, intelligence, astuteness, knavery, dissimulation, etc., rooted in the character of his folkdom, serve him as weapons thereto. They are as much stratagems in his war of survival as those of other peoples in combat.

In foreign policy he tries to bring nations into a state of unrest, to divert them from their true interests, and to plunge them into reciprocal wars and in this way gradually rise to mastery over them with the help of the power of money and propaganda.

His ultimate goal is the denationalization, the promiscuous bastardization of other peoples, the lowering of the racial level of the highest peoples as well as the domination of this racial mish-mash through the extirpation of the folkish intelligentsia and its replacement by the members of his own people.

The end of the Jewish world struggle therefore will always be a bloody Bolshevization. In truth this means the destruction of all the intellectual upper classes linked to their peoples so that he can rise to become the master of a mankind become leaderless.

Stupidity, cowardice and baseness, therefore, play into his hands. In bastards he secures for himself the first openings for the penetration of an alien nation.

Hence the result of Jewish domination is always the ruin of all culture and finally the madness of the Jew himself. For he is a parasite of nations and his victory signifies his own end as much as the death of his victim.

With the collapse of the ancient world the Jews encountered young, in part still completely unspoiled, peoples sure in racial instinct who protected themselves against being infiltrated by them. He was a foreigner and all his lies and dissimulation helped him little for nearly one and a half thousand years.

It was the feudal domination and the government of the princes which first created a general situation which allowed him to attach himself to the struggle of an oppressed social class, indeed to make this struggle his own in a short time. He received civil equality with the French Revolution. With that the bridge was constructed over which he could stride to the conquest of political power within nations.

The nineteenth century gave him a dominating position within the economy of nations through the building up of loan-capital based on ideas regarding interest. Finally, through the subterfuge of stock-holdings he placed himself in possession of a great part of the production sites and with the help of the stock exchanges he gradually became not only the ruler of public economic life but ultimately also of political life. He supported this rule by means of the intellectual contamination of nations with the help of Freemasonry as well as by the work of the press become dependent upon him. He found the potential strength for the destruction of the bourgeois intellectual regime in the newly rising fourth estate of the handicraftsmen, just as once before the bourgeoisie had been the means for the demolition of feudal domination. At the same time bourgeois stupidity and dishonest lack of principle, avarice and cowardice worked into

28

his hands. He formed the vocational estate of the handicraftsmen into a special class which he now allowed to take up the struggle against the national intelligentsia. Marxism became the spiritual father of the Bolshevik revolution. It is the weapon of terror which the Jew now applies ruthlessly and brutally.

The economic conquest of Europe by the Jews was pretty much completed around the turn of the century, and now he began to safeguard it politically. That means, the first attempts to extirpate the national intelligentsia were undertaken in the form of revolutions.

He utilized the tensions between European nations, which are in great part to be ascribed to their general need for territory with the consequences which arise therefrom, for his own advantage by systematically inciting them to the World War.

The aim is the destruction of inherently anti-Semitic Russia as well the destruction of the German Reich which in the administration and the army still offers resistance to the Jew. The further aim is the overthrow of those dynasties which had not yet been made subject to a democracy dependent upon and led by Jews.

This Jewish war aim has at least in part been completely achieved. Czarism and Kaiserism in Germany were eliminated. With the help of the Bolshevik revolution the Russian upper classes and also the Russian national intelligentsia were murdered and completely extirpated amid inhuman agonies and atrocities. For the Russian people the total number of victims of this Jewish struggle for hegemony in Russia amounted to 28-30 million people in number of dead. This is fifteen times more than the World War cost Germany. After the successful revolution he completely tore down [further] the bonds of order, of morality, of custom, etc., abolished marriage as a lofty institution and instead proclaimed a general copulation with the aim of breeding a general inferior human mish-mash, by way of a chaotic bastardization, which by itself would be incapable of leadership and which ultimately would no longer be able to do without the Jews as its only intellectual element.

The future will show to what extent this has succeeded and to what extent now forces of a natural reaction can still bring about a change of this most terrible crime of all times against mankind.

At the moment, he exerts himself to lead the remaining states toward the same condition. Thereby he is supported and covered in his strivings and his actions by the bourgeois national parties of the so-called national fatherland leagues, whereas Marxism, democracy and the so-called Christian Center emerge as aggressive shock troops.

The bitterest struggle for the victory of Jewry at the present time is being waged in Germany. Here it is the National Socialist movement which alone has taken upon itself the struggle against this execrable crime against mankind. . . .

Hitlers Zweites Buch — Ein Dokument aus dem Jahr 1928, Stuttgart, 1961. English translation : *Hitler's Secret Book*, New York, 1961, pp. 212-215.

6 RESULTS OF ELECTIONS TO THE GERMAN REICHSTAG, 1919–1933

	Nat.Vers. 19.1.1919		Reichstag 6.6.1920		Reichstag 4.5.1924		Reichstag 7.12.1924		Reichstag 20.5.1928		Reichstag 14.9.1930		Reichstag 31.7.1932		Reichstag 6.11.1932		Reichstag 5.3.1933		Reichstag 12.11.1933	
Wahlberechtigt*	36.8		35.9		38.4		39.0		41.2		43		44.2		44.2		44.3		45.2	
Abgegebene Stimmen**	30.5		28.5		29.7		30.7		31.2		35.2		37.2		35.7		39.3		43.1	
	83.0%		79.2%		77.4%		78.8%		75.6%		81.9%		84.0%		80.6%		88.5%		95.3%	
	%	***	%	***	%	***	%	***	%	***	%	***	%	***	%	***	%	***	%	***
Nationalsoz. deutsche Arbeiterpartei	—		—		6.6	32	3.0	14	2.6	12	18.3	107	37.3	230	33.1	196	43.7	288	92.1	661
Deutschnationale Volkspartei	10.3	44	15.1	71	19.5	95	20.5	103	14.2	73	7.0	41	5.9	37	8.8	52	8.0	52	—	
Christl.-soz. Volksd.	—		—		—		—		—		—	14	—	3	1.2	5	1.0	4	—	
Landbund	—		—		—	10	—	8	—	3	—	3	—	2	—	2	—		—	
Volksrechtpartei	—		—		—		—		—	2	—		—	1	—		—		—	
Deutsche Volkspartei	4.4	19	13.9	65	9.2	45	10.1	51	8.7	45	4.5	30	1.2	7	1.9	11	—		—	
Christl.-natl. Bauern- und Landvolkpartei	—		—		—		—		—	10	—	19	—		—		1.1	4	—	
Dtsch.-Hannov. Partei	—	1	—	5	—	4	—	4	—	3	—	3	—		—		{		—	
Wirtschaftspartei	—		—		2.4	10	3.3	17	4.5	23	3.9	23	0.4	2	0.3	1	—		—	
Deutsche Bauernpartei	—		—		—		—		—	8	—	6	—	2	0.4	3	—		—	
Bayr. Volkspartei	—		—	21	—	16	—	19	—	16	—	19	—	22	3.1	20	3.1	19	—	
Zentrum	19.7	91	13.6	64	13.4	65	13.6	69	12.1	62	11.8	68	12.4	75	11.9	70	11.0	73	—	
Deutsche Staatspartei	18.6	75	8.3	39	5.7	28	6.3	32	4.9	25	3.8	20	1.0	4	1.0	2	0.9	6	—	
Sozialdemokratische Partei	37.9	165	21.6	102	20.5	100	26.0	131	29.8	153	24.5	143	21.6	133	20.4	121	18.2	119	—	
Unabhängige Sozialdemokraten	7.6	22	17.9	84	0.8	—	0.3	—	0.1	—	—		—		—		—		—	
Kommunistische Partei	—		2.1	4	12.6	62	9.0	45	10.6	54	13.1	77	14.3	89	16.9	100	12.2	81	—	
Andere Parteien	—	2	—		—		—		—		—		—	1	0.7	1	—		—	

* No. of persons entitled to vote (in millions).

** No. of votes cast (in millions).

*** No. of delegates.

7

ORGANIZATION OF THE ANTI-JEWISH BOYCOTT OF APRIL 1, 1933 — INSTRUCTIONS GIVEN BY THE NATIONAL-SOCIALIST PARTY

An Order to the Whole Party !

The following order is accordingly issued to all Party offices and Party organizations.

Point 1 :
Action Committees for the Boycott against the Jews

In every local branch and oganizational section of the NSDAP [National-Socialist German Workers' Party] Action Committees are to be formed immediately for the practical systematic implementation of a boycott of Jewish shops, Jewish goods, Jewish doctors and Jewish lawyers. The Action Committees are responsible for making sure that the boycott will not affect innocent persons, but will hit the guilty all the harder.

Point 2 :
Maximum Protection for all Foreigners

The Action Committees are responsible for ensuring maximum protection for all foreigners, without regard to their religion, origin or race. The boycott is solely a defensive measure, directed exclusively against the German Jews.

Point 3 :
Propaganda for the Boycott

The Action Committees will immediately use propaganda and information to popularize the boycott. The principle must be that no German will any longer buy from a Jew, or allow Jews or their agents to recommend goods. The boycott must be general. It must be carried out by the whole nation and must hit the Jews in their most sensitive spot.

Point 4 :

Central Direction : Party Comrade Streicher

In doubtful cases the boycott of the store concerned is to be postponed until definite instructions are received from the Central Committee in Munich. The Chairman of the Central Committee is Party Member Streicher.

Point 5 :

Supervision of Newspapers

The Action Committees will scrutinize newspapers most stringently with a view to observing the extent to which they take part in the information campaign against Jewish atrocity propaganda abroad.* If any newspaper fails to do this or does so to a limited extent only, then they are to be excluded immediately from every house in which Germans live. No German person and no German business may place advertisements in such newspapers. They [the newspapers] must be subjected to public contempt, as written for members of the Jewish race, and not for the German people.

Point 6 :

The Boycott as a Measure for the Protection of German Labor

The Action Committees, together with Party cells in industry, must carry into the enterprises explanatory propaganda on the consequence of Jewish atrocity campaigns for German production, and therefore for the German worker, and explain to the workers the need for a national boycott as a defensive measure to protect German labor.

Point 7 :

Action Committees Right Down into the Smallest Village !

The Action Committees must reach out right into the smallest peasant village in order to strike particularly at Jewish traders in the countryside. On principle, it is always to be stressed that this is a matter of a defensive measure which has been forced on us.

Point 8 :

The Boycott Will Start on April 1 !

The boycott is not to begin piecemeal, but all at once; all preparations to this end are to be made immediately. Orders will go out to the SA and SS to post guards outside Jewish stores from the moment that the boycott comes into force, in order to warn the public against entering the premises. The start of the boycott will be made known with the aid of posters, through the press and by means of leaflets, etc. The boycott will start all at once at exactly 10:00 a.m. on Saturday, April 1. It will continue until the Party leadership orders its cancellation.

Point 9 :

Mass [meetings] to Demand the Numerus Clausus *!*

The Action Committees will immediately organize tens of thousands of mass meetings, reaching down to the smallest village, at which the demand will be raised for the introduction of a limited quota for the employment of Jews in all professions, according to their proportion in the German population. In order to increase the impact of this step the demand should be limited to three areas for the time being :

    a) attendance at German high schools and universities;
    b) the medical profession;
    c) the legal profession.

Point 10 :

The Need for Explanations Abroad

The Action Committees also have the task of ensuring that every German who has any kind of connections abroad will make use of these in letters, telegrams and telephone calls. He must spread the truth that calm and order reign in Germany, that the German people has no more ardent wish than to go about its work in peace and to live in peace with the rest of the world, and that its fight against Jewish atrocity propaganda is solely a defensive struggle.

34

Point 11 :
Quiet, Discipline and No Violence!
The Action Committees are responsible for ensuring that this entire struggle is carried out in complete calm and with absolute discipline. In future, too, do not harm a hair on a Jew's head ! We will deal with this atrocity campaign simply through the incisive weight of the measures listed. More than ever before it is now necessary for the whole Party to stand in blind obedience, as one man, behind the leadership. . . .

Völkischer Beobachter (Süddeutsche Ausgabe), No. 88, March 29, 1933.

* This was the phrase used by the Nazis for press accounts of atrocities against Jews in the Third Reich.

8

FROM GOEBBELS' DIARY ON THE BOYCOTT

April 1, 1933
The boycott against the international atrocity propaganda has burst forth in full force in Berlin and the whole Reich. I drive along the Tauentzien Street in order to observe the situation. All Jews' businesses are closed. SA men are posted outside their entrances. The public has everywhere proclaimed its solidarity. The discipline is exemplary. An imposing performance ! It all takes place in complete quiet; in the Reich too. . .

In the afternoon 150,000 Berlin workers marched to the Lustgarten, to join us in the protest against the incitement abroad. There is indescribable excitement in the air.

The press is already operating in total unanimity. The boycott is a great moral victory for Germany. We have shown the world abroad that we can call up the entire nation without thereby causing the least turbulence or excesses. The Führer has once more struck the right note.

At midnight the boycott will be broken off by our own decision. We are now waiting for the resultant echo in the foreign press and propaganda.

April 2, 1933

The effects of the boycott are already clearly noticeable.
The world is gradually coming to its senses. It will learn to understand that it is not wise to let itself be informed on Germany by the Jewish émigrés. We will have to carry out a campaign of mental conquest in the world as effective as that which we have carried out in Germany itself.

In the end the world will learn to understand us.

J. Goebbels, *Vom Kaiserhof zur Reichskanzlei* ("From the Emperor's Court to the Reich Chancellery"), Munich, 1937, pp. 291-292.

9

EXCHANGE OF LETTERS BETWEEN HINDENBURG AND HITLER CONCERNING THE STATUS OF JEWS WHO SERVED IN THE GERMAN ARMY

Berlin, April 4, 1933

The President of the Reich
To
The Reich Chancellor
Adolf Hitler
Berlin

Dear Mr. Chancellor!

Recently, a whole series of cases has been reported to me in which judges, lawyers, and officials of the Judiciary who are disabled war veterans and whose record in office is flawless, have been forcibly sent on leave, and are later to be dismissed for the sole reason that they are of Jewish descent.

It is quite intolerable for me personally...that Jewish officials who were disabled in the war should suffer such treatment, [especially] as, with the express approval of the Government, I addressed a Proclamation to the German people on the day of the national uprising, March 21, in which I bowed in reverence before the dead of the war and remembered in gratitude the bereaved families of the war dead, the disabled, and my old comrades at the front. I am certain, Mr. Chancellor, that you share this human feeling, and request you, most cordially and urgently, to look into this matter yourself, and to see to it that there is some uniform arrangement for all branches of the public service in Germany. As far as my own feelings are concerned, officials, judges, teachers and lawyers who are war invalids, fought at the front, are sons of war dead, or themselves lost sons in the war should remain in their positions unless an individual case gives reason for different treatment. If they were worthy of fighting for Germany and bleeding for Germany, then they must also be considered worthy of continuing to serve the Fatherland in their professions...

April 5, 1933

The Chancellor

Dear Mr. President!

In a most generous and humane manner you, Mr. Field Marshal, plead the cause of those members of the Jewish people who were once compelled, by the requirements of universal military service, to serve in the war. I entirely understand these lofty sentiments, Mr. Field Marshal. But, with the greatest respect, may I point out that members and supporters of my movement, who are Germans, for years were driven from all Government positions, without consideration for their wives and children or their war service... Those responsible for this cruelty were the same Jewish [political] parties which today complain when their supporters are denied the right to official positions, with a thousand times more justification, because they are of little use in these positions but can do limitless harm... Nevertheless, Mr. Field Marshal, in consideration of your noble motives, I had already discussed the preparation of a law with Minister of the Interior Frick which would remove the solution of these questions from arbitrary individual action and provide a uniform law. And I pointed out to the Reich Minister of Interior the cases for which you, Mr. Field Marshal, wished to see exceptions made. The law in question received preliminary discussion at several meetings last week and will provide consideration for those Jews who either served in the war themselves, were disabled in the war, have other merits, or never gave occasion for complaint in the course of a long period of service. In general, the primary aim of this cleansing process is only to restore a certain sound and natural balance, and, secondly, to remove from official positions of national significance those elements to which one cannot entrust [the choice between] Germany's survival or destruction. For it will not be possible to avoid, in the next few years, [the need] to make sure that certain processes which must not be communicated to the rest of the world for reasons of the highest national interests, will indeed remain secret. This can only be guaranteed by the inner homogeneity of the administrative bodies concerned.

I beg you, Mr. President, to believe that I will try to do justice to your noble feelings as far as is possible. I understand your inner motivations and myself, by the way, frequently suffer under the harshness of a fate which forces us to make decisions which, from a human point of view, one would a thousand times rather avoid.

Work on the law in question will proceed as quickly as possible, and I am convinced that this matter, too, will then find the best possible solution.

I am, in sincere and profound respect,

Your ever devoted,
signed   Adolf Hitler

Yad Vashem Archives, JM/2462.

10

**Law for the Restoration of the Professional Civil Service,
April 7, 1933**

The Reich Government has enacted the following Law, promulgated herewith :

§ 1

1) To restore a national professional civil service and to simplify administration, civil servants may be dismissed from office in accordance with the following regulations, even where

there would be no grounds for such action under the prevailing Law.

2) For the purposes of this Law the following are to be considered civil servants: direct and indirect officials of the Reich, direct and indirect officials of the *Länder*, officials of Local Councils, and of Federations of Local Councils, officials of Public Corporations as well as of Institutions and Enterprises of equivalent status... The provisions will apply also to officials of Social Insurance organizations having the status of civil servants...

§ 2

1) Civil servants who have entered the service since November 9, 1918, without possessing the required or customary educational background or other qualifications are to be dismissed from the service. Their previous salaries will continue to be paid for a period of three months following their dismissal.

2) They will have no claim to temporary pensions, full pensions or survivors' benefits, nor to retain designation of rank or titles, or to wear uniforms or emblems...

§ 3

1) Civil servants who are not of Aryan descent are to be retired (§ 8 ff.); if they are honorary officials, they are to be dismissed from their official status.

2) Section 1 does not apply to civil servants in office from August 1, 1914, who fought at the Front for the German Reich or its Allies in the World War, or whose fathers or sons fell in the World War. Other exceptions may be permitted by the Reich Minister of the Interior in coordination with the Minister concerned or with the highest authorities with respect to civil servants working abroad.

§ 4

1) Civil servants whose previous political activities afford no assurance that they will at all times give their fullest support to the national State, can be dismissed from the service....

Reich Chancellor
Adolf Hitler
Reich Minister of Interior
Frick
Reich Minister of Finance
Graf Schwerin von Krosigk

Reichsgesetzblatt, I, 1933, p. 175.

11

First Regulation for the Implementation of the Law for the Restoration of the Professional Civil Service, April 11, 1933

§ 2

. . .

[Amendment] to § 3

1) A person is to be considered non-Aryan if he is descended from non-Aryan, and especially from Jewish parents or grandparents. It is sufficient if one parent or grandparent is non-Aryan. This is to be assumed in particular where one parent or grandparent was of the Jewish religion.

2) Any civil servant who was not already serving on August 1, 1914, must bring proof that he is of Aryan descent or fought at the Front, or is the son or father of a soldier who fell in the World War. Such proof is to be supplied by the presentation of documents (birth certificates and marriage license of the parents, military documents).

41

3) In the event of Aryan descent being questionable, an opinion must be obtained from the expert on racial research attached to the Ministry of Interior...

Reichsgesetzblatt, I, 1933, p. 195.

12

INSTRUCTIONS BY MINISTER OF ECONOMICS ON THE POSITION OF JEWS IN GERMAN TRADE, SEPTEMBER 1933 *

... The legal regulations made by the Law for the protection of retail trade are completed for the time being. This means that the Reich Government will refrain from taking further measures such as have been demanded from various sides...

In this connection I see myself obliged... to point out once more that the absolutely essential further restoration of calm to the entire economy and its unified, organic reconstruction can only be achieved if those who have been appointed by the Reich Government to carry out its orders avoid any measure which could endanger the feeling of confidence in the Law as the result of their failure to observe existing laws and thereby introduce renewed uncertainty into the economy...

I therefore request that the lower-echelon offices and city magistrates in particular be emphatically instructed that such measures are to be absolutely avoided, and cancelled when necessary...

The groups directly interested in additional measures, and who have claimed up to now that their more far-reaching demands are in accordance with the economic policy of the Reich Government, are to be emphatically notified that the decision of the Reich

Government in this respect has now been made unmistakably clear, as I have stated before. The Reich Government cannot permit itself to be deprived of freedom of action by the creation of established facts, as the result of unauthorized intervention, directly or indirectly, in its decisions on the legal and economic position of the enterprises concerned. It will deal with such lack of discipline as offenses against the Führer Principle and as sabotage of economic reconstruction...

In the interest of maintaining the enterprises in question as places of work of very large numbers of German employees and [blue-collar] workers, and as providers of employment for much larger numbers still, boycotts and similar measures are to be avoided where they prevent business relations with suppliers or customers (i.e., the production of black or white lists, failure to include the enterprises in supply registers, refusal to accept advertisements, discouraging of customers by the posting of observers, distribution of leaflets, posters, threats, photographing of customers or interfering with them in other ways, etc.)...

Actions of this type have already been emphatically forbidden to members, officers and organizations of the NSDAP and its related bodies, by order of the Führer's Deputy, Rudolf Hess, of July 8, 1933, as well as by a subsequent order of August 8, 1933.

I therefore request that most decisive action be taken to prevent intervention of this type in future, and that organizations and associations rescind without delay any contrary directions and decisions, and that lower-echelon offices should receive instructions in accordance with this memorandum as soon as possible.

C.V.-Zeitung, No. 39, October 11, 1933.

* See Document 30.

13

PROPOSAL BY FRANK FOR A PAUSE IN
ANTI-JEWISH AGITATION

...The firm decision of the Reich authorities is that there should be a certain pause now in the continued disputation with the Jews. The Reich authorities further desire to state — in particular as far as the world [abroad] is concerned, that Jews living in Germany within the framework of German law may carry out their occupations without hindrance... [and that] *a certain agreement has now been achieved in the area of disputation with the Jews... that the security and life of the Jews in Germany is in no danger...*

Jüdische Rundschau, No. 79-80, October 4, 1933.

14

"WEAR IT WITH PRIDE, THE YELLOW BADGE,"
ARTICLE BY ROBERT WELTSCH

The first of April, 1933, will remain an important date in the history of German Jewry — indeed, in the history of the entire Jewish people. The events of that day have aspects that are not only political and economic, but moral and spiritual as well. The political and economic implications have been widely discussed in the press, though of course the need for agitation has frequently obscured objective understanding. To speak of the *moral* aspect, that is *our* task. For however much the Jewish question is now debated, nobody except ourselves can express what is to be said on these events from the Jewish point of view, what is happening in the soul of the German Jew. Today the Jews cannot speak except as Jews. Anything else is utterly senseless... Gone is the fatal misapprehension of many Jews that Jewish interests can be pressed under some other cover. On April 1 the German Jews learned a lesson which penetrates far more deeply than even their embittered and now triumphant opponents could assume...

We live in a new period, the national revolution of the German people is a signal that is visible from afar, indicating that the world of our previous concepts has collapsed. That may be painful for many, but in this world only those will be able to survive who are able to look reality in the eye. We stand in the midst of tremendous changes in intellectual, political, social and economic life. It is for us to see how the Jews will react.

April 1, 1933, can become the day of Jewish awakening and Jewish rebirth. If the Jews will it. If the Jews are mature and have greatness in them. If the Jews are not as they are represented to be by their opponents.

The Jews, under attack, must learn to acknowledge themselves.

Even in these days of most profound disturbance, when the stormiest of emotions have visited our hearts in face of the unprecedented display of the universal slander of the entire Jewish population of a great and cultural country, we must first of all maintain : composure. Even if we stand shattered by the events of these days we must not lose heart and must examine the situation without any attempt to deceive ourselves. One would like to recommend in these days that the document that stood at the cradle of Zionism, Theodor Herzl's "Jewish State," be distributed in hundreds of thousands of copies among Jews and non-Jews...

They accuse us today of treason against the German people : The National-Socialist Press calls us the "enemy of the Nation," and leaves us defenseless.

It is not true that the Jews betrayed Germany. If they betrayed anyone, it was themselves, the Jews.

45

Because the Jew did not display his Judaism with pride, because he tried to avoid the Jewish issue, he must bear part of the blame for the degradation of the Jews.

Despite all the bitterness that we must feel in full measure when we read the National-Socialist boycott proclamations and unjust accusations, there is one point for which we may be grateful to the Boycott Committee. Para. 3 of the Directives reads: "The reference is... of course to businesses owned by members of the Jewish race. Religion plays no part here. Businessmen who were baptized Catholic or Protestant, or Jews who left their Community remain Jews for the purpose of this Order." This is a [painful] reminder for all those who betrayed their Judaism. Those who steal away from the Community in order to benefit their personal position should not collect the wages of their betrayal. In taking up this position against the renegades there is the beginning of a clarification. The Jew who denies his Judaism is no better a citizen than his fellow who avows it openly. It is shameful to be a renegade, but as long as the world around us rewarded it, it appeared an advantage. Now even that is no longer an advantage. The Jew is marked as a Jew. He gets the yellow badge.

A powerful symbol is to be found in the fact that the boycott leadership gave orders that a sign "with a yellow badge on a black background" was to be pasted on the boycotted shops. This regulation is intended as a brand, a sign of contempt. We will take it up and make of it a badge of honor.

Many Jews suffered a crushing experience on Saturday. Suddenly they were revealed as Jews, not as a matter of inner avowal, not in loyalty to their own community, not in pride in a great past and great achievements, but by the impress of a red placard with a yellow patch. The patrols moved from house to house, stuck their placards on shops and signboards, daubed the windows, and for 24 hours the German Jews were exhibited in the stocks, so to speak. In addition to other signs and inscriptions one often saw windows bearing a large Magen

David, the Shield of David the King. It was intended as dishonor. Jews, take it up, the Shield of David, and wear it with pride!...

Jüdische Rundschau, No. 27, April 4, 1933.

"Wear It With Pride, The Yellow Badge," Robert Weltsch's article in the Zionist publication *Jüdische Rundschau*, April 4, 1933

15

PROCLAMATION BY THE CENTRAL COMMITTEE OF GERMAN JEWS FOR RELIEF AND RECONSTRUCTION *

Our Duty!

...There is great distress in German Jewry. We German Jews bore our share in the general distress in Germany. We contributed our contingent to the great army of people who were without work and without income, and seemed to be excluded from meaningful life. New distress has overtaken us. Jewish people are torn away from their work; the sense and basis of their lives has been destroyed.

The purpose of a community reveals itself in times of trouble. When the individual can no longer see any sense in his existence,

47

when he is alone, the community can direct him to a purpose and an aim; when he alone can no longer do anything, then the community must show its strength. In times of distress the community must grow anew, gain life and existence. It is from the community that the individual must draw the strength to live and be active.

The task of the community of the German Jews is great today. Need stands at the doors of our people, and their strength threatens to break. It is only from us, from the strength of the community, that relief can come.

We are faced with new tasks of unknown magnitude. It is not enough to give bread to those who do not know how they are to survive the next few days. Of course it is our first task to make sure that none of our people goes hungry or lacks a roof over his head. Of course we must make sure that the institutions remain that we have built for our children, for our old and our sick, as we have done in the past. They are more necessary than ever today, even though difficulties may force us to reduce considerably the demands we have made in the past concerning facilities in these institutions. But all that is not enough. We will not, and may not, consider that we have done enough if we offer charity to our brothers and sisters and provide for their simplest needs. Our duty is to help them to find a new basis for their existence, work with which they may make a living, which gives them once more a task and sense to their lives! It would of course be pointless if our people were to rush into various occupations that appeal to them in some way, without much thought. It will be the task of those responsible to investigate carefully where there is room and opportunity for the work of Jewish people, and then to offer them the opportunity to prepare themselves for this work.

Great demands will be made on the ability of our people to readjust, to find their way into new kinds of work and new circumstances. But much must also be demanded of the willingness to make sacrifices of those who are saved the need

48

to change their lives. Those who are lucky enough to have work and an income must help those who have lost everything. Anyone who is still able to give must sacrifice the maximum! The greatest possible demands must be made on everybody! Whoever evades this duty is an enemy of the community. Every sacrifice must be made, every sacrifice in aid for those who are now in need, but also every sacrifice in contribution to our communities, on whom innumerable persons now depend. Shame on those whose lack of willingness for sacrifice, whose criminal evasion of taxes forces our communities to dismiss officials or employees! *We* must not be the cause of making one of our own people lose his job or his bread!

The tasks that await us can only be carried out in unity and cooperation. All our differences of opinion, everything that divides us, must be put aside. The major organizations and social institutions of German Jewry have made the first move in this direction. They have united for joint effort in the Central Committee of the German Jews for Relief and Reconstruction. All special interests and personal wishes are silent there. The people who work together there labor only with one great common aim before them: The Aid organization of the German Jews!

This central organization will see to it that everything is done that must be done. It will see to it that there will be neither duplication nor competition but joint effort. The various organizations and offices will place their financial means at the disposal of the central organization... German Jews, show that you are able to rise to the magnitude of your task! Do not imagine that the problems of German Jewry can be solved without the greatest of sacrifices, by means of undirected emigration. There is no honor in leaving Germany in order to live untroubled on your income abroad, free of the fate of your brothers in Germany. It will not help anybody to go abroad aimlessly, with no prospect of making a living, but only increase the numbers there who are without work and means. Every prospect will be examined, every possibility exploited to help those who no longer have a prospect of earning a living in the German Fatherland to find some means of settling abroad! But don't leave Germany senselessly! Do your duty *here*! Don't push people off blindly to an uncertain fate.

Let nobody fail in his duty in this hour of trial! Let everybody contribute according to his ability, and in his own place, to the task of helping others! The hour of German Jewry has arrived, the hour of responsibility, the hour of trial. Let German Jewry prove itself capable of facing this hour.

C.V.-Zeitung, No. 17, April 27, 1933.

* *Zentralausschuss der deutschen Juden für Hilfe und Aufbau.*

16

THE POSITION OF THE GERMAN JEWS, AS SEEN BY ALFRED WIENER, OF THE LEADERSHIP OF THE CENTRALVEREIN *

Between Heaven and Earth

... The great majority of German Jews remains firmly rooted in the soil of its German homeland, despite everything. There may be some who have been shaken in their feeling for the German Fatherland by the weight of recent events. They will overcome the shock, and if they do not overcome it then the roots which bound them to the German mother earth were never sufficiently strong. But according to the ruling of the laws and regulations directed against us only the "Aryans" now belong to the German people. What are we, then? Before the Law we are non-Germans without equal rights; to ourselves we are Germans with full rights. We reject it, to be a folk or national minority, perhaps like the Germans in Poland or the Poles in Germany, because we cannot deceive our own innermost [feelings]. We wish to be subject as Germans with equal rights to the new Government and not to some other creation, whether it is called League of Nations or anything else. As far as we are concerned that also closes the question of Geneva,** which at present occupies Jewish people everywhere.

Thus we are suspended between heaven and earth. We will have to fight with courage and strength in order to get back to earth, in the eyes of State and Law too...

C.V.-Zeitung, No. 22, June 1, 1933.

* *Centralverein deutscher Staatsbürger jüdischen Glaubens* — Central Association of German Citizens of the Jewish Faith, commonly abbreviated as C.V.
** The reference is to the League of Nations, where Bernheim's Petition concerning the rights of the Jewish minority in Upper Silesia was discussed on the application of the *Comité des Délègations Juives.*

17

MARTIN BUBER ON THE TASKS OF THE CENTER FOR JEWISH ADULT EDUCATION *

The concept of "Jewish adult education" might have been understood even a short time ago to mean "elements of education" or "cultural values" that were to be passed on to those growing up and to the grown-up — for instance, giving an idea of "higher education" to those who were not privileged to obtain it, or to initiate those not familiar with Jewish subjects into some general knowledge of this community. When we gave this name to our newly founded experiment we obviously meant something else. The issue is no longer equipment with knowledge, but mobilization for existence. Persons, Jewish persons, are to be formed, persons who will not only "hold out" but will uphold some substance in life; who will have not only morale, but moral strength, and so will be able to pass on moral strength to others; persons who live in such a way that the spark will not die. Because our concern is for the spark, we work for "education." What we seek to do through the educating of individuals is the building of a community that will stand firm, that will prevail, that will preserve the spark. . . .

---

1. *Rundbrief der Mittelstelle für jüdische Erwachsenenbildung* ("First Circular Letter of the Center for Jewish Adult Education"), May 1934.

* *Mittelstelle für jüdische Erwachsenenbildung.*

18

ACTIVITIES OF THE STUDY INSTITUTE FOR JEWISH ADULT EDUCATION

New Paths for the Mannheim Study Institute

The Study Institute (*Lehrhaus*) in our community has become an important center of Jewish intellectual life in Mannheim since its establishment, and thus has preserved its original purpose. Creative forces have here found the right soil for their development, whether the occasion is a commemorative meeting with its effect of Jewish self-renewal, the discussion of more or less urgent topical problems, or even new artistic interpretations of ancient religious celebrations. For those with an acute ear the Study Institute always served as an indicator of the level of spiritual problems of the Jewish intellectual. . .

Great masses of people who formerly stood apart from whatever the Study Institute had to offer now crowd into its premises. Our previous efforts to supply the needs of the hour are now faced with entirely new tasks. The German Jew of the present day is in difficulties which direct his attention away from his current circumscribed position and far beyond his former sphere of activities. The well-known need for new occupations demands more varied qualifications than before from those involved. It is plainer than ever that one necessary requirement among the adults is the knowledge of foreign languages. The Study Institute was always a place for Jewish adult education, and now it must make itself available for the demands of occupational changes and "re-education." We accept this as a fruitful development of our original aim. . . .

Israelitisches Gemeindeblatt Mannheim, July 28, 1933.

19

CHAIM ARLOSOROFF ON THE NEED FOR HA'AVARA

. . . The liquidation of the immigrants' businesses and realization of their capital. Currency and transfer regulations make it very difficult for the immigrants to realize their capital in order to invest in Palestine. I believe that this problem *will not find its solution without negotiations and an agreement with the German Government.* Such negotiations would no doubt enjoy the support of the public in various countries, and a solution must be found based on concessions and advantages for both sides. It may be necessary to increase German exports to Palestine or to establish *a guarantor company* to insure the liquidation of immigrants' businesses over a long period. This matter requires study, effort and speedy attention. . . .

Ha'olam, No. 28, June 22, 1933.

20

REGULATIONS BY THE GERMAN MINISTRY OF ECONOMICS OF AUGUST 1933, CONCERNING CONDITIONS FOR HA'AVARA *

The following agreement has been made with the Jewish organizations concerned to enable German Jews to continue to emigrate to Palestine with the aid of allocations of the required funds, but without making excessive demands on the foreign-currency reserves of the Reichsbank. At the same time, German exports to Palestine will be increased.

Emigrants may obtain an endorsement from the Emigrants' Advisory Bureau to the effect that they require additional sums, over and above the minimum of LP 1,000 required for capitalist immigrants, which are necessary and adequate for the establishment of a livelihood in Palestine. This endorsement with respect to funds exceeding RM 15,000 [then equivalent to LP 1,000] will authorize them to pay the additional sum into Special Account I of the "Bank of the Temple Society" Ltd., established by the Reichshauptbank, in favor of a Jewish Trust Company to be established in Palestine (and in favor of the Anglo-Palestine Bank Ltd. until such time as the Trust Co. is established). For the time being a total of RM 3 million has been budgeted for Special Account I together with Special Account II, referred to below. Both will be administered by the Temple Society Bank as a Trust Account for the above Jewish Trust Co. Exports of German goods to Palestine will be paid for through this account. Funds accruing from the sale of the German goods in Palestine will be paid out by the Palestinian Trust Company in Palestine Pounds to the emigrants in accordance with their payments in Germany, and in the order and relative sums in which these payments were made into Special Account I. A "Palestine Trust Co. to Advise German Jews Ltd." has been established at Friedrichstrasse 218, Berlin, to advise German

. Jews in matters concerning this form of capital transfer to Palestine. I would request that when endorsements are issued the applicants [for such transfers] be emphatically advised to visit this office.

In addition, a Special Account II has been opened for the Bank of the Temple Society in the Reichshauptbank. The German Foreign Currency Authorities may, on application, give permission for the payment of sums up to a maximum of RM 50,000 per person to German citizens of Jewish nationality (*Volkstum*) who are not yet emigrating but nevertheless wish already to establish a home in Palestine. (These funds will also be paid in to the credit of a Jewish German Trust Company which is to be established in Palestine and to the Anglo-Palestine Bank Ltd. until this Trust Co. has been set up.) Special Account II, like Special Account I, will be used to pay for German exports to Palestine, with the difference that this account will be made use of only after Special Account I has been entirely disbursed. Special Account II may also be used by emigrants for deposits in excess of the sums authorized on their behalf as adequate by the Emigrants' Advisory Organization, but also in no case more than RM 50,000 per person (including sums allocated in foreign currency).

L. Pinner, *"Vermögenstransfer nach Palästina 1933-1939"* ("Transfer of Capital to Palestine 1933-1939"), *In zwei Welten—Siegfried Moses zum fünfundsiebzigsten Geburtstag ("In Two Worlds — for Siegfried Moses on His 75th Birthday"),* Tel Aviv, 1962, pp. 138-139.

* Transfer of Jewish property to Palestine.

Kundgebung

der neuen Reichsvertretung der deutschen Juden

In Tagen, die hart und schwer sind, wie nur je Tage der jüdischen Geschichte, aber auch bedeutungsvoll, wie nur wenige gewesen, ist uns durch die gemeinsame Entschließung der jüdischen Landesverbände, der großen jüdischen Organisationen und der Großgemeinden Deutschlands die Leitung und Vertretung der deutschen Juden übertragen worden.

Kein Parteigedanke, kein Sonderwunsch hat darin gesprochen, sondern allein und ganz die Erkenntnis dessen, daß Leben und Zukunft der deutschen Juden heute durch ihre Einigkeit und ihren Zusammenhalt bedingt sind. Darum ist es die erste Aufgabe, diese Einheit lebendig werden zu lassen. Jede Organisation und jeder Verband sollen in ihrer Lebenskraft und in ihrem Aufgabenkreise anerkannt sein, aber in allen großen und entscheidenden Aufgaben darf es nur die eine Gemeinschaft, nur die eine Gesamtheit der deutschen Juden geben. Wer heute Sonderwege geht, wer heute sich ausschließt, hat sich an das Lebensgebote der deutschen Juden vergangen.

Im neuen Staate ist die Stellung der einzelnen Gruppen, auch derer, die weit zahlreicher und stärker sind als wir, eine ganz andere geworden. Gesetzgebung und Wirtschaftsführung haben ihren gewiesenen Weg, eingliedernd und ausgliedernd. Wir sollen dies einsehen ohne Selbsttäuschung. Nur dann werden wir jede ehrenvolle Möglichkeit beobachten können und um jedes Recht, um jeden Platz, um jeden Lebensraum zu ringen imstande sein. Die deutschen Juden werden als arbeitnehmende und arbeitgebende schaffende Gemeinschaft im neuen Staate sich bewähren können.

Eigene Gedanken, eigene Aufgaben zu verwirklichen, ist uns nur auf einem Gebiete, aber einem entscheidenden, gewährt, auf dem unseres jüdischen Lebens und unserer jüdischen Zukunft. Hier sind die bestimmtesten Aufgaben gestellt.

Neue Pflichten jüdischer E r z i e h u n g sind zu erfüllen, neue Bereiche jüdischer S c h u l e sind zu schaffen und alte zu wahren und zu schützen, damit dem heranwachsenden Geschlechte seelische Festigkeit, innere Widerstandskraft, körperliche Tüchtigkeit gegeben werde. Zu Berufen, die ihr einen Platz im Leben zeigen, soll unsere Jugend in besonnener Auswahl herangebildet und umgeschichtet werden, damit ihr Dasein seinen Ausblick gewinne. Das Bestehende wie alles Begonnene und Versuchte soll hier zusammengeführt werden, um zu helfen und zu stützen. Allem Zersetzenden soll entgegengearbeitet, dem Aufbau auf dem religiösen Fundament des Judentums alle Kraft geweiht werden.

Viel von einstiger wirtschaftlicher Sicherheit ist uns deutschen Juden genommen oder beeinträchtigt worden. Innerhalb dessen, was bleibt, soll der Einzelne aus der Vereinzelung herausgeführt werden. Ständische Verbindungen und Zusammenschlüsse, soweit zulässig, können vorhandene Kräfte erhöhen und dem Schwachen einen Rückhalt geben, können Erfahrungen und Beziehungen für alle nutzbar machen. — So manchem wird die Stätte der Arbeit und des Berufes auf deutschem Boden versagt sein. Vor uns steht als Tatsache, der gegenüber alles Fragen und Meinen aufhört, die deutliche, geschichtliche Notwendigkeit, unserer Jugend Neuland zu bereiten. Es ist zur großen Aufgabe geworden, Plätze zu erkunden und Wege zu bahnen, wie auf dem heiligen Boden P a l ä s t i n a s, dem die Vorsehung eine neue Zeit gefügt hat, so überall, wo Charakter, Fleiß und Tüchtigkeit des deutschen Juden sich bewähren können, niemandem Brot nehmend, sondern anderen Brot schaffend.

Hierfür wie für alles das andere erhoffen wir den verständnisvollen Beistand der Behörden und die Achtung unserer nichtjüdischen Mitbürger, mit denen wir uns in der Liebe und Treue zu Deutschland begegnen.

Wir bauen auf den lebendigen Gemeinschaftssinn und das Verantwortungsbewußtsein der deutschen Juden wie auch auf die opferwillige Hilfe unserer Brüder überall.

Wir wollen zusammenstehen und im Vertrauen auf unseren Gott für die E h r e d e s j ü d i s c h e n N a m e n s arbeiten. Möge aus dem Leiden dieser Tage das Wesen des deutschen Juden neu erstehen!

Die Reichsvertretung der deutschen Juden

Proclamation of the *Reichsvertretung der deutschen Juden* in the Zionist publication *Jüdische Rundschau*, September 29, 1933

56

21

PROCLAMATION
OF THE (NEW) REICHSVERTRETUNG, SEPTEMBER 1933 *

At a time that is as hard and difficult as any in Jewish history, but also significant as few times have been, we have been entrusted with the leadership and representation of the German Jews by a joint decision of the State Association of the Jewish Communities (*Landesverbände*), the major Jewish organizations and the large Jewish communities of Germany.

There was no thought of party interests, no separate aims in this decision, but solely and wholly the realization that the lives and future of the German Jews today depend on their unity and cooperation. The first task is to make this unity live. There must be recognition of the vitality and aims of every organization and association, but in all major and decisive tasks there must only be one union, only the totality of the German Jews. Anyone who goes his own way today, who excludes himself today, has committed a wrong against the vital need of the German Jews.

In the new State the position of individual groups has changed, even of those which are far more numerous and stronger than we are. Legislation and economic policy have taken their own authorized road. including [some] and excluding [others]. We must understand this and not deceive ourselves. Only then will we be able to discover every honorable opportunity, and to struggle for every right, for every place, for every opportunity to continue to exist. The German Jews will be able to make their way in the new State as a working community that accepts work and gives work.

There is only one area in which we are permitted to carry out our own ideas, our own aims, but it is a decisive area, that of our Jewish life and Jewish future. This is where the most clearly defined tasks exist.

There are new duties in Jewish *education*, new areas of Jewish *schooling* must be created, and existing ones must be nurtured and protected, in order that the rising generation may find spiritual strength, inner resistance, and physical competence. There must be thoughtful selection in order to develop and re-direct our youth towards professions which offer them a place in life and prospects of a future.

All there is now, all that has been begun, all that has been attempted must be joined together here to give aid and support. All that is destructive must be opposed, and all our strength devoted to reconstruction on the religious base of Judaism.

Much of our former economic security has been taken from us German Jews, or at least reduced. Within the area that remains to us the individual must be drawn away from his isolation. Occupational connections and associations, where permissible, can increase existing strength and give support to the weak, can make experience and contacts useful for all. There will be not a few who will be refused a place of work or the exercise of their profession on German soil. We are faced by the fact which can no longer be questioned or opposed, of a clear, historic necessity to give our youth new [living] space. It has become a great task to discover places and open roads, as on the sacred soil of *Palestine,* for which Providence has decreed a new era, as everywhere where the character, industry and ability of the German Jews can prove themselves, robbing none of their bread, but creating a livelihood for others.

For this and all else we hope for the understanding assistance of the Authorities, and the respect of our gentile fellow citizens, whom we join in love and loyalty to Germany.

We place our faith in the active sense of community and of responsibility of the German Jews, as also in the willingness to sacrifice of our Brothers everywhere.

We will stand united and, in confidence in our God, labor for the *honor of the Jewish Name.* May the nature of the German Jews arise anew from the tribulations of this time!

Reichsvertretung der deutschen Juden
Leo Baeck

Otto Hirsch — Stuttgart	Siegfried Moses — Berlin
Rudolf Callmann — Cologne	Jacob Hoffmann — Frankfurt
Leopold L..n Jenberger — Nuremberg	Franz Meyer — Breslau
Julius L. Seligsohn — Berlin	Heinrich Stahl — Berlin

Jüdische Rundschau, No. 78, September 29, 1933.

* The reference is to the *Reichsvertretung der deutschen Juden* (National Representation of German Jews), established in September 1933, which replaced the "old" *Reichsvertretung.*

22

MEMORANDUM FROM THE ORGANIZATION OF INDEPENDENT ORTHODOX COMMUNITIES* TO THE GERMAN CHANCELLOR, OCTOBER 1933

...The position of German Jewry today, as it has been shaped by the German People, *is wholly intolerable, both as regards their legal position and their economic existence, and also as regards their public standing and their freedom of religious action.*

Following the passage of the Laws by the National Government the legal position of the German Jews is as follows. Jews have been excluded from national and local public service and have been removed from the spheres of culture, institutes of learning, and from science. Only a limited number of Jewish students and pupils will be admitted to universities and high schools, and even these will not be allowed to sit for certain examinations.

59

Jewish lawyers are forbidden to represent public and local organizations in court. Jewish physicians have lost the right to work for the sick funds. They have been removed from the public hospitals. The remaining exceptions, which apply to special categories of soldiers who fought at the front and their kin, do not affect the hopelessness of the position of the next generation of doctors. The Jews are excluded everywhere from the occupational structure of the new Reich.

In addition to that, even where no law applies, economic activity has been made extraordinarily difficult. Even if Jewish activity in the economic field has not been limited directly by the law, there is *in practice in all of Germany an anti-Jewish boycott*. National, local and public enterprises have been forbidden to buy from Jews, while the Nazi Party has made a similar ruling for all members of the NSDAP. In many cases even low-level Jewish employees have been removed from economic enterprises, to say nothing of Jewish members of their management.

As a result of this legal and actual situation tens of thousands of German Jews have suddenly lost all means of livelihood. Many additional tens of thousands see their position threatened with destruction as an indirect result. Where the logical consequence of the limitation of Jewish work in administration, the professions and business should be encouragement of the Jewish share in skilled trades and agriculture, if the Jews are to be left any living-space at all, there is no sign of any such effort on the part of the State. On the contrary, the boycott against the Jews is applied very emphatically in the craftsmen's organizations, and there is scarcely any opportunity for Jews to engage in agriculture.

This means, then, that the German Jew has been sentenced to a slow but certain death by starvation.

Added to this is the defamation of the Jews, whose good name is sullied, which prejudices the people even more sharply against the Jews and robs them of the air they need to breathe. In the official text of laws Jews are placed on a level with colored persons. School text-books represent all Jews without distinction as the height of evil, so that young people are taught enmity towards the Jews from the outset. In the press, radio and in speeches every evil act of any Jew is represented as the general rule, as Jewish crime, and Judaism identified with it.

There is also obstruction of Jewish religious life, which could be a source of moral education and ennoblement...

The religious educational system is collapsing and the religious communities — the framework for the only and last means of training their members as noble, deeply God-fearing people — can no longer maintain it for lack of Government support, and owing to the destruction of the livelihood of their members.

In addition to everything else there is the most severe personal deprivation for the Orthodox Jew, the ban on ritual slaughter.

Thus the position of German Jewry must be perceived as altogether desperate by the most objective of observers the world over, and one must understand that the German National Government might all too easily be suspected of aiming deliberately at the destruction of German Jewry. *This false concept must be disproved with concrete arguments if an information campaign is to have any effect.*

Orthodox Jewry is unwilling to abandon the conviction that it is not the aim of the German Government to destroy the German Jews. Even if some individuals harbor such an intention, we do not believe that it has the approval of the Führer and the Government of Germany.

But if we should be mistaken, if you, Mr. Reich Chancellor, and the National Government which you head, if the responsible members of the National Administration of the NSDAP have indeed set themselves the ultimate aim of the elimination of German Jewry from the German People, then we do not wish to cling to illusions any longer, and would prefer to know the bitter truth.

It is in your interest, and in that of the whole German People, to tell us the truth openly. We would then prefer to consider your intention as fact and make our arrangements accordingly.

We confess that this would be an unspeakable tragedy for us. We have learned to love the German soil. It contains the graves of our ancestors, of many great and holy Jewish men and women. Our link with this soil goes back through history for 2,000 years; we have learned to love the German sun; all through the centuries it has let our children grow and mature and has added special and good elements to their Jewish characteristics. And we have learned to love the German people. At times it hurt us, particularly in the Middle Ages. But we were also present at its rise. We feel closely linked to its culture. It has become a part of our intellectual being and has given us German Jews a stamp of our own.

And yet we would and could muster up the courage to bear our tragic fate and to leave its reversal confidently to the God of History.

But if the German National Government *does not* seek the destruction of the forces of German Jewry; if it seeks to force us away from influence on the structure of public life, reserving this for those of German racial origin, but will give us a place in the process of the reconstruction of the German Nation, if it is willing to maintain moral Jewry, which is the sworn enemy of materialism, then let it tell us this openly, too.

In view of the atmosphere that has been created we shall not demand of the German Government the cancellation overnight of all the regulations affecting the Jews, although we consider them a great, historic error; we do not wish to create difficulties for the National Government.

We would *today* have to accept some of the restrictions, if with an aching heart. Orthodox Jewry never sought dominance in economic life, which is in any case not possible for those who observe the religious precept of the holy Sabbath, which saves the Jews from materialism. Jewish Orthodoxy has always opposed baptism and mixed marriage in the sharpest possible manner.

But we do aspire to living space within the living space of the German people, *the possibility of practicing our religion and carrying out our occupations without threats and without abuse.* In accordance with our religious duties we will always remain loyal to the Government of the State. Within the framework of the German people the German Jew will gladly take part in the task of reconstruction of the German Nation and do what is within his power to win friends beyond the German borders.

In presenting this statement for your just examination, Mr. Reich Chancellor, we request the opportunity of a personal interview shortly, as representatives of the undersigned organizations, which have for decades cared for the religious requirements of Orthodox German Jewry. We are convinced that such a discussion would benefit, at the very least, the internal and external policy interests of Germany, which urgently require clarification of the situation and a gradual reduction of the tensions that have developed from the present situation.

In expectation of the gracious acceptance of our request, we remain, with deep respect,

Reich Union of Orthodox Synagogue Communities (*Reichsbund gesetzestreuer Synagogengemeinden*), Halberstadt
   signed Rabbi Dr. E. Schlesinger, Halberstadt
   Rabbi Dr. E. Munk, Berlin

Independent Association for the Interests of Orthodox Jewry (*Freie Vereinigung für die Interessen des Orthodoxen Judentums*), Frankfurt on Main
   signed Dr. S. Ehrmann   Dr. J. Breuer

National Organization of Agudas Jisroel in Germany (*Landesorganisation der Agudas Jisroel in Deutschland*), Berlin
   signed Rabbi Dr. M. Auerbach, Berlin
   Jacob Rosenheim, Frankfurt on Main
October 1933

Yad Vashem Archives, JM/2462.

* These organizations maintained a separate communal framework. They did not recognize the authority of the *Reichsvertretung der deutschen Juden,* but subsequently cooperated with them — see Document 38.

23

REQUEST OF THE REICH UNION OF JEWISH VETERANS * FOR THE CO-OPTING OF FORMER JEWISH FRONT-SOLDIERS FOR DUTIES IN THE GERMAN REICH, OCTOBER 1933

October 19, 1933

To
Dr. Lammers,
Secretary of State in the Office of the Reich Chancellor,
Berlin.

The Honorable Mr. Secretary of State,
Following the conversation of April 28 with your Excellency, I took the liberty of giving expression to wishes and thoughts concerning the regulation of the position of the German Jews within the German State in a letter addressed to the Reich Chancellor on May 6, 1933. In this letter I endeavored to describe the honest desire of our Union to serve the German People and German State, and to outline the way that might lead in such a direction. In view of the position of the German Reich abroad, which has been brought about by Germany's withdrawal from the League of Nations and the recall of the German Delegates from the Disarmament Conference, I wish to declare the happy approval of our Union of this energetic move, which at long last opens up new possibilities for German equality. Just as I declared at that time that our Union placed its manpower at the disposal of the Reich Government, so do the members of our Union wish to place themselves at the disposal of the Reich Government today. Today, as 19 years

ago, they wish to mobilize themselves entirely for the Fatherland, if that is what the hour requires.

I request your Excellency to inform the Reich Chancellor of our Declaration of Loyalty and of our readiness.

With the assurance of my most especial
respect, I beg to sign, your Excellency
Your obedient Servant
Dr. Löwenstein
Captain of Cavalry (Retired)
Chairman of the Union

German Foreign Ministry Archives Bonn.

* *Reichsbund jüdischer Frontsoldaten.*

24

INSTRUCTIONS FOR JEWISH PUBLIC ELEMENTARY SCHOOLS, JANUARY 1934

1. The Jewish school develops a special character as a result of the two-fold experience of life of every Jewish child living in Germany: Jewish and German. These two basic experiences are to be equally developed and made conscious; they are to be made fruitful and developed, both in parallel lines and in the tension between them.
2. The school is to be penetrated by a Jewish spirit that understands itself. The growing child is to have a secure and healthy awareness of himself as a Jew; he is to learn to take pleasure in the name, with all the pride and all the deprivation which it involves. In order to achieve this aim what is essentially Jewish is to be made the center of all subjects where this can

be done. To enable the child to carry out his tasks at home and in the synagogue, in the community and among the Jews in general, a vital understanding of the eternal values of the Jewish religion and of Jewish life at the present time, and particularly for the creative effort in Palestine, must be aroused and developed...

3. To supplement the official guide-lines for instruction in German language there should be emphasis on the mutual influence of everything that Jewish being and thinking has derived from the German spirit, and, on the other hand. everything that the Jewish spirit and Jewish work have contributed to the growth of German culture.

4. Despite the development of all intellectual abilities it is always to be taken into special consideration that the entire education must be directed towards the creation of determined and secure Jewish personalities. Apart from all other considerations this is made necessary by the urgent demands of the present: the Jewish child must be enabled to take up and master the exceptionally difficult struggle for survival which awaits him.

5. As a result, well-planned physical training and, in particular, the practice of gymnastics and sports are among the most important tasks of the school. The necessary change to different occupations can be prepared by means of manual training (drawing, needlework, technical crafts). In order to allow for the special situation of the German Jews, pupils at elementary schools should also be given the possibility of learning at least one modern Western European language, and also, in particular, modern Hebrew.

Arbeitsbericht des Zentralausschusses der deutschen Juden für Hilfe und Aufbau 1. Januar - 30. Juni 1934, Anlage (Report of the Central Committee of German Jews for Relief and Reconstruction, January 1 - June 30, 1934, Enclosure), 1934.

25

THE GERMAN AUTHORITIES AND THE CULTURAL ASSOCIAATION OF GERMAN JEWS

June 19, 1934

Hans Hinkel
Staatskommissar
NSDAP [Nazi Party] *Gau* Hessen-Nassau
District Office, Frankfurt on Main

In reply to your inquiry of June 6, 1934, I wish to state that, for a variety of reasons, it is to be permitted for the Jews to join together in an Organization, the Cultural Association of German Jews (*Kulturbund deutscher Juden*), which will be supervised by the State Police and other Party organizations. The main reasons for this [permission], apart from intentions connected with foreign policy, is the easier supervision and the concentration of the intellectual-artistic Jews in an organization where Jews will "make art" only for Jews. Permission has been given generally for the State of Prussia, because the Secret State Police, which is mainly responsible for the supervision, gave its express approval. The existence of this Jewish organization will depend on its observance of various conditions. One of these conditions is that the gatherings of the Association will not be advertised publicly. Immediately on receipt of your communication I was in touch with Dr. Singer, the head of the local central office of the Association, with the urgent request that he inform the associated organizations and responsible colleagues that in future publicly exhibited posters or announcements in shops would no longer be tolerated and would endanger the whole work of the Association.

Heil Hitler!

Hinkel Files, Wiener Library, Tel Aviv University.

26

ACTIVITIES OF THE CULTURAL ASSOCIATION OF GERMAN JEWS

The Cultural Association of German Jews needs you!

The need for the work of the Cultural Association has already been proved in Berlin. Cologne and Munich followed suit with plans and work. Frankfurt on Main, with its significant Jewish tradition and its special Jewish tasks, must also give a lead in these efforts. We have received authority from the State Commissioner for the independent organization of artistic and creative work. Like the centers of the Cultural Association in the main cities, so Frankfurt will be the starting-point for the work done in the District Rhein-Main. The smaller and smallest Jewish communities in cities and the countryside will join in actively and passively.

The creative artists appeal to you! Our program includes music, theater, lectures and art.

Finding work for members of artistic and crafts professions.

Training at all levels for Jewish musicians, painters and sculptors. There is a task here for the Youth Associations that is appropriate to our times.

The aim of our work is the cooperation of all those who take part, actively or passively, in Jewish cultural life, both artists and audience, and this can be achieved only if all Jewish organizations play their part. Every individual is jointly responsible and will decide with us on the success of our work.

Our appeal is addressed to all! We all need contact with elation, consolation, joy!

Therefore: Register as a member of the Cultural Association of German Jews, Frankfurt on Main.

_____

Frankfurter Israelitisches Gemeindeblatt, April 1934.

27

ACTIVITIES OF THE HILFSVEREIN * IN THE FIELD OF EMIGRATION

Urgent Tasks at the Present Time

The *Hilfsverein* has taken on a new task in addition to its former tasks: advice and assistance for those who emigrate from Germany.

The German Jews feel an inner bond with their Fatherland, and they wish to remain in their Homeland, whose fate they see as their own. Where this appears impossible for economic reasons and because of the future of their children, and emigration becomes economically and politically necessary, it becomes the duty of the Aid Association to prepare [emigration] and to help those who have made the grave decision to leave their Fatherland and establish a new life... The *Hilfsverein* advises persons emigrating to all countries with the exception of Palestine. Up to now it has assisted in emigration to 34 countries overseas.

In the course of the year 1933, 60,000 persons received advice and information of all kinds from the *Hilfsverein*. Financial assistance was given to 7,700 persons in the form of subsidies for tickets for railway and ship passage, visas, food, transport of luggage, furniture, machinery and instruments. A voluminous correspondence with authorities, communities, and aid committees has been maintained on behalf of many thousands of persons...

The Central Archives for the History of the Jewish People, A/176.

* *Hilfsverein der deutschen Juden* — Aid Association of German Jews.

REPORT ON THE ACTIVITIES OF THE HILFSVEREIN IN THE YEAR 1933

... The middle of March saw an increase in the number of persons who applied to our Central Office and our Committees in the Reich for advice and assistance in connection with emigration. The first great influx took place on March 29; during the ensuing months three hundred and more called every day asking for counsel. It was impossible to deal with them all at our office at No. 91 Martin Luther Street, and we therefore opened a special advisory department at No. 31 Oranienburger Street. In addition to applicants from Berlin we had daily callers from the various towns of the Reich. Letters asking for information in matters of emigration arrived in vastly increasing numbers, and in many months their numbers amounted to more than three thousand. . .

Constant communication is being kept up with no less than a hundred and eight organizations within the Reich; they are supplied with information of all kinds, and the *Hilfsverein* works together with them in cases where advice seems necessary. . .

The *Hilfsverein* recognized from the start that, having regard to the crisis reigning in all countries both in Europe and overseas, and in view of the many prohibitions against immigration and labor, the movement of larger groups of German Jews to countries abroad would meet with the greatest possible difficulties. The extent of the problem is shown by the fact that in recent years a considerable return of emigrants from overseas to Europe has taken place. . .

Events took place at such speed that the various assistance depots were absolutely unable to give to the impatient masses who were anxious to emigrate the required information to anything like the extent which would have been necessary. Having regard to the callings exercised by German Jews and to the economic conditions abroad, there is often a lack of the primary requisites for the reconstruction of a new life in those countries. Very often they are ignorant of foreign languages, agricultural and manual workers are relatively scarce, and for the numerous commercial employees and intellectuals there are hardly any openings abroad. Further, in the majority of cases the power of adaptability which is absolutely necessary for work in unaccustomed surroundings, especially overseas, is entirely wanting. Many rejoice in the childlike faith that accommodation can be found for an emigrant in any country, "somewhere abroad," without any special preparation being necessary...

Report of the Hilfsverein der Deutschen Juden on its Activities During 1933, Berlin, 1934.

29

PROTEST OF THE REICHSVERTRETUNG * AGAINST THE REFUSAL TO INCLUDE JEWS IN THE WEHRMACHT,** MARCH 1935

Reichsvertretung der deutschen Juden   March 23, 1935

To His Excellency,
The Reich Minister of War, *Generaloberst* von Blomberg
Berlin

The Government of the German Reich, on March 16, 1935, published the Law for the Reconstruction of the Wehrmacht. "Service in the Wehrmacht is based on general conscription." The duty of serving in the Army means the right to be a German soldier. This right and this duty is also claimed by the German Jews. In view of the legislation on Aryans the *Reichsvertretung der deutschen Juden* feels called upon to bring

71

this fact to your especial knowledge, Mr. Reich Minister of War, as it will be your responsibility to prepare the supplementary regulations to the Law.

Twelve thousand German Jews gave their lives for Germany in the World War. In memory of these dead, as representatives for the living, for ourselves and our children, we declare:

We German Jews are confident that we will not be denied participation in military service on equal terms with other Germans.

Reichsvertretung der deutschen Juden
signed Baeck

The Central Archives for the History of the Jewish People, A/171.

* *Reichsvertretung der deutschen Juden* — National Representation of German Jews.

** See Document 38.

30

RECOMMENDATION BY SCHACHT TO PREVENT DAMAGE TO JEWISH PLACES OF BUSINESS, JUNE 1935 *

Berlin, June 5, 1935
Immediate

The Reich and Prussian
Minister of Economics

To: The Minister-President
of Bavaria

I have seen from the daily papers that the leaders of the "Terror Gangs" who have caused an impermissible boycott of Jewish stores in the past weeks have been arrested. In view of the anxiety caused by these incidents and by the approaching Whitsun holiday business I will take this opportunity to request you to ensure that any further breaches of the law will be dealt with most severely, and that Whitsun sales can proceed without friction in the non-Aryan stores as well [as in others]...

Hjalmar Schacht
President of the Reichsbank

Yad Vashem Archives, JM/2858.

* See Document 12.

31

THE LEADERSHIP OF THE GERMAN GOVERNMENT ON THE EFFECT ON THE ECONOMY OF GERMAN POLICY TOWARDS THE JEWS, AUGUST 1935

At the... meeting of senior officials called on August 20, 1935, President of the Reichsbank Dr. Schacht first of all described the worrying effects that German policy with regard to Jews was having on the economic situation by quoting specific examples. His account was climaxed by the observation that he was forced to entertain serious doubts whether — in view of the increasingly radical trend in the policy on the Jews — it would be possible to achieve the economic targets set by the Führer, finding work for the unemployed and reconstruction of the Wehrmacht (and obtaining raw materials from abroad)... Schacht rejected any suggestion that he might be,called pro-Jewish. All he was doing was to point out the results for his field of operations of irresponsible incitement against the Jews. Schacht was most sharply critical of the independent operations of certain Party agencies, the Labor Front, the National Socialist Trade and Crafts Association (NS-Hago), as well as the activities of *Gauleiter* Streicher.

Reich Minister of the Interior Frick supported Mr. Schacht's criticism in general and had a memorandum read, which was directed to the Governments of the German *Länder*, which, in a sharp tone, demanded determined intervention by the police against illegal individual operations directed against Jews. Frick added the explanation that the police would remain absolutely passive if Party Organizations themselves carried out anti-Semitic operations. In that case, however, the responsibility would remain exclusively that of the Party.

Minister of State Wagner, as Representative of the Party, declared that the Party also disapproved of individual operations. But nevertheless the State must take the anti-Semitic mood of the population into account, and proceed with the gradual elimination of the Jews from the economy by means of legislation. This would reduce the unrest that now existed within the population.

Secretary of State von Bülow pointed out the importance of the Jewish Question in foreign affairs. Foreign affairs suffered considerably from the backlash following excesses against the Jews by irresponsible organizations. In view of the approaching Olympics, whose importance for foreign relations could not be overestimated, some arrangement must be made to prevent incidents such as that on the Kurfürstendamm,* in consideration of the expected influx of foreigners.

It emerged from the discussion that, generally speaking, the Party's Jewish Program should be retained as to substance, but the methods applied be subjected to criticism. There would be legal measures to put a stop to the limitless growth of anti-Semitic activities on the part of irresponsible organizations and private individuals in every possible area of life. But at the same time there would be special legislation to control Jewry in certain areas, particularly in all economic matters; as for the rest, they were on principle to retain their freedom of movement.

No general and unified aim of German policy with respect to the Jews was produced by the debate. The arguments of Ministers responsible for various departments merely revealed that the Jewish Question made their political task more difficult. The observation made by Mr. Schacht that he would not be able to accept responsibility for the completion of the program of Reconstruction unless something were done about anti-Semitic excesses, sounded, in its various forms, like an ultimatum. But Mr. Schacht did not draw the conclusion that he must demand a radical change in the Party's Jewish Program, or even the methods by which it was carried out, for example, a ban on the *Stürmer*. On the contrary, he maintained the fiction of the 100-percent execution of the Jewish Program.

Both Mr. Schacht and the Party Representative pointed out during the debate that in this question there was a divergence in the basic attitudes of Party and State, which was significant in principle beyond the concrete question under discussion. The representatives of the departments in most cases pointed out practical disadvantages which developed in their areas, while the Party based the need for radical steps against the Jews on political-emotional and abstract-philosophical grounds.

Yad Vashem Archives, JM/2245.

* The reference is to anti-Semitic disturbances which occurred on July 15, on the Kurfürstendamm, Berlin.

Reichsbürgergesetz.

Vom 15. September 1935.

Der Reichstag hat einstimmig das folgende Gesetz beschlossen, das hiermit verkündet wird:

§ 1

(1) Staatsangehöriger ist, wer dem Schutzverband des Deutschen Reiches angehört und ihm dafür besonders verpflichtet ist.

(2) Die Staatsangehörigkeit wird nach den Vorschriften des Reichs- und Staatsangehörigkeitsgesetzes erworben.

§ 2

(1) Reichsbürger ist nur der Staatsangehörige deutschen oder artverwandten Blutes, der durch sein Verhalten beweist, daß er gewillt und geeignet ist, in Treue dem Deutschen Volk und Reich zu dienen.

(2) Das Reichsbürgerrecht wird durch Verleihung des Reichsbürgerbriefes erworben.

(3) Der Reichsbürger ist der alleinige Träger der vollen politischen Rechte nach Maßgabe der Gesetze.

§ 3

Der Reichsminister des Innern erläßt im Einvernehmen mit dem Stellvertreter des Führers die zur Durchführung und Ergänzung des Gesetzes erforderlichen Rechts- und Verwaltungsvorschriften.

Nürnberg, den 15. September 1935,
am Reichsparteitag der Freiheit.

Der Führer und Reichskanzler
Adolf Hitler

Der Reichsminister des Innern
Frick

The Reich Citizenship Law of September 15, 1935

32

NUREMBERG LAWS ON REICH CITIZENSHIP, SEPTEMBER 15, 1935

Reich Citizenship Law
September 15, 1935

The Reichstag has unanimously enacted the following law, which is promulgated herewith:

§ 1

1) A subject of the State is a person who enjoys the protection of the German Reich and who in consequence has specific obligations towards it.

2) The status of subject of the State is acquired in accordance with the provisions of the Reich and State Citizenship Law.

§ 2

1) A Reich citizen is a subject of the State who is of German or related blood, who proves by his conduct that he is willing and fit faithfully to serve the German people and Reich.

2) Reich citizenship is acquired through the granting of a Reich Citizenship Certificate.

3) The Reich citizen is the sole bearer of full political rights in accordance with the Law.

§ 3

The Reich Minister of the Interior, in coordination with the Deputy of the Führer, will issue the Legal and Administrative orders required to implement and complete this Law.

Nuremberg, September 15, 1935
at the Reich Party Congress of Freedom

The Führer and Reich Chancellor
Adolf Hitler
The Reich Minister of the Interior
Frick

Reichsgesetzblatt, I, 1935, p. 1146.

33

NUREMBERG LAW FOR THE PROTECTION OF GERMAN BLOOD AND GERMAN HONOR, SEPTEMBER 15, 1935

Law for the Protection of German Blood and German Honor September 15, 1935

Moved by the understanding that purity of the German Blood is the essential condition for the continued existence of the German people, and inspired by the inflexible determination to ensure the existence of the German Nation for all time, the Reichstag has unanimously adopted the following Law, which is promulgated herewith:

§ 1

1) Marriages between Jews and subjects of the state of German or related blood are forbidden. Marriages nevertheless concluded are invalid, even if concluded abroad to circumvent this law.

2) Annulment proceedings can be initiated only by the State Prosecutor.

§ 2

Extramarital intercourse between Jews and subjects of the state of German or related blood is forbidden.

§ 3

Jews may not employ in their households female subjects of the state of German or related blood who are under 45 years old.

§ 4

1) Jews are forbidden to fly the Reich or National flag or to display the Reich colors.

2) They are, on the other hand, permitted to display the Jewish colors. The exercise of this right is protected by the State.

§ 5

1) Any person who violates the prohibition under § 1 will be punished by a prison sentence with hard labor.

2) A male who violates the prohibition under § 2 will be punished with a prison sentence with or without hard labor.

3) Any person violating the provisions under § § 3 or 4 will be punished with a prison sentence of up to one year and a fine, or with one or the other of these penalties.

§ 6

The Reich Minister of the Interior, in coordination with the Deputy of the Führer and the Reich Minister of Justice, will issue the Legal and Administrative regulations required to implement and complete this Law.

§ 7

The Law takes effect on the day following promulgations except for § 3, which goes into force on January 1, 1936.

Nuremberg, September 15, 1935
at the Reich Party Congress of Freedom

> *The Führer and Reich Chancellor*
> *Adolf Hitler*
> *The Reich Minister of the Interior*
> *Frick*
> *The Reich Minister of Justice*
> *Dr. Gürtner*
> *The Deputy of the Führer*
> *R. Hess*

Reichsgesetzblatt, I, 1935, pp. 1146-1147.

34

First Regulation to the Reich Citizenship Law
November 14, 1935

. . .

§ 4

1) A Jew cannot be a Reich citizen. He has no voting rights in political matters; he cannot occupy a public office.

2) Jewish officials will retire as of December 31, 1935...

§ 5

1) A Jew is a person descended from at least three grandparents who are full Jews by race...

2) A *Mischling* who is a subject of the state is also considered a Jew if he is descended from two full Jewish grandparents

> a) who was a member of the Jewish Religious Community at the time of the promulgation of this Law, or was admitted to it subsequently;
>
> b) who was married to a Jew at the time of the promulgation of this Law, or subsequently married to a Jew;
>
> c) who was born from a marriage with a Jew in accordance with paragraph 1, contracted subsequently to the promulgation of the Law for the Protection of German Blood and German Honor of September 15, 1935 (*Reichsgesetzblatt*, I, p. 1146);
>
> d) who was born as the result of extramarital intercourse with a Jew in accordance with Paragraph 1, and was born illegitimately after July 31, 1936...

Reichsgesetzblatt, I, 1935, p. 1333.

35

EXTRACTS FROM HITLER'S SPEECH IN THE REICHSTAG ON THE NUREMBERG LAWS, SEPTEMBER 1935

This international unrest in the world would unfortunately seem to have given rise to the view amongst the Jews within Germany that the time has come openly to oppose Jewish interests to those of the German nation. From numerous places vigorous complaints have been received of the provocative action of individuals belonging to this people, and the remarkable frequency of these reports and the similarity of their contents point to a certain system of operation.

... The only way to deal with the problem which remains open is that of legislative action. The German Government is in this controlled by the thought that through a single secular solution it may be possible still to create a level ground [*eine Ebene*] on which the German people may find a tolerable relation towards the Jewish people. Should this hope not be fulfilled and the Jewish agitation both within Germany and in the international sphere should continue, then the position must be examined afresh.

The third [law] is an attempt to regulate by law [the Jewish] problem, which, should this attempt fail, must then be handed over by law to the National-Socialist Party for a final solution.

Behind all three laws there stands the National-Socialist Party and with it and supporting it stands the German nation.

N. H. Baynes, ed., *The Speeches of Adolf Hitler*, I, London, 1942, pp. 731-732.

36

EXTRACT FROM HITLER'S SPEECH ON THE IMPORTANCE OF THE NUREMBERG LAWS, AT A MEETING OF PARTY LEADERS

At this meeting the Führer expressed his gratitude to the responsible heads of the Reich Party organization for their work, made use of the opportunity to emphasize the importance of the new Laws, and to point out that National-Socialist legislation offered the only possibility of achieving a tolerable relationship with the Jews living in Germany. The Führer emphasized especially that in accordance with these Laws the Jews in Germany were offered opportunities of living their own national (*völkisch*) life in all areas, as they had never been able to do in any other country. With a view to this the Führer reiterated his order to the Party to avoid all individual actions against Jews, as before.

M. Domarus, ed., *A. Hitler — Reden und Proklamationen 1932-1945* ("A. Hitler — Speeches and Proclamations 1932-1945"), I. Neustadt a.d. Aisch, 1962, pp. 538-539.

37

COMMENT IN THE GERMAN NEWS AGENCY ON THE NUREMBERG LAWS *

After years of struggle the new Laws passed by the Reichstag at the Party Congress of Freedom... establish *absolutely clear relations between the German Nation (Deutschtum) and Jewry.* Unmistakably clear expression has been given to the fact that the German people has no objection to the Jew as long as he wishes to be a member of the Jewish people and acts accordingly, but that, on the other hand, he declines to look on the Jew as a fellow-member of the German Nation (*Volksgenosse*) and to accord him the same rights and duties as a German.

The International Zionist Congress has just been in session in Switzerland, a Congress which also put an end very plainly to any talk of Judaism being simply a religion. The speakers at the Zionist Congress stated that the *Jews are a separate people* and once again put on record the national claims of Jewry.

Germany has merely drawn the practical consequences from this and is meeting the demands of the International Zionist Congress when it declares the Jews now living in Germany to be a national minority. Once the *Jews have been stamped a national minority* it is again possible to establish normal relations between the German Nation and Jewry. The new Laws give the Jewish minority in Germany their own cultural life, their own national life. In future they will be able to shape their own schools, their own theater, their own sports associations; in short, they can create their own future in all aspects of national life. On the other hand, it is evident that from now on and for the *future* there can be *no interference* in questions connected with the Government of the German people, that there can be no interference in the national affairs of the German Nation.

The German people is convinced that these Laws have performed a healing and useful deed, for Jewry in Germany itself, as for the Germans. Germany has given the Jewish minority the opportunity to live for itself and is offering State protection for this separate life of the Jewish minority: Jewry's process of growth into a nation will thereby be encouraged and a contribution will be made to the establishment of more tolerable relations between the two nations.

Jüdische Rundschau, No. 75, September 17, 1935.

* Written by the editor, A. I. Berndt.

38

RESPONSE OF THE REICHSVERTRETUNG * TO THE NUREMBERG LAWS **

The Statement by the Reichsvertretung

The *Reichsvertretung der Juden in Deutschland* announces the following:

I

"The Laws decided upon by the Reichstag in Nuremberg have come as the heaviest of blows for the Jews in Germany. But they must create a basis on which a tolerable relationship becomes possible between the German and the Jewish people. The *Reichsvertretung der Juden in Deutschland* is willing to contribute to this end with all its powers. A precondition for such a tolerable relationship is the hope that the Jews and Jewish communities of Germany will be enabled to keep a moral and economic means of existence by the halting of defamation and boycott.

The organization of the life of the Jews in Germany requires governmental recognition of an autonomous Jewish leadership. The *Reichsvertretung der Juden in Deutschland* is the agency competent to undertake this. It has the support, with few exceptions, of the totality of the Jews and Jewish Communities, particularly the State Association of Jewish Communities (*Landesverbände*) and all the City Communities, as well as the independent Jewish organizations: Zionist Federation of Germany (*Zionistische Vereinigung für Deutschland*), Central Organization of Jews in Germany (*Zentralverein der Juden in Deutschland*), Union of Jewish Veterans (*Reichsbund jüdischer Frontsoldaten*), Association for Liberal Judaism (*Vereinigung für das religiös-liberale Judentum*), the Organized Orthodox Community (*die organisierte Gemeinde-Orthodoxie*), Union of Jewish Women (*Jüdischer Frauenbund*), Reich Committee for Jewish Youth Organizations (*Reichsausschuss der jüdischen Jugendverbände*).

The most urgent tasks for the *Reichsvertretung*, which it will press energetically and with full commitment, following the avenues it has previously taken, are:

1. Our own Jewish educational system must serve to prepare the youth to become upright Jews, secure in their faith, who will draw the strength to face the onerous demands which life will make on them from conscious solidarity with the Jewish community, from work for the Jewish present and faith in the Jewish future. In addition to transmitting knowledge, the Jewish schools must also serve in the systematic preparation for future occupations. With regard to preparation for emigration, particularly to Palestine, emphasis will be placed on guidance toward manual work and the study of the Hebrew language. The education and vocational training of girls must be directed to preparing them to carry out their responsibilities as upholders of the family and mothers of the next generation.

An independent cultural structure must offer possibilities of employment to Jews who are artistically and culturally creative, and serve the separate cultural life of the Jews in Germany.

2. The *increased need* for emigration will be served by large-scale planning, firstly with respect to *Palestine*, but also to all other available countries, with particular attention to young people. This includes study of additional possibilities for emigration, *training* in professions suited for emigrants, particularly agriculture and technical skills; the creation of ways and means to mobilize and liquidate the property of persons who are economically independent, the broadening of existing means of transferring property and the creation of additional such means.

3. Support and care of the needy, sick or aged must be assured through further systematic expansion of the Jewish *welfare services* provided by the communities to supplement government social services.

4. An impoverished community cannot carry out these varied and difficult tasks. The *Reichsvertretung* will try by every means to safeguard the economic position of the Jews by seeking to *protect the existing means of livelihood*. Those who are econo-

mically weak will be assisted by the further development of such *economic aids* as employment bureaus, economic advice, and personal or mortgage loans.

5. *We are given strength in the present and hope for the future by the vitality of the progress in the construction of a Jewish Palestine.* In order to draw the Jews of Germany even more closely into this development, the *Reichsvertretung* itself has joined the *Palestine Foundation Fund* (Keren Hayesod) and appeals warmly to Jewish communities and organizations to follow its example. The *Reichsvertretung* offers its services to establish organizational links between the institutions of the Jews in Germany and the work of reconstruction in Palestine.

*

In full awareness of the magnitude of the responsibilities involved and the difficulties of the task, the *Reichsvertretung* calls on the Jewish men and women, and on all Jewish youth, to join together in unity, to maintain high Jewish morale, to practise strictest self-discipline, and show a maximum willingness to make sacrifices.

II

In accordance with a proposal made in the presidium of the *Reichsvertretung,* the *Reichsvertretung,* the state Federations and the communities are requested to cooperate closely in taking such organizational and personnel measures as are required in the Jewish bodies in order to ensure the vigorous and systematic carrying out of the new working program by all Jewish official bodies."

Jüdische Rundschau, No. 77, September 24, 1935.

* *Reichsvertretung der Juden in Deutschland* — National Representation of the Jews in Germany.
** See Document 29.

39

PRAYER COMPOSED BY RABBI LEO BAECK FOR ALL JEWISH COMMUNITIES IN GERMANY FOR THE EVE OF THE DAY OF ATONEMENT, OCTOBER 10, 1935 *

At this hour the whole House of Israel stands before its God, the God of Justice and the God of Mercy. We shall examine our ways before Him. We shall examine what we have done and what we have failed to do; we shall examine where we have gone and where we have failed to go. Wherever we have sinned we will confess it: We will say "we have sinned" and will pray with the will to repentance before the Lord and we will pray: "Lord forgive us!"

We stand before our God and with the same courage with which we have acknowledged our sins, the sins of the individual and the sins of the community, shall we express our abhorrence of the lie directed against us, and the slander of our faith and its expressions: this slander is far below us. We believe in our faith and our future. Who brought the world the secret of the Lord Everlasting, of the Lord Who is One? Who brought the world understanding for a life of purity, for the purity of the family? Who brought the world respect for Man made in the image of God? Who brought the world the commandment of justice, of social thought? In all these the spirit of the Prophets of Israel, the Revelation of God to the Jewish People had a part. It sprang from our Judaism, and continues to grow in it. All the slander drops away when it is cast against these facts.

We stand before our God: Our strength is in Him. In Him is the truth and the dignity of our history; In Him is the source of our survival through every change, our firm stand in all our trials. Our history is the history of spiritual greatness, spiritual dignity. We turn to it when attack and insult are directed against us, when need and suffering press in upon us. The Lord led our fathers from generation to generation. He will continue to lead us and our children through our days.

We stand before our God; we draw strength from His Commandments, which we obey. We bow down before Him, and we stand upright before Men. Him we serve, and remain steadfast in all the changes around us. We put our faith in Him in humility and our way ahead is clear, we see our future.

The whole House of Israel stands before its God at this hour. Our prayer, our faith, and our belief is that of all the Jews on earth. We look upon each other and know ourselves, we raise our eyes to the Lord and know what is eternal.

"Behold, He that guardeth Israel shall neither slumber nor sleep."

"He who maketh peace in His high places, may He make peace for us and for all Israel, and say ye, Amen."

We are filled with sorrow and pain. In silence will we give expression to all that which is in our hearts, in moments of silence before our God. This silent worship will be more emphatic than any words could be.

The Attorney-General of the Government of Israel v. Adolf Eichmann, Minutes of Session No. 14, Jerusalem, 1961.

* The reading of this prayer was banned by order of the Gestapo, and Rabbi Leo Baeck and Otto Hirsch were arrested for a short period by the Germans.

40

EXTRACT FROM A MEMORANDUM BY HITLER ON THE TASKS OF THE FOUR YEAR PLAN, 1936

The Political Situation

Politics is the conduct and process of the historical struggle for the life of nations. The aim of these struggles is survival. Idealistic struggles over world views (*Weltanschaung*) also have their ultimate causes, and draw their deepest motivating power from purposes and aims in life that derive from national (*völklich*) sources But religions and world views can give such struggles an especial sharpness and by this means endow them with a great historic effectiveness. They can put their mark on the character of centuries. It is then not possible for nations and states which exist within the sphere of influence of such conflicts of philosophical or religious nature to stand apart or exclude themselves from these events. . .

Since the beginning of the French Revolution the world has been drifting with increasing speed towards a new conflict, whose most extreme solution is named Bolshevism, but whose content and aim is only the removal of those strata of society which gave the leadership to humanity up to the present, and their replacing by international Jewry. . .

It is not the purpose of this memorandum to prophesy when the intolerable situation in Europe will become an open crisis. In these lines I wish only to record my conviction that this crisis cannot and will not fail to arrive, and that Germany has a duty to make its own existence secure by all possible means in face of this catastrophe and to protect itself against it; a number of conclusions follow from this necessity, and these involve the most important tasks that our nation has ever faced. For a victory of Bolshevism over Germany would not lead to a Versailles Treaty, but to the final destruction, even the extermination of the German people. . .

The extent of such a catastrophe cannot be foreseen. How, indeed, would the whole of densely populated Western Europe (including Germany) after a collapse into Bolshevism, live through probably the most gruesome catastrophe for the peoples which has been visited upon mankind since the downfall of the States of antiquity.

Faced with the need to fend off this danger, all other considerations must be relegated to the background as totally without significance. . .

Akten zur deutschen auswärtigen Politik 1918-1945 ("Documents on German Foreign Policy 1918-1945"), series E (1933-1937), Vol. V, 2. Göttingen, 1977, pp. 793-795.

41

Second Regulation for the Law on the Reunification of Austria with the German Reich, March 18, 1938

Based on Article III of the Law on the Reunification of Austria with the German Reich of March 13, 1938 (*Reichsgesetzbl.* I, p. 237), the following is ordered :

§ 1
The *Reichsführer* SS and Head of the German Police in the Reich Ministry of the Interior may take measures necessary for Security and Order even beyond the legal limits otherwise set for this purpose.

§ 2
The *Reichsführer* SS and Head of the German Police in the Reich Ministry of the Interior can transfer his authority to other offices.

§ 3
This Regulation takes effect on the date of promulgation.

Berlin, March 18, 1938

Reich Minister of the Interior
signed Frick

Reichsgesetzblatt, I, 1938, p. 262.

42

ABOLITION OF THE LEGAL STATUS OF THE JEWISH COMMUNITIES, MARCH 1938

Law Concerning the Legal Status of the Jewish Religious Communities, March 28, 1938

The Reich Government has enacted the following law, which is promulgated herewith:

§ 1

1) Jewish religious communal organizations and their roof organizations obtain legal standing by means of registration in the Register of Associations.

2) At the end of March 31, 1938, Jewish religious organizations and their roof organizations will lose the status of Corporations under public law, insofar as they possessed such status up to the present time. From this date on they will be private Associations with legal status under civil law. Entry in the Register of Associations must be carried out...

Berlin, March 28, 1938

The Führer and Reich Chancellor
Adolf Hitler
The Reich Minister for Church Affairs
Kerrl
The Reich Minister of the Interior
Frick

Reichsgesetzblatt, I, 1938, p. 338.

43

THE SITUATION OF THE JEWS IN AUSTRIA, APRIL 1938

Report

Submitted to the Executive of the Zionist Organization by Dr. Leo Lauterbach *

... Generally speaking the situation in Vienna seemed to be, both on the non-Jewish and the Jewish side, characterized by confusion, uncertainty and a state of flux. The mission of Sir Wyndham Deedes was greatly handicapped by the fact that, at the time of his and my visit, there seemed to be no established authority from whom the official policy could be reliably ascertained and whose intervention could be solicited. The position might have changed since, but at the time it appeared that the chief authority was vested in the Gestapo, whose officials were at that time in Berlin and who, as we learned there afterwards, returned to Vienna with, it was stated, a full measure of independence from their headquarters in Berlin. Possibly the Gestapo are now under instructions from Herr Bürckel. A clear policy with regard to the Jewish problem in Austria has neither been announced in public, nor was it conveyed to us in the few interviews we succeeded in having. One cannot, however, avoid the impression that this policy will be essentially different from that adopted in Germany and that it may aim at a complete annihilation of Austrian Jewry. To all appearances, it is intended to eliminate them from economic life, to deprive them of all their financial resources, and to compel them either to starve or to leave the country without means, at the expense of the great Jewish organizations abroad and with the help of such countries as may be willing to receive them.

For reasons of their own the authorities seem to wish to deal with Austrian Jews without any interference by the Jews in Germany. One cannot help feeling that, after the protracted campaign of intimidation, the Jews of Austria have become a pliable instrument in the hands of their oppressors, who may think that they will achieve their ends more easily if they deal directly with people whose moral backbone has been broken.

If this analysis is correct, no effort should be spared on our side to counteract such tendencies and to give the Austrian Jews not only material support, but also moral encouragement. For that purpose it would seem to be the most urgent task of the moment to delegate to Austria representatives of the great Jewish and Zionist organizations abroad who, with permission of the authorities, would be allowed to act there, even if only temporarily, as advisers and helpers of the local leaders. In addition, any future financial support given by Jewish institutions abroad ought to be made dependent as far as possible upon the establishing of a permanent contact between the Jewish institutions in Vienna and those in Berlin...

(sgd) Leo Lauterbach

London,
29th April, 1938

Zionist Archives, S5/653.

* Director of the Organization Department of the World Zionist Organization.

44

EICHMANN TAKES CONTROL OF JEWISH LIFE IN AUSTRIA

"Vienna — May 8, 1938 — Dear Herbert ! * Today I want to write you a little letter again. I have just been to all our sub-sections. I gave the people working there a general idea of the subject under discussion, which they received with appreciation for, after all, they had had no notion up to now. I hope that I will shortly be in possession of the Jewish year-books of all neighboring states, which I will then send you. I consider them an important aid. All Jewish organizations in Austria have been ordered to make out weekly reports. These will go to the appropriate experts in II 112 in each case, sub-sections and sections. The reports are to be divided into a report on the situation and a report on activities. They are due each week on a Monday in Vienna, and on the Thursday of each week in the provinces. I hope to be able to send you the first reports by tomorrow. The first issue of the Zionist *Rundschau* is to appear on the Friday of next week. I have had the manuscript sent to me and am on the boring job of censorship just now. You will of course get the newspaper, too. This will in time, up to a point, become "my paper." In any case I have got these gentlemen on the go, you may believe me. They are now already working very busily. I demanded an emigration figure of 20,000 Jews without means for the period from April 1, 1938 to May 1, 1939, of the Jewish Community and the Zionist Organization for Austria, and they promised me that they would keep to this...

Tomorrow I will again check on the offices of the Jewish Community and the Zionists. I do that at least once every week. They are completely in my hands here, they dare not take a step without checking with me first. That is the way it should be, because it gives better possibilities of control. We can save ourselves the creation of a fourth Jewish roof-organization, similar to the *Hilfsverein*. I have instructed the Jewish Community to establish a central emigration office within the Community for all countries apart from Palestine. The preparatory work for this has already been set in motion. Just in quite basic lines the situation is now as follows : according to the Decree, *Gauleiter* Bürckel will deal with Aryanization, Jews in the economy, etc. The far more difficult business of getting the Jews to emigrate is the task of the SD. Now that the Jewish Community and the Jewish Association in Austria have been reorganized, their work is also aimed at emigration. I hope that with this I have put you in the picture again briefly...

Regards to all the comrades on II 112, your old Adolf.

The Attorney-General of the Government of Israel v. Adolf Eichmann,
Minutes of Session No. 18, Jerusalem, 1961.

* Herbert Hagen, Eichmann's colleague in the Gestapo Department of Jewish Affairs.

45

DECISIONS TAKEN AT THE EVIAN CONFERENCE ON JEWISH REFUGEES, JULY 1938

(The Intergovernmental Committee)
Adopted by the Committee on July 14th, 1938

"Having met at Evian, France, from July 6th to July 13th, 1938 :
1. Considering that the question of involuntary emigration has assumed major proportions and that the fate of the unfortunate people affected has become a problem for intergovernmental deliberation;
2. Aware that the involuntary emigration of large numbers of people, of different creeds, economic conditions, professions and trades, from the country or countries where they have been established, is disturbing to the general economy, since these persons are obliged to seek refuge, either temporarily or permanently, in other countries at a time when there is serious unemployment; that, in consequence, countries of refuge and settlement are faced with problems, not only of an economic and social nature, but also of public order, and that there is a severe strain on the administrative facilities and absorptive capacities of the receiving countries;

3. Aware, moreover, that the involuntary emigration of people in large numbers has become so great that it renders racial and religious problems more acute, increases international unrest, and may hinder seriously the processes of appeasement in international relations;

4. Believing that it is essential that a long-range programme should be envisaged, whereby assistance to involuntary emigrants, actual and potential, may be co-ordinated within the framework of existing migration laws and practices of Governments;

5. Considering that if countries of refuge or settlement are to co-operate in finding an orderly solution of the problem before the Committee they should have the collaboration of the country of origin and are therefore persuaded that it will make its contribution by enabling involuntary emigrants to take with them their property and possessions and emigrate in an orderly manner;

6. Welcoming heartily the initiative taken by the President of the United States of America in calling the Intergovernmental Meeting at Evian for the primary purpose of facilitating involuntary emigration from Germany (including Austria), and expressing profound appreciation to the French Government for its courtesy in receiving the Intergovernmental Meeting at Evian;

7. Bearing in mind the resolution adopted by the Council of the League of Nations on May 14th, 1938, concerning international assistance to refugees :

Recommends :

8. a) That the persons coming within the scope of the activity of the Intergovernmental Committee shall be 1) persons who have not already left their country of origin (Germany, including Austria), but who must emigrate on account of their political opinion, religious beliefs or racial origin, and 2) persons as defined in 1) who have already left their country of origin and who have not yet established themselves permanently elsewhere;

b) That the Governments participating in the Intergovernmental Committee shall continue to furnish the Committee for its strictly confidential information, with 1) details regarding such immigrants as each Government may be prepared to receive under its existing

laws and practices and 2) details of these laws and practices;
c) That in view of the fact that the countries of refuge and
settlement are entitled to take into account the economic and
social adaptability of immigrants, these should in many cases
be required to accept, at least for a time, changed conditions of
living in the countries of settlement;
d) That the Governments of the countries of refuge and settlement
should not assume any obligations for the financing of involuntary
emigration;
e) That, with regard to the documents required by the countries
of refuge and settlement, the Governments represented on the
Intergovernmental Committee should consider the adoption of
the following provision :
In those individual immigration cases in which the usually required documents emanating from foreign official sources are
found not to be available, there should be accepted such other
documents serving the purpose of the requirements of law as
may be available to the immigrant, and that, as regards the
document which may be issued to an involuntary emigrant by
the country of his foreign residence to serve the purpose of a
passport, note be taken of the several international agreements
providing for the issue of a travel document serving the purpose
of a passport and of the advantage of their wide application;
f) That there should meet at London an Intergovernmental Committee consisting of such representatives as the Governments
participating in the Evian Meeting may desire to designate. This
Committee shall continue and develop the work of the Intergovernmental Meeting at Evian and shall be constituted and
shall function in the following manner : There shall be a Chairman
of this Committee and four Vice-Chairmen; there shall be a
director of authority, appointed by the Intergovernmental Committee, who shall be guided by it in his actions. He shall undertake negotiations to improve the present conditions of exodus
and to replace them by conditions of orderly emigration. He shall
approach the Governments of the countries of refuge and settlement with a view to developing opportunities for permanent

97

settlement. The Intergovernmental Committee, recognising the value of the work of the existing refugee services of the League of Nations and of the studies of migration made by the International Labor Office, shall co-operate fully with these organizations, and the Intergovernmental Committee at London shall consider the means by which the co-operation of the Committee and the Director with these organizations shall be established. The Intergovernmental Committee, at its forthcoming meeting at London, will consider the scale on which its expenses shall be apportioned among the participating Governments;

9. That the Intergovernmental Committee in its continued form shall hold a first meeting at London on August 3rd, 1938."

Proceedings of the Intergovernmental Committee, Evian, July 6th to 15th, 1938... Record of the Plenary Meetings of the Committee. Resolutions and Reports, London, July 1938.

46

REGULATION REQUIRING JEWS TO CHANGE THEIR NAMES, AUGUST 1938

Second Regulation for the Implementation of the Law Regarding the Changing of Family Names and Given Names, August 17, 1938

§ 2

1) Insofar as Jews have given names other than those which they are permitted to bear according to § 1,* they are required as from January 1, 1939, to take an additional given name; males will take the given name Israel, females the given name Sara. . .

98

Berlin, August 17, 1938

The Reich Minister of the Interior
signed for Dr. Stuckart
The Reich Minister of Justice
Dr. Gürtner

Reichsgesetzblatt, I, 1938, p. 1044.

* The reference is to conspicuously Jewish names, which were published in a separate list.

47

ESTABLISHMENT OF THE CENTRAL OFFICE FOR JEWISH EMIGRATION IN VIENNA, AUGUST 1938 *

The *Reichskommissar*
for the Reunification of
Austria with the German Reich
        Staff

Vienna I, August 20, 1938

To all offices of the Party and State in Austria

Undesirable interruptions and delays have occurred in the emigration of Jews; in addition, the question of Jewish emigration has been dealt with inefficiently by certain offices.

To assist and expedite arrangements for the emigration of Jews from Austria a Central Office for Jewish Emigration has therefore been set up in Vienna IV, at Prinz Eugen Strasse 22.

The Central Office will be responsible for dealing with the following matters, in cooperation with the Government Offices concerned :

1. The creation of opportunities for emigration through negotiations for entry permits with the competent German and other
emigration organizations.

2. Obtaining the foreign currency required for emigration.

3. Establishment and supervision of professional re-training
centers.

4. Cooperation with travel agencies and shipping companies to
ensure the technical arrangements for emigration.

5. Supervision of Jewish political and other emigration associations with regard to their attitude concerning emigration.

6. The issuing of guidelines and continuous contacts with all
offices connected with the emigration of Jews from Austria...

All Party offices and other authorities are instructed to pass
on all applications for emigration to the Central Office for
Jewish Emigration immediately and without taking action of
their own for the time being, and to send all Jews anxious to
emigrate to the above office. Jews who wish to emigrate are
in future to apply only to the Central Office for Jewish Emigration.
This office will control further procedures and, in particular,
obtain the permits required for emigration from the competent
offices, and supervise the final emigration.

This Regulation applies, for the time being, to the *Gau* Vienna
and Lower Danube. The procedures in other areas are regulated
by the Central Office for Jewish Emigration in consultation
with the local *Gauleiters*.

A central office for Jewish Planning in conjunction with the
Central Office for Jewish Emigration is definitely still under
consideration.

I entrust the general direction of these Central Offices to the
SD-Führer of the SS Section Upper Danube and Inspector of
the Security Police, SS *Standartenführer* Governmental Director
Dr. Stahlecker. He is herewith invested with the necessary powers
to carry out his commission. In particular, he is entitled to

order the transfer of officials of the Authorities concerned with emigration to the Central Office for Jewish Emigration.

Heil Hitler !
signed Bürckel
Gauleiter

Österreichisches Staatsarchiv — Abteilung : Allgemeines Verwaltungsarchiv. Der Reichskommissar für die Wiedervereinigung Österreichs mit dem Deutschen Reiche (Austrian State Achives — Department: General Administrative Archives. The *Reichskommissar* for the Reunification of Austria with the German Reich), 1762/2.

* See Document 57.

48

FIRST ATTEMPT OF THE NAZI PARTY TO EXPEL VIENNESE JEWRY, OCTOBER 1938

Security Service of the *Reichsführer* SS
Vienna 4

Vienna, October 5, 1938

To the
SD Sub-Section
Vienna

Re : Operation against Jews
Previous corresp. : None

At yesterday's meeting of leading representatives [of the Nazi Party] at the Local Group "Goldegg" (Vienna, sub-District 3), it was announced by the head of the local group that in accordance with instructions from the *Gau*, a stepped-up operation against the Jews was to take place through October 10, 1938. As many Jews as possible should be caused to emigrate. If the Jews have

no passports, then they will be pushed over the Czech border
to Prague without a passport. If the Jews have no cash money
they would be given RM 40— by the *Gau* for their departure.

In this operation against the Jews the impression is to be
avoided that it is a Party matter; instead, spontaneous demonstrations by the people are to be caused. There could be use
of force where Jews resist.

Manager
SD Branch, Vienna

Yad Vashem Archives, O-5/1-2.

49

RIOTS OF KRISTALLNACHT * —
HEYDRICH'S INSTRUCTIONS, NOVEMBER 1938

Secret
*Copy of Most Urgent telegram from Munich, of November
10, 1938, 1:20 A.M.*
To
All Headquarters and Stations of the State Police
All Districts and Sub-districts of the SD
Urgent! For immediate attention of Chief or his deputy!

Re : *Measures against Jews tonight*

Following the attempt on the life of Secretary of the Legation
vom Rath in Paris, demonstrations against the Jews are to be
expected in all parts of the Reich in the course of the coming
night, November 9/10, 1938. The instructions below are to be
applied in dealing with these events :

1. The Chiefs of the State Police, or their deputies, must
immediately upon receipt of this telegram contact, by telephone,
the political leaders in their areas — *Gauleiter* or *Kreisleiter* —

who have jurisdiction in their districts and arrange a joint meeting with the inspector or commander of the Order Police to discuss the arrangements for the demonstrations. At these discussions the political leaders will be informed that the German Police has received instructions, detailed below, from the *Reichsführer* SS and the Chief of the German Police, with which the political leadership is requested to coordinate its own measures:

a) Only such measures are to be taken as do not endanger German lives or property (i.e., synagogues are to be burned down only where there is no danger of fire in neighboring buildings).
b) Places of business and apartments belonging to Jews may be destroyed but not looted. The police is instructed to supervise the observance of this order and to arrest looters.
c) In commercial streets particular care is to be taken that non-Jewish businesses are completely protected against damage.
d) Foreign citizens — even if they are Jews — are not to be molested.

2. On the assumption that the guidelines detailed under para. 1 are observed, the demonstrations are not to be prevented by the Police, which is only to supervise the observance of the guidelines.

3. On receipt of this telegram Police will seize all archives to be found in all synagogues and offices of the Jewish communities so as to prevent their destruction during the demonstrations. This refers only to material of historical value, not to contemporary tax records, etc. The archives are to be handed over to the locally responsible officers of the SD.

4. The control of the measures of the Security Police concerning the demonstrations against the Jews is vested in the organs of the State Police, unless inspectors of the Security Police have given their own instructions. Officials of the Criminal Police, members of the SD, of the Reserves and the SS in general may be used to carry out the measures taken by the Security Police.

5. As soon as the course of events during the night permits the release of the officials required, as many Jews in all districts — especially the rich — as can be accommodated in existing prisons are to be arrested. For the time being only healthy male Jews, who are not too old, are to be detained. After the detentions have been carried out the appropriate concentration camps are to be contacted immediately for the prompt accommodation of the Jews in the camps. Special care is to be taken that the Jews arrested in accordance with these instructions are not ill-treated. . . . .

signed Heydrich,
SS *Gruppenführer*

PS — 3051.

* "Night of the Broken Glass."

50

DESCRIPTION OF THE RIOT AT DINSLAKEN

. . . I recognized a Jewish face. In a few words the stranger explained to me: "I am the president of the Jewish community of Düsseldorf. I spent the night in the waiting-room of the Gelsenkirchen Railway Station. I have only one request — let me take refuge in the orphanage for a short while. While I was traveling to Dinslaken I heard in the train that anti-Semitic riots had broken out everywhere, and that many Jews had been arrested. Synagogues everywhere are burning!"

With anxiety I listened to the man's story; suddenly he said with a trembling voice: "No, I won't come in! I can't be safe in your house! We are all lost!" With these words he disappeared into the dark fog which cast a veil over the morning. I never saw him again.

104

In spite of this Job's message I forced myself not to show any sign of emotion. Only thus could I avoid a state of panic among the children and tutors. Nonetheless I was of the opinion that the young students should be prepared to brave the storm of the approaching catastrophe. About 7:30 A.M. I ordered 46 people — among them 32 children — into the dining hall of the institution and told them the following in a simple and brief address:

"As you know, last night a Herr vom Rath, a member of the German Embassy in Paris, was assassinated. The Jews are held responsible for this murder. The high tension in the political field is now being directed against the Jews, and during the next few hours there will certainly be anti-Semitic excesses. This will happen even in our town. It is my feeling and my impression that we German Jews have never experienced such calamities since the Middle Ages. Be strong! Trust in God! I am sure we will withstand even these hard times. Nobody will remain in the rooms of the upper floor of the building. The exit door to the street will be opened only by myself! From this moment on everyone is to heed my orders only!"

After breakfast the pupils were sent to the large study-hall of the institution. The teacher in charge tried to keep them busy.

At 9:30 A.M. the bell at the main gate rang persistently. I opened the door: about 50 men stormed into the house, many of them with their coat- or jacket-collars turned up. At first they rushed into the dining room, which fortunately was empty, and there they began their work of destruction, which was carried out with the utmost precision. The frightened and fearful cries of the children resounded through the building. In a stentorian voice I shouted: "Children, go out into the street immediately!" This advice was certainly contrary to the order of the Gestapo. I thought, however, that in the street, in a public place, we might be in less danger than inside the house. The children immediately ran down a small staircase at the back, most of them without hat or coat — despite the cold and wet weather. We tried to reach the next street crossing, which

105

was close to Dinslaken's Town Hall, where I intended to ask for police protection. About ten policemen were stationed here, reason enough for a sensation-seeking mob to await the next development. This was not very long in coming; the senior police officer, Freihahn, shouted at us: "Jews do not get protection from us! Vacate the area together with your children as quickly as possible!" Freihahn then chased us back to a side street in the direction of the backyard of the orphanage. As I was unable to hand over the key of the back gate, the policeman drew his bayonet and forced open the door. I then said to Freihahn: "The best thing is to kill me and the children, then our ordeal will be over quickly!" The officer responded to my "suggestion" merely with cynical laughter. Freihahn then drove all of us to the wet lawn of the orphanage garden. He gave us strict orders not to leave the place under any circumstances.

Facing the back of the building, we were able to watch how everything in the house was being systematically destroyed under the supervision of the men of law and order — the police. At short intervals we could hear the crunching of glass or the hammering against wood as windows and doors were broken. Books, chairs, beds, tables, linen, chests, parts of a piano, a radiogram, and maps were thrown through apertures in the wall, which a short while ago had been windows or doors.

In the meantime the mob standing around the building had grown to several hundred. Among these people I recognized some familiar faces, suppliers of the orphanage or trades-people, who only a day or a week earlier had been happy to deal with us as customers. This time they were passive, watching the destruction without much emotion.

At 10:15 A.M. we heard the wailing of sirens! We noticed a heavy cloud of smoke billowing upward. It was obvious from the direction it was coming from that the Nazis had set the synagogue on fire. Very soon we saw smoke-clouds rising up, mixed with sparks of fire. Later I noticed that some Jewish houses, close to the synagogue, had also been set alight under the expert guidance of the fire-brigade. Its presence was a necessity, since the firemen had to save the homes of the non-Jewish neighborhood...

In the schoolyard we had to wait for some time. Several Jews, who had escaped the previous arrest and deportation to concentration camps, joined our gathering. Many of them, mostly women, were shabbily dressed. They told me that the brown hordes had driven them out of their homes, ordered them to leave everything behind and come at once, under Nazi guard, to the schoolyard. A stormtrooper in charge commanded some bystanders to leave the schoolyard "since there is no point in even looking at such scum!"

In the meantime our "family" had increased to 90, all of whom were placed in a small hall in the school. Nobody was allowed to leave the place. Men considered physically fit were called for duty. Only those over 60 — among them people of 75 years of age — were allowed to stay. Very soon we learned that the entire Jewish male population under 60 had already been transferred to the concentration camp at Dachau. During their initial waiting period, while still under police custody, the Jewish men had been allowed to buy their own food. This state of affairs, however, only lasted for a few hours.

I learned very soon from a policeman, who in his heart was still an anti-Nazi, that most of the Jewish men had been beaten up by members of the SA before being transported to Dachau. They were kicked, slapped in the face, and subjected to all sorts of humiliation. Many of those exposed to this type of ill-treatment had served in the German army during World War I. One of them, a Mr. Hugo B.C., had once worn with pride the Iron Cross First Class (the German equivalent of the Victoria Cross), which he had been awarded for bravery....

Y. S. Herz, "*Kristallnacht* at the Dinslaken Orphanage," *Yad Vashem Studies*, XI, 1976, pp. 345-349.

51

DISCUSSIONS BY THE AUTHORITIES FOLLOWING
KRISTALLNACHT

Stenographic Report of the Meeting on the Jewish Question held under the Chairmanship of Field Marshal Göring in the Reich Air Ministry at 11 A.M. on November 12, 1938

Göring: Gentlemen! Today's meeting is of decisive importance. I have received a letter on the Führer's orders by the Head of Staff of the Führer's deputy, Bormann, with instructions that the Jewish Question is to be summed up and coordinated once and for all and solved one way or another. A phone call from the Führer to me yesterday again gave me instructions that decisive coordinated steps must now be outlined.

As the problem is in the main a large-scale economic matter, it is from this angle that it will have to be tackled. This will, of course, produce a number of legal measures, in the jurisdiction of the Justice Minister as well as the Minister of Interior; and then the resultant propaganda measures which fall into the area of the Propaganda Minister; and of course also measures by the Finance Minister and Economics Minister.

At the meeting at which this question was discussed for the first time and it was decided to Aryanize the German economy, to get the Jew out of the economy, to make them debtors on a pension, we unfortunately only made very fine plans, but then dragged our feet in following them up...

Heydrich: After all the elimination of the Jew from economic life, in the end there is still always the basic problem of getting the Jew out of Germany. May I make a few suggestions in this connection?

Following a suggestion made by the *Reichskommissar* we have set up a Reich Central Office for Jewish Emigration in Vienna* with the aid of which we have taken at least 50,000 Jews away from Austria, while only 19,000 Jews were taken out of the Reich during the same period. It was made possible by coordination between the Ministry of Economics, which was responsible, and the foreign aid organizations.

Göring: First of all you cooperated with the local leader of the "green border" [clandestine border crossing]. That is the main thing.

Heydrich: That involved only very small numbers, Mr. Field Marshal. The illegal —

Göring: The story has gone through the entire world press. In the first night the Jews were expelled to Czechoslovakia. Next morning the Czechs caught them and pushed them across into Hungary. From Hungary they were returned to Germany and then to Czechoslovakia. That way they travelled around and around. In the end they finished up on an old barge on the Danube. They stayed there and wherever they tried to land they were turned away again.

Heydrich: That's what was reported. There were not even as many as 100 Jews.

Göring: For two weeks, in effect, a number of Jews emigrated every midnight. That was in Burgenland.

Heydrich: At least 45,000 Jews got away by legal means.

Göring: How was that possible?

Heydrich: Through the Jewish Community Council we took a certain sum off the rich Jews who wanted to emigrate. That was how it was done. With this money and some additional foreign currency it was then possible to get out a number of poor Jews. After all, the problem is not to get the rich Jews out, but the Jewish mob.

Göring: But, fellows, have you ever thought about this properly? It doesn't really help us even if we get a few hundred thousand of the Jewish mob away from Germany. Have you ever considered whether this procedure may not, in the long run, cost so much foreign currency that we cannot continue with it permanently?

Heydrich: Only the foreign currency that every Jew received.
(Göring: agrees.)

109

This way. May I suggest that we set up a similar bureau in the Reich, with the cooperation of the government agencies concerned, and that we make use of this experience [Austria] in order to find a solution for the Reich, at the same time avoiding the mistakes which the Field Marshal has so rightly pointed out to us?

(Göring: agrees.)

A second way of getting the Jews out would be an emigration operation for the Jews in the rest of the Reich, spread over at least 8 to 10 years. We cannot get out more than the maximum of 8,000 to 10,000 Jews a year. That would leave a great many Jews here. Because of Aryanization and other restrictions Jewry will become unemployed. We will see the remaining Jews becoming proletarians. I would have to take measures in Germany to isolate the Jews, on the one hand, so that they will not enter into the normal life of the Germans. On the other hand, I must create possibilities of permitting the Jews certain activities, in the matter of lawyers, doctors, barbers, etc., while yet limiting them to the smallest possible circle of customers. This question will have to be studied.

As far as isolation is concerned, I should like to put forward a few suggestions, purely police matters, which are important in part for their psychological effect on public opinion. For instance, the identification of the Jews, saying: Every person who is a Jew in accordance with the Nuremberg Laws must wear a certain distinguishing mark. This is a possibility which would simplify many other matters — I don't see any danger of excesses against the Jews — and it would make our relationship with foreign Jews easier.

Göring: A uniform!

Heydrich: Badge. This would also prevent the foreign Jews, whose external appearance is no different from that of the local Jews, from suffering the same disadvantages.

Göring: But my dear Heydrich, you will not be able to avoid having ghettos in the cities on a really big scale. They will have to be established.

110

Heydrich: As for the matter of ghettos, I would like to make my position clear right away. From a police point of view I think that a ghetto, in the form of a completely segregated district with only Jews, is not possible. We would have no control over a ghetto where the Jew gets together with the whole of his Jewish tribe. It would be a permanent hideout for criminals and first of all [a source] of epidemics and the like. The situation today is that the German population... [which lives together with the Jews] forces the Jews to behave more carefully in the streets and the houses.· The control of the Jews by the watchful eyes of the whole population is better than putting thousands upon thousands of Jews together in a single district of a city where uniformed officials will be unable to check on their daily activities.

Göring: We only have to cut off the telephone link with the outside.

Heydrich: I could not stop the movements of Jewry out from this district completely.

Göring: And in cities really all their own?

Heydrich: Yes, if I put them into cities entirely their own. But then this city would become such a center for criminal elements that it would be very dangerous. I would try a different way...

Göring: I shall choose the definition that the German Jews as a whole, as a punishment for their abominable crimes, etc., etc., will have to pay a *Kontribution* (fine) of one billion. That will do it. The swine won't hurry to commit another murder. In general I must say once again: I should not like to be a Jew in Germany.

v. Krosigk: That is why I would like to emphasize what Mr. Heydrich said at the beginning: we must try everything in the way of more export, of getting the Jews out abroad. It will always be the decisive point that we do not have to keep this whole proletarian company here. It will always be a terrible burden to deal with them.

(Frick: and a danger.)

111

I also do not imagine that if we are forced to have ghettos it would be very pleasant. The likelihood of having to have ghettos is not pleasant. Therefore the aim must be what Heydrich said: out with whoever can be got out!

Göring: The second point is the following. If the German Reich should in the near future become involved in conflict abroad then it is obvious that we in Germany will first of all make sure of settling accounts with the Jews. Apart from that the Führer is now at last to make a major move abroad, starting with the Powers which have brought up the Jewish question, in order really to get around to the Madagascar solution. He explained this to me in detail on November 9. There is no longer any other way. He is also going to say to the other nations: "Why do you keep talking about the Jews? — Take them!". . .

Funk: The decisive question is whether the Jewish stores will have to be re-opened or not?

Göring: That depends on the extent to which these Jewish stores have a relatively large turnover. If that is the case it is a sign that the German people are simply forced to buy there although it is a Jewish store, because there is a need. If all the Jewish stores that are shut now were to be shut before Christmas many would go empty-handed.

Fischböck: We already have a precise plan for this in Austria, Mr. Field Marshal General. In Vienna there are 12,000 Jewish artisans' businesses and 5,000 Jewish retail stores. Even before the *Umbruch*** there was a plan for all the tradesmen involved in these 17,000 open businesses; of the 12,000 artisans' shops almost 10,000 were to be closed for good, and 2,000 kept going. Of the 5,000 retail stores, 1,000 were to be kept going, that is they were to be Aryanized, and 4,000 were to be shut. According to this plan, then, 3,000 to 3,500 of the total of 17,000 businesses would remain open, and all the others would be closed. This is calculated on the basis of investigation for each separate branch and in accordance with local requirements. It has been settled with all the competent authorities and could

112

start tomorrow, as soon as we get the Law which we requested in September, which would authorize us to withdraw trade licenses generally, without any connection with the Jewish Question. It would be quite a short Law.

Göring: I will issue the regulation today.

Fischböck: We had been promised this for Austria within the framework of our general economic plan. I think that it was not settled only because of ongoing negotiations between the Reich Ministry of Economics and [the Ministry of] Nutrition. There was agreement on principle. As soon as we have it we can close these 10,000 businesses officially. That's just paperwork. In order to carry it out it will then still be necessary for somebody to see to what is to be done with the goods in these businesses. Up to last week we had had the intention of leaving the liquidation of stores more or less to the Jews themselves. That will now no longer be possible. We plan to create an economic agency for all these businesses together, which will see to it that use is made of these goods. In general this will be done best by handing them over to the branch concerned, which can then divide them up among the Aryan businesses, who can either take them on commission or pay for them.

If this is carried out along the proposed lines we will be left with only about another 3,000 businesses slated for Aryanization in accordance with the plans for the various branches. There are already firm buyers for about half these stores, and their purchase contracts have been checked sufficiently for immediate authorization. In many cases the authorization has not been finalized only because we were waiting for the definitive decision on the planning issue. Negotiations have also proceeded quite far for the other 15,000 businesses. We are of the opinion that we should set ourselves a deadline, which might be the end of this year. If no definite buyer has been found by the end of the year for the retail stores that are to be Aryanized we will check again whether they should not be liquidated after all. That should usually be possible: artisans' shops are very

113

individual businesses. As far as retail stores are concerned the matter would never be so urgent that it could be said that the economic damage was too great. That would leave us with just a very few stores that have been judged necessary but for which there are no buyers : they would have to be taken on by the Public Trustee's Office. I don't think that it would come to as many as 100 businesses, probably fewer. In this way we could have eliminated all publicly visible Jewish businesses by the end of the year.

Göring: That would be excellent!

Fischböck: Then 12,000 or 14,000 of 17,000 businesses would be closed and the rest Aryanized or transferred to the State Trustee.

Göring: I must say that this proposal is marvelous. Then the whole business would really be cleared out by Christmas or the end of the year in Vienna, one of the chief Jewish cities, so to say.

Funk: We can do it here [in Germany] too. I have prepared a Regulation for this matter which states that from January 1, 1939, Jews are forbidden to operate retail stores and commission agencies, or to operate independent artisans' businesses. They are also forbidden to hire employees for this purpose, to offer such services, to advertise them or to accept orders. Where any Jewish trade is carried out it will be closed by the Police. From January 1, 1939, a Jew can no longer be the manager of a business, in accordance with the Law for the Organization of National Labor, of January 20, 1934. Where a Jew is in a leading position in an economic enterprise without being the official manager his employment can be terminated by the manager with six weeks' notice. At the end of the period of notice all claims of the employee deriving from the terminated contract will be void, including pension rights where these existed. That is always very unpleasant and a great danger. A Jew cannot be a member of a cooperative. Jewish membership in cooperatives is terminated on December 31, 1938. No special

114

authorization is required. The Reich Ministers concerned are being authorized to issue the Regulations necessary for the implementation of the Law. . . .

PS — 1816.

* See Document 47.
** Austrian expression for *Anschluss*.

52

Regulation for the Elimination of the Jews from the Economic Life of Germany, November 12, 1938

On the basis of the regulation for the implementation of the Four Year Plan of October 18, 1936 (*Reichsgesetzblatt*, I, p. 887), the following is decreed:

§ 1

1) From January 1, 1939, Jews (§ 5 of the First Regulation to the Reich Citizenship Law of November 14, 1935, *Reichsgesetzblatt*, I, p. 1333) are forbidden to operate retail stores, mail-order houses, or sales agencies, or to carry on a trade [craft] independently.
2) They are further forbidden, from the same day on, to offer for sale goods or services, to advertise these, or to accept orders at markets of all sorts, fairs or exhibitions.
3) Jewish trade enterprises (Third Regulation to the Reich Citizenship Law of June 14, 1938 — *Reichsgesetzblatt*, I, p. 627) which violate this decree will be closed by police.

§ 2

1) From January 1, 1939, a Jew can no longer be the head of an enterprise within the meaning of the Law of January 20,

1934, for the Regulation of National Work (*Reichsgesetzblatt,* I, p. 45).

2) Where a Jew is employed in an executive position in a commercial enterprise he may be given notice to leave in six weeks. At the expiration of the term of the notice all claims of the employee based on his contract, especially those concerning pension and compensation rights, become invalid.

§ 3

1) A Jew cannot be a member of a cooperative.

2) The membership of Jews in cooperatives expires on December 31, 1938. No special notice is required.

§ 4

The Reich Minister of Economy, in coordination with the Ministers concerned, is empowered to publish regulations for the implementation of this decree. He may permit exceptions under the Law if these are required as the result of the transfer of a Jewish enterprise to non-Jewish ownership, for the liquidation of a Jewish enterprise or, in special cases, to ensure essential supplies.

Berlin, November 12, 1938

> *Plenipotentiary for the Four Year Plan*
> *Göring*
> Field Marshal General

Reichsgesetzblatt, I, 1938, p. 1580.

53

Regulation for the Payment of an Expiation Fine by Jews who are German Subjects, November 12, 1938

The hostile attitude of Jewry toward the German People and Reich, which does not even shrink from cowardly murder, calls for determined resistance and severe expiation. Based on the Decree of October 18, 1936, for the Implementation of the Four Year Plan (*Reichsgesetzblatt*, I, p. 887) I therefore order the following:

§ 1

The totality of Jews who are German subjects will pay a *Kontribution* (fine) of 1,000,000,000 (one billion) Reichsmarks to the German Reich.

§ 2

The Reich Minister of Finance in cooperation with the other Ministers concerned will issue regulations for the implementation of this order.

Berlin, November 12, 1938

Plenipotentiary for the Four Year Plan
Göring
Field Marshal General

Reichsgesetzblatt, I, 1938, p. 1579.

54

SS VIEWS ON THE SOLUTION OF THE JEWISH QUESTION
Jews, What Next?

...In 1933 and later we were simple-hearted and naive. When so-called public opinion in the world lost control of itself because our "barbaric ways" prevented the Jews from abusing our wives and daughters, then we took it very seriously, and tried to explain the Jewish Question to the others from the beginning — what holy simplicity! As though one of these waterproof democrats ever had the least interest in it!

What is the real position? Neither Mr. Roosevelt, nor an English Archbishop, nor any other prominent diploma-democrat would put his dear daughter in the bed of a greasy Eastern European Jew; only, when it is a question of Germany, they suddenly know nothing of any Jewish question, only of the

Das Schwarze Korps, no. 47, 24.11.1938

"Jews, What Next?" An article from the SS publication *Das Schwarze Korps*, November 24, 1938

"persecution of innocents because of their religion," as though we had ever been interested in anything a Jew believes or doesn't believe.

The real situation and truth is that these diploma-democrats know the Jewish question very well, in fact — one need only look at their immigration regulations and their fear of Jewish immigrants — and even derive practical conclusions from them, but pretend to be stupid and ignorant when they think they can harm Germany by this means.

Well then, that might still have surprised us a couple of years ago. Today we react to their screeching as to a continuous noise that is not capable of becoming any louder. It is known that the human ear can hear sounds only up to a certain level of vibration. Sounds and noises of still higher frequencies are not heard. We have become immune to any increase in the great screaming of world Jewry.

Simple people derive an unshakable wisdom from this...

There is a view that is heard at every step: if we had solved the Jewish Question completely and by the most brutal methods back in 1933, the outcry would have been no worse than it has been all the time since then, because we are solving the Jewish Question piecemeal, by single measures forced on us by the Jews themselves and their friends. This view is correct in itself. But it had to remain theoretical because at that time we lacked the *military might that we possess today.* At that time the Jews might have succeeded in inciting the nations into a war of revenge against us; today the loudest of the democratic screechers will be the ones to hesitate the longest.

Because it is necessary, because we no longer hear the world's screaming, and finally because no power in the world can stop us, we shall therefore now take the Jewish Question towards its total solution. The program is clear.

It is:

total elimination, complete separation!

119

What does that mean?

It means *not only* the elimination of the Jews from the German national economy, a position which they brought upon themselves following their murderous attack and their incitement to war and murder.

It means much more!

It can no longer be asked of any German that he should continue to live under one roof with Jews, a race stamped with the mark of murderers and criminals, and deadly enemies of the German people.

The Jews must therefore be driven out of our apartment houses and residential areas and put into series of streets or blocks of houses where they will be together and have as little contact as possible with Germans. They must be marked and the right must be taken from them to own houses or land or a share in either, because it cannot be expected of a German that he should submit to the power of a Jewish landlord and maintain him by the work of his hands.

Into a criminal existence

But once this nation of parasites is in every way dependent on itself and isolated, it will become impoverished because it is unwilling and incapable of doing work itself. Even if the Jews still call billions their own today, and even if there are still many hundreds of millionaires among them, and even if the individual so-called "poor" Jew has disguised and hidden enough, they will still very soon have eaten up their capital, once the vital artery of these parasites has been blocked.

And if we force the rich Jews to support the "poor" comrades of their race, which may prove necessary, they will still all sink down into a criminal existence, in accordance with their deepest blood-conditioned nature.

But let nobody believe that we will calmly watch such a development. The German People has not the least wish to put up with hundreds of thousands of criminals in its territory, who will seek not only to secure their existence by means of crime, *but also to take revenge!*

Least of all do we wish to see a breeding-ground for Bolshevism and a roof-organization for the political and criminal sub-humans who crumble away from the edge of our own nation as the result of a process of natural elimination. . . .

Das Schwarze Korps, No. 47, November 24, 1938.

55

LETTER DESCRIBING THE DEPORTATION TO ZBASZYN,* DECEMBER 1938

My dear ones!

You have probably already heard of my fate from Cilli. On October 27 of this year, on a Thursday evening at 9 o'clock, two men came from the Crime Police, demanded my passport, and then placed a deportation document before me to sign and ordered me to accompany them immediately. Cilli and Bernd were already in bed. I had just finished my work and was sitting down to eat, but had to get dressed immediately and go with them. I was so upset I could scarcely speak a word. In all my life I will never forget this moment. I was then immediately locked up in the Castle prison like a criminal. It was a bad night for me. On Friday at 4 o'clock in the afternoon we were taken to the main station under strict guard by Police and SS. Everybody was given two loaves of bread and margarine and was then loaded on the freight cars. It was a cruel picture.

Weeping women and children, heart-breaking scenes. We were then taken to the border in sealed cars and under the strictest police guard. When we reached the border at 5 o'clock on Saturday afternoon we were put across. A new terrible scene was revealed here. We spent three days on the platform and in the waiting rooms, 8,000 people. Women and children fainted, went mad, people died, faces as yellow as wax. It was like a cemetery full of dead people. I was also among those who fainted. There was nothing to eat except the dry prison bread, without anything to drink. I never slept at all, for two nights on the platform and one in the waiting room, where I collapsed. There was no room even to stand. The air was pestilential. Women and children were half dead. On the fourth day help at last arrived. Doctors, nurses with medicine, butter and bread from the Jewish Committee in Warsaw. Then we were taken to barracks (military stables) where there was straw on the floor on which we could lie down...

H. J. Fliedner, *Die Judenverfolgung in Mannheim 1933-1945* ("The Persecution of the Jews in Mannheim 1933-1945"), II, Stuttgart, 1971, pp. 72-73.

* This was the first deportation of Jews from Germany on October 27 and 28, 1938, which involved Jews holding Polish nationality. The Poles refused to allow the Jews to enter Poland, and they were concentrated near the border city of Zbaszyn.

56

EMMANUEL RINGELBLUM'S NOTES ON THE REFUGEES IN ZBASZYN

Srodborow, December 6, 1938

Dear Raphael,

I am on holiday in Srodborow. I worked in Zbaszyn for five weeks. Apart from Ginzberg, I am among the few who managed to hold out there for a long time. Almost all the others broke down after a more or less short time. I have neither the strength nor the patience to describe for you everything that happened in Zbaszyn. Anyway, I think there has never been so ferocious, so pitiless a deportation of any Jewish Community as this German deportation. I saw one woman who was taken from her home in Germany while she was still in her pajamas (this woman is now half-demented). I saw a woman of over 50 who was taken from her house paralyzed; afterwards she was carried all the way to the border in an armchair by young Jewish men. (She is in hospital until this day.) I saw a man suffering from sleeping sickness who was carried across the border on a stretcher, a cruelty not to be matched in all history.

In tne course of those five weeks we (originally Giterman, jinzberg and I, and after ten days I and Ginzberg, that is), set up a whole township with departments for supplies, hospitalization, carpentry workshops, tailors, shoemakers, books, a legal section, a migration department and an independent post office (with 53 employees), a welfare office, a court of arbitration, an organizing committee, open and secret control services, a cleaning service, and a complex sanitation service, etc. In addition to 10-15 people fron Poland, almost 500 refugees from Germany are employed in the sections I listed above. The most important thing is that this is not a situation where some give and some receive. The refugees look on us as brothers who have hurried to help them at a time of distress and tragedy. Almost all the

123

responsible jobs are carried out by refugees. The warmest and most friendly relations exist between us and the refugees. It is not the mouldering spirit of philanthropy, which might so easily have infiltrated into the work. For that reason all those in need of our aid enjoy receiving it. Nobody's human feelings are hurt. Every complaint of bad treatment is investigated, and more than one "philanthropist" has been sent away from here.

We have begun on cultural activities. The first thing we introduced was the speaking of Yiddish. It has become quite the fashion in the camp. We have organized classes in Polish, attended by about 200 persons, and other classes. There are several reading rooms, a library; the religious groups have set up a Talmud Torah [religious school]. There are concerts, and a choir is active.

. . . Zbaszyn has become a symbol for the defenselessness of the Jews of Poland. Jews were humiliated to the level of lepers, to citizens of the third class, and as a result we are all visited by terrible tragedy. Zbaszyn was a heavy moral blow against the Jewish population of Poland. And it is for this reason that all the threads lead from the Jewish masses to Zbaszyn and to the Jews who suffer there. . .

Please accept my warmest good wishes and kisses from

Emmanuel

R. Mahler, *"Mikhtavei E. Ringelblum mi-Zbaszyn ve'al Zbaszyn"* ("Letters of E. Ringelblum from and about Zbaszyn"), *Yalkut Moreshet*, No. 2 (1964), pp. 24-25.

57

ESTABLISHMENT OF THE REICH CENTRAL OFFICE FOR JEWISH EMIGRATION, JANUARY 1939 *

Berlin, January 24, 1939

Plenipotentiary for the Four Year Plan

To
The Reich Minister of the Interior
Berlin

The emigration of the Jews from Germany is to be furthered by all possible means.

A Reich Central Office for Jewish Emigration is being established in the Reich Ministry of the Interior from among representatives of the agencies concerned. The Reich Central Office will have the task to devise uniform policies as follows:

1. Measures for the *preparation* of increased emigration of Jews. This will include the creation of a Jewish organization that can prepare uniform applications for emigration; the taking of all steps for the provision and efficient use of local and foreign funds; and a decision on suitable target countries for emigration, to be selected in coordination with the Reich Center for Emigration.

2. The *direction* of emigration, including, for instance, preference for the emigration of the poorer Jews.

3. The speeding up of emigration in *individual cases,* by means of speedy and smooth provision of the State documents and permits required by the individual emigrant, through central processing of applications for emigration.

The Reich Center for Emigration will be headed by the Chief of the Security Police. He will appoint a Responsible Manager and make rules for the operation of the Reich Center.

Regular reports on the work of the Reich Center will be

125

forwarded to me. I will be consulted continuously on measures requiring decisions of principle.

In addition to representatives of other agencies involved, the Committee will include Ambassador Eisenlohr, who is responsible for official inter-state negotiations, and Ministerial Director Wohlthat, who is responsible for the negotiations in connection with the Rublee Plan.

Signed Göring

NG-2586-A.

* See Document 47.

58

GERMAN FOREIGN MINISTRY MEMORANDUM ON POLICY REGARDING JEWS IN 1938

Foreign Ministry Circular

Berlin, January 25, 1939
83 — 26 19/1

Subject : The Jewish Question as a Factor in Foreign Policy in 1938.

1. Germany's Jewish policy as condition and consequence of foreign policy decisions in 1938.

2. The aim of German Jewish policy: emigration.

3. Means, ways and destinations of Jewish emigration.

4. The Jewish émigré as the best propaganda for Germany's Jewish policy.

It is probably no coincidence that the fateful year of 1938 brought not only the realization of the concept of a Greater Germany, but at the same time has brought the Jewish question close to solution. For the Jewish policy was both pre-condition and consequence of the events of 1938. More than the power politics and hostility of the former enemy Allies of the World War it was the penetration of Jewish influence and the corrupting Jewish mentality in politics, economy and culture which paralyzed the strength and the will of the German people to rise once more. The cure of this disease of the body politic was probably one of the most important pre-conditions for the strenuous effort which in 1938 enforced the consolidation of the Greater German Reich against the will of a whole world.

But the need for a radical solution of the Jewish question also resulted from the developments in foreign affairs which added 200,000 persons of the Jewish faith in Austria to the 500,000 living in the old Reich. The influence of the Jews in the Austrian economy, which had increased beyond measure under the Schuschnigg system, made it necessary to take immediate steps to eliminate the Jews from the German economy and to apply Jewish financial resources in the public interest. The campaign launched in reprisal for the assassination of Secretary of Legation vom Rath has speeded up this process so greatly that Jewish retail trade — so far with the exception of foreign-owned stores — has vanished completely from our streets. The liquidation of Jewish wholesale and manufacturing enterprises, and of houses and real estate owned by Jews, is gradually progressing so far that within a limited period of time the existence of Jewish property will in Germany be a thing of the past...

The ultimate aim of Germany's Jewish policy is the emigration of all Jews living in German territory...

The Jew has been eliminated from politics and culture, but until 1938 his powerful economic position in Germany and his tenacious determination to hold out until the return of "better times" remained unbroken.

...As long as the Jew could still make money in the German economy there was, in the eyes of world Jewry, no need to give up the Jewish bastion in Germany.

But the Jew had underestimated the consistency and strength of the National-Socialist idea. Together with the complex of states in Central Europe created at Versailles for the purpose of holding Germany down, the Jewish position of strength in Vienna and Prague also collapsed. With its race legislation, Italy took its place by the side of Germany in the struggle against Jewry. In Bucharest Professor Goga, an expert on the Jewish question, took over the government with a program directed against the Jews, but was unable to assert himself against the overwhelming international pressure from Paris and London. In Hungary and Poland the Jews were subjected to special legislation. The German political success at Munich, like an earthquake with distinct tremors, is beginning to shatter the position which the Jews have consolidated for centuries even in distant countries.

It is understandable that world Jewry, which "has chosen America as its headquarters" recognizes as its own defeat the Munich agreement, which in the American view signifies the collapse of the democratic front in Europe. Experience has shown that the system of parliamentary democracy has always aided the Jews to obtain wealth and political power at the expense of the host nation. It is probably for the first time in modern history that Jewry must now retreat from a previously secure position.

This decision was only taken in 1938. It took shape in the efforts of the Western democracies, and the United States of America in particular, to extend international control and protection to the now finally decided Jewish withdrawal from Germany, that is, the emigration of the Jew. The American President Roosevelt, "who, as is known, included a number of spokesmen of Jewry amongst his close advisers," convened an international conference to discuss the refugee question as early as the middle of 1938, which took place in Evian without producing any notable practical results. The two questions which needed to be answered as a condition of organized Jewish emigration remained open: first, of *how* this emigration was to be organized and financed; and, secondly, the question of *where* the emigration was to be directed.

International Jewry, in particular, seemed disinclined to make a contribution towards the solution of the first question. Rather, it considered the Conference — and the Committee subsequently established in London by the Conference under the leadership of an American named Rublee — as having for its main aim to create international pressure on Germany to enforce the release of Jewish funds to the largest possible extent...

The second question, to which countries the organized emigration of the Jews should be directed, could be solved just as little by the Evian Conference;* each of the countries taking part expressed its agreement in principle to help solve the refugee problem, but declared that it was unable to accept large masses of Jewish émigrés into its territory. While in the years 1933/34 more than 100,000 Jews from Germany made their way abroad, legally or illegally, and were able to gain a foothold in a new host nation, either with the aid of relatives living abroad, or the pity of humanitarian circles, by now almost all countries in the world have sealed their borders hermetically against the burdensome Jewish intruders...

Even the migration of only about 100,000 Jews has been sufficient to waken the interest in, if not the understanding of, the Jewish danger in many countries, and it can be foreseen that the Jewish question will develop into an international political problem when large numbers of Jews from Germany, Poland, Hungary and Rumania are set in motion by the increasing pressure of their host nations. Even for Germany the Jewish question will not be solved when the last Jew has left German soil...

Palestine, which has already been designated by a popular catchword as the target of emigration, cannot be considered as such because its absorptive capacity for a mass influx of Jews is insufficient. Under pressure of Arab resistance the British Mandatory Government has limited Jewish immigration into Palestine to a minimum.

129

At first the emigration of German Jews to Palestine received extensive support from Germany through the conclusion of an agreement with Jewish representatives in Palestine permitting the transfer of Jewish funds by means of additional exports (the Ha'avara Agreement).** Apart from the fact that this method enabled only a small number of well-to-do Jews to emigrate, but not the mass of Jews without property, there were also basic considerations of principle and of foreign policy which created an objection to this form of emigration : the transfer of Jewish property from Germany contributed in no small measure to the development of a Jewish State in Palestine. But Germany is obliged to discern the danger in the creation of a Jewish State, which even in a miniature form could provide world Jewry with a basis for action similar to that of the Vatican State for political Catholicism, and could absorb only a fraction of the Jews. The realization that Jewry will always be the implacable enemy of the Third Reich forces us to the decision to prevent any strengthening of the Jewish position. A Jewish State would give world Jewry increased power in international law and relations. Alfred Rosenberg formulated this thought in his address at Detmold on January 15, 1939, in the following manner :

"Jewry is striving today for a Jewish State in Palestine. Not in order to offer a home to Jews from all over the world, however, but for other reasons: world Jewry must have a little miniature state in order to send ambassadors and delegates with extraterritorial rights to all countries in the world and through them to promote its lust for domination. But above all they want a center for Jewry, a Jewish State where Jewish swindlers from the whole world can be given refuge when they are pursued by the police of other countries, supplied with new passports and then sent to other parts of the world. It would be desirable if the friends of the Jews in the world, and particularly in Western democracies, which have at their command so much space all over the earth, were to provide the Jews with an area outside Palestine, *but of course not in order to set up a Jewish State, but a Reservation for the Jews."*

That is the program of German foreign policy as regards the Jewish question. Germany has an important interest in seeing the splintering of Jewry maintained. Those who argue that this will cause the creation of sources of boycott and anti-German centers all over the world disregard a development already evident, that the influx of Jews arouses the resistance of the native population in all parts of the world and thus provides the best propaganda for Germany's policy towards the Jews.

In North America, in South America, in France, in Holland, Scandinavia and Greece — wherever the stream of Jewish migrants has poured in, a clear increase in anti-Semitism has already been recorded. It must be an aim of German foreign policy to strengthen this wave of anti-Semitism...

The poorer the Jewish immigrant is and the greater the burden he constitutes for the country into which he has immigrated, the stronger the reaction will be in the host country, and the more desirable the effect in support of German propaganda. The aim of this German policy is a future international solution of the Jewish question, dictated not by false pity for a "Jewish religious minority that has been driven out" but by the mature realization by all nations of the nature of the danger that Jewry spells for the national character of the nations.

for/Schumburg

Akten zur deutschen auswärtigen Politik 1918-1945 ("Documents on German Foreign Policy 1918-1945"), series D (1937-1945), Vol. V, Baden-Baden, 1953, pp. 780-785.

* See Document 45.
** See Document 20.

59

EXTRACT FROM THE SPEECH BY HITLER,
JANUARY 30, 1939 *

... In connection with the Jewish question I have this to say: it is a shameful spectacle to see how the whole democratic world is oozing sympathy for the poor tormented Jewish people, but remains hard-hearted and obdurate when it comes to helping them — which is surely, in view of its attitude, an obvious duty. The arguments that are brought up as an excuse for not helping them actually speak for us Germans and Italians.

For this is what they say:

1. "We," that is the democracies, "are not in a position to take in the Jews." Yet in these empires there are not even 10 people to the square kilometre. While Germany, with her 135 inhabitants to the square kilometre, is supposed to have room for them!

2. They assure us: We cannot take them unless Germany is prepared to allow them a certain amount of capital to bring with them as immigrants.

For hundreds of years Germany was good enough to receive these elements, although they possessed nothing except infectious political and physical diseases. What they possess today, they have by a very large extent gained at the cost of the less astute German nation by the most reprehensible manipulations.

Today we are merely paying this people what it deserves. When the German nation was, thanks to the inflation instigated and carried through by Jews, deprived of the entire savings which it had accumulated in years of honest work, when the rest of the world took away the German nation's foreign investments, when we were divested of the whole of our colonial possessions, these philanthropic considerations evidently carried little noticeable weight with democratic statesmen.

Today I can only assure these gentlemen that, thanks to the brutal education with which the democracies favoured us for fifteen years, we are completely hardened to all attacks of sentiment. After more than eight hundred thousand children of the nation had died of hunger and undernourishment at the close of the War, we witnessed almost one million head of milking cows being driven away from us in accordance with the cruel paragraphs of a dictate which the humane democratic apostles of the world forced upon us as a peace treaty. We witnessed over one million German prisoners of war being retained in confinement for no reason at all for a whole year after the War was ended. We witnessed over one and a half million Germans being torn away from all that they possessed in the territories lying on our frontiers, and being whipped out with practically only what they wore on their backs. We had to endure having millions of our fellow countrymen torn from us without their consent, and without their being afforded the slightest possibility of existence. I could supplement these examples with dozens of the most cruel kind. For this reason we ask to be spared all sentimental talk. The German nation does not wish its interests to be determined and controlled by any foreign nation. France to the French, England to the English, America to the Americans, and Germany to the Germans. We are resolved to prevent the settlement in our country of a strange people which was capable of snatching for itself all the leading positions in the land, and to oust it. For it is our will to educate our own nation for these leading positions. We have hundreds of thousands of very intelligent children of peasants and of the working classes. We shall have them educated — in fact we have already begun — and we wish that one day they, and not the representatives of an alien race, may hold the leading positions in the State together with our educated classes. Above all, German culture, as its name alone shows, is German and not Jewish, and therefore its management and care will be entrusted to members of our own nation. If the rest of the world cries out with a hypocritical mien against this barbaric expulsion from Germany of such an irreplaceable and culturally eminently valuable element, we can only be astonished at the conclusions they draw from this situation. For how thankful they must be that we are releasing these precious apostles of culture, and placing them at the disposal of the rest of the world. In accordance with their own declarations they cannot find a single reason to excuse themselves for refusing to receive this most valuable race in their own countries. Nor can I see a reason why the members of this race should be imposed upon the German nation, while in the States, which are so enthusiastic about these "splendid people," their settlement should suddenly be refused with every imaginable excuse. I think that the sooner this problem is solved the better; for Europe cannot settle down until the Jewish question is cleared up. It may very well be possible that sooner or later an agreement on this problem may be reached in Europe, even between those nations which otherwise do not so easily come together.

The world has sufficient space for settlements, but we must once and for all get rid of the opinion that the Jewish race was only created by God for the purpose of being in a certain percentage a parasite living on the body and the productive work of other nations. The Jewish race will have to adapt itself to sound constructive activity as other nations do, or sooner or later it will succumb to a crisis of an inconceivable magnitude.

One thing I should like to say on this day which may be memorable for others as well as for us Germans: In the course of my life I have very often been a prophet, and have usually been ridiculed for it. During the time of my struggle for power it was in the first instance the Jewish race which only received my prophecies with laughter when I said that I would one day take over the leadership of the State, and with it that of the whole nation, and that I would then among many other things settle the Jewish problem. Their laughter was uproarious, but I think that for some time now they have been laughing on the other side of their face. Today I will once more be a prophet: If the international Jewish financiers in and outside Europe should succeed in plunging the nations once more into a world war, then the result will not be the bolshevization of the earth, and thus the victory of Jewry, but the annihilation of the Jewish race in Europe!

... The nations are no longer willing to die on the battle-field so that this unstable international race may profiteer from a war or satisfy its Old Testament vengeance. The Jewish watchword "Workers of the world unite" will be conquered by a higher realization, namely "Workers of all classes and of all nations, recognize your common enemy!"

N. H. Baynes, ed., *The Speeches of Adolf Hitler*, I, London, 1942, pp. 737-741.

* See Document 4.

60

APPEAL BY LÖWENHERZ FOR THE RENEWAL OF RELIGIOUS SERVICES IN VIENNA *

Up to March 11, 1938, there were in Vienna 23 synagogues in their own buildings, and 70 prayer houses in smaller premises. In all these premises religious services were held regularly twice a day, and were attended by all sectors of the Jewish population of Vienna.

After the reorganization of the situation, the Community Synagogue of Vienna-Floridsdorf was occupied by Nazi Party organs, while 31 prayer houses were disbanded by the Commissar for the Aryanization of clubs, associations and organizations. Religious services were held as before in all other synagogues.

Since all synagogues existing in Vienna on November 10, 1938, were withdrawn from their [normal] purpose, the lack of a religious service has become painfully noticeable among the Jews living in Vienna. Even if the main aim of the Jewish

135

population is emigration, and the means of survival until the time of their departure, it would still be of great importance to make at least some public religious services available once more to the Jews living in Vienna. The provision of religious services would not only help to satisfy the religious requirements of the Jewish population, but also create an opportunity for the Jewish Community to transmit directly important announcements by order of the Authorities, or of importance for emigration, as used to be the practice.

We therefore beg that it be permitted to hold religious services in the auditorium of the Community House I, 4 Seitenstetten Street; in the auditorium of Community House II, 3 Tempel Street; and in the Hall [District] XX, 35 Denis Street.

The General Director
Löwenherz,
Head of the Jewish Community, Vienna

The Central Archives for the History of the Jewish People. A/W165,3.

* Written on March 8, 1939, to the Central Office for Jewish Emigration, the Gestapo Headquarters and the Commissar for the Aryanization.

61

EICHMANN PROTECTS THE STATUS OF THE VIENNA JEWISH COMMUNITY IN ORDER TO FACILITATE EMIGRATION

Central Office for   Vienna, IV., June 12, 1939
Jewish Emigration

To
SS *Obersturmbannführer* Krüger
Ministry for Interior and
Cultural Affairs

Vienna, I.,

Re: Withdrawal of [status as] legally recognized public corporation
from the Jewish Community of Vienna.

Proceedings: Conversation between Privy Councillor SS *Obersturm-bannführer* Krüger and SS *Hauptsturmführer* Eichmann of June
6, 1939.

With reference to the above conversation concerning the withdrawal
of status as legally recognized public corporation from the
Jewish Community of Vienna, we wish to report the following:
    Contrary to the position in Berlin, we were able to arrange
back in the middle of last year that the Jewish financial institutions
abroad, such as the "Council for German Jewry," the "American
Joint Distribution Committee," "Hicem," etc., provide considerable
sums in foreign currency for Jewish emigration from Germany,
after, on the one hand, the responsible leaders of the Jewish
organizations had undergone the appropriate handling, and, on
the other, various agreements could be made with the Reich
Ministry of Economics. Subsequently, about $1,400,000 was trans-
ferred in foreign currency from Paris and London to Vienna.
These sums in foreign currency are controlled and administered
by the Central Office for Jewish Emigration in cooperation with
the Foreign Currency Department in Vienna.

In view of the purpose for which these sums are to be used, the Reich Ministry of Economics has authorized the release of these sums from the required levy and, in addition, permits this foreign currency to be paid to the Jews in the *Ostmark* [Austria] at unlimited exchange rates.

This foreign currency made it possible, on the one hand, for the emigration of Jews to be carried out, as this currency enabled them to produce the sums required as landing money, and, on the other hand, the requirements of the Jewish organizations in the *Ostmark* could be financed. (The monthly budget of the Jewish Community in Vienna, for instance, amounted to more than 1,200,000 Reichsmarks. For understandable reasons the tax income of the Jewish Community is dropping continuously. At the present time about 36,000 Jews must receive assistance for food, etc., from the Jewish Community, and the whole network of Jewish employees has to be maintained in the interest of speeding the emigration of the Jews, etc.)

With the aid of this income in foreign currency and the resultant funds here, and also through the creation of other, additional opportunities for immigration, it was possible by June 10, 1939, to get 106,672 Jews from the *Ostmark* to emigrate legally.

As the Jewish organizations abroad would stop further transfers of foreign currency immediately if the Jewish Community in Vienna were to lose its status as a legally recognized public corporation, it is requested that, in view of the resultant consequences and in the interest of continued increased emigration of the Jews from the *Ostmark*, this cancellation should not be carried out for the time being, and the status quo be maintained or permitted to continue until the end of January 1940. This is particularly so as the organizations abroad are now making difficulties insofar as they take the stand that the 77,000 Jews of Mosaic religion can no longer receive the same sums in foreign currency as were provided for 185,000 Jews of Mosaic religion. Their aim is to reduce the monthly allowance of

$100,000 to $50,000 in view of the drop in the number of Jews of Mosaic religion.

I thereupon threatened the Jewish organizations abroad that if they failed to maintain the payments at the level of $100,000, the Jewish Community would immediately lose its rights as a corporation.

The Jewish organizations abroad have in fact been intimidated by this threat, and the sums for May and June were sent to Vienna in full in foreign currency.

Head of the Central Office
for Jewish Emigration
signed   Eichmann

Österreichisches Staatsarchiv — Abteilung : Allgemeines Verwaltungsarchiv. Der Reichskommissar für die Wiedervereinigung Österreichs mit dem Deutschen Reiche (Austrian State Archives — Department : General Administrative Archives. The *Reichskommissar* for the Reunification of Austria with the German Reich), 1762/1.

62

THE ESTABLISHMENT OF THE REICHSVEREINIGUNG,* JULY 1939 **

Tenth Regulation to the Reich Citizenship Law

July 4, 1939

Pursuant to § 3 of the Reich Citizenship Law of September 15, 1935 (*Reichsgesetzbl.* I, P. 1146), the following Order is made:

Article I
Reichsvereinigung der Juden

§ 1

1) The Jews will be organized in a *Reichsvereinigung.*

139

2) The *Reichsvereinigung* is a legally recognized Association. Its name is *"Reichsvereinigung der Juden in Deutschland,"* and it is located in Berlin.

3) The *Reichsvereinigung* will use the Jewish Communities as [its] local branches.

§ 2

1) The purpose of the *Reichsvereinigung* is to further the emigration of the Jews.

2) The *Reichsvereinigung* is also
    a) Responsible for the Jewish school system;
    b) Responsible for the independent Jewish welfare system.

3) The Reich Minister of the Interior is authorized to transfer further responsibilities to the *Reichsvereinigung*.

§ 3

1) All Jewish Subjects of the State as well as stateless Jews resident in the area of the Reich, or who normally live there, belong to the *Reichsvereinigung*.

2) In a mixed marriage the Jewish spouse is a member only if
    a) the husband is the Jewish spouse and there are no progeny from the marriage, or
    b) if the progeny are considered Jews.

3) Jews of foreign nationality and those maintaining a mixed marriage, who are not already members under section 2), may join the *Reichsvereinigung* voluntarily.

§ 4

The *Reichsvereinigung* is subject to the supervision of the Reich Minister of the Interior; its statutes require his approval.

§ 5

1) The Reich Minister of the Interior may disband Jewish Associations, Organizations, and Institutions or order them to be incorporated in the *Reichsvereinigung*.

140

2) In the event of disbandment the rules of Civil Law will apply... After the liquidation has been completed the funds of the disbanded Jewish organizations will be transferred to the *Reichsvereinigung.*

3) In the event of incorporation the property of the Jewish organizations concerned will be transferred to the *Reichsvereinigung.* There will be no liquidation in this case. The *Reichsvereinigung* will be fully liable with its entire property for the obligations of the incorporated organizations.

4) The Reich Minister of the Interior may revoke or amend statutes and decisions of Jewish Associations, Organizations, and Institutions, where they contain regulations not in accordance with the above Orders on the disposal of funds...

Article II
Jewish School System

§ 6

1) The *Reichsvereinigung* is obligated to provide schooling for Jews.

2) To this end the *Reichsvereinigung* will establish the required number of primary schools and maintain them. In addition it may maintain intermediate and high schools, as well as professional and technical schools and other schools or courses intended to assist the emigration of the Jews.

3) The *Reichsvereinigung* is responsible for the training and higher training of teachers at the schools which it maintains.

4) The schools maintained by the *Reichsvereinigung* are considered to be private schools.

§ 7

Jews may attend only the schools maintained by the *Reichsvereinigung.* They are obligated to attend these schools in accordance with the general regulations on compulsory education.

§ 8

1) Existing public and private Jewish schools and ... other Jewish educational establishments will be disbanded if the *Reichsvereinigung* fails to incorporate them by a date to be set by the Reich Minister for Science, Education and Popular Instruction.

2) The property of Jews which had been used for Jewish educational establishments is to be ceded on request to the *Reichsvereinigung* in return for suitable compensation...

§ 9

Teachers at Jewish schools who have Civil Service status will be retired as of June 30, 1939. They are obligated to accept employment at a Jewish school offered to them by the *Reichsvereinigung...*

§ 10

The Regulations made in Reich and *Länder* Law concerning the education of Jews, in particular the admission of Jews to schools, the establishment and maintenance of public Jewish schools, as well as the provision of public funds for the purpose of instruction in the Jewish Religion are revoked.

§ 11

The Jewish school system is subject to the supervision of the Reich Minister for Science, Education and Popular Instruction.

Article III
Jewish Social Welfare

§ 12

The *Reichsvereinigung* as the body responsible for Jewish independent Welfare is obligated ... to assist adequately Jews in need in accordance with its means, so that Public Welfare is not called upon. It is required to provide institutions intended solely for the use of Jews who are in need of institutional care.

142

Article IV
Final General Regulations

§ 13

No compensation will be provided for disadvantages occasioned by this regulation.

§ 14

1) The Reich Minister of the Interior will promulgate the Provisions required to carry out this Regulation.

2) Where the Jewish School System is concerned the Provisions will be made by the Reich Minister for Science, Education and Popular Instruction in coordination with the Reich Minister of the Interior. . .

Berlin, July 4, 1939

Reich Minister of the Interior — Frick
Deputy to the Führer — R. Hess
Reich Minister for Science, Education and Popular Instruction
— Rust
Reich Minister for Church Affairs — Kerrl

Reichsgesetzblatt, I, 1939, pp. 1097-1099.

* *Reichsvertretung der Juden in Deutschland* — Reich Association of the Jews in Germany.
** See Document 21.

63

DEPORTATION OF JEWS FROM AUSTRIA TO NISKO (LUBLIN), OCTOBER 1939 *

Further to the Note on the conversation between SS *Hauptsturmbannführer* Eichmann, Dr. Ebner of the Gestapo and the Special Representative of *Reichskommissar* Dr. Becker, it is stated that the Resettlement operation to Poland will begin at 22.00 hours on October 20, 1939, with the first transport of 1,000 Jews fit for work, from the Aspang Rail Station in Vienna.

The Jews were supplied by the Jewish Community with tools for the erection of a barracks village at Nisko, where transports of Jews fit for work have already been sent from *Mährisch-Ostrau*. The Jews on the transport will also be given foodstuffs for 4 weeks.

Further transports will leave regularly on Tuesdays and Fridays of each week with 1,000 Jews. The second and third transports will consist of Jews and Jewesses at present under arrest in Vienna, whose departure date has been set by the Gestapo. From the fourth transport on, complete families will already be sent.

When the barrack village at Nisko has been completed, the Jews who arrived with the first transport will in continuous progression be distributed to the interior to the formerly Jewish villages in that area.

The composition of the transports is arranged by the Jewish Community of Vienna (as long as this remains possible) and a Jewish transport management is responsible for the transports. In addition, each transport is accompanied by 25 police (*Schupo*) officers under the command of a police captain, who must prevent all danger of escape by use of arms.

Dokumentationsarchiv des österreichischen Widerstandes (Document Archives of the Austrian Resistance), 2536.

* Report by the Central Office for Jewish Emigration, October 18, 1939.

64

INSTRUCTIONS FOR THE DEPORTATION OF THE JEWS
FROM THE PALATINATE (PFALZ), OCTOBER 1940

Secret

Notes for the Responsible Officials

1. Ony full Jews will be deported. *Mischlinge,* partners in *mixed marriages* and *foreign Jews,* as long as they are not citizens of enemy nations or of areas occupied by us, will be excluded from the *Aktion.* Stateless Jews will, on principle, be detained. Every Jew is considered fit to be moved; the only exceptions are Jews who are actually bedridden.

2. In order to assemble the Jews collection points have been established in... The transport of those who are being held will be by buses. Every bus will be accompanied by a Crime Police official as transport leader. He will have with him, according to need, regular police, Gendarmerie or Crime Police. The transport leader is responsible for the assembly, transport and supervision of his group until the departure of the train from the collection point.

3. Every transport leader will receive a list at the concentration point, noting the bus which he has been allocated, the police officials who will work with him, and the names and addresses of the persons to be detained. Where the names of the officials to work with him have not yet been listed they will be inserted later by the transport leader.

4. The transport leader will inform the officials working with him of the names and addresses of the persons to be detained.

5. When the officials appointed for this purpose have received the personal information on the Jews, they will go to the homes of those concerned. They will then convey to them that they have been detained in order to be deported; it is to be pointed out at the same time that they must be ready to move in two hours. Possible queries are to be communicated to the head

of the collection point, who will clarify the issue; no delay in the preparations is to be permitted.

6. Those who have been detained should take with them, as far as possible:

a) A suitcase or parcel with clothing for each Jew; the weight permitted is 50 kg. for each adult, 30 kg. per child.

b) A complete set of clothing.

c) A woollen blanket for every Jew.

d) Food for several days.

e) Utensils for eating and drinking.

f) Up to RM 100 in cash per person.

g) Passports, identity cards or other identification papers. These are not to be packed but to be carried by each individual...

7. ...

8. A questionnaire is to be filled in for every head of a family or single Jew, in accordance with the sample provided, and is to be signed by the official in charge.

9. Attention should be paid to the following before the apartment is vacated :

a) Livestock and other live animals (dogs, cats, cage birds) are to be handed over to the local head official, chairman of the local farmers' association or other suitable person against a receipt,

b) Perishable foodstuffs are to be placed at the disposal of the NSV [Nazi welfare organization],

c) Open fires are to be extinguished,

d) Water and gas supply is to be turned off,

e) Electrical fuses are to be disconnected,

f) The keys to the apartment are to be tied together and provided with a tie-on label with the name, city, street and number of the house of the owner.

g) As far as possible the persons detained are to be searched before their departure for weapons, ammunition, explosives, poison, foreign currency, jewelry, etc.

10. After the apartment has been vacated the entrance to the apartment is to be locked by the official and sealed with

the adhesive strip provided for this purpose. The key-hole must be covered by the adhesive strip.

11. After the persons detained have been taken to the bus the official will hand over to the transport leader the objects or valuables, questionnaires and keys, for delivery at the concentration point.

12. After the transport leader has handed over the detainees at the concentration point he will check the list which he received, amend it if required, and mark it as having been dealt with.

13. It is absolutely necessary that the Jews will be dealt with in a proper manner when they are detained. Excesses are in any case to be avoided absolutely.

P. Sauer, ed., *Dokumente über die Verfolgung der jüdischen Bürger in Baden-Württemberg durch das nationalsozialistische Regime 1933-1945* ("Documents on the Persecution of the Jewish Citizens of Baden-Württemberg by the National-Socialist Regime 1933-1945"), II, Stuttgart, 1966, pp. 236-237.

65

CASES OF SUICIDE TO ESCAPE DEPORTATION *

... The arrest and information of the deportation was a terrible experience for those concerned. It was inevitable that some souls could not face this trial. There were several cases of suicide and attempted suicide in the course of the first hours of the *Aktion*. In Mannheim (with 2,500 deportees) there were about 10 cases, and as many in Baden-Baden (with scarcely 100 members of the community). These cases of suicide — there were others during the journey — involved almost exclusively Jews who had moved far from Judaism, had left the community or were baptized. The fate of these people was tragic: the road into exile forced them back (to Judaism, to being a Jew) where

147

their own efforts had taken them away. They no longer wanted to be Jews and now were forced to be Jews. . . .

H. D. Fliedner, ed., *Die Judenverfolgung in Mannheim 1933-1945* ("The Persecution of the Jews in Mannheim 1933-1945"), II, Stuttgart, 1971, p. 79.

* From a report prepared by Dr. Eugen Netter, one of the heads of the Mannheim Community.

66

YOUTH ALIYA SCHOOL IN VIENNA, 1940

The Community of the JUAL Group

An invisible link of genuine cooperation and a sense of belonging brings together all who attend the JUAL School; the atmosphere which these young people see as surrounding their future lives is already present. These youths are already friends, not chance comrades; they share the same fate, they wish to tread their road together, and together to reach their goal. We must also recall the teachers and educators, who are the friends of their pupils. Here we have the happy synthesis that is the necessary condition for successful work with young people, a relationship of trust between teachers and students that could scarcely be finer or more free. The young people feel at home, but they study no less well. The head of the Vienna Youth Aliyah, Aron *Menczer,* has at his disposal for this educational task a staff of assistants which is made up mainly of high school teachers and youth educators, who join in discussing the direction and methods for what has now become the largest Jewish school in Vienna.

In order to maintain this aim, on which the school has embarked as completely as possible, the idea came up of consulting with the parents, and this is now to become a permanent feature.

The catalogue for an exhibition held by Youth Aliya in Vienna,
September 1940

New suggestions are expected from this side, too, and they are to be given far-reaching consideration where the welfare of our youth is considered. Every class at the school forms a community that tries to help every individual, and, if possible, to lighten even his private burdens. The social welfare with its admittedly very modest means also tries to help in the most urgent cases.

Yad Vashem Archives, O-30/30.

67

THE SITUATION OF THE JEWS IN GERMANY
IN THE SUMMER OF 1941*

At present, the number of Jews taken for labor service in Berlin is approximately 26,000 (possibly as many as 28,000), of these 55 percent are males and 45 percent females. In the remainder of the *Altreich* (Germany before 1938) an addition of probably 25,000 Jews have been conscripted for labor service.

Those employed are men aged 14-60 years and women aged 16-50 years. Where persons are physically fit these age limits are sometimes exceeded; in most cases such older persons, together with members of the regular age groups of reduced working capacity, are used for so-called short hours (i.e., low-level auxiliary work for approximately 40 hours a week), unless they are qualified or specialist workers who can be used in their trade...

In general, these workers are used only in enterprises in which it is possible to keep them separated from the Aryan workers, as required by law, which is mainly in industry. A large part, particularly of the women workers and youth, are employed in the various Siemens enterprises, in several chemical works and enterprises of the wood industry. In part (as at Siemens) the employment is on the assembling and adjusting, etc., of apparatus and instruments for airplanes, etc., and in part sorting, packing, loading, etc.

In addition, a fairly large number of men is employed on the building of roads and laying of railway tracks. Auxiliary workers of both sexes are used to handle goods for forwarding agents and in enterprises for the treating and re-use of scrap materials, etc.

Only in special cases is use made [of Jews] in small places of work, and usually only specially trained workers. Recently the City Administration has taken on Jews for street-cleaning.

The working time depends on the occupation and averages 40-55 hours for women and youth per week, and up to 60 hours for men. . .

The supply of foodstuffs is carried out within the framework of the War Economy Organization on the basis of the ration cards generally used in the Reich (marked with the letter J); it is regularly announced in the *Jüdisches Nachrichtenblatt* when the ration cards intended for Jewish households must be collected from the various offices concerned. There is no central office for the issuing of ration-cards to Jews, and this would be difficult to carry out owing to the large distances involved and the wide scattering of Jewish residences. Jews are permitted to visit the ration-card offices for other purposes only once a week (for several hours set in the late afternoon). Purchases may be made in any retail store between 16.00 and 17.00 hours daily. . .

There are no other restrictions concerning sources of supply, but, particularly in certain parts of the city (such as the West, which is heavily populated by Jews), the number of stores is constantly increasing that will not sell to Jews, with the result that there is an automatic concentration on some (usually large) stores. It is increasingly common for announcements to be displayed in food stores that goods not on ration or in short supply are not sold to Jews. As regards the re-soling and repair of shoes, which is linked to the Reich Clothes Ration-Card for the rest of the population, an arrangement has been made to the effect that Jews may apply only to one enterprise (Repair Station ALSI), which has branches in all parts of the city...

The *Reichsvereinigung der Juden in Deutschland*** set up by the Implementation Order to the Reich Citizenship Law created an organization for the Jewish population which, on the one hand, established obligatory membership in place of the former customary voluntary adherence to local religious associations; and, on the other, extended the organization to the total stratum of persons who are to be considered as Jews in the sense of the Reich Citizenship Law, and is thus in a position to operate as an organization representing all Jews. At the same time there are clear indications of a maximum possible centralization of Jewish organizations. Where the predecessor of the *Reichsvereinigung,* the *Reichsvertretung der Juden in Deutschland* was a federal roof organization for Jewish organizations in the *Länder,* the former separate bearers of the *Reichsvertretung* now become branches of the *Reichsvereinigung...*

The number of places of religious accommodation has not been greatly reduced in the recent period. At present there are 11 synagogues and prayer houses available in Berlin; in addition, most closed institutions (in particular the Old Age Homes) have synagogues, but these are intended only for the inmates. As in other areas of Jewish settlement in the *Altreich,* Berlin also has representatives of the various types of rites formerly common (Conservative, Liberal, Reform, etc.). The synagogues have in part remained in their former locations, and in part halls in school buildings or other public institutions of the Jewish community are used.

The religious personnel has been given up completely as a result of economy measures. Some are employed in other administrative departments of the Community, so that the' performance of their religious functions has now become an additional occupation. Others, younger volunteer functionaries (including rabbis), have been taken for labor service.

Expenditure for religious purposes is minimal, consisting of RM 7,000 per month... for the whole *Altreich*.

Leo Baeck Institute, Jerusalem.

* From a report dated August 18, 1941, by Robert Prochnik, Vienna Jewish Community official in charge of Emigration, in which capacity he was sent temporarily to Berlin.
** See Document 62.

68

ORDER BANNING THE EMIGRATION OF JEWS FROM THE REICH, OCTOBER 1941

Reich Security Main Office (*Reichssicherheitshauptamt*)

Berlin, October 23, 1941

IV B 4 b(Rz) 2920/41 g (984)

To...

The Officer appointed by the Chief of the Security Police and the SD for Belgium and France

SS *Brigadeführer Thomas*

Brussels

Secret

Re: Emigration of Jews

Reference: none

The *Reichsführer* SS and Chief of the German Police has decreed that the *emigration* of Jews is to be prevented, taking effect immediately. (Evacuation *Aktionen* will remain unaffected.)

I request that the internal German Authorities concerned in the area of service there may be informed of this order.

153

Permission for the emigration of individual Jews can only be approved *in single very special cases*; for instance, in the event of a genuine interest on the part of the Reich, and then only after a *prior* decision has been obtained from the Reich Security Main Office.

signed Müller

Yad Vashem Archives, TR — 3/1209.

69

THE LAST DAYS OF THE ZIONIST YOUTH MOVEMENT IN GERMANY, 1942

Report on Scouts' Day

Young Maccabi — Union of Scouts
Troop *Emuna* [Faith]

Berlin, March 1942

To our Members in the Countries of the Diaspora and in the Land of Israel,

Even though we do not know whether, in fact, this letter will ever reach you, we will write it in the hope that at least one of us will remain alive and hand it over to you when the day comes.

It is already a few weeks since our troop discussed the approaching Scouts' Day. Shall we be able to celebrate it in the accustomed manner this year, too? For we are living in very difficult times. Many of our members are no longer with us. They have already been taken to Poland, a place where an unknown fate awaits them. But the Jewish Scout is told never to despair, and we are therefore determined that, *despite everything*, we shall meet this year, to honor this special day. We therefore met on that Wednesday afternoon in one of the classrooms of the school in Wilsnacker Street. Despite the danger involved almost all came in their white shirts (under jackets), and there was an atmosphere of high spirits and joy in the room. We had gathered together all the Jewish scouts who still remained in Berlin, boys and girls, about 50 altogether, from all circles. As guests of honor we had Herbert Growald and Fanny Bergas, from the *Hakhshara* [training] Kibbutz at Neuendorf, and also Alfred Selbiger, a member of the Movement's leadership. We sat in a big circle, and the room echoed to the sound of our singing "Be Prepared..." and all the other songs. The candles flickered gaily and the members looked into the flames.

After that one of our members, Mary Simon, read us a story about trees and plants in our Jewish Homeland which made us forget the dangers and the sorrows. After that we sang again, and several poems were read... We stood to attention to sing the anthem of the Movement. When we unfolded the flag after that — which we had kept with us despite all the danger — we gave the Scouts' salute and sang the song of the flag: "Carry it to Zion, the Banner and the Flag"... Then one of our members, Erwin Tichauer, stepped forward — at first we had no idea what he was about to do — and read to his group the names of all those who had been taken from us during the past months, since the deportations had begun, and as he read each name the members replied as one: "Here," that is to say, that even those who were missing were with us on this occasion, for we are always with them in our thoughts, just as they are surely with us in their thoughts...

At this difficult time we send our good wishes to all of you, outside. Do not forget us, just as we will not forget you — those already living in the Land of Israel and building our future, and those who are living a free life in other countries. We will all be united in spirit until the day comes when we can once more all be together. We send our good wishes and send you Shalom! Be of good courage!

Y. Schwersenz, *Mahteret Halutzim be-Germanya Hanazit* ("Pioneer Underground in Nazi Germany"), Tel Aviv, 1969, pp. 55-57.

70

RESPONSA BY RABBIS IN GERMANY DURING 1943

Should a Public Fast be Appointed ?

Question: Hamburg, Sunday of the [Torah] Portion "and let them make me a Sanctuary" [Terumah], 5703 [1943].
To: The distinguished Rabbi in Berlin

I wish to tell you, Sir, what happened to us last week. During the winter we assemble to pray in one of the rooms in the Community House — and in this room there stands a cupboard in which there are two large Scrolls of the Law. We therefore brought a third, a smaller one, from the Synagogue, to exchange it. And when we looked at the small Scroll we saw that it had several imperfections, there were letters that had faded, erasures and corrections, and therefore we decided not to read from it in congregation. And when we took out another Scroll it happened, may the Merciful Lord Preserve us, that the small Scroll fell to the ground.

And now, according to the common custom we must declare a fast for all the people who were in the room and who saw what took place; and this matter touches upon another matter, which is this: the people who always or sometimes are concerned with the ritual cleansing and burying of the dead must try their

156

souls [fast] on the eve of the New Moon before the month
of *Nisan,* and in my humble view this is a great trial, especially
so because some of these people are not in sufficient health.
I thought to myself that perhaps the two fasts should be observed
together on the eve of the New Moon referred to above.

I beg forgiveness that this time, too, I trouble you with my
question. But what shall I do? For my people look to me, and I
knew myself that I was not fit to instruct them, and particularly
as long as the voice of the *Torah* is heard in our land, praise
be to the Almighty, from the mouth of his honor, who is
distinguished in the *Torah.*

Set down by Jacob Hacohen Katzenstein.

Reply: With God's help, Berlin, Wednesday in the week of
the Portion of Terumah 5703.

We must not impose upon the people, on the contrary, because
of and owing to the troubles and persecutions that are breaking
our spirit — this is not the time to torture ourselves. For this
reason it is to be preferred to be sparing with scourging and
torture. . .

With respect
Your faithful servant
Michael Chaim Gescheit

Building a Mikveh [ritual bath]

With God's help, Hamburg, on the eve of the holy Sabbath
[Thursday night], of the Portion "And I will show them the
way" [*Yitro*], 5703.
To the Rabbi, our Teacher and Mentor, Rabbi Michael Chaim
Dr. Gescheit, in Berlin.

Herewith I send a copy of a memorial scroll which I composed
in honor of the Almighty and in praise of the people who
labored and troubled on the building of the new *mikveh,*

157

which has now been completed with the aid of Heaven, and this scroll has been hidden among the stones of the wall of the *mikveh* in order to fulfill the commandment "Let the stones cry out from the wall..."

To his Honor, the great scholar and outstanding rabbinical authority, Rabbi Jacob Katzenstein in Hamburg.

I received your esteemed letter of Thursday in the Week of the Portion *Yitro,* together with the copy of the memorial document and I am indebted to your honored Excellence for much gratitude, for despite the sad contents I read your beautiful verses with great pleasure. We must assuredly mourn the shrinking of the Hamburg community, but it nevertheless remains a great city in Israel and, despite the very difficult conditions, its leaders carry out their duties as it is commanded. Through this service they will hasten the day when sons will return to the Land, and when you will inscribe on a stone plaque on the wall what you have now hidden between the stones of the wall, in order to tell future generations of the devotion of the spirit and courage of your heart at a time of trial and oppression.

It has also been an example for us, for what happened to you happened to us. The building in Raben Street, which housed our *mikveh* has been sold, and we may perhaps be able to use its purification water for the present week... and may the Almighty open up for us soon wells of purification and the wells of salvation... Amen.

Your faithful servant,
Michael Chaim Gescheit

"She'elot u-Teshuvoth ben Hamburg le Berlin" ("Responsa Between Hamburg and Berlin"), *Beth Jacob, Yarhon le-Inyene Hinuh, Sifrut u-Mahshava* ("Monthly for Education, Literature and Philosophy"), No. 22 (1961), p. 23.

71

EICHMANN INFORMS THE JEWS ON DEPORTATIONS FROM AUSTRIA AND ON THE THERESIENSTADT GHETTO

Vienna, June 1, 1942

Memorandum on the visit to the Reich Security Main Office, Reich Ministry of the Interior, Department IV B 4, on Friday, May 29, 1942, at 10:30 A.M. and to SS Obersturmbannführer Eichmann on Saturday, May 30, 1942, at 12:00 noon at the same office.

1. In accordance with an order received I reported to the Reich Security Main Office, Dept. IV B 4, on May 29, 1942, together with Dr. Benjamin Israel Murmelstein, the six members of the Presidium of the *Reichsvereinigung der Juden in Berlin*: Baeck, Eppstein, Henschel, Kozower, Kreindler and Lilienthal, as well as the two representatives of the Jewish Community of Prague: Janovic and Friedmann. There we were informed that in connection with a sabotage attack on the exhibition "The Soviet Paradise" in Berlin, in which five Jews had been actively involved, 500 Jews had been arrested in Berlin and of these 250 had been shot and 250 sent to a camp. We were further informed that additional measures of this kind were to be expected in the event of any other act of sabotage in which Jews took part.

An instruction was given that this position was to be made known to the Jews in a suitable manner in order to make clear to them what the result of such acts would be.

2. During the visit to SS *Obersturmbannführer* Eichmann I reported on the situation in Vienna, the position [reached] by the emigration transports, the probable number of Jews over 65, who were to be taken to Theresienstadt for permanent residence, as well as on financial questions.

SS *Obersturmbannführer* Eichmann informed me that the total evacuation of the Jews was planned from the *Altreich* [Germany before 1938], the *Ostmark* [Austria] and the Protec-

159

torate. Jews under 65 years old would emigrate to the East, and those over 65, as well as some groups of those under 65, such as men seriously disabled in the War, and those who received medals in the World War, etc., would be sent to Theresienstadt for permanent residence.

In accordance with the Regulation of February 16, 1942, the Czechs living in Theresienstadt must leave the locality by May 31, 1942, so that the entire area of the city will be available for the Jews. After this a start will be made on transporting the Jews designated for permanent residence there. The administration of the city is to be carried out independently by the Council of Jewish Elders (*Judenältestenrat*). In addition to the old people, several thousand young people are to remain there in order to carry out necessary work in the city and countryside (about 650 (?) acres of land are available) and to look after the old people.

Institutions necessary for the maintenance of the Jews are also to be set up or, where possible, existing institutions will be enlarged. According to the instructions of the Council of Elders the Jews will be accommodated partly in the existing large barracks, or privately in the houses. A part will be catered for in communal kitchens, and a part privately. In addition to personal luggage up to 50 kgs. per person, a large quantity of equipment and furniture for apartments and dormitories, as well as tools are to be sent to Theresienstadt. The number of items of this type will be decided on each occasion by the Central Office for Jewish Emigration in Vienna, in accordance with the freight cars available.

Special importance will be accorded to the provision and maintenance of sanitary installations. Good doctors and nurses will go to Theresienstadt to look after the health of the Jews and, in particular, to prevent epidemics. This will also to a large extent be the task of the Council of Elders.

The financial maintenance of the Jewish population settled in Theresienstadt will be provided by the funds of the three organizations, the *Reichsvereinigung der Juden in Berlin*, and the Jewish Communities of Vienna and Prague. These organizations in general have considerable funds at their disposal.

The budget will be decided in accordance with requirements for certain periods at a time, and the necessary sum made available to the Council of Elders in Theresienstadt. The capacity of Theresienstadt to accommodate Jews is quite large. When I was asked how many Jews from Vienna might be considered for Theresienstadt, I named a figure of about 12,000 persons; SS *Obersturmbannführer* Eichmann declared that that number of Jews from Vienna could be settled there.

I pointed out that a total evacuation of Jews from Vienna was scarcely possible, because as a result of the large-scale emigration and the unusually high age of the remaining population there is a disproportionate number of aged and sick persons, who must be considered as incapable of travelling. In any case a fairly large number of Jews will remain in Vienna owing to the exclusion from deportation of [members of] Jewish mixed marriages.

I also asked that a part of the Jews designated for emigration, particularly the children at present in youth and children's homes, who are under my care as guardian of orphans, should be sent to Warsaw with the personnel looking after them, because I could then be sure that they will receive the proper care and attention in a large Jewish center.

SS *Obersturmbannführer* Eichmann declared that the destination for emigration was decided together with departments of the Wehrmacht, and that it was not possible to say in advance where the transports would go; he would see what could be done in this matter.

signed   Dr. Josef Israel Löwenherz
General Director and Head
of the Jewish Community, Vienna

Yad Vashem Archives, TR-3/1156.

72

FROM HITLER'S TESTAMENT

Adolf Hitler

My Political Testament

More than thirty years have passed since I contributed my modest strength in 1914 as a volunteer in the First World War, which was forced upon the Reich.

In these three decades only love and loyalty to my people have guided me in my thinking, my actions and my life. They gave me the strength to make the difficult decisions, such as have never before confronted mortal man. I have used up my time, my working strength and my health in these three decades.

It is untrue that I or anybody else in Germany wanted war in 1939...

But nor have I left any doubt that if the nations of Europe are once more to be treated only as collections of stocks and shares of these international conspirators in money and finance, then those who carry the real guilt for this murderous struggle, this people will also be held responsible: the Jews! I have further left no one in doubt that this time it will not be only millions of children of Europeans of the Aryan peoples who will starve to death, not only millions of grown men who will suffer death, and not only hundreds of thousands of women and children who will be burned and bombed to death in the cities, without those who are really responsible also having to atone for their crime, even if by more humane means...

But before everything else I call upon the leadership of the nation and those who follow it to observe the racial laws most carefully, to fight mercilessly against the poisoners of all the peoples of the world, international Jewry.

Set down in Berlin, April 29, 1945, 4.00 o'clock.

Adolf Hitler

Witnesses:

Dr. Joseph Goebbels   Wilhelm Burgdorf
Martin Bormann   Hans Krebs

PS-3569.

Part Two
Poland

INTRODUCTION

The selection of documents in this section covers, geographically, the areas of central Poland (known as the Government-General during the period of the occupation), Polish areas in the west that were annexed to the Reich (*Reichsgau* Wartheland and the east of Upper Silesia), as well as the district (*Bezirk*) of Bialystok. Chronologically, the selection starts with the beginning of the occupation (September 1939 in the Government-General and the western areas, and June 1941 in the district of Bialystok and in eastern Galicia) and ends with the liquidation of Jewish population centers in the course of the "final solution," and of the evacuation and liquidation of the extermination and concentration camps. The selection includes key documents in several fields:

1) Political and legislative trends, and the policy employed by various German authorities towards the Jews;

2) The organization and activities of Judenräte (Jewish Councils) and the struggle of the Jews to survive;

3) The attitudes of the Jewish Underground, the development of armed groups, and the active revolt movement in the final phases of the period;

4) The attitude of the Polish population and the Polish Underground to the Jews during the period of the occupation and during the stage of destruction;

5) A description of the reality of the concentration and extermination camps and of revolts that took place in these camps.

The first practical steps of the occupation authorities, mainly the establishment of Judenräte, the expulsion of the Jews from the western areas and their concentration in the large cities, are laid down in the *Schnellbrief* sent by Heydrich to the commanders of the *Einsatzgruppen*, dated September 21, 1939, as well as in other documents (Documents 73, 78, 82, 83). The

Germans ordered the setting up of Judenräte as instruments through which they could transmit their orders to the Jewish population and ensure that they were carried out. Many of the Jews, on the other hand, who undertook the responsibility of leading a Judenrat, or who became members of one, hoped and believed that they would be able to build up an institution bearing a traditional Jewish character and which would represent Jewish interests (Documents 80, 90, 110, 120).

During the fighting in September 1939, and in the early period of the occupation, hundreds of thousands of Jews escaped to the eastern areas that had been occupied by the Soviet Union (Document 81).

In the first months of the occupation, when the administration was in the hands of the military authorities and the *Einsatzgruppen,* and later, when civilian authority began to establish itself in the Government-General, a number of orders were issued whose purpose was to degrade the Jewish population, to stamp them as criminals, to exclude the Jews from the economy and to take over their property, and also to prevent the free movement of Jews from one locality to another (Documents 74, 77, 79, 87). At this stage Jews were hunted in the streets of the cities for forced labor; later an order was issued by the authorities imposing organized forced labor on the Jews for the use of the Germans (Documents 75, 79, 80).

The establishment of ghettos, with a few exceptions, began in the spring of 1940, and policies were defined by the Germans that remained in force until the phase of total extermination. The German authorities sought to separate the Jews from the non-Jews in accordance with racist principles, to shut away the Jewish population in ghettos and to starve it. At the same time the Germans discovered that there were many skilled workers among the Jews and forced them to perform work needed for the war economy (Documents 84, 85, 96, 99, 101, 114, 115).

During this period the Jewish population sought to defend itself, even at great risk, particularly by contravening the orders and opposing the plans of the authorities. The Polish Jews had in the past, too, been forced more than once to outflank hostile government decrees, and their experience helped them to adjust rapidly to a situation that continuously changed and grew worse. Foodstuffs were smuggled into the ghettos, illegal workshops existed, schools functioned without permission, and public prayers were held although this was forbidden. Some of the Judenräte, for example in Lodz, tried to recruit Jews for work and believed that a greater contribution made by the Jews to production would assure them the essential supplies they needed to stay alive. At the same time there was also increasing criticism of the Judenräte, which were accused of slavish loyalty to the authorities and of corruption. A Jewish welfare organization, the JSS and ZSS, was set up separately from the Judenräte, and functioned throughout the Government-General. The self-help organization took over a number of institutions that had existed earlier (Centos, TOZ, ORT and others) and benefited from the financial assistance of the Joint. The social-welfare institution obtained recognition from the German authorities and was included in a roof organization that consisted of Poles, Ukrainians and Jews. At the same time, the institution, especially in Warsaw, also operated in illegal ways and did much to mobilize funds from the local Jewish public. The social-welfare institution operated soup-kitchens and aided individuals in its endeavor to match the desperate material needs, but its many efforts were insufficient to overcome the steadily worsening distress. Hunger and disease caused mass deaths in the ghettos and weakened the powers of resistance of the population (Documents 88, 89, 91, 92, 102-105, 109, 114, 120).

Underground cells were also formed in the occupied countries. Organized secret operations took place within the field of cultural activities, but Underground work was concentrated mainly within the youth movements and political parties. Groups from the parties concentrated mainly on mutual aid, information and cultural organizations and maintained contact with foreign countries, while the youth movements developed widespread activities in the fields of education and mutual aid and, despite conditions of terror, published secret newspapers and maintained contact among the isolated Jewish communities. The youth movements organized groups that went out for agricultural training and seasonal work in agriculture. Underground historical archives, known by the name of *Oneg Shabbat*, were set up in the Warsaw ghetto by Emmanuel Ringelblum; documents, diaries, newspapers and the work of writers were collected. There were also efforts to facilitate emigration to Israel, both legally and by illegal means, but these experiments had only minimal success (Documents 93-95, 104, 107, 108, 111).

In the summer of 1941, with the start of "Operation Barbarossa" — the German invasion of the Soviet Union — the "final solution" entered a new phase, the total destruction of the Jewish people in Europe.

Two interim plans for the concentration of Jews in the Lublin area and in Madagascar produced no far-ranging results. The *Einsatzgruppen*, which had accompanied the regular German forces on the Soviet front, began to carry out systematic mass murder. On July 31, 1941, Göring ordered Heydrich to prepare a plan for the "final solution of the Jewish question." In January 1942, representatives of the various German authorities and ministries met under the chairmanship of Heydrich to discuss the coordination and implementation of the elimination of the Jews of Europe. At the end of 1941, an extermination camp was put into operation at Chelmno, and in the spring of 1942 the extermination process was set in motion in other camps in the occupied areas of Poland (Auschwitz, Belzec, Treblinka, and Sobibor). Special units of the German Police and SS inspected the ghettos and carried out *Aktionen* — deportation of the Jews to the death camps. Those who remained behind after the *Aktionen* were ostensibly defined as workers essential to the German war effort. There was an ongoing argument between the various German authorities with regard to Jewish manpower; the Wehrmacht tried to hold on to the Jewish workers employed by them as a matter of their own interest. Most of the ghettos in the occupied country were liquidated during the years 1942 and 1943, and only a small fraction of those who were sent to the extermination camps were actually put to work (Documents 97, 98, 106, 116, 117, 122, 124, 128, 131-134, 158-164).

The first news of mass exterminations in the Vilna district (Ponary) and in other areas in the east reached Warsaw and other ghettos by means of Underground emissaries in the final months of 1941. The mass murder in the camp at Chelmno became known in January 1942. There was uncertainty and confusion among the Jewish population. It was assumed that the extermination was partial and would not continue. In some places the Judenräte believed it was possible to save the working section of the Jewish population, and that the price to be paid was acceptance of the loss of the weak and unemployed. From this derived the view that it was obligatory to cooperate in the *Aktionen* in order to moderate them, to reduce their effect and to gain time. The Jewish Underground, and particularly the Underground youth movements, came to the conclusion that the Germans were aiming at the total physical destruction of the Jewish people. From the spring of 1942 onwards attempts were made in Warsaw to set up a fighting organization. The Jewish Fighting Organization (ZOB) was founded at the time of the large-scale deportations from Warsaw, which began in July 1942, and, later, set up organizations in other ghettos. A second fighting organization — the Jewish Military Association (ZZW) — was set up in the Warsaw Ghetto. In Warsaw and in other ghettos the Underground fighters sought to establish contact with Polish organizations, and, as a result, a limited amount of help was received in Warsaw, but no help at all was received in other places (Documents 111-113, 118, 119, 121, 125-127, 129, 130, 135-136, 138-142).

On April 19 the revolt broke out in the Warsaw Ghetto under the command of Mordecai Anielewicz. The Germans were forced to send in regular troops, and a lengthy military struggle ensued before they were able to suppress the revolt. The revolt was not carried out by the Fighters alone : tens of thousands of Jews took a passive part by hiding and refusing to obey the orders of the Germans. We have in our possession the reports written by SS General Jürgen Stroop, the commander of the German forces employed against the rebelling Jews. The revolt and the Jewish military effort achieved a wide response. In Bialystok there was a debate in the branches of the fighting organization whether it should concentrate solely on the struggle within the ghetto itself or whether the struggle in the ghetto should be linked with fighting alongside the partisans in the forests (Documents 137, 143-154).

Many thousands of Jews from the Warsaw Ghetto and also from other ghettos escaped and sought refuge among the Polish population, either by hiding or in disguise as non-Jews. Most of the Polish population reacted with indifference and some even with enmity towards the Jews, even at the time of their great tragedy. On the other hand, a group of devoted people was aroused and attempted to save Jews through an organization named *Zegota*, which operated under the control of the general Polish Underground. Another part of the population systematically searched out Jews, blackmailed them for their property and handed them over to the Nazis (Documents 155-157).

In the last phase of the war, the only surviving Jews remained in concentration camps. Only a tiny proportion of those who had been brought there survived the selections, the working and living conditions in the camps. Revolts broke out in the extermination camps, and there were attempts at escape by large groups of prisoners. The few who survived in the concentration camps until the eve of the liberation believed that the Jewish world in Poland had been totally destroyed; there were even those who thought there was no longer any purpose in their staying alive (Documents 165-168).

Yisrael Gutman

73

INSTRUCTIONS BY HEYDRICH ON POLICY AND OPERATIONS CONCERNING JEWS IN THE OCCUPIED TERRITORIES, SEPTEMBER 21, 1939

The Chief of the Security Police   Berlin, September 21, 1939

Schnellbrief
To Chiefs of all Einsatzgruppen of the Security Police
Subject: *Jewish Question in Occupied Territory*

I refer to the conference held in Berlin today, and again point out that the *planned total measures* (i.e., the final aim — *Endziel*) are to be kept *strictly secret.*

Distinction must be made between:
1. the final aim (which will require extended periods of time) and
2. the stages leading to the fulfillment of this final aim (which will be carried out in short periods).

The planned measures require the most thorough preparation with regard to technical as well as economic aspects.

It is obvious that the tasks ahead cannot be laid down from here in full detail. The instructions and directives below must serve also for the purpose of urging chiefs of the *Einsatzgruppen* to give practical consideration [to the problems involved].

I

For the time being, the first prerequisite for the final aim is the concentration of the Jews from the countryside into the larger cities.

This is to be carried out speedily.

In doing so, distinction must be made
1) between the zones of Danzig and West Prussia, Poznan, Eastern Upper Silesia, and
2) the other occupied zones.

173

As far as possible, the areas referred to under 1) are to be cleared of Jews; at least the aim should be to establish only few cities of concentration.

In the areas under 2), as few concentration centers as possible are to be set up, so as to facilitate subsequent measures. In this connection it should be borne in mind that only cities which are rail junctions, or are at least located on railroad lines, should be selected as concentration points.

On principle, Jewish communities of *less than 500 persons* are to be dissolved and transferred to the nearest concentration center.

This decree does not apply to the area of *Einsatzgruppe* 1, which is situated east of Cracow and is bounded roughly by *Polanice, Jaroslaw,* the new line of demarcation, and the former Slovak-Polish border. Within this area only an approximate census of Jews is to be carried out. Furthermore, Councils of Jewish Elders (*Jüdische Ältestenräte*), as outlined below, are to be set up.

II
Councils of Jewish Elders

1) In each Jewish community a Council of Jewish Elders is to be set up which, as far as possible, is to be composed of the remaining authoritative personalities and rabbis. The Council is to be composed of up to 24 male Jews (depending on the size of the Jewish community).

The Council is to be made *fully responsible,* in the literal sense of the word, for the exact and prompt implementation of directives already issued or to be issued in the future.

2) In case of sabotage of such instructions, the Councils are to be warned that the most severe measures will be taken.

3) The Judenräte (Jewish Councils) are to carry out an approximate census of the Jews of their areas, broken down if possible according to sex (and age groups): a) up to 16 years, b) from 16 to 20 years, and c) above; and also according to the principal occupations. The results are to be reported in the shortest possible time.

4) The Councils of Elders are to be informed of the date and time of the evacuation, the means available for evacuation, and, finally, the departure routes. They are then to be made personally responsible for the evacuation of the Jews from the countryside.

The reason to be given for the concentration of the Jews in the cities is that the Jews have taken a decisive part in sniper attacks and plundering.

5) The Councils of Elders in the concentration centers are to be made responsible for the appropriate housing of the Jews arriving from the countryside.

For reasons of general police security, the concentration of the Jews in the cities will probably call for regulations in these cities which will forbid their entry to certain quarters completely and that — but with due regard for economic requirements — they may, for instance, not leave the ghetto, nor leave their homes after a certain hour in the evening, etc.

6) The Councils of Elders are also to be made responsible for the suitable provisioning of the Jews during the transport to the cities.

There is no objection to the evacuated Jews taking with them their movable possessions in so far as that is technically possible.

7) Jews who fail to comply with the order to move into cities are to be given a short additional period of grace where there was sufficient reason for the delay. They are to be warned of the most severe penalties if they fail to move by the later date set.

III

All necessary measures are, on principle, always to be taken in closest consultation and cooperation with the German civil administration and the competent local military authorities.

In the execution [of this plan], it must be taken into consideration that economic requirements in the occupied areas do not suffer.

1) Above all, the needs of the army must be taken into consideration. For instance, for the time being, it will scarcely be possible to avoid, here and there, leaving behind some trade Jews who are absolutely essential for the provisioning of the

175

troops, for lack of other possibilities. But in such cases the prompt Aryanization of these enterprises is to be planned and the move of the Jews to be completed in due course, in cooperation with the competent local German administrative authorities.

2) For the preservation of German economic interests in the occupied territories, it is obvious that Jewish-owned war and other essential industries, and also enterprises, industries and factories important to the Four Year Plan, must be maintained for the time being.

In these cases also, prompt Aryanization must be aimed at, and the move of the Jews completed later.

3) Finally, the food situation in the occupied territories must be taken into consideration. For instance, as far as possible, land owned by Jewish settlers is to be handed over to the care of neighboring German or even Polish farmers to work on commission to ensure the harvesting of crops still standing in the fields, and replanting.

With regard to this important question, contact is to be made with the agricultural expert of the Chief of the Civil Administration.

4) In all cases in which it is not possible to coordinate the interests of the Security Police on the one hand, and the German civil administration on the other, I am to be informed by the fastest route and my decision awaited before the particular measures in question are carried out.

IV

The Chiefs of the *Einsatzgruppen* are to report to me continuously on the following matters:

1) Numerical survey of the Jews present in their areas (according to the above classifications, if possible). The numbers of Jews evacuated from the countryside and of those already in the cities is to be listed separately.

2) Names of the cities which have been designated as concentration centers.

3) The dates set for the Jews to move to the cities.

4) Surveys of all the Jewish [owned] war and other essential industries and enterprises, or those important to the Four Year Plan in their areas.

If possible, the following should be specified:

a) Type of enterprise (with a statement on possible conversion to really vital or war-important enterprises or ones of importance to the Four Year Plan);

b) which factories should be most urgently Aryanized (in order to forestall possible losses);

What kind of Aryanization is proposed? Germans or Poles? (the decision to depend on the importance of the enterprise);

c) The number of Jews working in these factories (specify those in leading positions).

Can operations at the enterprise be continued without difficulty after the removal of the Jews, or will it be necessary to allocate German or possibly Polish workers in their place? In what numbers?

If Polish workers have to be used care should be taken that they are drawn mainly from the former German provinces so as to begin to ease the problem there. These matters can be carried out only by means of coordination with the German Labor Offices which have been set up.

V

In order to reach the planned aims, I expect the fullest cooperation of the whole manpower of the Security Policy and the SD.

The Chiefs of neighboring *Einsatzgruppen* are to establish contact with each other immediately in order to cover the areas in question completely.

VI

The High Command of the Army; the Plenipotentiary for the Four Year Plan (attention: Secretary of State *Neumann*), the Reich Ministry for the Interior (attention: State Secretary *Stuckart*), for Food and the Economy (attention: State Secretary *Landfried*), as well as the Chiefs of Civil Administration of the Occupied Territories have received copies of this decree.

Signed Heydrich

PS–3363.

74

IDENTIFYING MARKS FOR JEWS IN THE GOVERNMENT-GENERAL, NOVEMBER 23, 1939

Regulation for the Identification of Jewish Men and Women in the Government-General, November 23, 1939

Pursuant to § 5, Para. 1, of the Edict of the Führer and Reich Chancellor on the Administration of the Occupied Polish Territories, dated October 12, 1939 (*Reichsgesetzblatt* I, p. 2077), I order:

§ 1

All Jews and Jewesses within the Government-General who are over ten years of age are required, beginning December 1, 1939, to wear on the right sleeve of their inner and outer garments a white band at least 10 cm. wide, with the Star of David on it.

§ 2

Jews and Jewesses must procure these armbands themselves, and provide them with the required distinguishing mark.

§ 3

1) Violations will be punished by imprisonment.
2) Cases will be judged by Special Courts.

§ 4

Orders required for the implementation of this regulation will be issued by the Chief of the Internal Administration Division in the Governor General's office.

Cracow, November 23, 1939

The Governor General
for the Occupied Polish Territories
Frank

VBlGG, 1939, p. 61.

75

BAN ON CHANGES OF PLACE OF RESIDENCE BY JEWS WITHIN THE AREA OF THE GOVERNMENT-GENERAL, DECEMBER 11, 1939

Implementation Order No. 1 for the Regulation of October 26, 1939, for the Introduction of Forced Labor for the Jewish Population in the Government-General, December 11, 1939

Pursuant to § 2 of the Regulation for the introduction of Forced Labor for the Jewish population of October 26, 1939 (*Verordnungsbl.* G.G.P.p.6), I order the following:

1. As from January 1, 1940, it is forbidden for all Jews within the Government-General of the Occupied Polish Territories to move their place of residence or lodging, without the written permission of the local German Administrative Authority, beyond the limits of the community of their place of residence, or to cross the border of this community and to move away after giving up their permanent residence or lodging.

2. All Jews moving into, or transferred into, the Government-General are required to register immediately with the Mayor of the locality when they have taken up residence, but no later than 24 hours after entering the Government-General, and to

179

inform the local Judenrat of their presence. The Judenrat will record this information in writing and submit it to the Mayor on the Monday of each week, against written acknowledgement.

3. After having obtained accommodation, all Jews referred to in § 2 must comply with the requirements of § 1.

4. All Jews within the Government-General are forbidden to enter or use pathways, streets and public squares between the hours of 9:00 P.M. and 5:00 A.M. without written authority specifying the times and places, issued by the local German authorities. Orders by local German authorities containing more severe restrictions are not affected by this regulation.

5. The restrictions of § 4 do not apply in cases of public or personal emergency.

6. Jews contravening the regulations under § § 1 through 4 will be sent immediately to prolonged hard forced labor. This does not affect punishment provided by other orders.

7. The orders under § § 1 through 6 do not apply to Jews who have moved under the provisions permitting them to do so in accordance with the Law setting out an "Agreement between the German Reich Government and the Government of the U.S.S.R. concerning the transfer of the Ukrainian and Byelorussian population out of the area belonging to the Zone of Interest of the German Reich."

8. The public announcement of these instructions will be carried out by the Mayors according to orders by the sub-district Commander (*Kreishauptmann*) or the City Commander (*Stadthauptmann*). The Judenräte will be instructed by the Mayors.

9. These orders are effective immediately.

Cracow, December 11, 1939

> *Higher SS and Police Leader (Höherer SS-und Polizeiführer)*
> *in the Government-General*
> *of the Occupied Polish Territories*
> *Krüger*
> *SS Obergruppenführer*

VBlGG, 1939, pp. 231-232.

76

SUPPLEMENTARY REGULATIONS FOR THE BAN ON CHANGES OF RESIDENCE BY JEWS IN THE GOVERNMENT-GENERAL, OCTOBER 15, 1941

Third Regulation for Restrictions of Residence in the Government-General, October 15, 1941

... § 4b

1) Jews who leave without authorization the district assigned for their residence will suffer the death penalty. The same penalty will apply to persons who knowingly give shelter to such Jews.

2) Instigators and helpers will be punished like the culprits, and attempted acts as though they had been completed. In less serious cases prison with hard labor or prison may be imposed.

3) Cases will be judged by the Special Courts.

This Regulation takes effect on the day of promulgation.

Warsaw, October 15, 1941

The Governor General
Frank

VBlGG, 1941, p. 595.

77

BAN ON THE USE OF THE RAILROADS BY JEWS IN THE GOVERNMENT-GENERAL, JANUARY 26, 1940

Regulation for the Use of the Railroad by Jews in the Government-General, January 26, 1940

§ 1

1) The use of the Railroad by Jews is prohibited until further notice.

2) This does not apply to journeys for which there is an order in writing from the Governor General, his office, or of a District Commander.

§ 2

1) Contraventions will be punished with a prison sentence and an unlimited fine, or one of these penalties.
2) A special court will handle these cases.

§ 3

This Regulation takes effect on the day of promulgation.

Cracow, January 26, 1940

The Governor General
for the Occupied Polish Territories
Frank

VBlGG, 1940, p. 45.

78

FROM A DISCUSSION ON THE COMPULSORY EVACUATION OF THE JEWISH POPULATION OF THE WARTHELAND TO THE GOVERNMENT-GENERAL, JANUARY 30, 1940

1. SS *Gruppenführer Heydrich* stated that today's meeting was called on the instructions of the *Reichsführer* SS for the purpose of achieving a uniform policy in the offices involved in carrying out the tasks of resettlement ordered by the Führer. The evacuations carried out up to now have consisted of approximately 87,000 Poles and Jews from the Warthegau in order to make room for the Baltic Germans* who are to be settled there. In addition there has been a spontaneous, so-called illegal, emigration.

Following statements by Reich Minister SS *Gruppenführer* Seyss-Inquart and SS *Obergruppenführer* Krüger, SS *Gruppenführer* Heydrich noted that no objections in principle were raised against the evacuation in the direction of the Government-General by the competent authorities of the Government-General. The objections raised up to now had only been directed against the fact that in the earlier evacuations the figures originally set had been exceeded, and not kept to. The creation of Section IV D 4 for the central regulation of all evacuation measures will eliminate the objections that were raised.

It is of prime importance to move out 40,000 Jews and Poles from the Warthegau into the Government-General to free space for Baltic Germans. The policy for the selection is the Order of the *Reichsführer* SS, according to which, among other points, no persons of German origin are to be moved, regardless of their record. . . .

3. After the two mass evacuations:

a) of 40,000 Poles and Jews in the interests of the Baltic Germans and

b) of about 120,000 Poles in the interests of the Germans from Volhynia, there is now to be a final mass movement to shift

183

all Jews from the new *Ostgau*** (Eastland) and 30,000 Gypsies from the area of the Reich into the Government-General. As it has been decided that the removal of 120,000 Poles is to begin about March 1940, the evacuation of Jews and Gypsies will have to be postponed until after the completion of *Aktionen* referred to above. In any case the Government-General is to supply information on the system of distribution [of the evacuees] in order that planning can begin.

SS *Obergruppenführer Krüger* stated that fairly considerable training areas would have to be prepared in the Government-General for the Wehrmacht, *Luftwaffe* and SS, which would necessitate the relocation of about 100,000-120,000 persons within the Government-General itself. It was therefore desirable to take this fact into account in the evacuations in the direction of the Government-General in order to avoid double resettlement. SS *Gruppenführer* Heydrich observed in this connection that the building of the [defensive] ramparts and other plans in the East would probably occasion the concentration of several 100,000 Jews in forced-labor camps. Their families would be distributed among Jewish families already living in the Government-General, which would solve the problem referred to. . . .

In the middle of February 1940, he observed, 1,000 Jews from Stettin, whose apartments were urgently needed for purposes of the war economy, would also be evacuated to the Government-General.

SS *Gruppenführer Seyss-Inquart* recapitulated the number of persons which would have to be absorbed by the Government-General in the immediate future, as follows:

40,000 Jews and Poles,

120,000 Poles and also all the Jews from the new *Ostgau* and 30,000 Gypsies from the *Altreich**** and the *Ostmark* [Austria].

He referred to the transport difficulties which the German Railways would have to solve and, finally, also to the poor food situation in the Government-General, which would not improve before the next harvest. This would make it necessary for the

184

Reich to continue its subventions. Reich Minister *Seyss-Inquart* requested SS *Gruppenführer Heydrich* to support him on this issue if it should become necessary to obtain further food subventions for the Government-General.

SS *Brigadeführer Wächter* requested that the evacuees, who came from areas where the food situation was considerably better than in the Government-General, should be provided with the appropriate foodstuffs.

SS *Gruppenführer Heydrich* noted in connection with the transport difficulties referred to by Reich Minister *Seyss-Inquart,* that this had already been taken into consideration, as all transport was supervised centrally by the Reich Ministry of Transport, so as to avoid the inefficient use of rolling stock.

NO — 5322.

* Persons of German descent living in the Baltic countries, who were to be concentrated within the area of the Reich in accordance with the Nazi-German plan.
** The reference is to formerly Polish areas, which had been annexed to the German Reich.
*** Germany before 1938.

79

ATTACK ON THE JEWS OF WLOCLAWEK FOLLOWING THE GERMAN OCCUPATION *

A few days after they entered Wloclawek, the Germans burst into a private house where Jews were standing in prayer on the eve of the Day of Atonement, and ordered those present to get out and run. Then they gave the order "Stop," but some of the Jews did not hear this order being given and went on running; then the Germans opened fire and killed 5 or 6 of them. On the Day of Atonement itself the Germans burned down the two large synagogues. The fire also spread to several private homes. The Jews threw their possessions out [to save them] and there they were robbed by the Polish mob. These fires were set mostly by the men of the SS. The Jews tried to save the burning houses. The Germans then took all the Jewish men from one of the buildings, 26 persons, and forced them to sign a declaration that they themselves had set fire to the building. After the Germans had obtained this declaration they told the men who had been arrested that they would be punished for committing arson and could save themselves only if they paid a ransom of 250,000 zloty. The Jewish population of Wloclawek collected the necessary sum amongst themselves and the men were released. Then [the Germans] began to launch hunting expeditions into the houses. They caught about 350 Jews and put some of them in barracks and some of them in the Mühsam factory. From there they were taken out to work every day, but given no food — only their families were permitted to bring them food. After many pleas those who had been arrested were permitted, after many checkings, to visit their homes from time to time in accordance with a special leave-of-absence permit, in order to wash, change their clothes, eat, and so on. The regular work of the 350 who had been arrested did not by any means stop the abduction for work of Jews in the streets of the city. And apart from that there was the Jewish Council (Judenrat), which had been appointed in place of the former Community authorities; its activities were limited to nothing but carrying out the orders of the German authorities — it would supply a certain number of Jewish workers every day, in accordance with German demands. Those who had been taken away and those who were abducted for work were beaten and abused unmercifully. How they treated the Jews while they were working is shown by the fact that one of these Jews, Jacob Heiman, 52 years old and too weak for physical labor, was beaten and stabbed with a dagger while he was working, and a few days after he returned home he died of his injuries. In October the Germans decreed that the

Jews must attach a yellow badge to their clothes in back, and that they must not step on the sidewalks of the streets but walk in the middle of the streets. When they had collected the ransom of 250,000 zloty from the Jews for the imaginary arson, they imposed a new fine on the Jewish population after a short while, of 500,000 zloty, for the imaginary offense of not obeying the ban on using the sidewalk. The schools were closed.

A few days after they moved into the city the Germans closed and confiscated the factories and stores belonging to Jews. The Jews were required to register all their property, and a Jew was not permitted to keep more than 200 zloty in his home (in Warsaw — 2,000 zloty). There were many cases of Jews being beaten and tortured. They used to beat them not only during forced labor and not only when they had some complaint, but also for no reason at all: they would simply go up to Jews passing in the street, cry *"Zhid"* and stop to hit them. . . .

B. Mintz and I. Klausner, eds., *Sefer ha-Zeva'ot* ("Book of Abominations"), I, Jerusalem, 1945, p. 86.

* From evidence given in Israel on June 7, 1940, by a woman who left Poland at the beginning of the war.

80

FROM A REPORT ON THE SITUATION OF THE JEWS IN WARSAW AFTER THE OCCUPATION *

Until the entry of the Germans into Warsaw the Jews suffered equally with the Poles. There were dead and injured from among both peoples. From the day the war broke out people escaped, panic stricken. Tens and perhaps hundreds of thousands escaped. Main roads and side roads were crowded with refugees. Men and women, old men and youths, all escaped, most of them on foot, because it was impossible to obtain a cart, to say nothing of an automobile. In the confusion wives were separated from their husbands and children from their parents. To add to the panic German airplanes continuously fired on the refugees at all times and on all the roads. Tens of thousands died on the roads. Of course most of these were Jews, as most of the refugees came from the cities, and the villagers remained in their homes. . . .

The Council of Elders

On October 4, 1939, the Gestapo disbanded the Jewish Community Council and appointed in its place a Council of Elders. This was composed of 24 members presided over by the Engineer Czerniakow. It was not the duty of this Council to manage the affairs of the Community but — as was set out in the document appointing the members — to carry out Gestapo orders. It was thus not a body representing the Jews, but one carrying out Gestapo [orders] with regard to Jews. This Supreme Council does not represent the community and cannot supply the needs of the Jews. Nor was it in a position to carry out any serious action. The Jewish schools had been closed, and there were no means available to the Council to provide social welfare for the Jewish population.

In general the Council was not permitted to do anything. Every time it began some action, the Gestapo came and interfered. As soon as it was set up it received an order to hold a census of the Jewish population, and the whole Council had to busy itself with the census; when the census was finished, at the end of October, and the Council started to do something, there was the business of the ghetto, and again the Council could do nothing but attend to this matter; when the business of the ghetto was finished — on November 10** — and then there was the question of the Contribution [forced levy]; when the matter of the Contribution was finished — came the matter of the Jewish hospital, then — the business of the epidemic. And that is how it was in other cities too, and in the small towns. . . .

One of the most troubling economic measures was this: the picking up of people in the streets, or in their homes, for forced labor. This situation robbed the Jews of all opportunity of carrying on any kind of activity; no business, no office run by Jews can operate, because neither the owner nor the employees can be sure that they will get to their place of work. Even the employees of the Jewish Council are picked up while they are on their way to work. . . .

B. Mintz and I. Klausner, eds., *Sefer ha-Zeva'ot* ("Book of Abominations"), I, Jerusalem, 1945, pp. 1-2.

* The report was written by Apolinary Hartglas, one of the leaders of Polish Jewry, whose evidence was recorded in Israel in 1940.
** The Warsaw ghetto was not set up in November 1939, but only in November 1940.

81

ESCAPE OF JEWS FROM POLAND TO THE SOVIET UNION AT THE BEGINNING OF THE WAR

November 15, 1939

. . . There is no present and no future for young Jews. They escape for their lives. They get away by different methods: on foot, by auto, train, carts and every other kind of transport. The border is open. The Soviets do nothing to prevent it.* The occupying forces have no fixed system. You can never know what is forbidden and what is allowed. In a word — one day they are lenient and one day severe. It is understandable Where the heart is harsh and cruel there is no set and fixed system. And, in addition, what one authority permits, the other forbids. At the beginning of the Occupation the border was open. Anybody could cross without written permission, and those who wanted to stand in a queue for three days were not prevented from getting written permission; this stated clearly that the bearer of the letter was permitted to cross the border to Russia with his goods and chattels and that he was authorized to make use of any form of transport. That is what it said in writing. In reality the roads were beset with dangers. According to the "Regulations" persons crossing the border could take only 20 zloty with them. This was a sadistic law that could not be observed. Devices were therefore thought up in order to smuggle larger sums across, and here many failed. People were robbed and beaten on the way and left naked, with everything gone. The Border Guards know that the blood and the money of the Jews were outside the law. And they dealt with people crossing the border as the spirit moved them. From this time the border crossers preferred to cross without permission. They had no confidence in the legalisms of the Occupying Power. When they crossed quietly they were more secure. There simply was no refugee who did not take with him a sum of money larger than that which the "Regulations" permitted. And so the "green border" [clandestine border crossing] became known among the refugees, together with the expert guides who earned huge sums from this "trade."

It is reliably estimated that more than a million** refugees escaped to Russia. However many came they were still well received. But — where was this great mass of people to go? A small part, particularly those with a trade, have already been moved to the interior of Russia. As to the majority — either they had money with them and could eat, or they had nothing and hungered and thirsted. . . .

C. A. Kaplan, *Megilat Yissurin* — *Yoman Getto Varsha, September 1, 1939* — *August 4, 1942*, Tel Aviv-Jerusalem, 1966, p. 83 (English version :

Scroll of Agony — The Warsaw Diary of Chaim A. Kaplan, New York, 1965).

* The Soviets left the border freely open to traffic until the end of October 1939. From then until the end of 1939 a small number of persons still crossed the border, and after that it was completely sealed.
** It is estimated that the number of refugees who crossed from the part of Poland occupied by the Germans to the areas annexed by the Soviet Union totalled about 300,000.

82

ESTABLISHMENT OF JUDENRÄTE (JEWISH COUNCILS) IN THE OCCUPIED TERRITORIES, NOVEMBER 28, 1939

Regulation for the Establishment of the Judenräte, November 28, 1939

1. In each community a body representing the Jews will be formed.
2. This representation of the Jews, known as the Judenrat, will consist of 12 Jews in communities with up to 10,000 inhabitants, and in communities with more than 10,000 inhabitants, of 24 Jews, drawn from the locally resident population. The Judenrat will be elected by the Jews of the community. If a member of the Judenrat leaves, a new member is to be elected immediately.
3. The Judenrat will elect a chairman and a deputy from among its members.
4. 1) After these elections, which must be completed not later than December 31, 1939, the membership of the Judenrat is to be reported to the responsible sub-district Commander (*Kreishauptmann*), in urban districts to the City Commander (*Stadthauptmann*).
   2) The sub-district Commander (City Commander) will decide

whether the Judenrat membership submitted to him should be approved. He may order changes in the membership.

5. It is the duty of the Judenrat through its chairman or his deputy to receive the orders of the German Administration. It is responsible for the conscientious carrying out of orders to their full extent. The directives it issues to carry out these German decrees must be obeyed by all Jews and Jewesses.

Cracow, November 28, 1939

The Governor General
for the Occupied Polish Territories
Frank

VBlGG, 1939, pp. 72-73.

83

REPORT BY UEBELHOER ON THE ESTABLISHMENT OF THE GHETTO IN LODZ, DECEMBER 10, 1939

Top secret !

Establishment of a Ghetto in the City of Lodz

In Greater Lodz there are today 320,000 Jews* according to my estimate. Their immediate evacuation is not possible. Thorough investigations by all offices concerned indicate that it is possible to collect all the Jews in a closed ghetto. The Jewish question in the city of Lodz must be solved in the following manner for the time being:

1. The Jews living north of the line formed by Listopada Street... will be collected in a closed ghetto. Firstly, an area around the *Freiheitsplatz*, required for the establishment of a German power center, will be cleansed of Jews; and, secondly, the northern part of the city, which is inhabited almost exclusively by Jews, will be included in the ghetto.

192

2. Jews fit for work living in other parts of the city of Lodz will be collected for labor battalions, housed in barracks and guarded.

Preparations and execution of this plan will be carried out by a staff which will include representatives of the following authorities and offices:

1. N.S.D.A.P. (Nazi Party)
2. The [branch] office in Lodz of the Local Governor in Kalisch.
3. The City Administration of Lodz (Departments of Housing, Building, Health, Nutrition, etc.)
4. Order Police
5. Security Police
6. Death's Head Unit (*Totenkopfverband*) [of the SS]
7. Chamber of Trade and Industry
8. Finance Department

I shall serve as Chairman of the Staff for this operation....

... The first task of the Staff will be to decide on the borders of the ghetto that is to be established, and the settling of problems that will arise, such as the re-aligning of thoroughfares, tramway lines, etc. Further, it is to be ascertained immediately how many Germans and Poles still live in the area of the future ghetto, and will have to be resettled. At the same time, new apartments must be found for this group of persons and made available in order to ensure that the resettlement can be carried out without friction. As far as Germans are concerned, this will be done by the Party and the City Administration; as regards the Poles, it will be done by the City Administration alone....

After the preparations have been completed and sufficient guard personnel has been made available, the establishment of the ghetto will be carried out all at once, on a date to be decided by myself; this means that at a certain hour the intended border line of the ghetto will be manned by the guards provided for this purpose, and the streets closed by means of barbed-wire barriers and other measures. At the same time a start will be made on the blocking-up and sealing of the fronts of houses at the edge of the ghetto by Jewish labor to be taken from the ghetto. A Jewish autonomous administration will be set up immediately in the ghetto, consisting of the Jewish Elder (*Judenältester*) and a much enlarged Community Council. This Council of the ghetto must carry out the following tasks:

1. Department of Nutrition. . .
2. Department of Health. . .
3. Department of Finance. . .
4. Department of Security. . .
5. Department of Housing. . .
6. Department of Registration. . .

The Nutrition Department of the city of Lodz will deliver the required foodstuffs and fuel at locations in the ghetto still to be decided, and hand these over to the representative of the Jewish administration for distribution. The principle must be that foodstuffs and fuel can be paid for only by means of an exchange of materials, such as textiles, etc. In this way we should succeed in getting from the Jews all their hoarded and hidden items of value. . . .

At the same time, i.e., shortly after the establishment of the ghetto, Jews living outside the ghetto who are unfit for work are to be moved off into the ghetto (Security Police, Order Police, City Administration). The apartments vacated in other parts of the city as a result of the removal of the Jews must be guarded against illegitimate interference. The strongest measures are to be taken against Jews who carry out malicious damage when they are forcibly moved from their apartments. . . .

The creation of the ghetto is, of course, only a temporary measure. I reserve to myself the decision concerning the times and the means by which the ghetto and with it the city of Lodz will be cleansed of Jews. The final aim (*Endziel*) must in any case bring about the total cauterization of this plague spot.

Signed Uebelhoer

Eksterminacja, pp. 77-81.

* The City of Lodz, which housed the second largest Jewish population in Poland, was included in the areas annexed to the Reich. According to the Record of *Pinkas ha-Kehillot Polin*, I, *Lodz ve-ha-Galil* ("Encyclopaedia of Jewish Communities, Poland, I, The Communities of Lodz and its Region"), Jerusalem, 1976, p. 24, the estimated number of Jews in Lodz in 1939 was 219,866.

84

DIRECTIVES ISSUED BY THE HEAD OF DEPARTMENT FOR JEWISH AFFAIRS ON POLICIES CONCERNING TREATMENT OF JEWS IN THE GOVERNMENT-GENERAL, APRIL 6, 1940

In order to preserve uniformity in dealing with all Jewish affairs, it is necessary to reach an understanding concerning the basis on which our future work will be built up.

On taking over the department of Jewish affairs in the Office of the Governor General, I am therefore turning to the advisers in this field and would like to outline briefly the attitude that will be appropriate in confrontation with Jewry. This will at the same time indicate the targets at which we must aim (*Basic Working Principles* 1-9). These working principles are roughly as follows:

1. Spacial separation between Poles and Jews. In the decision whether a person is a Jew or a non-Jew,* the sole essential factors are his racial origins and blood, and his acceptance of Judaism (through marriage of a non-Jew with a Jew): not simply membership in a religious community.

2. A full Jew (*Volljude*) [here] — unlike in the Nuremberg Laws — is a person who has two or more Jewish grandparents or is married to a Jew and does not dissolve this connection.

3. As a matter of principle Jews are to work for Jews; for instance, only Jews are to be used for the building of accommodations for Jews.

4. The Jews are to establish their own social insurance system and are not to pay contributions to non-Jewish insurance

schemes, nor make claims on non-Jewish facilities.

5. The property and funds of such Jewish organizations will be under the protection of the German Administration. The same applies to Jewish welfare establishments.

6. It should be considered whether, as a temporary measure, the Polish Red Cross may be used by Jews if Jews had up to now supported and helped this institution.

7. All measures must be directed at the target that later the whole of Jewry will be concentrated in a specific district and in one area of Jewish settlement, as a self-supporting society under the control of the Reich.

8. Preparation of a plan for the resettlement of 400,000 Jews who will enter the area of the Government-General after May 1, 1940.

9. Creation of archives on Polish Jews and Jews in general (newspaper reports, regulations, laws, culture, races, health care, etc.).

In addition you are requested to answer the following questions, as far as possible, in accordance with the situation in your district:

1. In which districts and which sub-districts do the largest number of Jews live at the present time, and what percentage do they form of the general population in those areas (with maps, if possible)?

2. Which areas are the least valuable economically as regards the nature of the soil? How large are they? Where are they situated (map)?

3. Which areas are least closely populated, how large are they, how many people live there at the present time? Why are they so sparsely populated? What nationalities live there (Numbers!)? To what extent would it be possible to resettle the non-Jewish nationalities? Is the area suited for a purely Jewish colony?

4. What property is still in Jewish hands? Where is the Jewish property and of what does it consist? What additional means would have to be supplied for the settlement of the 400,000 Jews who will arrive here after May 1, 1940?

5. What proposals can you make for the accommodation of the deportees? What possibilities of work are there for the deportees in the various districts (preferably in public services)? What temporary arrangements — camps, etc. — are still available at the present time?

6. What has been done up to now in order to prevent as far as possible the likelihood of infection or disease being passed on to non-Jews? What is the position concerning health and hygiene among the Jews in the area of the Government-General, particularly where living conditions are cramped and close contact between Jews and non-Jews cannot be avoided?

In addition, I request a report on all plans for work and the dispatch of a record of all measures taken up to now by your office in any Jewish affairs.

(for) Dr. Gottong
Head of Department for Jewish Affairs

Eksterminacja, pp. 48-51.

* See Documents 32, 33, 34, 96.

85

FROM A SPEECH BY FRANK ON THE NEED TO REMOVE THE JEWS FROM CRACOW, APRIL 12, 1940

... if the authority of the National-Socialist Reich is to be upheld, then it is unacceptable that representatives of the Reich should be obliged to meet Jews when they enter or leave the house, and are in this way liable to infection with epidemics. He [Frank] therefore intends to clear the city of Cracow of Jews, as far as at all possible, by November 1, 1940. There will be a major operation to move the Jews, on the grounds that it is absolutely intolerable that thousands upon thousands of Jews should go slinking around and occupy apartments in the city which the Führer has granted the great honor of becoming the seat of a high Reich Authority. . . .

H. Frank, *Das Diensttagebuch des deutschen Generalgouverneurs in Polen 1939-1945* ("The Official Diary of the German Governor General of Poland, 1939-1945"), Stuttgart, 1975, p. 165.

86

HIMMLER ON THE TREATMENT OF ETHNIC GROUPS AND JEWS IN THE EAST, IN A SECRET MEMORANDUM TO HITLER, MAY 25, 1940

In the treatment of the alien populations of the East we shall have to endeavor to recognize and nurture as many individual peoples as possible; that is, in addition to the Poles and Jews also the Ukrainians, the Byelorussians, the Gorals (*Goralen*), Lemcos (*Lemken*), and the Cashubes (*Kaschuben*). And if there are any other splinter peoples to be found anywhere, then these too.

I wish to say by this that we have the greatest interest in not uniting the population of the East, but, on the contrary, in dividing it into as many parts and splinters as possible.

. . . I hope that the concept of Jews will be completely extinguished through the possibility of large-scale emigration of all Jews to Africa or some other colony. It must also be possible, in a somewhat longer period of time, to let the national concept of Ukrainians, Gorals and Lemcos disappear in our territory. Whatever is said concerning these splinter peoples applies on a correspondingly larger scale to the Poles.

...Cruel and tragic as every individual case may be, this method is the mildest and best if, out of inner conviction, we reject the Bolshevist method of physical destruction of a people as un-Germanic and impossible....

NO-1880.

87

JEWISH MEMORANDUM TO THE AUTHORITIES ON THE ECONOMIC SITUATION OF THE JEWS FOLLOWING THE OCCUPATION *

...Right from the beginning of the New Order in Poland a number of regulations were published that damaged the Jewish economy. At the beginning of October of last year [1939], that is, shortly after the cessation of military operations in Poland, a regulation was published, dated September 18, concerning currency in circulation.

This regulation contains the following severe restrictions in respect to the economic activities of the Jews in this country:

1. A maximum of 500 zloty may be paid out in cash to a Jew, and the rest must be deposited in a blocked account in a financial institution.
2. Banks may pay out to a Jew a maximum of 250 zl. a week from his accounts, or credit his accounts with this sum.
3. A Jewish family may not possess more than 2,000 zl. not deposited in a bank....

The above regulations make it impossible for Jews to conclude any business transaction or fill any orders, as a businessman must have at his disposal large sums of money for the purchase of goods or the execution of large orders, particularly now as transactions on credit have completely disappeared. How can a Jewish trader or craftsman buy the necessary goods or raw materials if he may possess only 2,000 zl. and may only collect 500 zl. a month of monies owing to him, has to pay cash and then may often wait several months until he can sell his goods? As a result, hundreds of Jewish enterprises had to be liquidated immediately after these regulations were made known. . . .

. . . The Regulation of September 29, 1939, provides for officially appointed Administrators only in cases where the individual authorized to manage the enterprise up to then is abroad, or where the rational management of the enterprise is not possible for special reasons. In actual fact, official Administrators have been appointed in many Jewish firms where the owner is present, and there is no reason for complaint concerning the management. . . .

In a number of Jewish enterprises the Adminstrators and trustees first of all brought about the removal of Jewish employees and workers. . . .

Paragraph 6 of the Regulation of December 12, 1939, concerning the introduction of forced labor for Jews, forbids all Jews ordered to carry out forced labor to sell their work-tools or machinery, or to make any disposition concerning their use, without written permission from the German authorities. This restriction applies to all Jewish craftsmen and greatly increases the difficulties of their position, as it is now often necessary to liquidate the workshops that have been destroyed, to set up cooperatives, and to sell the workshops of persons who have died or emigrated. . . .

In addition, Jews may not be on the roads between 9:00 o'clock in the evening and 5:00 o'clock in the morning. Further, Jews may not move their place of residence from one locality to another without special permission from the Authorities, according to a Regulation dated December 11 of last year.** Jewish manufacturers, traders, and craftsmen therefore have no opportunity of making contact with the merchants in other cities. . . .

Pension rights and social insurance have been withdrawn from former government officials who are Jews, and from invalids, widows and dependents of Jews entitled to social insurance.

This has increased the number of Jews who have lost all means needed for their living expenditures. . . .

Eksterminacja, pp. 154-157.

* The memorandum was completed in July 1940.
** See Document 75.

88

EXTRACTS FROM THE WARSAW GHETTO DIARY OF CHAIM A. KAPLAN, 1940

March 10, 1940

The gigantic catastrophe which has descended on Polish Jewry has no parallel, even in the darkest periods of Jewish history. Firstly — the depth of the hatred. This is not hatred whose source is simply in a party platform, invented for political purposes. It is a hatred of emotion, whose source is some psychopathic disease. in its outward manifestation it appears as physiological hatred, which sees the object of its hatred as tainted in body, as lepers who have no place in society.

The masses have accepted this sort of objective hatred. Their limited understanding does not grasp ideological hatred; psychology is beyond them, and they are incapable of understanding it. They have absorbed their masters' teaching in a concrete bodily form. The Jew is filthy; the Jew is a swindler and evil; the Jew is the enemy of Germany and undermines its existence; the Jew was the prime mover in the Versailles Treaty, which reduced Germany to a shambles; the Jew is Satan, who sows dissension between the nations, arousing them to bloodshed in order to profit from their destruction. These are easily understood concepts whose effect on day-to-day life can be felt immediately.

But the founders of Nazism and the party leaders created a theoretical ideology with deeper foundations. They have a complete doctrine which represents the Jewish spirit inside and out. Judaism and Nazism are two attitudes to the world that are incompatible, and for this reason they cannot co-exist side by side. For 2,000 years Judaism has left its imprint, culturally and spiritually, on the nations of the world. It stood fast, blocking the spread of German paganism, whose teaching was different and whose culture was drawn from a different source. Two kings cannot wear one crown. Either humanity would be Judaic, or it would be pagan-German. Up until now it was Judaic. Even Catholicism is a child of Judaism, and the fruit of its spirit, and thus afflicted by all the shortcomings inherited from its mother. The new world which Nazism would fashion would be pagan, primordial, in all its attitudes. It is therefore ready to fight Judaism to the finish...

It is our good fortune that the conquerors failed to understand the nature and strength of Polish Jewry. Logically, we are obliged to die. According to the laws of nature, our end is destruction and total annihilation. How can an entire community feed itself when it has no grip on life? For there is no occupation, no trade which is not limited and circumscribed for us.

But even this time we did not comply with the laws of nature. There is within us some hidden power, mysterious and secret, which keeps us going, keeps us alive, despite the natural law. If we cannot live on what is permitted, we live on what is forbidden. That is no disgrace for us. What is permitted is no more than an agreement, and what is forbidden derives from the same agreement. If we do not accept the agreement, it is not binding on us. And particularly where this forbidden and permitted comes from a barbarous conqueror, who limits life to one made in his image, his murderous and larcenous views.

... The Jews of Poland — oppressed and broken, shamed and debased, still love life, and do not wish to leave this world before their time. Say what you like, the will to live amidst terrible suffering is the manifestation of some hidden power whose nature we do not yet know. It is a marvelous, life-preserving power that only the most firmly established and strongest of the communities of our people have received as a blessing.

The fact that we have hardly any suicides is worthy of special emphasis.

We have remained naked. But as long as that secret power is concealed within us, we shall not yield to despair. The strength of this power lies in the very nature of the Polish Jew, which is rooted in our eternal tradition that commands us to live....

October 2, 1940
Eve of the New Year, 5701

We have no public prayers even on the High Holy Days....

Even for the High Holy Days permission was not received for public prayers, although I do not know whether the Community [Council] tried to get it. And if it did not try that is only because it knew that its request would be refused. Even in the darkest days of our exile we did not suffer this trial....

The wonder is that despite all this we go on living. Our life may be one of scorn and debasement as it is seen from outside, but our human emotions have become so numbed that we no longer feel, and the awareness of insult that is concealed within every human being no longer rises up in protest against even the most barbarous and cruel of such insults.

To what can this matter be compared? To a vicious dog who does not treat you with respect; would you, then, be insulted? Is not that why he is a dog?

Again: everything is forbidden to us; and yet we do everything! We make our "living" in ways that are forbidden, and not by permission.

It is the same with community prayers: secret *minyanim**
in their hundreds all over Warsaw hold prayers together and do not leave out even the most difficult hymns. Neither preachers nor sermons are missing; everything is in accordance with

the ancient traditions of Israel. Where there is no informer the enemy does not know what is going on. And surely no member of the Community of Israel, even if he was born in Poland, will go to lay information against Jews standing before their Maker.

Near the main synagogue some side room is chosen with windows facing the courtyard, and there hearts are poured out to the God of Israel in whispered supplications. This time it is without cantors and without choirs; there are only whispered prayers, but the prayer comes from the heart; even tears may be wept secretly, and the gates of the tears cannot be locked....

C. A. Kaplan, *Megilat Yissurin — Yoman Getto Varsha* ("Scroll of Agony — Warsaw Ghetto Diary"), *September 1, 1939 — August 4, 1942,* Tel Aviv-Jerusalem, 1966, pp. 201-202, 350.

* The group of ten adult males making a quorum for Jewish community prayers.

89

EXTRACTS FROM THE WARSAW GHETTO DIARY OF AVRAHAM LEVIN, 1942

Friday, June 5, 1942

... One of the most surprising side-effects of this war is the clinging to life, the almost total absence of suicides. People die in great numbers of starvation, the typhus epidemic or dysentery, they are tortured and murdered by the Germans in great numbers, but they do not escape from life by their own desire. On the contrary, they are tied to life by all their senses, they want to live at any price and to survive the war. The tensions of this historic world conflict are so great that all wish to see the outcome of the gigantic struggle and the new regime in the world, the small and the great, old men and boys. The old have just one wish: the privilege of seeing the end and surviving Hitler.

I know a Jew who is all old age. He is certainly about 80. Last winter a great tragedy befell the old man. He had an only son who was about 52. The son died of typhus. He has no other children. And the son died. He did not marry a second time and lived with his son. A few days ago I visited the old man. When I left — his mind is still entirely clear — he burst out crying and said: "I want to see the end of the war, even if I live only another half an hour! "

Why should the old man wish so much to stay alive? There it is: even he wants to live, "if only half an hour" after the last shot is fired. This is the burning desire of all the Jews.

A. Levin, *Mi-Pinkaso shel ha-More mi-Yehudiya* ("From the Notebook of the Teacher from Yehudiya"), Beit Lohamei ha-Geta'ot, 1969, p. 70.

90

ACTIVITIES OF THE JUDENRAT, REFLECTED IN THE GAZETA ZYDOWSKA,* 1940

The latest events and regulations have brought about a fundamental change in Jewish life, and caused a number of basic differences. There were basic changes also in the nature and work of the Jewish Community [Council] or the Jewish Committee. Before the war the Community [Council] had been responsible for a very limited field of work, of matters concerning religion and welfare. . . .

The Community [Council] has now taken on an entirely different character, of an *Office for the Jews,* for all matters concerning the Jewish population. With the creation of Jewish

Quarters [ghettos], this character is becoming stronger and more conspicuous. The Council is responsible for dealing with the obligations which the authorities have imposed on the Jewish public, and at the same time it conveys to the authorities the requirements of this same population. In this way the Council has become the sole *representative and mediator* between the Jewish population and the authorities. For this purpose it has received certain rights, and authority in some matters. The Council has become the central place where all the various Jewish affairs are organized. This gives it certain rights but also imposes duties. The maintenance of balance between these rights and duties is a difficult task, but an important one, and the satisfactory relationship between the Council and the public depends on its achievement.

Gazeta Zydowska, No. 46, December 23, 1940.

* *Gazeta Zydowska* ("Jewish Newspaper"), a Jewish newspaper that was put out with the approval of the German authorities in the Government-General.

91

ACTIVITY OF THE JOINT IN OCCUPIED POLAND *

When the war broke out the Joint did not have large sums of money available, scarcely sufficient for a few months. It was very difficult to maintain contact with the headquarters [of the Joint], which moved from place to place, and, as a result, the transfer of funds from abroad was inadequate for so difficult a period. Later, when war broke out between America and Germany, in 1941, there were no more direct transfers of funds. . . .

As the social-welfare organization required huge sums of money, the Management of the Joint, consisting of Messrs. Guzik, Giterman and Neustadt, set about obtaining very large loans for the Joint from private persons. These transactions, which continued right through the period of the war, were forbidden from the beginning. This illegal transfer could have cost the heads of the Management of the Joint, particularly as the matter became an open secret about which all Warsaw talked. Guzik was imprisoned for nine months in connection with illegal transfers. . . .

Ringelblum, II, pp. 133-134.

* The various parts of Ringelblum's writings, which carry no date, were written between the end of 1942 and the spring of 1944.

92

JEWISH SELF-HELP IN WARSAW

It is in difficult times that the noble side of people sometimes reveals itself. It has never before been possible to witness so many examples of devotion and self-sacrifice as at this hour. Countless individuals hurry to answer every call for help from the Jewish Community or the Jewish Self-Help,* and sometimes, on their own initiative, they give aid where the need arises.

. . . A Social Welfare department was set up under ZSS with sections for: *Finance, Clothes Collection, Emergency Aid, Sanitation and Housing for the Homeless.* In addition, *Local Committees* have been set up in the various sections of the city. In this way a fairly complicated and widespread system of public assistance has penetrated through every level and part of the Jewish public, and reaches into the most distant areas populated by Jews. . .

A separate chapter worth noting in the work of the House Committees is *child care.* Owing to the fact that the schools are not operating, many children of school and kindergarten age have remained without care and supervision, particularly where their parents are sometimes obliged to leave their homes in order to make a living. The House Committees, under the auspices of the ZSS, have undertaken to set up child-care centers in many houses, and particularly for children become abandoned. The Centers are managed by first-rate pedagogical personnel under the supervision of devoted public workers, who do everything possible to ensure that the children receive proper care. In this way the Centers play an important part in easing the suffering and poverty of the Jewish population of Warsaw, together with the Child Feeding Stations of the ZSS, which are intended mainly for the children of the refugees. The number of House Committees has grown steadily, and their work has been extended. There are now at least 2,200 active [House Committees] with 10,000 devoted workers.

Gazeta Zydowska, No. 2, July 26, 1940.

* *Zydowska Samopomoc Spoleczna* — ZSS.

93

THE WORK OF A JEWISH POLITICAL PARTY, FROM AN UNDERGROUND PUBLICATION, 1940 *

... There have often been discussions among the members concerning our working methods. At one discussion the question under review was: what are our aims at this time? What should our task be in this war? Two answers were given.

There were members who were of the opinion that at the present time we should occupy ourselves only with economic problems, helping the large number of members who are in difficulties, looking for means to help them, and very often to see to it that there should be a piece of bread and a bowl of soup for those in need. [In their view] all our efforts should be aimed in this direction and we should not occupy ourselves with any other activities.

Another group of members considered that it was by no means the purpose of our movement to turn itself into a charitable organization and to provide aid for individuals. According to them, such tasks were never our responsibility nor that of movements similar to ours, and we should not occupy ourselves with them, even though conditions have changed. We should turn to cultural activities, build up organizational cells, hold frequent discussions among the members to broaden our educational activities and to make use of this time for deeper thought.

And if this debate was in place a few months ago, then today, owing to the realities of the situation and the experience of more than a year, it is no longer the time for it now. All the members were right, those who said one thing and those who said the other: we are working in both directions at once, and the two views have merged into one. . . .

Yad Vashem Archives, JM/219/3.

* From the underground newspaper of the Po'alei Zion ZS in Warsaw, *Befrayung* ("Liberation"), December 1940.

94

THE AIMS OF JEWISH YOUTH AT THE PRESENT TIME, FROM AN UNDERGROUND PUBLICATION, 1940 *

. . . We, the Jewish youth, cannot free ourselves from the influence of the situation as a whole on young people in general. To this is added the specific lack of contact with the land of the Jews and the special hatred that accompanies us as Jews. The

war and the Nazi Occupation have revealed the tragedy of
our Jewish youth very sharply. We have become a group that
is ostracized, attacked and humiliated, the object of scorn and
derision. Jewish youth has been worn down and has withered
physically and spiritually in the Nazi labor camps. Jewish
children are cut off from school and education. First of all
there hangs over us the sword of want and unemployment, which
cuts short the existence and lives of thousands of individuals,
which ages Jewish youth before their time, turns them into
worn-out people, apathetic and full of doubts, without faith
and without the ability to change their lives.

ר. ד א פ ס .י

די יידישע יוגנט אין איצטיקן מאמענט.

די איצטיקע חקומה אין הכבער מיר לעפון, קען באצייכנם חירן אלס א*רנ
פון די כרויעריקסטע אין דער מיודעלטעכער גי*רכסט. אלע יסודות סון כיד אויצטיק*ן
לכבן זיבחן דערי*ס׳ולרם גימהורן. און קען גיער זיכנין גאך בים אנסטחאנצן. דז*ד
יובגער דור, ה*לבן ט קם* אוים צו לעבן און צום איטסחן אין אזא איכבורד גאבנבם
צ*ט גמפרוב* ורי ט דט מקור פונהתנטין צו זיין זון גיסטיטקע רבוקה, און ס*ה*י אבב־.
כאונין א גיםעקי*ר קרידים, הלכבר סרהי טו דעגנבעראצייע און דכרכרהגנבם צו א
גמערלקלכדר אנאמכיב אין דעם גאמבן ארם דסנקץ און מילן סון דער יובנם.

די יוגנט, הסלכב בילרסם אין דער גיזעלטמאמה א באזוונדרטיב פסיכאלאגישמ
פסרסמצגיע, און ירחירדטם זיך סון די טלחטרים דערהים, האם מיר באטור איד ברויונב
און איר מרר גמיל*ם-סאמפלפטסםכפם און אינבמדכבסיאהסר. די גיסילן סון יובגסטלככן זיבטן א
אקומולצאטער, ה*לבור זאמפלק ארן אין זיך אלט אידנדרוקן סון ארום, און סון ד
כאסן זיך בים יובגהלכלכן הסארקט אימפולסן, נאגאחיאהט און מאזיירחיהט, אמסחגניק
סון ארה אוון צר אין הילכבר די יובגט לרבם. דרסמאר חאקף אוירי בים קען צומאל,
האב די יובגב חאח אין אלץ סאציאלט און באציאנאל-מרג*רסטסיה* אידריין זיהין גי־
האון אוירסגימראבגן דורך דער יובגמי.

די היסטסריטע רטלס סון דער יובגם חאט זיך אבירסל גטמבדטרם. די כור־
זוואזר ורכרציער האבן מי* דער חילף סום זיהיר מלוכהטן און קולטור-אפאראטם גי־חאם
רכי סקלצדבכפרם צו לעבגזן די סגדרגיש סון דער יובגם אין א מארכסרמחטר ריכטולנב..
די יונגנדהלכבד לדנבהמאם צו _אחן מעפס נדים האבן זי גיגכבן אן אוילסגאהנם-סובנעפ
אין ד דר זארם סון סאסן א ני*ר ארדנגנג: א מסינסטפרטסר. די יוגנכלטכטם כונסאריש־

"Jewish Youth at the Present Time," an article from the underground
newspaper *Dror*, August 1940

What must we do in this situation? In which direction shall
we turn our attention? It is only natural that we cannot speak
of one road for the whole of Jewish youth. There are different
diseases and different forms of cure. There is one situation
for the youth that fills the streets and courtyards, who are
without schools and supervision, in whom one can see all
the undesirable aspects of the whole adult world. They spend

210

their time buying and selling. The situation is different for the youth which has an opportunity of acquiring education. But this youth withdraws into itself, and is unwilling to descend into the life of the Jewish masses.

The first group must be enabled to acquire an elementary education; we must arrange courses in reading and writing Yiddish, Hebrew, and in arithmetic, etc.; to draw the street youth into warm social surroundings, to attend as far as possible to their personal future, and to implant in them a feeling of solidarity and responsibility; and with the aid of singing and games to create a youthful atmosphere for a Jewish youth that has become old before its time.

The other part of Jewish youth must be helped to a consciousness of its common fate with the Jewish masses; it must be brought down from Olympus; its feeling for the people must be awakened; it must be given an awareness of Socialism; it must be drawn into public activities in every part of Jewish life; enriched with the spiritual treasures which the Jewish people have created through the ages. And, finally, we must gather together the best of the Jewish youth, which has already received its education in our movement, and forge it into a cadre that is prepared for battle and that will lead the way for Jewish youth. . . .

Yad Vashem Archives, JM/215/1.

* From the article by R. Domski (T. Borzykowski) in the underground newspaper of the Dror-He-Halutz movement in Warsaw, *Dror*, No. 3, August 1940.

95

EDUCATIONAL PROBLEMS IN THE UNDERGROUND
YOUTH MOVEMENT IN THE GHETTO *

...The [Youth] Movement now has before it far more tasks to fulfill than before the war. In the group named "Mitorerim" it has now become necessary to set up a self-help organization for members who are in need. This self-help can take two forms, according to the capacity of the "Nest" (club) and the objective conditions: it can either consist of an educational element alone, or it can develop into a successful combination of the educational element and economic "Nest" that will really be able to supply the material needs of the members. Both in the first case and in the second it will fulfill the high aim of a home working constructively for the future of the spirit of Jewish youth. There is no social education based on a single element: the educator must here find the exact synthesis that he requires.

But the task of "Mitorerim" does not end with the fulfillment of these demands. Apart from educational aims which must be fulfilled from the point of view of the young people's own needs, there is the problem of national existence. These times are marked by the total loss of the will to fight among the Jews. The invader's terror methods have entirely broken the will to opposition — to say nothing any longer of any opposition in the physical sense — and it is the adolescent youth that must become the stronghold and tower of the Jewish spirit of freedom. The need of the hour is to spread among the Jewish masses faith in our aims and real existence. Our youth which gather in the groups of "Mitorerim" and "Magshimim" must therefore set up *cells of spiritual opposition*, which will awaken in the Jewish masses faith in a better future and the desire to survive. To fight against the spreading pessimism and the mood of depression — here, this is one of the most important tasks of the older youth, which they must carry out among the general Jewish population. And they themselves, when they have guarded in their hearts their faith in the future existence of the Jewish people as a whole, will have to be ready also for the practical effort that will be demanded of them by the reality of Eretz Israel after the war. . . .

It thus becomes completely clear that the aims and demands of the educational youth movement, and the work program planned in the days before the war, have lost nothing of their value.

If in the years before the war education within the Movement was directed towards the pioneering effort in Eretz Israel, then at this time we must emphasize that in the education of the youth we must combine the demand for pioneering effort in Eretz Israel with the need to be active here, in order that we may stand fast, and exist and remain alive. In this way the framework of education has been greatly extended.

We cannot, therefore, omit anything at all from the educational program of former years, but must add to it the campaign to accept life at this time. For we shall not succeed in shaping the future of our life in Eretz [Israel] if we do not succeed in preserving the position of the youth in this period. It is equally necessary to have concern for material lives and for *the creation of suitable conditions for their continuous spiritual development.* . . .

Yad Vashem Archives, JM/210.

* From the underground newspaper of Gordonia youth, *Slowo Mlodych* ("Youth Speaks"), No. 25 (II), June 1942.

96

OFFICIAL DEFINITION OF THE TERM "JEW" IN THE GOVERNMENT-GENERAL, JULY 24, 1941

Regulation for the Definition of the Term "Jew" in the Government-General July 24, 1940

§ 1

Where the word "Jew" is used in Legal and Administrative Provisions in the Government-General, it is to be interpreted as follows:

1) Anyone who is a Jew, or is considered a Jew, in accordance with the Legal Provisions in the Reich;

2) Anyone who is a Jew, or is considered a Jew, and is a former Polish citizen or stateless person, under § 2 of this Regulation.

§ 2

1) A Jew is a person descended from at least three fully Jewish grandparents by race.

2) A person is considered a Jew if he is descended from two grandparents who are full Jews by race and

a) if he was a member of the Jewish Religious Community on September 1, 1939, or joined such a community subsequently;

b) if he was married to a Jew on the date on which this Regulation came into force, or married a Jew subsequently;

c) if he is the product of extra-marital intercourse with a Jew in accordance with para. 1 and was born after May 31, 1941.

3) A grandparent is automatically considered a full Jew if he was a member of a Jewish community.

§ 3

1) Where the concept [person of] Jewish *Mischling* is used in Legal and Administrative Provisions of the Government-General, it is to be interpreted as follows:

214

a) a person who is a Jewish *Mischling* in accordance with the Reich Legal Provisions;

b) any person who is a former Polish citizen or stateless, and is descended from one or two grandparents who are full Jews by race, unless he is considered a Jew under § 2, para. 2.

2) The provisions under § 2, para. 3 apply similarly.

§ 4

1) A business enterprise is considered Jewish if the owner is a Jew in accordance with § 1.

2) A business enterprise which is owned by a Limited Company is considered Jewish if one or more members who are personally responsible are Jews. . . .

3) A place of business is also considered Jewish if it is in practice under the dominant influence of Jews.

4) The provisions under para. 1-4 also apply to Associations, Endowments, Institutions and other organizations which are not business enterprises.

§ 5

Legal and Administrative Provisions issued for Jews apply to Jewish *Mischling* only where this is expressly stated.

§ 6

This Regulation comes into effect on August 1, 1940.

Cracow, July 24, 1940

The Governor General
for the Occupied Polish Territories
Frank

VBlGG, 1940, pp. 231-232.

97

THE MADAGASCAR PLAN, JULY 1940

The Jewish Question in the Peace Treaty

The approaching victory gives Germany the possibility, and in my view also the duty, of solving the Jewish question in Europe. The desirable solution is: all Jews out of Europe. The task of the Foreign Ministry in this is:

a) To include this demand in the Peace Treaty and to insist on it also by means of separate negotiations with the European countries not involved in the Peace Treaty;

b) to secure the territory necessary for the settlement of the Jews in the Peace Treaty, and to determine principles for the cooperation of the enemy countries in this problem;

c) to determine the position under international law of the new Jewish overseas settlement;

d) as preparatory measures:

1) clarification of the wishes and plans of the departments concerned of the Party, State and Research organizations in Germany, and the coordination of these plans with the wishes of the Reich Foreign Minister, including the following:

2) preparation of a survey of the factual data available in various places (number of Jews in the various countries), use of their financial assets through an international bank;

3) negotiations with our friend, Italy, on these matters.

With regard to beginning the preparatory work, Section D III has already approached the Reich Foreign Minister via the Department Germany [interior affairs], and has been instructed by him to start on the preparatory work without delay. There have already been discussions with the Office of the *Reichsführer* SS in the Ministry of Interior and several departments of the Party. These departments approve the following plan of Section D III:

216

Section D III proposes as a solution of the Jewish question: In the Peace Treaty France must make the island of Madagascar available for the solution of the Jewish question, and to resettle and compensate the approximately 25,000 French citizens living there. The island will be transferred to Germany under a mandate. Diégo Suarez Bay and the port of Antsirane, which are [sea-] strategically important, will become German naval bases (if the Navy wishes, these naval bases could be extended also to the harbors — open road-steads — Tamatave, Andevorante, Mananjara, etc.). In addition to these naval bases, suitable areas of the country will be excluded from the Jewish territory (*Judenterritorium*) for the construction of air bases. That part of the island not required for military purposes will be placed under the administration of a German Police Governor, who will be under the administration of the *Reichsführer* SS. Apart from this, the Jews will have their own administration in this territory: their own mayors, police, postal and railroad administration, etc. The Jews will be jointly liable for the value of the island. For this purpose their former European financial assets will be transferred for use to a European bank to be established for this purpose. Insofar as the assets are not sufficient to pay for the land which they will receive, and for the purchase of necessary commodities in Europe for the development of the island, the Jews will be able to receive bank credits from the same bank.

As Madagascar will only be a Mandate, the Jews living there will not acquire German citizenship. On the other hand, the Jews deported to Madagascar will lose their citizenship of European countries from the date of deportation. Instead, they will become residents of the Mandate of Madagascar.

This arrangement would prevent the possible establishment in Palestine by the Jews of a Vatican State of their own, and the opportunity for them to exploit for their own purposes the symbolic importance which Jerusalem has for the Christian and Mohammedan parts of the world. Moreover, the Jews

217

will remain in German hands as a pledge for the future good behavior of the members of their race in America.

Use can be made for propaganda purposes of the generosity shown by Germany in permitting cultural, economic, administrative and legal self-administration to the Jews; it can be emphasized at the same time that our German sense of responsibility towards the world forbids us to make the gift of a sovereign state to a race which has had no independent state for thousands of years: this would still require the test of history.

Berlin, July 3, 1940
signed Rademacher

NG — 2586 — B.

98

FROM A SPEECH BY FRANK ON THE MADAGASCAR PLAN, JULY 12, 1940

... Another very important point is the decision of the Führer, which he made at my request, that there will be no more transports of Jews into the area of the Government-General. As a general political observation I would like to state that it is planned to transport the whole pack of Jews (*Judensipp-schaft*) from the German Reich, the Government-General and the Protectorate, in the shortest conceivable time after peace has been made, to an African or American Colony. Madagascar is being considered, to be ceded by France for this purpose. There will be ample room here for a few million Jews on an area of 500,000 sq. kms. I have tried to let the Jews in the Government-General also share in this advantage, of building up a new life on new land. This has been accepted so that there should be a tremendous easing within sight. ...

Eksterminacja, pp. 51-52.

218

99

REGULATION FOR THE BAN ON JEWISH EMIGRATION FROM THE GOVERNMENT-GENERAL, NOVEMBER 1940 *

In a Decree of October 25, 1940, the Reich Security Main Office (*Reichssicherheitshauptamt*) has informed me of the following:

"Owing to the fact that the emigration of Jews from the Government-General still further considerably reduced the already shrinking opportunities for emigration for Jews from the *Altreich*,** the *Ostmark* [Austria] and the Protectorate of Bohemia and Moravia, contrary to the wish of the Reich Marshal, I request that no such emigration be considered.

"The continued emigration of Jews from Eastern Europe [to the West] spells a continued spiritual regeneration of world Jewry, as it is mainly the Eastern Jews who supply a large proportion of the rabbis, Talmud teachers, etc., owing to their orthodox-religious beliefs, and they are urgently needed by Jewish organizations active in the United States, according to their own statements. Further, every orthodox Jew from Eastern Europe spells a valuable addition for these Jewish organizations in the United States in ther constant efforts for the spiritual renewal of United States Jewry and its unification. It is United States Jewry in particular, which is endeavoring, with the help of newly immigrated Jews, especially from Eastern Europe, to create a new basis from which it intends to force ahead its struggle, particularly against Germany.

"For these reasons it can be assumed that after a certain number of emigration permits have been issued, creating a precedent for Jews from the Government-General, so to speak, a large part of the entry visas, [which are] mainly for the United States, will in future only be made available for Jews from Eastern Europe."

I fully accept the point of view of the Reich Security Main Office and request that you will not pass on to the office here for decision any more applications by Jews to emigrate. Such applications would of course have to be rejected here.

I empower you to reject without further investigation any applications by Jews from the Government-General for permission to emigrate. It is requested that applications to emigrate shall be forwarded here only if they involve Jews holding foreign citizenship. As there is no further question of emigration by Jews from the Government-General as a matter of principle, there is also no need for a Jew to receive a permit to visit the Reich for the purpose of obtaining a visa from a foreign consulate in the German Reich. It is requested that even applications by Jews for the issuing of a permit for the purpose of obtaining a visa from a foreign consulate in the Reich should also be rejected.

(for) Eckhardt

Eksterminacja, pp. 55-56.

* From a memorandum dated November 23, 1940, addressed to District Governors in the Government-General.
** Germany before 1938.

100

ORDER BY FISCHER ON THE ESTABLISHMENT OF A GHETTO IN WARSAW, OCTOBER 2, 1940

1. On the basis of the Regulation for Restrictions on Residence in the Government-General of September 13, 1940 (V.Bl.G.G.I., p. 288), a Jewish quarter is to be formed in the city of Warsaw, in which the Jews living in the city of Warsaw, or still to move there, must take up residence. The [Jewish] quarter will be set off from the rest of the city by the following streets: [here follows a list of streets and sections of streets]. . . .

2. Poles residing in the Jewish quarter must move their domicile into the other part of the city by October 31, 1940. Apartments will be provided by the Housing Office of the Polish City Hall.

Poles who have not given up their apartments in the Jewish quarter by the above date will be forcibly moved. In the event of forcible removal they will be permitted to take only refugee [style] luggage (*Flüchtlingsgepäck*), bed-linen, and articles of sentimental value.

Poles are not permitted to move into the German quarter.

3. Jews living outside the Jewish quarter must move into the Jewish area of residence by October 31, 1940. They may take only refugee luggage and bed-linen. Apartments will be allocated by the Jewish Elder (*Judenältester*).

4. The Appointed Mayor of the Polish City Hall and the Jewish Elder are responsible for the orderly move of the Jews to the Jewish quarter, and the punctual move of the Poles away from the Jewish quarter, in accordance with a plan yet to be worked out, which will provide for the evacuation by stages of the individual Police districts.

5. The Representative of the District Governor of the city of Warsaw will give the necessary detailed instructions to the Jewish Elder for the establishing and permanent closure of the Jewish quarter.

6. The Representative of the District Governor of the city of Warsaw will issue regulations for the execution of this Decree.

7. Any person contravening this Decree, or the Regulations for its execution, will be punished in accordance with the existing laws on punishment.

Head of the Warsaw District
Dr. Fischer
Governor

Eksterminacja, pp. 95-97.

101

FROM A LECTURE ON THE STEPS LEADING TO THE ESTABLISHMENT OF THE WARSAW GHETTO, JANUARY 20, 1941 [1] *

Introduction

The establishment of Jewish quarters and limitations of the right of Jews to take up residence or establish an economic existence are not new in the history of the East [i.e., Eastern Europe]. Their beginnings go back to the 13th century and have been observed again and again in the course of history, down to the establishment of the Polish Republic.[2] *

A new method is being applied when these limitations are imposed according to National-Socialist principles and perception.

Back in February 1940 — shortly after the establishment of the Department for Resettlement — the idea came up for the creation of a Jewish quarter in Warsaw, and the first preparations were made. It had originally been planned by the Governor to place the Jewish quarter in a suburb of Warsaw which is bordered on the east by the [River] Vistula.

The head of the Department of Resettlement was instructed to carry this out.

It was clear that this idea must at first appear to be incapable of execution, owing to the specific and extremely complicated conditions in the city of Warsaw. Objections were raised on various sides, and in particular by the City Administration. It was argued that the forming of a ghetto would cause serious disruption to industry and the economy. As about 80 percent of all the skilled labor was Jewish, it was indispensable and could not be shut away. Finally it was argued that the feeding of the Jews would not be possible if they were concentrated in a closed area.

222

The discussion on March 8, 1940, produced the conclusion that the plan for the establishment of a ghetto should be postponed for the time being.

About the same time it was being considered in the Government-General that the district of Lublin might be declared a collection area for all the Jews in the Government-General, and in particular for the evacuated Jews arriving there, and refugee Jews.

Cases of illegal emigration of Jews and unauthorized border crossings by Jews increased greatly at that time, particularly on the border of the sub-districts of Lowicz and Skierniewice. Conditions had become dangerous in the city of Lowicz as a result of the illegal move there of Jews, both as regards hygiene and from the point of view of the Security Police. The sub-district Commander (*Kreishauptmann*) of the Lowicz sub-district rightly considered that he should remove these dangers by means of the establishment of areas of Jewish residence in Lowicz and Glowno. The experience of the establishment of the Jewish quarters in Lowicz and Glowno have shown that these methods are the only ones that are correct to banish the dangers that emanate from the Jewish world (*Judenwelt*).

At the beginning of April 1940 we were informed by the Higher SS and Police leader (*Höherer SS-und Polizeiführer*) in Cracow that it was not intended to concentrate the Jews in the district of Lublin.

The Department of Resettlement then turned once more to the preliminary work for the establishment of Jewish quarters in the Warsaw district. The Governor gave instructions that the establishment of the Jewish quarters should be begun by a date which would make it possible to carry out the resettlement before the beginning of winter.

The plan now submitted by the Department of Resettlement provided for the establishment of two ghettos, both situated on the outskirts of the city — one in the west, including the suburbs of Kolo and Wola, and in the east of the city the suburb of Grochow. This idea was based on the realization that these ghettos on the outskirts of the city would cause the least

223

harm and disruption to the economy, industry and traffic of the city of Warsaw. The start of these *Aktionen* was set for July 1, 1940, in order to complete the most important measures in time before the onset of winter.

In the first stage of the preparations, orders were sent out from Cracow that all work on the establishment of the ghettos should be stopped in view of the fact that, according to the plan of the Führer, after the war all the Jews of Europe would be resettled in Madagascar,[3] * and that the creation of ghettos was therefore in fact illusory.

Upon this, the preliminary work of the Department of Resettlement was halted again. At the end of August 1940 the establishment of ghettos was once more pushed ahead by the Department for Health Care, in view of the increasing concentration of troops in the Warsaw District, and for the protection of the German Army and population. The Department for Interior Administration in the office of the Governor General on August 20, 1940, confirmed that it was necessary to establish Jewish areas of residence, but these would not be hermetically closed ghettos, but Jewish districts which would permit just enough economic contact with the Aryan surroundings to keep the Jewish quarter viable.

It was now already very late [in the year] to establish ghettos on the outskirts of the city, and this would have taken at least four to five months, as it would have involved regrouping almost 600,000 persons. But the resettlement *Aktionen* had to be completed by November 15, in particular according to the recommendation of the District Medical Officer, or at the latest by the end of November, as there was always an increased incidence of epidemics during the winter months, and these would have been speeded up dangerously by the resettlement operation.

The plan for ghettos on the outskirts of the city was therefore abandoned. The area chosen now was one that had been marked as endangered by epidemics (*Seuchensperrgebiet*), which in its present condition offered no secure protection against epidemics.

After voluminous preliminary discussions and negotiations, visits to the area and preparations, a promising plan was submitted to the Governor.

On October 2, 1940, general instruction went out from the Governor of the Warsaw District to all local leaders and the representatives of the District Governor of the city of Warsaw to begin work by November 15, 1940, on the resettlement required for the establishment of Jewish quarters. It was clear that this problem would have to be attacked all along the line if there were to be certainty of success.

On the same day the Governor issued Decree No. 40/50 concerning the establishment of a Jewish quarter in the city of Warsaw, and instructed the head of the Department of Resettlement to take charge of the whole resettlement operation.

The reasons for the establishment of a Jewish quarter in the Warsaw District, apart from general principles concerning ethnic restructuring (*Volkstumsordnung*) in this area, are as follows:

1. The German Army and population must in any case be protected against the Jews, the immune carriers of the bacteria of epidemics.

2. The separation of the Jews from the rest of the population, both Poles and ethnic Germans (*Volksdeutsche*)[*] is a political and moral requirement. Jewish thinking and action had up to now dominated the population of the eastern lands. The beneficial effects of the elimination of Jewish influence can now already be seen. If the German task of reconstruction is to be successful at all, then the freedom of Jewry to act in the area must be ended.

3. A further reason derives from the need to secure the execution of war economy measures and the safeguarding of the nutrition level in general by stopping the black market and the raising of prices.

225

The Resettlement Aktionen in Warsaw

The resettlement *Aktionen* started at the beginning of October 1940. The first date set for the completion of the operation was October 31, 1941.

For a start, 700 *Volksdeutsche* had to be pulled out of the section which had been declared a Jewish quarter and moved into the provisional German area.

Altogether, 113,000 Poles and 138,000 Jews were exchanged. As the Jews who had been living outside the Jewish area in most cases had fairly large apartments, it was possible to carry out the change without disturbances by placing several Polish families in one of these larger apartments. A total of 11,567 Aryan apartments were vacated in the Jewish quarter and about 13,000 Jewish apartments taken over outside the Jewish quarter. . . .

It is surprising that the resettlement of roughly 250,000 persons was carried out in the comparatively short period of not quite six weeks without any blood being shed and with the aid of police pressure only in the final stage. This was done by bringing in the Polish mayor on the one hand and the Judenrat, on the other, to give their help.

On November 16, 1940, a major police *Aktion* was carried out under the direction of the head of the Department of Resettlement, in which all parts of the city outside the Jewish quarter were combed and 11,130 Jews caught and taken forcibly to the Jewish quarter. On the same day 1,170 food stores and 2,600 other stores owned by Jews were sealed by the police, handed over to the appropriate departments and organizations and cleared by them. . . .

The Appearance of the Jewish Quarter

The Jewish quarter extends over about 1,016 acres. According to the figures supplied by the Judenrat, which claims to have carried out a census, about 410,000 Jews live in this area;

according to our own observations and various estimates, carried out by other bodies, they number between 470,000 and 590,000.[5] *

Based on the statistics supplied by the Judenrat, and subtracting empty spaces and cemeteries, there are [in the Jewish quarter] 1,108 persons living on a built-up area of one hectare (2.5 acres), i.e., 110,800 persons per sq. km. [approx. 277,000 per sq. mile]. The population density of the city of Warsaw is 14,400 persons per sq. km. of the total area and 38,000 per sq. km. of built-up and inhabited area.

It should be noted that the number will be increased by the new resettlement of 72,000 Jews from the western section of the District. This is needed in order to make room for 62,000 evacuated Poles.

In the Jewish area of residence there are about 27,000 apartments with an average number of 2½ rooms. Occupancy therefore works out at 15.1 persons per apartment and 6 to 7 persons per room. The Jewish area of residence is separated from the rest of the city by the use of partition walls and fire-proof walls and by walls sealing off streets, windows, entrances and spaces between houses. The walls are three meters high and are raised another meter by means of a barbed-wire extension. Additional control is assured by motorized and mounted police patrols.

At first 22 gates in the surrounding wall were retained for the maintenance of necessary traffic, but these have since been reduced to 15. Reinforced German police guards were at first posted at these openings; these were later replaced by Polish police, with German police taking over mainly the supervision.

The units of the German police for the Jewish quarter — consisting of 87 men under the command of an *Oberleutnant* — are accommodated in three posts outside the wall. . . .

Permits to pass these gates are issued for absolutely essential passenger traffic: the permit cards are yellow for German citizens, ethnic Germans and Poles, for Jews there are yellow

227

cards with an oblique blue bar. The permits are valid only together with an identity card with a photograph. . . .

Eksterminacja, pp. 99-104.

1 * Lecture by Waldemar Schön, Head of the Department of Resettlement in the Warsaw District.
2 * The reference is to the independent Polish Republic between the two wars.
3 * See Documents 97, 98.
4 * *Volksdeutsche* — persons of German origin or persons who declared themselves to be of German origin and lived outside Germany.
5 * The German estimate is deliberately exaggerated. According to J. Ziemian, *Gvulot Getto Varsha ve-Shinuyehem* ("The Borders of the Warsaw Ghetto and their Changes"), Jerusalem 1971, p. 17, the population census taken on Jan. 1, 1941 gave the number of persons in the ghetto as 380,740. According to the calculations of the Judenrat, based on the food-ration cards of Jan. 1, 1941, the number of Jews was 394,836.

102

THE SMUGGLING OF FOOD INTO THE WARSAW GHETTO

Smuggling began at the very moment that the Jewish area of residence was established; its inhabitants were forced to live on 180 grams [6½ oz.] of bread a day, 220 grams of sugar a month, 1 kg. [2.2 lbs.] jam and ½ kg. of honey, etc. It was calculated that the officially supplied rations did not cover even 10 percent of normal requirements. If one had wanted really to restrict oneself to the official rations then the entire population of the ghetto would have had to die of hunger in a very short time. . . .

The German authorities did everything to seal off the ghetto hermetically and not to allow in a single gram of food. A wall was put up around the ghetto on all sides that did not leave a single millimeter of open space. . . .

They fixed barbed wire and broken glass to the top of the wall. When that failed to help, the Judenrat was ordered to make the wall higher, at the expense of the Jews, of course....

Several kinds of guards were appointed for the walls and the passages through them; the categories [of guards] were constantly being changed and their numbers increased. The walls were guarded by the gendarmerie together with the Polish police; at the ghetto wall there were gendarmerie posts, Polish police and Jewish police... The victims of the smuggling were mainly Jews, but they were not lacking either among the Aryans [Poles]. Auerswald, too, employed sharply repressive measures to stop the smuggling. Several times smugglers were shot at the central lock-up on Gesiowka* Street. Once there was a veritable slaughter (100 persons were shot near Warsaw). Among the Jewish victims of the smuggling there were tens of Jewish children between 5 and 6 years old, whom the German killers shot in great numbers near the passages and at the walls....

And despite that, without paying attention to the victims, the smuggling never stopped for a moment. When the street was still slippery with the blood that had been spilled, other [smugglers] already set out, as soon as the "candles" ** had signalled that the way was clear, to carry on with the work....

The smuggling took place — a) through the walls, b) through the gates, c) through underground tunnels, d) through sewers, and e) through houses on the borders....

Ringelblum, II, pp. 274-277.

* The reference is to the Jewish prison in the Warsaw ghetto which was called "Gesiowka."
** Smugglers' look-outs.

103

EXTRACT FROM THE DIARY OF CHAIM A. KAPLAN ON THE WARSAW JUDENRAT, 1941

April 23, 1941

The Community Council — the Judenrat, in the language of the Occupying Power — is an abomination in the eyes of the Warsaw Community. When the Council is so much as mentioned, everyone's blood begins to boil. If it were not for fear of the Authorities there would be bloodshed. I am certain that at the first opportunity, if we are only freed a little from the Nazi tutelage, we will fall upon Grzybowska 26,* and pour out our fury upon it, and not leave one stone standing upon another. It was not elected by the Community, but reached its position of power through appointment and with the support of the Nazi Authorities, and as a result of the general situation. In accordance with its system, the Authorities gave the Council autonomous rights, not only in cultural matters but also in official affairs. Starzynski appointed Czerniakow, whom nobody had known prior to this appointment. There were thousands like him... Everything depended on his taste and on his personal judgment concerning every individual, and he took everything he could lay his hands on. According to rumor, the President is a decent man. But the people around him are the dregs of humanity. There are two or three exceptions, who have no influence, like Prof. M. Balaban** and A. Wolfowicz; all the rest are the scum of the [Jewish] public. I shall not list their names because they are not worthy of having their names recorded officially in the history of the Jewish Community of Warsaw. They are known as scoundrels and corrupt persons, who did not avoid ugly dealings even in the period before the war. The Community has become for them a milch-cow and an unending opportunity to take bribes, to rob the poor and crush the oppressed. Everything is done in the name of the President. But in truth, everything is done without his knowledge and even without his consent, and perhaps also against his decisions and wishes. . . .

Moreshet Archives, D.2.138.

* This was the house where the Warsaw Jewish Community Council had its offices before the war, and the Judenrat during the war.
** Meir Balaban, the historian of Polish Jewry. He was for a short time a member of the first Judenrat in the Warsaw Ghetto.

104

APPEAL NOT TO GO TO LABOR CAMPS, FROM AN UNDERGROUND PUBLICATION *

There is no justification for the despicable creatures who have become servants of violence for filthy lucre.

There is no justification for the defilement that is spreading among the Jews, that is imposing the whole burden of the camps on the shoulders of the tired and starved poor of the ghetto.

The labor camps were and continue to be an act of violence on the part of the Fascist rulers; they shall meet with passive but determined resistance on the part of conscious Jews.

We will not go to the labor camps! We will put obstacles in the way of the Community Council [Judenrat] at every step they take to carry out their jobs.

Let the [youth] leaders of the Nest [youth club] not cease their duties even for a moment. We shall prove that indeed nothing can break us and nothing can force us to stop our work. Let us give expression to the fact that the future is with us and not with them.

Yad Vashem Archives, JM/211/1-2.

* From the Ha-Shomer Ha-Za'ir publication *Iton Ha-Tenua* ("Newspaper of the Movement"), 1942.

105

THE DILEMMA OF JEWISH SELF-HELP

May 26, 1942

... Relief work doesn't solve the problem; it only keeps people going a little while. The people have to die anyway. It lengthens suffering but cannot save them; if it [the Jewish Self-Help] really wanted to do anything, it would have to have millions of zloty at its disposal every month, and it does not have them. It remains a proven fact that the people fed in the soup-kitchens will all die if they eat nothing but the soup supplied and the dry rationed bread. The question thus arises whether it would not serve the purpose better to reserve the available money for selected individuals, for those who are socially productive, for the intellectual elite, etc. But the situation is such that, first of all, the numbers even of such select individuals is quite considerable, and there would not be sufficient even for them. Secondly, the question arises why should one pronounce judgment on artisans, laborers and other useful persons, who were productive people back in their small towns, and only the ghetto and the war have turned them into non-people, into scrap, into human dregs, candidates for mass graves. There is left a tragic dilemma: What shall one do? Shall one [hand out the food] with little spoons to everybody, and then no one will live, or in generous handfuls to just a few...?

Ringelblum, I, p. 365.

106

GÖRING ORDERS HEYDRICH TO PREPARE A PLAN FOR THE "FINAL SOLUTION OF THE JEWISH PROBLEM," JULY 31, 1941

To the Chief of the Security Police and the SD,
SS *Gruppenführer* Heydrich
Berlin

In completion of the task which was entrusted to you in the Edict dated January 24, 1939, of solving the Jewish question by means of emigration or evacuation in the most convenient way possible, given the present conditions, I herewith charge you with making all necessary preparations with regard to organizational, practical and financial aspects for an overall solution (*Gesamtlösung*) of the Jewish question in the German sphere of influence in Europe.

Insofar as the competencies of other central organizations are affected, these are to be involved.

I further charge you with submitting to me promptly an overall plan of the preliminary organizational, practical and financial measures for the execution of the intended final solution (*Endlösung*) of the Jewish question.

Göring

PS-710.

107

RINGELBLUM ON COOPERATION BETWEEN JEWISH POLITICAL PARTIES IN THE UNDERGROUND

The war has confronted Jewish public circles with very important problems. The political relationships that existed before the war had to cease. A united Jewish front had to be created from Left to Right. The Hitlerist fight against the Jewish population took on the character of an extermination. It was directed against all strata and all classes of the Jewish population as a whole. As far as the Hitlerites were concerned there was no difference between the Zionists and members of the Bund — they hated both equally. They wanted to destroy both. A policy for struggle appropriate to this situation had to be developed by the Jewish population. A united national front had to be created to face the German Fascist powers of destruction. The Jews were confronted by such cardinal questions of life and death that no [section] could take the responsibility for deciding such crucial questions alone. It required united strength to find the answers to the problems which the situation continuously brought up. The institution of Party consultations of all political directions had no name, but it was a permanent body, and its views were consulted by the Joint, the Jewish Social Self-Help organization and by the Community itself more than once....

Ringelblum, II, p. 109.

108

"ONEG SHABBAT," THE JEWISH UNDERGROUND ARCHIVES IN THE WARSAW GHETTO

The ghetto archives were established by the group that called itself "Oneg Shabbat" ("Sabbath gathering") in the course of the three and a half years of war. The strange name derived from the fact that the discussions of this group were held on the Sabbath — for the sake of secrecy the entire institution was called "Oneg Shabbat." I laid the foundations of the archives in October 1939....

I began to collect material on current events in October 1939. As head of the Jewish Self-Help welfare organization (which was known then as the Coordinating Committee of the welfare organizations), I had daily personal contact with the life around me. Information reached me on everything that happened to Jews in Warsaw or the suburbs. The Coordinating Committee was at that time a branch of the Joint, and delegations from the smaller towns arrived almost daily to describe the difficulties experienced by the Jewish population. Whatever I heard in the course of the day I wrote down in the evening, and added my observations. In time these daily records made up a good-sized book of some hundreds of closely written pages, a mirror of that time. The daily records were replaced first by weekly summaries, and later monthly summaries. I did this at a time when the number of colleagues working for the "Oneg Shabbat" had already become larger...

In May 1940 I decided that it would be proper to find wider support for this important work. I made a careful choice of people for the job and as a result the work progressed in the right direction and could be carried out in sufficient measure. The secretary of "Oneg Shabbat," Hirsch W [Wasser] was appointed by the Committee of "Oneg Shabbat" at that time, and he has continued with the work to the present day....

The creation of the ghetto, and the shutting away of the Jews within the walls, brought about even greater opportunities for work on the archives. We reached the conclusion that the Germans took very little interest in what the Jews were doing amongst themselves. There were meetings on subjects and in a manner that would not have been possible before the war. One said everything that came to mind at every meeting of a house committee, in every soup-kitchen, and on the premises of every public institution, without interference. The Jewish Gestapo agents were busy looking for the rich Jews with hoarded goods, smugglers, etc. Politics interested them little. It went so far that illegal publications of all political directions appeared almost openly. In the cafés they were read practically in public; money was collected for the newspaper fund, there were arguments with opponents — in a word, people behaved almost like before the war. In conditions of such "freedom" among the slaves of the ghetto it was not surprising that the work of "Oneg Shabbat" could develop successfully. . . .

"Oneg Shabbat" grew and grew, and so much valuable material was collected that we came to the conclusion that even if the time had not yet come to consolidate the material we could in any case make summaries of various problems and important events in Jewish life. If this plan had been carried out it would have made a very important contribution to the history of the Jews in Hitler's time. It is very regrettable that only a part of the work planned was carried out. There was missing the quiet atmosphere that is needed for a task of such size and dimensions. The compilers of "Oneg Shabbat" who undertook to work on one chapter or another did not find it possible to complete their work up to the end. . . .

Ringelblum, II, pp. 76-80.

109

ADDRESS BY RUMKOWSKI TO THE OFFICIALS OF THE JUDENRAT IN LODZ

Bulletin No. 22

February 1, 1941

... Most of the propertied class left before the ghetto was closed. Those who remained were: the middle class, the poor, and the workers, who are to a large extent the element known as "the people from Baluti."* This element in particular causes great difficulties for the Community authorities, because it is ill-disciplined and tends to create chaos in the life of the ghetto. It forms a majority percentage of the criminal population in the ghetto.

I have made it my aim to regulate life in the ghetto at all costs. This aim can be achieved, first of all, by employment for all. Therefore, my main slogan has been *to give work to the greatest possible number of people.* It was not a simple matter to set up the workshops. Great difficulty was caused by the fact that there were scarcely any Jewish factories within the area of the ghetto. Despite that I succeeded in establishing a series of work-places, factories, carpentry workshops, a leather tannery, tailoring workshops, shoe-making workshops, establishments for the production of the most varied goods... My workshops are now already employing up to 10,000 workers. About 1,000 unskilled laborers are employed on public projects. About 1,600 persons have already been sent to work outside the ghetto; they use part of their wages to support the families who have remained here and whom I pay a regular weekly wage. ...

D. Dabrowska and L. Dobroszycki, eds., *Kronika getta lodzkiego* ("Lodz Ghetto Chronicle"), I, Lodz, 1965, p. 48.

* Baluti — a poor quarter of Lodz inhabited mainly by Jews. It was included in the area of the ghetto.

110

APPEAL FOR CONTRIBUTIONS BY THE JUDENRAT IN BIALYSTOK

Brothers and Sisters!

We appeal to you before the autumn and winter come and with them winds, cold and snow.

The urgent task awaits us of supplying the necessary daily needs of those who were burned out and are without a roof over their heads,* as well as of orphanages, children's homes, homes for the aged, hospitals and other institutions. Most important, we must find warm clothes and shoes for them, to protect them as far as possible from colds and infectious diseases, which are a grave danger for all of us.

In order to ward off these threats, the Judenrat announces a widely based collection campaign. Jews, remember that we have no one to rely on except ourselves alone.

Time is short and the need is terribly great, and because of that we must spare from ourselves whatever we can and give it to the campaign.

Please, therefore, receive our collectors with the warmth they deserve, and respond immediately and with a Jewish warmth of heart.

Let us ease from our own resources, if only by a little, the suffering in the winter days! Let the danger of epidemics be prevented!

Ask the collectors for receipts signed by the Judenrat.

Judenrat

Bialystok, September 8, 1941

Blumental, p. 330.

* The reference is to persons whose houses were burned down.

238

111

THE GIRL COURIERS OF THE UNDERGROUND MOVEMENT

May 19, 1942

The heroic girls, Chajka [Grosman], Frumke [Plotnicka] and others — theirs is a story that calls for the pen of a great writer. They are venturesome, courageous girls who travel here and there across Poland to cities and towns, carrying Aryan papers which describe them as Polish or Ukrainian. One of them even wears a cross, which she never leaves off and misses when she is in the ghetto. Day by day they face the greatest dangers, relying completely on their Aryan appearance and the kerchiefs they tie around their heads. They accept the most dangerous missions and carry them out without a murmur, without a moment's hesitation. If there is need for someone to travel to Vilna, Bialystok, Lvov, Kowel, Lublin, Czestochowa, or Radom to smuggle in such forbidden things as illegal publications, goods, money, they do it all as though it were the most natural thing. If there are comrades to be rescued from Vilna, Lublin, or other cities, they take the job on themselves. Nothing deters them, nothing stops them. If it is necessary to make friends with the German responsible for a train so as to travel beyond the borders of the Government-General, which is allowed only for people with special permits — they do it quite simply, as though it were their profession. They travel from city to city, where no representative of any Jewish institution has reached, such as Volhynia and Lithuania. They were the first to bring the news of the tragedy in Vilna. They were the first to take back messages of greeting and encouragement to the survivors in Vilna. How many times did they look death in the eye? How many times were they arrested and searched? But their luck held. "Those who go on an errand of mercy will meet no evil." With what modesty and simplicity do they deliver their reports on what they accomplished during their travels on trains where Christians, men and women, were picked up and taken away for work in Germany. Jewish women have written a shining page in the history of the present World War. The Chajkes and the Frumkes will take first place in this history. These girls do not know what it is to rest. They have hardly arrived from Czestochowa where they took forbidden goods, and in a few hours they would move on again: they do it without a moment's hesitation, and without a minute's rest.

Ringelblum, I, pp. 359-360.

112

SOME GHETTO THOUGHTS ON RESCUE AND REVENGE

June 10, 1942

... At a gathering of a few people there was a discussion concerning what should be done if there were a chance now of sending out one person into the wide world. Everyone agreed that, at all costs, the world must be awakened to the process of extermination being carried out against the Jews. There was no need to take into consideration that this might worsen our situation, we have nothing at all to lose. The extermination scheme will be carried out according to plan, systematically, in accordance with the scheme set out in advance. Only a miracle can save us: a sudden end to the war, otherwise we are lost. Should one demand revenge? Some [of the people] held that we should. One should gather together the few tens of thousands of Germans in America, lock them up in a concentration camp behind barbed wire, without food or water, and let them perish of hunger and need, as is done here in

240

Poland. Others thought that the demand for retaliation would incite the Germans even more and bring about the total extermination of the Jews. . . .

A second question that was discussed on this occasion was whether one should send abroad a list of the names of valuable persons in order to get foreign passports for them and save them in this way. Some pointed out that the elite should stay with the people and go down together with them. Others, again, made their stand on examples from Jewish history and tradition, which demand that even one single soul in Israel must be saved. . . .

Ringelblum, I, p. 372.

113

LETTERS FROM THE JEWISH UNDERGROUND YOUTH MOVEMENT *

Warsaw, Fall 1942

Lately I have been feeling ill. My health is not in order. I have lung disease and spit blood. I regret deeply that this will prevent me from entering into marriage with my beloved Moledet ["Homeland"]. Our love developed 15 years ago when we studied together at school, and I sang her love-songs while I was still a child. Eight years ago I began to work in her father's office [Zionist Movement], and I made progress in my work, steadily, which increased my chances of marriage [immigration]. To my great sorrow you will see that disease has struck me, and my dreams of life joined to hers [Eretz Israel] is doomed to remain a dream. But whatever happens, I will continue to bear great love for her, and the last words that I breathe before my death will be the name by which I have called her.

Gerushovitch [a play on *gerush*, Hebrew for deportation] and his brother Tevahovitch [*tevah* — slaughter] send you their greetings. My people labors and is going down to Killayon [*Killayon* — annihilation] with the aid of Yekes [the Germans]. I am only surprised that his rich aunt, Olamska [*Olam* — world], is not helping him at all. I suppose that she knows only very little about your people. . . .

Hrubieszow, 1942

My dear friend!

Do not let the pathos of the opening frighten you. It contains what I surely will not be able to express in the letter itself. I began to write to you times without number, but I was always overcome by the feeling of a senselessness in writing, and this saved me from absurd action. You understand. . . I always find myself accompanied by the realization that it is illusion and self-torture to cling to the shreds of the past and to bring them out into the light of day. Then why? For you have wiped us from your memory, and what are we? It is known that one cannot draw water from a poisoned spring. I am holding fast to my soul, in order not to allow escape to the bitterness that has mounted up against you and your friends, who have forgotten us in such a simple way. I am aggrieved against you, that you did not help me even with a few words. But it is not my wish today to settle accounts with you. Only the realization and certainty that we shall never meet again has caused me to write.

The sickness of Israel and my sickness — and you know how long we have been wrestling with it — has been revealed now as entirely without hope of cure, that is what the doctors have ruled. One must therefore slowly become accustomed to this thought. Perhaps it is terrible that there is no longer time enough to assimilate it. You would surely like to know

242

how the other members of the family are. Pra'otzki [*pra'ot* — pogrom] and Shehita [*Shehita* — killing] live with me and with Israel. There was nothing we could do against it. It has a fatal effect on the health of Israel, and I can see how it will bring about the end. But what can we do — this is the situation and no other. I am doing everything I can to prevent it but to my regret there are elements that can stop even the strongest will. Israel is dying before my eyes, and I wring my hands and can do nothing to help. Have you ever tried to beat your head against a wall? Two months ago I was in the city where you were born. There I met my friends from the Hurban [*hurban* — destruction] School. It is doing excellent business...

Hurban accompanied me faithfully and tried to make the days of my visit agreeable. For as regards the satisfaction of emotions he was always very civil. I saw Chajka. Apart from her I found nobody.

As regards our material existence, we manage somehow. We work as before. Josef [Kaplan] and I in our profession [leadership], and it works somehow. Only one thing has changed — the prospects. I have only one desire: to tell the world that Israel is so sick. For he is my best friend, and even if there cannot be much practical help, still the simple realization that somebody is with us, if only in their thoughts, on our road of suffering, makes it easier. But do not upset yourself too much, my friend. After all, there are theories concerning adaptation to conditions.

This has become a strange letter. At first it was intended to talk only about myself and about you: how I draw up from my memory details about you, and how sometimes when things are difficult I wonder what you would have done in the same case. But sometimes I cannot dredge up your appearance in my memory. I have not a single photograph. Who knows what will happen to me before you get this letter.

Don't give greetings to anyone. I don't want to know them! But you I would like to see again.

Tosia [Altman]

Adam! A few days ago I saw your parents. They are managing all right. We, too, remember them with affection. So you may feel reassured about them.

B. Habas, *Mihtavim min ha-Getta'ot* ("Letters from the Ghettos"), Tel Aviv, 1943, pp. 40-43.

* Many of the letters contain coded expressions taken from the Hebrew.

114

FROM A REPORT BY AUERSWALD, COMMISSAR OF THE WARSAW GHETTO, SEPTEMBER 26, 1941

The Office of the Commissar for the Jewish quarter was set up by order of the Governor General of April 19, 1941 (V.Bl.G.G., p. 211). Any report on the activities of this Office can therefore only begin from this date. But in the following a short account will be given of the development of the Jewish quarter in Warsaw.

From the beginning of the German Administration in Warsaw the idea arose inevitably, owing to the great number of Jews there, that they should be concentrated in a Jewish area of residence. The most important reason was, first of all, the desire to isolate the Jews from the Aryan world on general political and ideological grounds. In practice there were grave requirements in the fields of health and economy. . . .

The general situation in the Jewish quarter has up to now given no cause for anxiety. Even the beginning of the war with Russia and the introduction of the blackout did not change this.

The three most important problems in connection with the Jewish quarter were and are, the food situation, health and the economy.

The situation as regards food and health are closely linked. A sudden leap in the number of deaths in May of this year indicates that the food shortage had turned into starvation. The food supply was thus revealed as the most urgent task. [The aim] was first of all to improve nutrition by means of popular soup-kitchens, increasing both nutritional values and the number of food portions supplied. This improvement succeeded in large measure, as may be seen from the following figures: the number of food portions distributed daily by the Jewish Social Self-Help — less than 30,000 recently — was raised to about 50,000 by the end of May of this year, and to about 115,000 by June; in July and August it was maintained at about 120,000. This was done with the aid of special allocations. These special allocations included, in the period May through August of this year, altogether 170 tons oats, 125 tons rye flour, 20,000 kgs. of sugar, 24,000 kgs. [cooking] oil, 100,000 kgs. bread, 10,000 kgs. meat and some other supplies.

Nevertheless the quantity of legally supplied foodstuffs is far from enough to counter the acute starvation in the Jewish quarter effectively. The quantity of foodstuffs smuggled into the Jewish quarter is not small, but owing to the high cost it is available only to the wealthier section of the Jews. If there is to be any successful large-scale exploitation of Jewish labor, it will be necessary to increase their food supply considerably.

The increase in the food supply described above was insufficient to stop the rise in the number of deaths resulting from the generally wretched condition of the Jews since the beginning of the war. The following figures give an impressive picture of the number of deaths:

January 1941	. .	898	May 1941 . .	3,821
February 1941 .	.	1,023	June 1941 . .	4,290
March 1941	. .	1,608	July 1941 . .	5,550
April 1941	. .	2,061	August 1941 . .	5,560

It is seen that in August, for the first time, mortality remains unchanged at the level of the previous month. Improved nutrition appears now to be having its effect. This is confirmed by the preliminary figures for September, which indicate that the total for this month will scarcely exceed the figure for each of the past two months.

Another reason for the increase in deaths is the increase of typhus in the Jewish quarter. Despite energetic efforts to fight the typhus, the number of cases has risen steadily. Since July of this year the number of cases of typhus reported every week has remained fairly steady. They range from 320 to 450 new cases. The last figure for a month (August), at 1,788, is only slightly higher than the figure for the previous month at 1,736 cases. . . .

Auerswald

Eksterminacja, pp. 129-132.

115

FROM A SPEECH BY FRANK AT BERLIN UNIVERSITY, NOVEMBER 18, 1941

...A problem that occupies us in particular is the *Jews*. This merry little people (*Völklein*), which wallows in dirt, and filth, has been gathered together by us in ghettos and [special] quarters and will probably not remain in the Government-General for very long.

(Vigorous applause)

We will get these Jews marching and cause them — as they have already covered the distance from Jerusalem to Poland — to move eastward a few thousand kilometers. But these Jews are not that parasite gang alone, from our point of view, but strangely enough — we only realized it over there [in Poland] — there is another category of Jews, something one would never have thought possible. There are laboring Jews over there who work in transport, in building, in factories, and others are skilled workers such as tailors, shoemakers, etc. We have put together Jewish workshops with the help of these skilled Jewish workers, in which goods will be made which will greatly ease the position of German production, in exchange for the supply of food-stuffs and whatever else the Jews need urgently for their existence. These Jews may well be left to work in this way; in the way in which we are now using them it is something of an achievement for the work-Jews themselves; but for the other Jews we must provide suitable arrangements. It is always dangerous, after all, to leave one's native land. Since the Jews moved away from Jerusalem there has been nothing for them except an existence as parasites: that has now come to an end. If one looks at the Warsaw ghetto today in which 480,000 Jews — well, let us say — live, then one must realize that only the determination of the National-Socialist revolution was capable of successfully confronting even this problem. In 1919, at our first meetings in Munich, we proclaimed the motto: **An end must be put to the rule of the Jews in Europe**. . . .

Work Diary of Hans Frank, Yad Vashem Archives, JM/21.

116

FROM A SPEECH BY FRANK ON THE EXTERMINATION OF THE JEWS, DECEMBER 16, 1941

. . . One way or another — I will tell you that quite openly — we must finish off the Jews. The Führer put it into words once: should united Jewry again succeed in setting off a world war, then the blood sacrifice shall not be made only by the peoples driven into war, but then the Jew of Europe will have met his end. I know that there is criticism of many of the measures now applied to the Jews in the Reich. There are always deliberate attempts to speak again and again of cruelty, harshness, etc.; this emerges from the reports on the popular mood. I appeal to you: before I now continue speaking first agree with me on a formula: we will have pity, on principle, only for the German people, and for nobody else in the world. The others had no pity for us either. As an old National-Socialist I must also say that if the pack of Jews (*Judensippschaft*) were to survive the war in Europe while we sacrifice the best of our blood for the preservation of Europe, then this war would still be only a partial success. I will therefore, on principle, approach Jewish affairs in the expectation that the Jews will disappear. They must go. I have started negotiations for the purpose of having them pushed off to the East. In January there will be a major conference on this question in Berlin,* to which I shall send State Secretary Dr. Bühler. The conference is to be held in the office of SS *Obergruppenführer* Heydrich at the Reich Security Main Office (*Reichssicherheitshauptamt*). A major Jewish migration will certainly begin.

But what should be done with the Jews? Can you believe that they will be accommodated in settlements in the *Ostland*? In Berlin we were told: why are you making all this trouble? We don't want them either, not in the *Ostland* nor in the *Reichskommissariat*; liquidate them yourselves! Gentlemen, I must ask you to steel yourselves against all considerations of compassion. We must destroy the Jews wherever we find them, and wherever it is at all possible, in order to maintain the whole structure of the Reich... The views that were acceptable up to now cannot be applied to such gigantic, unique events. In any case we must find a way that will lead us to our goal, and I have my own ideas on this.

The Jews are also exceptionally harmful feeders for us. In the Government-General we have approximately 2.5 million [Jews], and now perhaps 3.5 million together with persons who have

Jewish kin, and so on. We cannot shoot these 3.5 million Jews,** we cannot poison them, but we will be able to take measures that will lead somehow to successful destruction; and this in connection with the large-scale procedures which are to be discussed in the Reich. The Government-General must become as free of Jews as the Reich. Where and how this is to be done is the affair of bodies which we will have to appoint and create, and on whose work I will report to you when the time comes. ...

PS-2233.

* See Document 117.
** The figures are not based on facts.

117

PROTOCOL OF THE WANNSEE CONFERENCE, JANUARY 20, 1942

Reich Secret Document
30 Copies

Protocol of Conference

I. The following took part in the conference on the final solution (*Endlösung*) of the Jewish question held on January 20, 1942, in Berlin, Am Grossen Wannsee No. 56-58:

Gauleiter Dr. Meyer and Reich Office Director Dr. Leibbrandt	Reich Ministry for the Occupied Eastern Territories
Secretary of State Dr. Stuckart	Reich Ministry of the Interior
Secretary of State Neumann	Plenipotentiary for the Four Year Plan

Secretary of State Dr. Freisler	Reich Ministry of Justice
Secretary of State Dr. Bühler	Office of the Governor General
Undersecretary of State Dr. Luther	Foreign Ministry
SS *Oberführer* Klopfer	Party Chancellery
Ministerial Director Kritzinger	Reich Chancellery
SS *Gruppenführer* Hofmann	Race and Settlement Main Office
SS *Gruppenführer* Müller	Reich Security Main Office
SS *Obersturmbannführer* Eichmann	Reich Security Main Office
SS *Oberführer* Dr. Schöngarth, Commander of the Security Police and the SD in the Government-General	Security Police and SD
SS *Sturmbannführer* Dr. Lange, Commander of the Security Police and the SD in the *Generalbezirk* Latvia as representative of the Commander of the Security Police and the SD for the *Reichskommissariat* for the *Ostland*	Security Police and SD

11. The meeting opened with the announcement by the Chief of the Security Police and the SD, SS *Obergruppenführer* Heydrich, of his appointment by the Reich Marshal [1] * as Plenipotentiary for the Preparation of the Final Solution of the European Jewish Question.[2] * He noted that this Conference had been called in order to obtain clarity on questions of principle. The Reich Marshal's request for a draft plan concerning the organizational, practical and economic aspects of the final solution of the European Jewish question required prior joint consideration by all central agencies directly involved in these questions, with a view to maintaining parallel policy lines.

Responsibility for the handling of the final solution of the Jewish question, he said, would lie centrally with the *Reichsführer* SS and the Chief of the German Police (Chief of the Security Police and the SD), without regard to geographic boundaries.

The Chief of the Security Police and the SD then gave a brief review of the struggle conducted up to now against this foe.

The most important elements are:

a) Forcing the Jews out of the various areas of life (*Lebensgebiete*) of the German people.

b) Forcing the Jews out of the living space (*Lebensraum*) of the German people.

In pursuit of these aims, the accelerated emigration of the Jews from the area of the Reich, as the only possible provisional solution, was pressed forward and carried out according to plan.

On instructions by the Reich Marshal, a Reich Central Office for Jewish Emigration[3] * was set up in January 1939, and its direction entrusted to the Chief of the Security Police and the SD. Its tasks were, in particular:

a) To take all measures for the *preparation* of increased emigration of the Jews;

b) To *direct* the flow of emigration;

c) To speed up emigration in *individual* cases.

The aim of this task was to cleanse the German living space of Jews in a legal manner.

The disadvantages engendered by such forced pressing of emigration were clear to all the authorities. But in the absence of other possible solutions, they had to be accepted for the time being.

In the period that followed, the handling of emigration was not a German problem alone, but one with which the authorities of the countries of destination or immigration also had to deal. Financial difficulties — such as increases ordered by the various foreign governments in the sums of money that immigrants were required to have and in landing fees — as well as lack of berths on ships and continually tightening restrictions or bans on immigration, hampered emigration efforts very greatly. Despite these difficulties a total of approximately 537,000 Jews were caused to emigrate between the [Nazi] assumption of power and up to October 31, 1941.

These consisted of the following:

From January 30, 1933:	from the *Altreich* [Germany before 1938]	Approx. 360,000
From March 15, 1938:	from the *Ostmark* [Austria]	Approx. 147,000
From March 15, 1939:	from the Protectorate of Bohemia and Moravia	Approx. 30,000

The financing of the emigration was carried out by the Jews or Jewish political organizations themselves. To prevent the remaining behind of proletarianized Jews, the principle was observed that wealthy Jews must finance the emigration of the Jews without means; to this end, a special assessment or emigration levy, in accordance with wealth owned, was imposed, the proceeds being used to meet the financial obligations of the emigration of destitute Jews.

In addition to the funds raised in German marks, foreign currency was needed for the monies which emigrants were required to show on arrival abroad and for landing fees. To conserve the German holdings of foreign currency, Jewish financial institutions abroad were persuaded by Jewish organizations in this country to make themselves responsible for finding the required sums in foreign currency. A total of about $9,500,000 was provided by these foreign Jews as gifts up to October 30, 1941.

In the meantime, in view of the dangers of emigration in war-time, and the possibilities in the East, the *Reichsführer* SS and Chief of the German Police has forbidden the emigration of Jews.[4] *

III. Emigration has now been replaced by evacuation of the Jews to the East, as a further possible solution, with the appropriate prior authorization by the Führer.

However, this operation should be regarded only as a provisional option; but it is already supplying practical experience of great significance in view of the coming final solution of the Jewish question.

In the course of this final solution of the European Jewish question approximately 11 million Jews may be taken into consideration, distributed over the individual countries as follows:

Country	Number
A. *Altreich*	131,800
Ostmark	43,700
Eastern Territories[5] *	420,000
Government-General	2,284,000
Bialystok	400,000
Protectorate of Bohemia and Moravia	74,200
Estonia — free of Jews	
Latvia	3,500
Lithuania	34,000
Belgium	43,000
Denmark	5,600
France: Occupied territory	165,000
France: Unoccupied territory	700,000
Greece	69,600
Netherlands	160,800
Norway	1,300
B. Bulgaria	48,000
England	330,000
Finland	2,300
Ireland	4,000
Italy, including Sardinia	58,000

Albania		200
Croatia		40,000
Portugal		3,000
Rumania, including Bessarabia		342,000
Sweden		8,000
Switzerland		18,000
Serbia		10,000
Slovakia		88,000
Spain		6,000
Turkey (in Europe)		55,500
Hungary		742,800
U.S.S.R.		5,000,000
Ukraine	2,994,684	
Byelorussia, without Bialystok	446,484	
Total:		over 11,000,000

As far as the figures for Jews of the various foreign countries are concerned, the numbers given include only Jews by religion (*Glaubensjuden*), since the definition of Jews according to racial principles is in part still lacking there. Owing to the prevailing attitudes and concepts, the handling of this problem in the individual countries will encounter certain difficulties, especially in Hungary and Rumania. For instance, in Rumania the Jew can still obtain, for money, documents officially certifying that he holds foreign citizenship.

The influence of the Jews in all spheres of life in the U.S.S.R. is well known. There are about 5 million Jews in European Russia, and barely another 250,000 in Asiatic Russia.

The distribution of Jews according to occupation in the European area of the U.S.S.R. was roughly as follows:

Agriculture	9.1%
Urban workers	14.8%
Trade	20.0%
State employees	23.4%
Professions — medicine, press, theater, etc.	32.7%

A.	Altreich	131.800
	Ostmark	43.700
	Ostgebiete	420.000
	Generalgouvernement	2.284.000
	Bialystok	400.000
	Protektorat Böhmen und Mähren	74.200
	Estland – judenfrei –	
	Lettland	3.500
	Litauen	34.000
	Belgien	43.000
	Dänemark	5.600
	Frankreich / Besetztes Gebiet	165.000
	Unbesetztes Gebiet	700.000
	Griechenland	69.600
	Niederlande	160.800
	Norwegen	1.300
B.	Bulgarien	48.000
	England	330.000
	Finnland	2.300
	Irland	4.000
	Italien einschl. Sardinien	58.000
	Albanien	200
	Kroatien	40.000
	Portugal	3.000
	Rumänien einschl. Bessarabien	342.000
	Schweden	8.000
	Schweiz	18.000
	Serbien	10.000
	Slowakei	88.000
	Spanien	6.000
	Türkei (europ. Teil)	55.500
	Ungarn	742.800
	UdSSR	5.000.000
	Ukraine 2.994.684	
	Weißrußland aus-	
	schl. Bialystok 446 484	
	Zusammen: über	11.000.000

A page from the protocol of the Wannsee Conference numerating the numbers of Jews from the various countries included in the "final solution of the Jewish question"

255

Under appropriate direction the Jews are to be utilized for work in the East in an expedient manner in the course of the final solution. In large (labor) columns, with the sexes separated, Jews capable of work will be moved into these areas as they build roads, during which a large proportion will no doubt drop out through natural reduction. The remnant that eventually remains will require suitable treatment; because it will without doubt represent the most [physically] resistant part, it consists of a natural selection that could, on its release, become the germ-cell of a new Jewish revival. (Witness the experience of history.)

Europe is to be combed through from West to East in the course of the practical implementation of the final solution. The area of the Reich, including the Protectorate of Bohemia and Moravia, will have to be handled in advance, if only because of the housing problem and other socio-political needs.

The evacuated Jews will first be taken, group by group, to so-called transit ghettos, in order to be transported further east from there.

An important precondition, SS *Obergruppenführer* Heydrich noted further, for the carrying out of the evacuation in general is the precise determination of the groups of persons involved. It is intended not to evacuate Jews over 65 years old, but to place them in an old-age ghetto — Theresienstadt is being considered.

In addition to these age groups — about 30% of the 280,000 Jews who were present in the *Altreich* and the *Ostmark* on October 31, 1941, were over 65 years old — Jews with severe war injuries and Jews with war decorations (Iron Cross, First Class) will be admitted to the Jewish old-age ghetto. This suitable solution will eliminate at one blow the many applications for exceptions.

The start of the individual major evacuation *Aktionen* will depend largely on military developments. With regard to the handling of the final solution in the European areas occupied by us and under our influence, it was proposed that the officials

256

dealing with this subject in the Foreign Ministry should confer with the appropriate experts in the Security Police and the SD.

In Slovakia and Croatia the matter is no longer too difficult, as the most essential, central problems in this respect have already been brought to a solution there. In Rumania the government has in the meantime also appointed a Plenipotentiary for Jewish Affairs. In order to settle the problem in Hungary, it will be necessary in the near future to impose an adviser for Jewish questions on the Hungarian Government.

With regard to setting in motion preparations for the settling of the problem in Italy, SS *Obergruppenführer* Heydrich considers liaison with the Police Chief in these matters would be in place.

In occupied and unoccupied France the rounding-up of the Jews for evacuation will, in all probability, be carried out without great difficulties.

On this point, Undersecretary of State Luther stated that far-reaching treatment of this problem would meet with difficulties in some countries, such as the Nordic States, and that it was therefore advisable to postpone action in these countries for the present. In view of the small number of Jews involved there, the postponement will in any case not occasion any significant curtailment. On the other hand, the Foreign Ministry foresees no great difficulties for the south-east and west of Europe.

SS *Gruppenführer* Hofmann intends to send a specialist from the Main Office for Race and Settlement to Hungary for general orientation when the subject is taken in hand there by the Chief of the Security Police and the SD. It was decided that this specialist from the Race and Settlement Main Office, who is not to take an active part, will temporarily be designated officially as Assistant to the Police Attaché.

IV. In the implementation of the plan for the final solution, the Nuremberg Laws are to form the basis,[6] * as it were; a precondition for the total clearing up of the problem will also require solutions for the question of mixed marriages and *Mischlinge.*

The Chief of the Security Police and the SD then discussed the following points, theoretically for the time being, in connection with a letter from the Chief of the Reich Chancellery:

1. *Treatment of first-degree* Mischlinge

    First-degree *Mischlinge* are in the same position as Jews with respect to the final solution of the Jewish question. The following will be exempt from this treatment:

    a) First-degree *Mischlinge* married to persons of German blood, from whose marriages there are children (second-degree *Mischlinge*). Such second-degree *Mischlinge* are essentially in the same position as Germans.

    b) First-degree *Mischlinge* for whom up to now exceptions were granted in some (vital) area by the highest authorities of the Party and the State. Each individual case must be re-examined, and it is not excluded that the new decision will again be in favor of the *Mischlinge*.

    The grounds for granting an exception must always, as a matter of principle, be the deserts of the *Mischling himself*. (Not the merits of the parent or spouse of German blood.)

    The first-degree *Mischling* exempted from evacuation will be sterilized in order to obviate progeny and to settle the *Mischling* problem for good. Sterilization is voluntary, but it is the condition for remaining in the Reich. The sterilized *Mischling* is subsequently free of all restrictive regulations to which he was previously subject.

2. *Treatment of second-degree* Mischlinge

    Second-degree *Mischlinge* are on principle classed with persons of German blood, *with the exception of the following cases,* in which the second-degree *Mischlinge* are considered equivalent to Jews:

    a) Descent of the second-degree *Mischling* from a bastard marriage (both spouses being *Mischlinge*).

    b) Racially especially unfavorable appearance of the second-degree *Mischling,* which will class him with the Jews on external grounds alone.

c) Especially bad police and political rating of the second-degree *Mischling*, indicating that he feels and behaves as a Jew.

Even in these cases exceptions are not to be made if the second-degree *Mischling* is married to a person of German blood.

3. *Marriages between full Jews and persons of German blood*
Here it must be decided from case to case whether the Jewish spouse should be evacuated or whether he or she should be sent to an old-age ghetto in consideration of the effect of the measure on the German relatives of the mixed couple.

4 *Marriages between first-degree* Mischlinge *and persons of German blood*

a) *Without children*
If there are no children of the marriage, the first-degree *Mischling* is evacuated or sent to an old-age ghetto. (The same treatment as in marriages between full Jews and persons of German blood, [see] para. 3.)

b) *With children*
If there are children of the marriage (second-degree *Mischlinge*), they will be evacuated or sent to a ghetto, together with the first-degree *Mischlinge, if they are considered equivalent to Jews*. Where such children *are considered equivalent to persons of German blood* (the rule), they and also the first-degree *Mischling* are to be exempted from evacuation.

5. *Marriages between first-degree* Mischlinge *and first-degree* Mischlinge *or Jews*
In such marriages all parties (including children) are treated as Jews and therefore evacuated or sent to an old-age ghetto.

6. *Marriages between first-degree* Mischlinge *and second-degree* Mischlinge

Both partners to the marriage, regardless of whether or not there are children, are evacuated or sent to an old-age ghetto, since children of such marriages commonly are seen to have a stronger admixture of Jewish blood than the second-degree Jewish *Mischlinge*.

SS *Gruppenführer* Hofmann is of the opinion that extensive use must be made of sterilization, as the *Mischling*, given the choice of evacuation or sterilization, would prefer to accept sterilization.

Secretary of State Dr. Stuckart noted that in this form the practical aspects of the possible solutions proposed above for the settling of the problems of mixed marriages and *Mischlinge* would entail endless administrative work. In order to take the biological realities into account, at any rate, Secretary of State Dr. Stuckart proposed a move in the direction of compulsory sterilization.

To simplify the problem of the *Mischlinge* further possibilities should be considered, with the aim that the Legislator should rule something like: "These marriages are dissolved."

As to the question of the effect of the evacuation of the Jews on the economy, Secretary of State Neumann stated that Jews employed in essential war industries could not be evacuated for the present, as long as no replacements were available.

SS *Obergruppenführer* Heydrich pointed out that those Jews would not be evacuated in any case, in accordance with the directives approved by him for the implementation of the current evacuation *Aktion*.

Secretary of State Dr. Bühler put on record that the Government-General would welcome it if the final solution of this problem *was begun in the Government-General*, as, on the one hand, the question of transport there played no major role and considerations of labor supply would not hinder the course of this *Aktion*. Jews must be removed as fast as possible from the Government-General, because it was there in particular that the Jew as carrier of epidemics spelled a great danger, and, at the same time, he caused constant disorder in the economic structure of the country by his continuous black-market dealings. Furthermore, of the approximately 2½ million Jews under consideration, the majority were in any case *unfit for work*.

Secretary of State Dr. Bühler further states that the solution of the Jewish question in the Government-General was primarily the responsibility of the Chief of the Security Police and the SD and that his work would have the support of the authorities of the Government-General. He had only one request: that the Jewish question in this area be solved as quickly as possible.

In conclusion, there was a discussion of the various possible forms which the solution might take, and here both *Gauleiter* Dr. Meyer and Secretary of State Dr. Bühler were of the opinion that certain preparatory work for the final solution should be carried out locally in the area concerned, but that, in doing so, alarm among the population must be avoided.

The conference concluded with the request of the Chief of the Security Police and the SD to the participants at the conference to give him the necessary support in carrying out the tasks of the [final] solution.

NG-2586-G.

1 * Reich Marshal Hermann Göring.
2 * See Document 106.
3 * See Document 57.
4 * See Document 68.
5 * The reference is to the districts of western Poland annexed to the Reich.
6 * See Documents 32, 33, 34.

118

FROM A PROTOCOL OF A SESSION OF THE JUDENRAT IN BIALYSTOK ON APRIL 4 AND 5, 1942

The Chairman, Rabbi Dr. Rosenman, opens the meeting and gives the floor to Engineer Barash to present his report.

Engineer Barash: ...We have called the meeting today specially to deal with the following matter. The ghetto is becoming larger through people coming in from the small towns and particularly because of those coming back from Pruzany.* Anyone who is familiar with the protocols of our meetings can see that we pointed regularly with great anxiety to the growth of the ghetto. We have now been warned by the Gestapo, and the position is dangerous. In Lida the arrival of refugees from Vilna and other places caused great tragedies. We are doing everything possible to keep punishment from the ghetto, but, after all, there is a relatively large population in Bialystok, and it can end in tragedy. We will have to take steps.

Engineer Barash asks Mr. Bergman, who was one of those present, how many persons had registered since October and receives the reply: About 800. Engineer Barash continues: The Gestapo states that Jews may not move [from place to place] without an official permit. In future we therefore cannot register anybody without the permission of the Gestapo. The authorities have demanded a list of all persons registered since February 1 of this year.

Mr. Y. Lifschitz expresses the opinion that the administration in the ghetto was too weak. "We have done nothing against the undesired new arrivals. The danger is so great that one must pick up a group of people and send them back to Pruzany; this will have an effect on others, that [people] should not come back any longer. The others who have come should have been told that they could use Bialystok only as a transit station." Mr. Lifschitz proposes the election of a committee that should,

by tomorrow, work out a series of disciplinary rules for new
arrivals. . .

*

Mr. Markus (speaking Polish): More than eight months have
already passed since the fence made a special "kingdom" for us,
the Jewish ghetto. In this "kingdom" the Judenrat carries out
the duties of a "government," and we, the Jewish police, must
carry out the difficult task of keeping order and maintaining
quiet in the ghetto. I asked Engineer Barash several times to
arrange talks with the population of the ghetto. The thing is
this: the regulations of the authorities are not being properly
observed. Perhaps I am at fault myself, I am too soft and
moderate, and our people do not take into account that we
are Jews. The evening curfew is not observed punctually: one
must go to bed at 9 o'clock, one is not allowed to be in the
street. Not keeping the regulations may cause somebody to
be shot; and Jews often take a walk after the curfew hour.
The [yellow] badge is not worn properly, one [man] forgets
it in front, and the next forgets it at the back. The same
happens about the black-out. There have been cases of whole
houses being lit up like for a celebration. There has already
been a tragic case in the ghetto: a woman was shot in her
home when the room was badly blacked out. The Jews are
a stiff-necked people. Street-trading never stops, especially on
Kupiecka Street, and all our efforts do not help. That shows
the need for a firm hand. There are telephone calls from the
4th [Police] Station outside the ghetto that Jewish children
have been caught without yellow badges and without papers
and that can cause a tragedy on some occasion. Parading up
and down the street with children in colored baby carriages
could also cause much annoyance. Let the mothers stop doing it.
Groups of Jews gather around the gates of the ghetto and
don't go away even when the Germans chase them off, and
the Jews might even be shot. Cleanliness is not satisfactory
either. Thousands are spent on cleaning, and it is dirty again
by the next morning; people don't take care, they don't want

to know that that is a danger. And again, thousands of Jews go to work, work in the sweat of their brows, and at the same time many others avoid work in various ways. The house committees are obliged to hand over such cases so that the members of the Jewish Police need not catch passers-by in the street and start fighting with Jews. That brings no credit either to the population or to the Jewish Police. If things go on like this for much longer, there is likely to be a catastrophe, for anyone who wants to live must work !...

Blumental, pp. 156, 166.

* The reference is to Jews from Bialystok who were deported to Pruzany in September and October 1941, and in the course of time many of them returned.

119

CELEBRATION SESSION ON THE FIRST ANNIVERSARY OF THE ESTABLISHMENT OF THE JUDENRAT IN BIALYSTOK, JUNE 29, 1942

... It is difficult to describe in detail the history of the establishment of the Judenrat. We placed before ourselves one aim: to co-opt for the work persons of influence, who were honest and capable — courageous people. There are such people among us, I will not praise them here. But one I will praise a little to his face, Engineer Barash, who is also the director of our industry, with his great ability and exceptional energy — everybody knows and respects him. The German Authorities have been persuaded that we work without profit to ourselves and the attitude towards us has, in time, become tolerable... Our industry has developed, as you know, and its importance to the ghetto is so great that we saw the need for *Eng. Barash to be in charge of this industry, and this has raised our reputation in the eyes of the Authorities.*

Today a year of labor has ended that has been hard but full of blessing, and a *new year* begins, and we pray that in this new year we may be remembered for life! May the Lord, Blessed be He, continue not to abandon us; that we may be able to continue with our tasks to the benefit and good fortune of the whole population.

Eng. Barash: We could not let this day pass without gathering together and talking at least with those who are closest to us. There is nobody who could describe what has happened to us, what we survived during these past 365 days — no artist, no writer, no painter. We can scarcely believe it ourselves, and I think nobody will believe it in future, all that has happened to us in this period. It is lucky that we cannot foresee the future, for if we could — we would not have lived and reached the present stage. If I were just to recite the record of our troubles, just a list, without describing them, it would take a long time, a very long time. I will just recall the worst and most unexpected of them. . . .

In short we did not have a single quiet day, one in which there was no scent of danger. Many of the dangers that threatened us were countermanded, as you know, as a result of our actions.

We did many useful things:

1. Our factories, which often had to "make bricks without straw," which caused admiration among those who hate us. 2. The exhibition that was arranged outside the ghetto demonstrated our achievements and our ability to succeed. 3. At the same time we established a system of schools and trade schools. 4. Our social welfare. . . hospitals, etc., in many cases are more extensive than similar institutions that we had before the war. 5. Our vegetable growing and other work show that the Jews are a very productive element.

There are differences of opinion concerning the actions of our Judenrat. But one must take the position of the Judenrat into account. After all, we are hostages, held responsible for everything that happens in the ghetto. And you have seen what that means in other cities. The members of the presidium went grey there before their time. The devotion, heart and soul, of the presidium cannot be described in words. If we survive, whole books will have to be written about it. Later there was a total change in our position, which distinguishes us from the people in all the other occupied areas and ghettos. There is nothing new to it, when the weak pay compliments to the strong, that is familiar flattery. *But that we, the weak,* hear compliments from those who are stronger, from those who have the power. This change came about as the result of our productive work.

I am full of admiration for the close harmony that reigns between the members of the Judenrat. Differences of opinion simply do not happen. All our decisions and actions are unanimous.

In truth, there is no place for optimism in the ghetto, but when I consider the road along which we have come and our burdens, then I am sure that we will take the Bialystok ghetto through to a happy end.

(Loud applause)....

Mr. Sobotnik: ... The Judenrat did not start out as what it is today: It developed in time as it worked, thanks to the efforts of its first members who created everything that we now have. As I said, we were not chosen by anybody. The respected Eng. Barash convinced us to accept the great and difficult duties because he understood the needs of the hour. Now it has become a government, so to say, with all the offices, departments, ministers. The official chairman, Dr. Rosenman, walks around by himself to find workers for the Germans. He has gone through a great deal. His most important contribution was to have appointed the respected Eng. Barash, because the Rabbi did not have the strength to do everything that was needed. I do not wish to praise the individual, what matters to me is the job, the achievement. The respected Eng. Barash is the prime minister in our "government," as well as minister of the interior, minister of industry, because in the ghetto everything must be concentrated in one hand. Industry, for instance, is connected with the Wehrmacht, so it becomes a matter of foreign policy. Sometimes we are surprised how he gets it all done, how it all works out. It seems like Divine intervention, particularly in the past few weeks. Everything gets done in the best possible way. The other responsibilities, it seems to me are carried out by the other members, but it is the spirit, the direction, which is the most important thing. . . .

What is our direction? In matters concerning the community we try always to reach agreement, compromise, so that everybody may be satisfied. From now on we shall have to stand by the letter of the law! Let him who is fearful and fainthearted return to his house! We shall have to cling to this principle if we wish to stay alive. And the ghetto must remain a productive element as well.

Of all our prayers for "Life," for a good life, for a livelihood, for a life without shame or disgrace, etc., we must today make do with just "Life"; and that thanks to Rosenman and Barash: we only help, but they, and especially Eng. Barash, labor for us! . . .

Blumental, pp. 214-220.

120

FROM THE DIARY OF ADAM CZERNIAKOW, CHAIRMAN OF THE JUDENRAT IN THE WARSAW GHETTO, 1942

January 7, 1942

The Community in the morning. To Auerswald afterwards. I suggested that he approach the higher authorities and request the release of the condemned men [in the Jewish prison]. It would be recompense for the furs that were supplied. I emphasized that I had asked for an additional food ration on those grounds, but that I would rather do without the food if there were a chance of saving so many people. I added that ordinarily the chain of official command runs from the Commissar to the Governor and from him to the Governor General. The Commissar replied that only the Governor had the authority to order persons released. I therefore asked him that in the name of humanity he submit a suitable proposal to the Governor. After a long discussion he promised that he would raise the matter of those condemned with the Governor.

I read the following in Zeromski's "Popioly." * "Have not I too under my command ruffians, strong-arm men and murderers? And still I watch over them and prize them, for they know more than others... they are the very ones able to rescue us from the danger in case of attack." These were the words of Captain Wyganowski.

In the afternoon three men of the *Schutzpolizei* (Police) appeared in my office, headed by a Lieutenant of the *Gettowache* (Ghetto Patrol), with machine-guns at the ready. They asked whether I was the person who had telephoned to them about an alleged attack by Poles on Jews in the ghetto. I told them that I knew nothing about it.

It is impossible to buy a calendar either in the ghetto or outside. I have been obliged to make a calendar for myself.

May 15, 1942

The Community in the morning. At home we expected the film crew at 8:30.** I asked them to hire some men and women for the film, to play parts in front of the camera.

They came at 8:45 and went on shooting until 12:30. They hung a signboard on the door with some inscription on it. They brought two women and some kind of "lover" to the apartment. Also an elderly Jew. They filmed a scene.

In town the rumors about deportations continue. People speak of tens of thousands. To work according to plan under such

268

conditions is remarkable. Nevertheless we do the job day by day. I always go back to what Dickens wrote: "A watch is not wound with tears."

In the afternoon the film people took pictures in the bedroom of the neighbors, the Zabludowski family. They brought in some woman who made up her face in front of the mirror.

...While they were making the film in my home they picked up an old Jew with a fine beard in the street. He sat in my apartment for several hours, but in the end they made no use of his photogenic qualities. I can just imagine what happened when he got home and tried to explain to his wife that he had earned no money because he had spent three hours being a "star"...

A. Czerniakow, *Yoman Getto Varsha* ("Warsaw Ghetto Diary") — *September 6, 1939–July 23, 1942,* edited by N. Blumental, A. Tartakower, N. Eck, J. Kermish, Jerusalem, 1959², pp. 257, 297-298. (English version: *The Warsaw Diary of Adam Czerniakow,* edited by R. Hilberg, S. Staron, J. Kermish, New York, 1979.)

* *Popioly* — "Ashes."
** The reference is to a German film crew which arrived in Warsaw to make a film of the ghetto.

121

PROTOCOL OF GENERAL MEETING OF THE JUDENRAT IN LUBLIN ON MARCH 31, 1942

In accordance with orders received from the Authorities carrying out the evacuation *Aktion,* the members of the Judenrat were assembled at 14:00: Dr. Alten, Bekker, Bursztyn, Cymerman, Dawidson, Goldsobel, Halbersztadt, Hochgemein, Hufnagel, Kantor, Kerszman, Kerszenblum, Kelner, Lewi, Lewinson, Lerner, Siegfried, Tenenbaum, Wajselfisz.

Members of the Judenrat who were absent: Kestenberg and Edelstein (who were arrested yesterday at the prison) and Rechtman.

In addition the following persons were invited today who do not belong to the Judenrat: Aizik Brodt, Daniel Kupferminc, Josef Rotrubin, Szulim Tajkef, Boleslaw Tenenbaum and Wolf Wiener.

After the arrival of representatives of the Authorities, Messrs. SS *Obersturmführer* Worthoff, SS *Untersturmführer* Walter, SS *Untersturmführer* Dr. Sturm, SS *Unterscharführer* Knitzky, Mr. Worthoff and Dr. Sturm made the following announcement: The evacuation of the Jewish population will continue in future with the difference that the valid document permitting a person to remain in Lublin will no longer be the *Arbeitsausweis* (work card) with the stamp of the *Sipo* (Security Police), but the *J.[uden] Ausweis*. Those in possession of the *J.-Ausweis* are entitled to remain in Lublin, all others will be evacuated.

The Jewish population is to be informed that those in possession of a *J.-Ausweis* are required to make certain that in their apartments in the ghetto, which have been inspected or will still be inspected, no persons without a *J.-Ausweis* are in hiding, as otherwise those who are in possession of a *J.-Ausweis* will also be evacuated.

As only a small percentage of the former Jewish population will remain in Lublin, the Judenrat will be reduced from 24 to 12 members.

The Authorities appointed the following members to the Judenrat:

From the previous membership: (1) Dr. Mark Alten, (2) Yitzhak Kerszman, (3) David Hochgemein, (4) Leon Hufnagel, (5) Jacob Kelner, (6) Nachman Lerner, (7) the clerk of the Judenrat Wolf Wiener; in addition to these, the following who were not formerly members of the Judenrat were appointed temporary members: (8) Aizik Brodt, (9) Daniel Kupferminc, (10) Josef Rotrubin, (11) Szulim Tajkef, (12) Boleslaw Tenenbaum.

Those members of the former Judenrat who were not included in the Judenrat appointed today will be evacuated together with their families and will leave Lublin today together with the first transport.

Those members of the former Judenrat who live outside the ghetto will go to their apartments accompanied by officials of the *Sipo*, and after they have taken belongings needed for their move, the apartments will be closed and sealed.

The former members of the Judenrat Engineer Bekker and Dr. Siegfried will be given administrative positions in the Judenrat and the JSS* in their new place of residence as persons with experience in these fields.

After the former members of the Judenrat had left the hall, Dr. Sturm made the following announcement:

Dr. Alten is appointed Chairman of the Judenrat.

Kerszman is appointed Deputy Chairman.

The Presidium of the Judenrat will include: Alten, Kerszman and Kupferminc.

The distribution of duties among the members of the Judenrat will be as follows, although it is possible that changes will be recommended:

Judenrat Member Kupferminc will deal with nutrition in the ghetto.

Judenrat Member Tenenbaum will deal with matters concerning the police, disinfection, elimination of lice and cleanliness in houses.

He will have M. Stockfisch as assistant. From today the office for the elimination of lice and for disinfection will be linked to the Judenrat and become part of it. Mendel Goldfarb is appointed Commander of the *Ordnungsdienst* (Jewish Police) as an operational instrument.

Judenrat Member Brodt will deal with labor affairs;

Judenrat Member Wiener will deal with housing;

Judenrat Member Hochgemein will deal with finance;

Judenrat Member Hufnagel will deal with Public Assistance;

Judenrat Member Rotrubin will deal with Public Health;

271

Judenrat Member Kelner will deal with registration and information;

Judenrat Member Tajkef will be responsible for the collection of taxes, together with Judenrat Member Hochgemein.

Dr. Alten is authorized to represent the Judenrat in appearances before the Authorities, but he is entitled to delegate his authority to the managers of other departments.

Judenrat members are obliged to carry out the instructions of the Chairman of the Judenrat, Dr. Alten.

No further recommendations of any kind for the issuing of a *J.-Ausweis* will be considered.

The Order Police is required to call for voluntary evacuation. Today 1,600 persons will be evacuated voluntarily.

(—) Deputy for Alten

(—) D. Hochgemein

N. Blumental, *Te'udot mi-Getto Lublin — Judenrat le-lo Dereh* ("Documents from Lublin Ghetto — Judenrat without Direction"), Jerusalem, 1967, pp. 314-318.

* *Jüdische Soziale Selbsthilfe* (Jewish Self-Help).

122

PROPOSAL FOR THE STERILIZATION OF 2-3 MILLION JEWISH WORKERS, JUNE 23, 1942

Reich Secret Document

Honorable Mr. *Reichsführer* !

On instructions from *Reichsleiter* Bouhler I placed a part of my men at the disposal of *Brigadeführer* Globocnik some considerable time ago for his Special Task. Following a further request from him, I have now made available more personnel. On this occasion *Brigadeführer* Globocnik pressed the view that the whole *Aktion* against the Jews should be carried out as quickly as it is in any way possible, so that we will not some day be stuck in the middle should any kind of difficulty make it necessary to stop the *Aktion.* You yourself, Mr. *Reichsführer,* expressed the view to me at an earlier time that one must work as fast as possible, if only for reasons of concealment. Both views are more than justified according to my own experience, and basically they produce the same results. Nevertheless I beg to be permitted to present the following consideration of my own in this connection:

According to my impression there are at least 2-3 million men and women well fit for work among the approx. 10 million European Jews. In consideration of the exceptional difficulties posed for us by the question of labor, I am of the opinion that these 2-3 million should in any case be taken out and kept alive. Of course this can only be done if they are at the same time rendered incapable of reproduction. I reported to you about a year ago that persons under my instruction have completed the necessary experiments for this purpose. I wish to bring up these facts again. The type of sterilization which is normally carried out on persons with genetic disease is out of the question in this case, as it takes too much time and is expensive. Castration by means of X-rays, however, is not only relatively cheap, but can be carried out on many thousands in a very short time. I believe that it has become unimportant at the present time whether those affected will then in the course of a few weeks or months realize by the effects that they are castrated.

In the event, Mr. *Reichsführer,* that you decide to choose these means in the interest of maintaining labor-material, *Reichsleiter* Bouhler will be ready to provide the doctors and other personnel needed to carry out this work. He also instructed me to inform you that I should then order the required equipment as quickly as possible.　　　　　　　　　　　Viktor Brack

SS *Oberführer*

NO-205.

123

SIGNED OBLIGATION BY SS MEN TAKING PART IN AN EXTERMINATION OPERATION TO OBSERVE SECRECY, JULY 18, 1942

concerning the obligation of [name of person]...........................
as a person with special duties in the execution of tasks in the
evacuation of Jews within the framework of *"Einsatz Reinhard,"*
[Operation Reinhard] under the SS Police Leader (*SS- und
Polizeiführer*) in the District of Lublin.

....[Name] declares :
I have been thoroughly informed and instructed by SS *Hauptsturmführer* Höfle, as Commander of the main division of
"Einsatz Reinhard" of the SS and Police Leader in the District
of Lublin :

1. that I may not under any circumstances pass on any form
of information, verbally or in writing, on the progress, procedure
or incidents in the evacuation of Jews to any person outside
the circle of the *"Einsatz Reinhard"* staff;

2. that the process of the evacuation of Jews is a subject
that comes under "Secret Reich Document," in accordance with
censorship regulation *Verschl. V. a;*

3. concerning the special regulations made by the SS and Police
Leader in the District of Lublin in this case, with explicit reference
to the fact that these regulations are "Orders concerning Duties,"
and/or "Orders and Prohibitions" in accordance with Para. 92b
of R.St.G.B.;

4. that there is an absolute prohibition on photography in
the camps of *"Einsatz Reinhard"*;

5. concerning Para. 88 through 93 R.St.G.B., of the formulation
of April 24, 1934, and the Regulation on Bribery and Revealing
of Secrets on the part of Persons who are not in Official Employ,
of May 3, 1917 and February 12, 1920;

6. concerning the paragraphs of R.St.G.B. 139 (Duty to lay
Information) and 353c Breach of the Official Secrets Act.

I am familiar with the above Regulations and Laws and am aware of the responsibilities imposed upon me by the task with which I have been entrusted. I promise to observe them to the best of my knowledge and conscience. I am aware that the obligation to maintain secrecy continues even after I have left the Service.

Eksterminacja, pp. 294-295.

124

ORDER BY HIMMLER ON JULY 19, 1942, FOR THE COMPLETION OF THE "FINAL SOLUTION" IN THE GOVERNMENT-GENERAL

I herewith order that the resettlement of the entire Jewish population of the Government-General be carried out and completed by December 31, 1942.

From December 31, 1942, no persons of Jewish origin may remain within the Government-General, unless they are in the collection camps in Warsaw, Cracow, Czestochowa, Radom, and Lublin. All other work on which Jewish labor is employed must be finished by that date, or, in the event that this is not possible, it must be transferred to one of the collection camps.

These measures are required with a view to the necessary ethnic division of races and peoples for the New Order in Europe, and also in the interests of the security and cleanliness of the German Reich and its sphere of interest. Every breach of this regulation spells a danger to quiet and order in the entire German sphere of interest, a point of application for the resistance movement and a source of moral and physical pestilence.

275

For all these reasons a total cleansing is necessary and therefore to be carried out. Cases in which the date set can not be observed will be reported to me in time, so that I can see to corrective action at an early date. All requests by other offices for changes or permits for exceptions to be made must be presented to me personally.

Heil Hitler!

H. Himmler

NO-5574.

125

CALL TO ARMED SELF-DEFENSE, FROM AN UNDERGROUND PUBLICATION *

...We know that Hitler's system of murder, slaughter and robbery leads steadily to a dead end and the destruction of the Jews. The fate of the Jews in the Soviet Russian areas occupied by the Germans, and in the Warthegau, marks a new period in the total annihilation of the Jewish population. The huge murder machine has been turned against Jewish masses that are weak, unarmed, brought low by hunger, camps and deportations. With satanic methods it liquidates the Jewish population centers one by one. The victory over the Jews will have to serve the Germans as recompense for the losses they have suffered at the front. Spilling the blood of defenseless Jews will have to take the place of Hitler's great dreams that failed to come true.

We also know that the march of Hitler's troops has been halted by the heroic Red Army and that the Spring Offensive will see the beginning of the far-reaching destruction of the Nazis in Europe. For the Jewish masses this will be a period of greater bloodshed than any in their history. There is no doubt that when Hitler feels that the end of his rule is approaching, he will seek to drown the Jews in a sea of blood. Jewish youth must prepare in the face of those difficult days. There must therefore be a start to the recruiting of all creative forces among the Jews. Despite the destruction many such forces still remain. For generation upon generation passivity and lack of faith in our own strength had pressed upon us; but our history also shows beautiful pages glowing with heroism and struggle. *It is our duty to join this period of heroism. . . .*

Yad Vashem Archives, JM/1178/1.

* From Ha-Shomer Ha-Za'ir newspaper in the Warsaw Underground *Jutrznia* ("Dawn"), March 28, 1942.

126

THE JEWISH POPULATION DISBELIEVES REPORTS OF THE EXTERMINATION *

. . . The liquidation of the Jews in the Government-General began at Passover 1942. The first victims were the Jews of the city of Lublin, and shortly after that the Jews of the whole District of Lublin. They were evacuated to Belzec, and there they were killed in new gas-chambers that had been built specially for this purpose. The Jewish Underground newspapers gave detailed descriptions of this mass slaughter. But [the Jews of] Warsaw did not believe it! Common human sense could not understand that it was possible to exterminate tens and hundreds of thousands of Jews. They decided that the Jews were being transported for agricultural work in the parts of Russia occupied by the Germans. Theories were heard that the Germans had begun on the productivization of the Jewish lower-level bourgeoisie! The Jewish press was denounced and charged with causing panic, although the *descriptions* of the "rooting out" of the population corresponded accurately to the reality. Not only abroad were the crimes of the Germans received with disbelief, but even here, close by Ponary, Chelmno, Belzec and Treblinka, did this information get no hearing! This unjustified optimism developed together with the lack of information, which was the result of total isolation from the outside world and the experience of the past. Had not the Germans for two and a half years carried out many deportations of Jews — from Cracow, from Lublin, from the Warsaw District and from the "Reich?" Certainly there had been not a few victims and blood had been shed during these deportations, but total extermination?

There were some people who believed it, however. The events at Ponary and Chelmno were a fact, but — it was said — "that was just a capricious act of the local authorities." For, after all, the German authorities in the Government-General did not have the same attitude to the ghettos in the cities and the small towns, not until death brought an equal fate to all. More than once, in various places, the reaction to the information we had about the liquidation of the Jews was: "that cannot happen to us here."

It was of course the Germans themselves who created these optimistic attitudes. Through two and a half years they prepared the work of exterminating the three and a half million Jews of Poland with German thoroughness. They rendered the Jewish masses helpless with the aid of individual killings, oppression and starvation, with the aid of ghettos and deportations. In years of unceasing experiments the Germans perfected their extermination methods. In Vilna they had needed several days to murder a thousand Jews, in Chelmno half an hour was enough to kill a hundred, and at Treblinka ten thousand were murdered every day! . . .

Yad Vashem Archives, O-25/96.

* From a report by Yitzhak Cukierman in Warsaw in March 1944, and sent to London on May 24, 1944, through the Polish Underground.

278

127

FROM THE DIARY OF ADAM CZERNIAKOW ON THE EVE OF THE DEPORTATION FROM THE WARSAW GHETTO, 1942

July 20, 1942

At the Gestapo at 7:30 in the morning. I asked Mende how much truth there was in the rumors. He answered that he had heard nothing about it. After this I asked Brandt; he answered that he knew of nothing of the kind. To the question whether a thing like that could nevertheless happen, he answered that he knew nothing. I came away unsure. I went to his superior officer, Commissar Böhm. He said that it was not his department, that perhaps Hoheman* might be able to make some statement in connection with the rumors. I observed that according to the rumors the deportation was due to start at 19:30 today. He answered that he would certainly know something if it were so.

For lack of any other choice I went to Scherer, the Deputy Director of Section 3. He said he was amazed at the rumor and claimed that he too knew nothing about it.

Finally I asked whether I could inform the population that there was no reason for fear. He said I could, that all the reports were nonsense and rubbish (*Unsinn und Quatsch*).

I gave orders to Lejkin that he should make this known through the area station....

July 22, 1940 [1942]

At the Community at 7:30 in the morning. The borders of the small ghetto are guarded by a special unit in addition to the usual one....

At 10 o'clock *Sturmbannführer* Höfle appeared with his people. We disconnected the telephone lines. The children were moved out of the little garden opposite.

The entry dated July 20, 1942, from the diary of Adam Czerniakow, chairman of the Judenrat in the Warsaw Ghetto

It was announced to us that the Jews, without regard to sex or age, apart from certain exceptions, would be deported to the East. Six thousand souls had to be supplied by 4 o'clock today. And this (at least) is how it will be every day....

Sturmbannführer Höfle (*Beauftragter* — [person in charge] — of the deportation) called me into the office and informed me that my wife was free at the moment, but if the deportation failed she would be the first to be shot as a hostage.**

A. Czerniakow, *Yoman Getto Varsha* ("Warsaw Ghetto Diary") — *September 6, 1939–July 23, 1942*, edited by N. Blumental, A. Tartakower, N. Eck, J. Kermish, Jerusalem 1959², pp. 325-327.

* The reference is apparently to Hömann, an SS officer in Warsaw.
** The next day Czerniakow committed suicide.

128

ANNOUNCEMENT OF THE EVACUATION OF THE JEWS FROM THE WARSAW GHETTO, JULY 22, 1942 *

The Judenrat is informed of the following:

1. All Jewish persons living in Warsaw, regardless of age and sex, will be resettled in the East.

2. The following are excluded from the resettlement:
   a) All Jewish persons employed by German Authorities or enterprises, and who can show proof of this fact;
   b) All Jewish persons who are members or employees of the Judenrat (on the day of the publication of this regulation).
   c) All Jewish persons who are employed by a Reich-German company and can show proof of this fact.

d) All Jews capable of work who have up to now not been brought into the labor process are to be taken to the barracks in the Jewish quarter.

e) All Jewish persons who belong to the staff of the Jewish hospitals. This applies also to the members of the Jewish Disinfection Team;

f) All Jewish persons who belong to the Jewish Police (*Jüdischer Ordnungsdienst*);

g) All Jewish persons who are first-degree relatives of the person listed under a) through f). Such relatives are exclusively wives and children.

h) All Jewish persons who are hospitalized in one of the Jewish hospitals on the first day of the resettlement and are not fit to be discharged. Fitness for discharge will be decided by a doctor to be appointed by the Judenrat

3. Every Jew being resettled may take 15 kgs. of his property as baggage. All valuables such as gold, jewelry, money, etc., may be taken. Food is to be taken for three days.

4. The resettlement will begin at 11:00 o'clock on July 22, 1942. In the course of the resettlement the Judenrat will have the following tasks, for the precise execution of which the members of the Judenrat will answer with their lives. . . .

Eksterminacja, pp. 300-302.

* The Regulation and detailed instructions for carrying it out were dictated to the Judenrat in Warsaw by Höfle, who was in charge of the evacuation.

129

RUMKOWSKI'S ADDRESS AT THE TIME OF THE DEPORTATION OF THE CHILDREN FROM THE LODZ GHETTO, SEPTEMBER 4, 1942

... The ghetto has been struck a hard blow. They demand what is most dear to it — children and old people. I was not privileged to have a child of my own and therefore devoted my best years to children. I lived and breathed together with children. I never imagined that my own hands would be forced to make this sacrifice on the altar. In my old age I am forced to stretch out my hands and to beg: "Brothers and sisters, give them to me! — Fathers and mothers, give me your children..." (Bitter weeping shakes the assembled public)... Yesterday, in the course of the day, I was given the order to send away more than 20,000 Jews from the ghetto, and if I did not — "we will do it ourselves." The question arose: "Should we have accepted this and carried it out ourselves, or left it to others?" But as we were guided not by the thought: "how many will be lost?" but "how many can be saved?" we arrived at the conclusion — those closest to me at work, that is, and myself — that however difficult it was going to be, we must take upon ourselves the carrying out of this decree. I must carry out this difficult and bloody operation, I must cut off limbs in order to save the body! I must take away children, and if I do not, others too will be taken, God forbid... (terrible wailing).

I cannot give you comfort today. Nor did I come to calm you today, but to reveal all your pain and all your sorrow. I have come like a robber, to take from you what is dearest to your heart. I tried everything I knew to get the bitter sentence cancelled. When it could not be cancelled, I tried to lessen the sentence. Only yesterday I ordered the registration of nine-year-old children. I wanted to save at least one year — children from nine to ten. But they would not yield. I succeeded in one thing — to save the children over ten. Let that be our consolation in our great sorrow.

There are many people in this ghetto who suffer from tuberculosis, whose days or perhaps weeks are numbered. I do not know, perhaps this is a satanic plan, and perhaps not, but I cannot stop myself from proposing it: "Give me these sick people, and perhaps it will be possible to save the healthy in their place." I know how precious each one of the sick is in his home, and particularly among Jews. But at a time of such decrees one must weigh up and measure who should be saved, who can be saved and who may be saved.

Common sense requires us to know that those must be saved who can be saved and who have a chance of being saved and not those whom there is no chance to save in any case. . . .

I. Trunk, *Lodzsher Geto* ("Lodz Ghetto"), New York, 1962, pp. 311-312.

130

NOTES BY A JEWISH OBSERVER IN THE LODZ GHETTO FOLLOWING THE DEPORTATION OF THE CHILDREN *

Lodz Ghetto   September 16, 1942

On September 5 the situation became clearer, and the frightening whispers of the past days became terrifying fact. The evacuation of children and old people took on the shape of reality. A small piece of paper on the wall in a busy part of the city announced an address by the President in an urgent matter. A huge crowd in Fire Brigade Square. The "Jewish Elder" will reveal the truth in the rumors. For it concerns the young, for whom he has great love, and the aged, for whom he has much respect. "It cannot be that they will tear the babes from their mothers' breasts, and drag old fathers and old mothers to some unknown place. The German is without mercy, he wages a terrible war, but he will not go as far as that in cruelty." Everybody has faith in the President** and hopes for words of comfort from him.

The representative of the ghetto is speaking. His voice fails him, the words stick in his throat. His personal appearance also mirrors the tragedy. One thing was understood by everybody: 20,000 persons must leave the ghetto, children under 10 and old people over 65. . . .

Everybody is convinced that the Jews who are deported are taken to destruction. . . People ran here and there, crazed by the desire to hide the beloved victims. But nobody knew who would direct the *Aktion*: the Jewish Police, the Gestapo in the ghetto, or a mobile unit of the SS. The President, in coordination with the German authorities (Biebow) decided in his area of responsibility to carry out the deportation (with his own forces). It was the Jewish Police that had to tear the children from the mothers, to take the parents from their children. . . It was to be expected that parents and relatives would try in this situation to make changes and corrections in registered ages. Errors and inaccuracies that had not been corrected up to now did exist. Something that gives you the right to live today may well decide your fate tomorrow. There was a tendency to raise the age of the children, because a child from the age of 10 up could go to work and so be entitled to a portion of soup. Other parents lowered the age, because a younger child had a prospect of getting milk. Yesterday the milk and the soup were the most important things, today there is literally a question of staying alive. The age of the old people also moved up and down for various reasons.

An unprecedented migration began to the Registration Office. The officials tried to manage the situation. They worked without stopping, day and night. The pressure of the people at the office windows increased all the time. The applicants yelled, wept and went wild. Every second could bring the death sentence, and hours passed in the struggle to restrain their passion... On Saturday the Gestapo already began on the operation [deportation], without paying any attention to the feverish work of registration that had been going on at No. 4 Church Square. Everyone had supposed that the Order Police [Jewish Police] would not stand the test. It could not itself carry out the work of the hangmen....

The little ones who were loaded on the cart behaved quietly, in submission, or yelling, according to their ages. The children of the ghetto, boys and girls less than 10 years old, are already mature and familiar with poverty and suffering. The young look around them with wide-open eyes and do not know what to do. They are on a cart for the first time in their lives, a cart that will be pulled by a real horse, a proper horse. They are looking forward to a gay ride. More than one of the little ones jumps for joy on the floor of the wagon as long as there is enough space. And at the same time his mother has almost gone out of her mind, twisting about on the ground and tearing the hair from her head in despair. It is difficult to overcome several thousand mothers. It is difficult to persuade them to give their children up willingly to death, as a sacrifice. It is difficult to take out the old people who hide in the smallest and most hidden corners.

All this was to be expected. The President imposed a general curfew which came into force at 5 o'clock on Sunday afternoon. Anyone who broke it was threatened with deportation.

Dokumenty i materialy, II, *Akcje i wysiedlenia* ("Documents and Records, II, *Aktionen* and Deportations"), Warsaw..., 1946, pp. 243-246.

* From the description written by O.S. (Oscar Singer), a refugee from Czechoslovakia, a journalist who managed the Jewish archives in Lodz at the time of the Occupation.
** The reference is to Rumkowski.

131

MEMORANDUM BY GENERAL VON GINANT TO THE GENERAL STAFF OF THE WEHRMACHT IN REACTION TO THE REMOVAL OF THE JEWS FROM INDUSTRIAL PRODUCTION, SEPTEMBER 18, 1942

I. To date, the following orders have been in force for the Government-General:

1) Polish and Ukrainian workers are to be replaced by Jewish workers, in order to release the former for work in the Reich; the enterprises concerned will set up camps for the Jews.
2) For the full exploitation of Jewish labor for the war effort, purely Jewish enterprises and Jewish sections of enterprises will be established.

The evacuation of the Jews without advance notice to most sections of the Wehrmacht has caused great difficulties in the replacement of labor and delay in correct production for military purposes. Work for the SS, with priority "Winter," cannot be completed in time.

II. Unskilled workers can be replaced in part, if the Commissioner General for Labor is prepared to relinquish the 140,000 Poles who were assigned for work in the Reich, and if the Police is successful in rounding them up. Previous experience gives cause for doubt in this respect.

A small proportion of the skilled labor can be supplied by students at present in government technical schools.

Fully skilled labor would first have to be trained. The training of labor drawn mainly from agriculture requires several months to a year, and more in the case of particularly highly qualified workers and craftsmen.

Whether the solution of this especially complex problem, on which the continued productivity of the Government-General for the war economy depends primarily, can be speeded up by the release of skilled workers from the Reich is beyond my competence to judge.

III. According to the figures supplied by the Government-[General's] Central Labor Office, manpower in industry totals a little over a million, of which 300,000 are Jews. The latter include roughly 100,000 skilled workers.

In the enterprises working for the Wehrmacht, the proportion of Jews among the skilled workers varies from 25% to 100%; it is 100% in the textile factories producing winter clothing. In other enterprises — for instance the important motor manufacturing works which produce the "Fuhrmann" and "Pleskau" models — the key men, who do the wheel-work, are mainly Jews. With few exceptions all the upholsterers are Jews.

A total of 22,700 workers are employed at the present time on reconditioning uniforms in private firms, and, of these, 22,000 (97%) are Jews. Of these, 16,000 are skilled textile and leather workers.

A purely Jewish enterprise with 168 workers produces metal parts for harnesses. The entire production of harnesses in the Government-General, the Ukraine and, in part, in the Reich depends on this enterprise.

IV. The immediate removal of the Jews would cause a considerable reduction in Germany's war potential, and supplies to the front and to the troops in the Government-General would be held up, at least for the time being.
1) There would be a serious drop in production in the armaments industry, ranging from 25% to 100%.
2) There would be an average decrease of about 25% in the work done at the motor vehicle repair workshops, i.e., about 2,500 vehicles fewer would be put back into working order per month.
3) Reinforced units would be required to maintain supplies.

V. Unless work of military importance is to suffer, Jews cannot be released until replacements have been trained, and then only step by step. This can only be done locally, but should be centrally directed from a *single* office in coordination with the Higher SS and Police Leader (*Höher SS- und Polizeiführer*).

It is requested that the orders may be carried out in this manner. The general policy will be to eliminate the Jews from work as quickly as possible without harming work of military importance.

VI. It has now been noted that a great variety of Wehrmacht offices have placed military orders of the highest priority, particularly for winter needs, in the Government-General, without the knowledge of the Armaments Department or the Military Commander of the Government-General. The evacuation of the Jews makes it impossible for these orders to be completed in time.

It will take some time to register systematically all the enterprises involved.

It is requested that the evacuation of Jews employed in industrial enterprises may be postponed until this has been done.

Yad Vashem Archives, 04/4 - 2.

132

RESPONSE BY HIMMLER TO THE MEMORANDUM FROM GENERAL VON GINANT

Reichsführer SS
Journal No. AR 31/22/42

Field Command
October 9, 1942

Secret !

With reference to the memorandum from the Commander of the Military District (*Wehrkreisbefehlshaber*) in the Government-General to the OKW [High Command of the Wehrmacht] concerning the replacement of Jewish labor by Poles, I have the following comments:

1. I have given orders that all so-called armament workers who are actually employed solely in tailoring, furrier and shoe-making workshops be collected in concentration camps on the spot, i.e., in Warsaw and Lublin, under the direction of SS *Obergruppenführer Krüger* and SS *Obergruppenführer Pohl.* The Wehrmacht will send its orders to us, and we guarantee the continuous delivery of the items of clothing required. I have issued instructions, however, that ruthless steps be taken against all those who consider they should oppose this move in the alleged interest of armaments needs, but who in reality only seek to support the Jews and their own businesses.

2. Jews in real war industries, i.e., armament workshops, vehicle workshops, etc., are to be withdrawn step by step. As a first stage they are to be concentrated in separate halls in the factories. In a second stage in this procedure the work teams in these separate halls will be combined, by means of exchange, into closed enterprises wherever this is possible, so that we will then have simply a few closed concentration-camp industries in the Government-General.

3. Our endeavor will then be to replace this Jewish labor force with Poles and to consolidate most of these Jewish concentration-camp enterprises into a small number of large Jewish concentration-camp enterprises — in the eastern part of the Government-General, if possible. But there, too, in accordance with the wish of the Führer, the Jews are some day to disappear.

signed   H. Himmler

Distribution:

1. SS *Obergruppenführer* Pohl
2. SS *Obergruppenführer* Krüger
3. SS *Brigadeführer* Globocnik
4. Reich Security Main Office (*Reichssicherheitshauptamt*)
5. SS *Obergruppenführer* Wolff.

NO-1611.

133

SECURITY POLICE PLANS TO ALLOW 30,000 JEWISH WORKERS TO REMAIN IN BIALYSTOK,* FEBRUARY–MARCH 1943

... The representative of the Security Police Commander stated at this discussion that it was not expected that there would be any further resettlement of Jews for the time being. The continued presence of 30,000 Jews in the ghetto was likely until the end of the war. This fact would have to be taken into account from the point of view of the economy, as the Reich Security Main Office (*Reichssicherheitshauptamt*) was expected to accede to this attitude of the local Security Police.

This created a new picture for the labor position and the maintenance of economic productivity.

1. The ghetto will remain, with new borders, but roughly the same size.

2. Factories situated within the ghetto would continue to operate, but with Jewish personnel.

3. Without any connection with the tasks of the city in the future peace, it is the target of the political and security-police to have the 4,000 Jews outside the ghetto disappear [from the Aryan side] in the near future and work only in the ghetto....

The local Security Police intends to allow the ghetto to remain for the time being and in a certain size: the Reich Security Main Office in Berlin is to take a final decision in the matter in the course of the month.

Yad Vashem Archives, M11/26.

* From documents dated February and March 1943, found in the Underground archives of the Bialystok ghetto.

134

HIMMLER ORDERS THE DESTRUCTION OF THE WARSAW GHETTO, FEBRUARY 16, 1943

Reichsführer SS   Field Command
Journal No. 38/33/43 g.   February 16, 1943

Secret!

To:

Higher SS and Police Leader (*Höher SS- und Polizeiführer*), East
SS *Obergruppenführer* Krüger, Cracow

For reasons of security I herewith order that the Warsaw Ghetto
be pulled down after the concentration camp has been moved:
all parts of houses that can be used, and other materials of
all kinds, are first to be made use of.

The razing of the ghetto and the relocation of the concentration camp are necessary, as otherwise we would probably
never establish quiet in Warsaw, and the prevalence of crime
cannot be stamped out as long as the ghetto remains.

An overall plan for the razing of the ghetto is to be submitted to me. In any case we must achieve the disappearance
from sight of the living-space for 500,000 sub-humans (*Unter-
menschen*) that has existed up to now, but could never be suitable
for Germans, and reduce the size of this city of millions —
Warsaw — which has always been a center of corruption and
revolt.

signed   H. Himmler

NO-2494.

135

FROM A REPORT OF THE JEWISH FIGHTING ORGANIZATION IN THE WARSAW GHETTO ON ITS ACTIVITIES *

...On Wednesday, July 22, 1942 [the eve of Tisha be-Av, Day of Mourning], the liquidation of the Warsaw ghetto was begun. The Public Committee was immediately summoned to find out what the situation was and to take measures. Those attending the meeting included: L. Bloch, Shmuel Bresler [Breslav], Dr. A. Berman, Yitzhak Cukierman, Zisha Friedman, Josef Finkelstein-Lewartowski, D. Guzik, Yitzhak Giterman, Josef Kaplan, Menachem Kirszenbaum, Alexander Landau, M. Orzech, Dr. Emmanuel Ringelblum, Josef Sack, Szachna Sagan and Dr. Yitzhak Schiper. Opinions were divided. Representatives of the left-wing Zionist parties and of He-Halutz [Zionists] and also some of the men in public life called for active intervention in some way or other. The majority wanted to wait. How long? Until the situation became clearer. For rumors were circulating that no more than 50,000 to 70,000 Jews would be deported from Warsaw (old people, the sick, prisoners, beggars, etc.), and [after that] the *Aktion* would be finished....

On July 28, 1942, a meeting was held of He-Halutz and its youth-movement branches: Ha-Shomer Ha-Za'ir, Dror, and Akiva. It was decided to set up the Jewish Fighting Organization YKA (*Yidishe-Kamf-Organizatsie*). The organization signed proclamations which it issued in the Polish language with the initials ZOB-*Zydowska Organizacja Bojowa* — Jewish Fighting Organization. The members of the Command were: Bresler, Cukierman, Zivia Lubetkin, Mordecai Tenenbaum and Josef Kaplan. A delegation was sent to the Aryan side [i.e., outside the ghetto], to the Poles: Tosia Altman, Plotnicka, Leah Perlstein and Arie-Jurek Wilner, in order to make contact with the Polish Underground and to obtain weapons for the ghetto.

The fighting organization had been set up, but all the weapons there were in the ghetto at that time consisted of just one pistol...!

Yad Vashem Archives, O-25/96.

* From a report by Yitzhak Cukierman in Warsaw, March 1944. See document 126.

136

FROM NOTES BY HERSH BERLINSKI ON THE AIMS OF THE JEWISH FIGHTING ORGANIZATION [1] *

... At the end of October 1942 a meeting was held at the Ha-Shomer [Left-wing Zionist] Club in 61 Mila Street. Those present were: Ha-Shomer — Mordecai [Anielewicz]; He-Halutz — Yitzhak [Cukierman]; and Po'alei Zion Smol [Left Labor Zionists] — Pola [Elster], Berlinski, Wasser ... agenda ... the defense of the Warsaw ghetto. After an exhaustive discussion in which the following members took part — Pola, Berlinski, Wasser, Mordecai and Yitzhak — we reached a joint conclusion: (1) That the Jewish Fighting Organization has been established in order to prepare the defense of the Warsaw ghetto, (2) In order to teach a lesson to the Jewish Police, the *Werkschutz*, [2] * the managers of the "shops" [3] * and all kinds of informers. When we reached the issue of appointing the leadership, a touchy discussion developed. Should there be one authority or two, military or military and political? The members of Ha-Shomer and He-Halutz strongly oppose two-fold authority. Two-fold authority will lead to arguments that will hamper the work. It will take us back to the days on the eve of the Destruction, when the parties argued and did nothing. The members of Ha-Shomer and He-Halutz speak with derision and scorn of the political parties. The parties have no right to interfere in our affairs. Apart from

294

the youth, after all, they will do nothing. They will only get in the way. One single military leadership must be established, so we can start on the job.

The members of Po'alei Zion Smol point out the faulty assumption of Ha-Shomer and He-Halutz on what they term the death of honor: "We are fighting for our lives. If a few of us fall in battle we will not make a tragedy of it. Every war claims its victims. If the political parties made certain mistakes it is not you who are entitled to judge them. It was not you who led the political struggle and not you who will lead it in the future... One must not sanction irresponsible acts that are likely to bring about the liquidation of the Warsaw ghetto before its time. A group or organization that carries out weapon training contains within itself the aspiration and expectation of the happy moment when it will use these arms. We consider it to be an essential condition that a second authority be established which can judge clearly, from a political point of view, what the appropriate time is for the use of arms. Why are you so anxious, why are you so much afraid? Justice will always conquer. And even if we start out from the assumption that the ghetto will be destroyed and that we shall not be accountable to anyone for our actions, as a political party we declare that we are responsible for our actions before the Jewish masses in the world and before our comrades abroad. We do not want anybody to stone our graves because we advised irresponsible action. If you do not agree that the political parties will control the fighting organization then you are creating conditions for us that do not permit us to continue to take part..."

As soon as there is agreement on two-fold authority: military ad political, the foundation stone will have been laid for the joint Jewish Fighting Organization. We have decided to widen the area of our work and to draw the Bund closer to us...

Yad Vashem Archives, JM/2598.

1 * Member of the military staff of the Jewish Fighting Organization.

2 * *Werkschutz* — the guard at places of employment and factories — the "shops."

3 * "Shop" — Code name for a German enterprise, or an enterprise working by authority, and on behalf of the Germans.

137

THE DISCUSSION ON FIGHTING AIMS BY THE ACTIVISTS OF THE BIALYSTOK MEMBERS OF THE DROR MOVEMENT, FEBRUARY 27, 1943

Mordecai [Tenenbaum-Tamaroff]: It's a good thing that at least the mood is good. Unfortunately, the meeting won't be very cheerful. This meeting may be historic, if you like, tragic if you like, but certainly sad. That you people sitting here are the last *halutzim* in Poland; around us are the dead. You know what happened in Warsaw, not one survived, and it was the same in Bendin and in Czestochowa,* and probably everywhere else. We are the last. It is not a particularly pleasant feeling to be the last: it involves a special responsibility. We must decide today what to do tomorrow. There is no sense in sitting together in a warm atmosphere of memories! Nor in waiting together, collectively, for death. Then what shall we do?

We can do two things: decide that when the first Jew is taken away from Bialystok now, we start our counter-*Aktion*. That nobody will go to the factories from tomorrow, that none of us are allowed to hide when the *Aktion* starts.

Everybody will be mobilized for the job. We can see to it that not one German leaves the ghetto, that not one factory remains whole. It is not impossible that after we have completed our task someone may by chance still be alive.

But we will fight to the last, till we fall. We can also decide to get out into the forest. The possibilities must be considered realistically. Two of our people went off today to prepare a place, but in any event military discipline will be in force after the meeting today. We must decide for ourselves now. Our daddies will not take care of us. This is an orphanage. There is one condition: our approach must be ideological, the ideas of the Movement must be our guide. Anyone who wishes, or believes or hopes that he has a real chance of staying alive and wants to make use of it — well and good. We will help him any way we can. Let everyone decide for himself whether to live or die. But together we must find a collective answer to our common question. As I do not want to impose my views on anybody, I will not come out with my one answer for the time being.

Yitzhak [Engelman]: We are today discussing two ways of dying. To move out into attack means certain death for us. The second way means death two or three days later. We must examine both ways, perhaps there is something that could be done. As the exact details are not known to me, I would like to hear more from better informed comrades. If some comrades believe that they could stay alive, then we should think about it.

Hershl [Rosental]: ... Here in Bialystok we are fated to live out the last act of this blood-stained tragedy. What can we do and what should we do? The way I see it the situation really is that the great majority in the ghetto and of our group are sentenced to die. Our fate is sealed. We have never looked on the forest as a place in which to hide, we have looked on it as a base for battle and vengeance. But the tens of young people who are going into the forests now do not seek a battle-field there, most of them will lead beggars' lives there and most likely will find a beggar's death. In our present situation our fate will be the same, beggars all.

Only one thing remains for us: to organize collective resistance in the ghetto, at any cost; to let the ghetto be our Musa Dagh,** to write a proud chapter on Jewish Bialystok and on our Movement. ...

Our way is clear: when the first Jew is taken away, the

counter-*Aktion* will begin. If anyone succeeds in taking a rifle from one of the murderers and getting to the forest — fine. A young armed person can find his place in the forest. If we still have time left to prepare the departure to the forest, then it is a place for battle and revenge.

I have lost everything, all those close to me; and yet, subconsciously, one wants to live. But there is no choice. If I thought that there might be escape, not just for individuals, but for 50 or 60% of the ghetto Jews to survive, I would say that the way of the Movement should be to stay alive at all costs. But we are condemned to death.

Sarah [Kopinski]: Comrades! If it is a question of honor, we have already long since lost it. In most of the Jewish communities the *Aktionen* were carried out smoothly without a counter-*Aktion*. It is more important to stay alive than to kill five Germans. In a counter-*Aktion* we will without doubt all be killed. In the forest, on the other hand, perhaps 40 or 50% of our people may be saved. That will be our honor and that will be our history. We are still needed, we will yet be of use. As we no longer have honor in any case, let it be our task to remain alive.

Hanoch [Zelaznogora]: No illusions! We can expect nothing but death down to the last Jew. We have before us two possibilities of death. The forest will not save us, and the counter-*Aktion* will certainly not save us. The choice that is left us is to die with dignity. The outlook for our resistance is poor. I don't know whether we have the necessary means for combat. It is the fault of all of us that our means are so small, but that is in the past, we must make do with what we have. Bialystok will be liquidated completely like all the other Jewish cities. Even if the factories were exempted, their manpower left untouched in the first *Aktion*, nobody can believe now that they will be spared this time. Obviously the forest offers greater possibilities of revenge, but we must not go there to live on the mercy of the peasants, to buy food — and our lives — for money.

298

To go to the forest means to become active partisans, and for that one needs the proper weapons. The arms that we have are not suitable for the forest. If there is still time we should try to get arms and go to the forest. If the *Aktion* starts first, then we must respond when the first Jew is taken.

Chaim [Rudner]: There are no Jews left, only a few remnants have remained. There is no Movement left, only a remnant. There is no sense speaking about honor. Everyone must save himself as best he can. It does not matter how they will judge us. We must hide, go to the forest....

Mordecai: If we want it sufficiently, and make it our aim, we could protect the lives of our people to the end, as long as Jews remain in Bialystok. I want to ask a drastic question: do those members who favor going to the "forest" think we should hide and not react during the coming *Aktion,* so as to escape into the forest later?

(Voices from all sides: No, not that!)

We have heard two opinions, from Sarah and Chaim on the one side, and from Hershl and Hanoch on the other. You decide. One thing is certain, we won't go off to the factories and pray to God there that they should take away the people in the streets in order that we may be saved. Nor will we watch from the factory windows when our comrades from another· factory are taken away.

We can take a vote — Hershl or Chaim...

Shmulik [Zolty]: This is the first time in my life that I have taken part in a meeting on death. We are planning the counter-*Aktion* not in order to write history but to die an honorable death, as befits a young Jew at this time... Now about the *Aktion.* All our experience teaches us that we can have no confidence in the Germans despite their promises that the factories would be safe, and that only those who are not working will be taken away, etc. Only with the aid of deception and confusion did they succeed in taking thousands of Jews to slaughter. But despite all that we have a chance of surviving the *Aktion* alive and safely.

Everybody is playing for time, and we must do the same. In the short time that is left to us we must work to improve our weapons, which are at present poor and small in number.

We must also do what we can as regards the forest, where we can fulfill a double task. I don't want to be misunderstood and have the fact that we hid during the *Aktion* judged as cowardice.

No, no, no! Man's instinct to live is so great that we must consider our self-interest first here. I don't care if others go in our stead. We have a much better claim to life than others, and by right.

We have an aim in life — to stay alive at all costs. We were brought here from Vilna because there was a threat of total liquidation there and some witnesses must stay alive. For that reason, if there is not to be total liquidation here, we must wait and try to gain time. But if there is to be liquidation let all join in the counter-*Aktion,* and let me die with the Philistines. . . .

Ethel [Sobol]: Practically speaking, if an *Aktion* should take place within the next few days then there is only one way left open to us, to start the counter-*Aktion.* But if we should have more time at our disposition then we should think in the direction of getting away to the forest.

I hope I will be able to carry out the duties that will be imposed on us. Perhaps, in the course of events I will find myself stronger. I am determined to do everything that needs to be done.

Hershl was right when he said that we are starting out on a desperate move. Whether we want it or not, our fate is already sealed. It only remains for us to decide between one kind of death and another. I am calm and cool.

Mordecai: The opinion of the comrades is clear — we should do everything to get out as many people as possible to join the partisans' battle in the forest. Everyone of us who is in the ghetto when the *Aktion* begins must move as soon as the first Jew is taken. There can be no bargaining with us over life; one must understand the situation as it is.

The most important thing of all is to maintain until the end the character and pride of the Movement.

Yad Vashem Archives, M—11/7.

* This estimate is the result of lack of information on what happened in Warsaw. In the deportation that took place in Warsaw in January, the Jewish Fighting Organization lost only part of its people. The information on Bendin and Czestochowa is also based on incomplete knowledge of the situation.
** The reference is to the book by F. Werfel, *The Forty Days of Musa Dagh,* which describes the mass murder of the Armenians by the Turks during World War I.

138

CALL TO RESISTANCE BY THE JEWISH FIGHTING ORGANIZATION IN THE WARSAW GHETTO, JANUARY 1943

To the Jewish Masses in the Ghetto

On January 22, 1943, six months will have passed since the deportations from Warsaw began. We all remember well the days of terror during which 300,000 of our brothers and sisters were cruelly put to death in the death camp of Treblinka. Six months have passed of life in constant fear of death, not knowing what the next day may bring. We have received information from all sides about the destruction of the Jews in the Government-General, in Germany, in the occupied territories. When we listen to this bitter news we wait for our own hour to come, every day and every moment. Today we must understand that the

301

Nazi murderers have let us live only because they want to make use of our capacity to work to our last drop of blood and sweat, to our last breath. We are slaves. And when the slaves are no longer profitable, they are killed. Everyone among us must understand that, and everyone among us must remember it always.

During the past few weeks certain people have spread stories about letters that were said to have been received from Jews deported from Warsaw, who were said to be in labor camps near Minsk or Bobruisk. *Jews in your masses, do not believe these tales. They are spread by Jews who are working for the Gestapo.* The blood-stained murderers have a particular aim in doing this: to reassure the Jewish population in order that later the next deportation can be carried out without difficulty, with a minimum of force and without losses to the Germans. They want the Jews not to prepare hiding-places and not to resist. Jews, do not repeat these lying tales.

Do not help the [Nazi] agents. The Gestapo's dastardly people will get their just deserts. *Jews in your masses,* the hour is near. You must be prepared to resist, not to give yourselves up like sheep to slaughter. *Not even one Jew must go to the train. People who cannot resist actively must offer passive resistance, that is, by hiding.* We have now received information from Lvov that the Jewish Police there itself carried out the deportation of 3,000 Jews. Such things will not happen again in Warsaw. The killing of Lejkin proves it. Now our slogan must be:

Let everyone be ready to die like a man!

January 1943

Archiwum Zydowskiego Instytutu Historycznego w Polsce (Archives of the Jewish Historical Institute in Poland), ARII/333.

139

CALL FOR RESISTANCE BY THE JEWISH MILITARY ORGANIZATION IN THE WARSAW GHETTO, JANUARY 1943 *

We are rising up for war!
We are of those who have set themselves the aim of awakening the people. Our wish is to take this watchword to our people:

Awake and fight!
Do not despair of the road to escape!

Know that escape is not to be found by walking to your death passively, like sheep to the slaughter. It is to be found in something much greater: in war!

Whoever defends himself has a chance of being saved! Whoever gives up self-defense from the outset — he has lost already!
Nothing awaits him except only a hideous death in the suffocation-machine of Treblinka.

Let the people awaken to war!

Find the courage in your soul for desperate action!
Put an end to our terrible acceptance of such phrases as:
We are all under sentence of death!
It is a lie!!!
We also were destined to live! We too have a right to life!
One only needs to know how to fight for it!
It is no great art to live when life is given to you *willingly*!
But there is an art to life just when they are trying to rob you of this life.

Let the people awaken and fight for its life!

Let every mother be a lioness defending her young!
Let no father stand by and see the blood of his children in silence!
Let not the first act of our destruction be repeated!
An end to despair and lack of faith!
An end to the spirit of slavery amongst us!

Let the tyrant pay with the blood of his body for every s u!
in Israel!
Let every house become a fortress for us!

Let the people awaken to war!
In war lies your salvation!
Whoever defends himself has a hope of escape!
We are rising in the name of the war for the lives of the helpless
masses whom we seek to save, whom we must arouse to action!
It is not for ourselves alone that we wish to fight. We will
be entitled to save ourselves only when we have completed
our duty! *As long as the life of a Jew is still in danger, even
one, single, life, we have to be ready to fight*!!!!

Our watchword is:
Not even one more Jew is to find his end in Treblinka!
Out with the traitors to the people!
War for life or death on the conqueror to our last breath!

Be prepared to act!
Be ready!

Archiwum Zydowskiego Instytutu Historycznego w Polsce (Archives of
the Jewish Historical Institute in Poland), ARII/333.

* The appeal is attributed to the Jewish Military Organization (*Zydowski
Zwiazek Wojskowy — ZZW*).

140

RESPONSE OF THE COMMANDER OF THE AK
TO THE JEWISH REQUEST FOR ARMS *

After all, Jews from all kinds of groups, including Communists,
are turning to us and asking for arms as though our depots
were full. By way of experiment I gave them a few revolvers.
I have no assurance whatsoever that they will use these arms

at all. I will not give them any more arms, because, as you know, we have none ourselves, we are waiting for a new consignment. Inform us what contacts our Jews have with London.

Kalina

Yad Vashem Archives, O-25/93.

* This message was sent by General Rowecki, Commander of the AK, to the Polish Government in London on January 4, 1943. AK — *Armia Krajowa* — Fatherland Army: the military arm of the Polish Underground under the orders of the Government-in-Exile in London.

141

APPEAL OF THE JEWISH FIGHTING ORGANIZATION TO THE POLISH UNDERGROUND, ASKING FOR ARMS

March 13, 1943

Dear Sirs !

... The coming days are likely to see the end of the Jews of Warsaw.

Are we ready? From a material point of view it is very bad. Of the 49 weapons that have been allocated to us only 36 can be used, for lack of ammunition. Our position as regards arms has worsened after the many operations of the past few weeks, during which much ammunition was used. At the present moment there are no more than 10 bullets for each weapon. This is a catastrophic situation.

Please inform the authorities in our name that if large-scale help does not arrive immediately we shall look on it as indifference on the part of the representatives and the authorities to the fate of the Jews of Warsaw. The allocation of weapons without ammunition is a cynical mockery of our fate, and confirms the assumption that the poison of anti-Semitism continues to pervade the leading circles in Poland, despite the

305

cruel and tragic experiences of the past three years. It is not our intention to persuade anybody concerning our willingness and ability to fight. Since January 18 the Jews of Warsaw have been in a state of continuous struggle with the invader and his servants. Anyone who denies this or casts doubt upon it is nothing but a deliberate anti-Semite.

We do not expect only "understanding" from the authorities and the *delegatura*,* but also that they should consider the murder of millions of Jews, who are Polish citizens, to be the main problem of our current life. We regret most deeply that it is not possible for us to make direct contact with the Allied governments, with the Polish Government and the Jewish organizations abroad in order to inform them about our situation and the attitude towards us on the part of the Polish authorities and public.

Dear Sirs !

We request that you take the necessary steps immediately with the Army Authorities and Government Representatives. We request that you read them this letter and demand immediately at least 100 grenades, 50 revolvers, 10 rifles and several thousand bullets of various diameters. I am prepared to submit within two days accurate plans of our positions, with maps, so that there need be no doubt whatsoever concerning the necessity of the supply of arms.

Commander, Jewish Fighting Organization

(—) Kalachi**

B. Mark, *Powstanie w getcie warszawskim* ("The Warsaw Ghetto Revolt"), Warsaw, 1963, pp. 221-223.

* The reference is to the Polish Underground leadership, which operated under the Polish Government-in-Exile in London.
** This is an error and should read Malakhi, underground name of Mordecai Anielewicz.

142

SURVEY OF PROBLEMS OF JEWISH RESISTANCE BY AN AK OFFICER IN CHARGE OF THE JEWISH AFFAIRS DEPARTMENT [1] *

... In the military field the demands of the Jews were directed towards obtaining arms and technical instruction for the preparation of the last, final battle for the Warsaw ghetto. The Jewish Fighting Organization took a decisive stand, saying that the fate of the Warsaw ghetto, like the fate of all the other concentrations of Jews, had been decided, and that total annihilation awaited it sooner or later. In view of this they asked to die with honor, that is — with arms in their hands. In December (1942), after insistent requests, the Jewish Fighting Organization received 10 revolvers and a limited amount of ammunition, by order of the Central Command. These weapons were in very poor condition and only a part were fit for use. The Jewish Fighting Organization considered this gift as covering only a very small part of their requirements. It therefore demanded incomparably more efficacious help, and said it was willing to budget a large part of the funds [2] * which it had at its disposal at its central offices for the purchase of arms. This request could be satisfied only in very small part. Prior to January 17, [3] * 1943 (the date of the liquidation of the Warsaw ghetto, which then numbered 50,000 souls), the Jewish Fighting Organization received another 10 revolvers, [4] * instructions for sabotage action, a formula for the production of bottle fire-bombs and instruction in military operations. The period up to January 17, 1943, was marked by feverish preparations by the Jewish Fighting Organization for the coming struggle, persistent, continuous calls for help to the army, which reacted to these appeals with lack of confidence and much reserve. The liquidation of the ghetto, which began on January 17, 1943, met with stubborn armed resistance that undoubtedly caused consternation among the German troops and caused the *Aktion* to be stopped after

307

four days. The Jewish Fighting Organization judged its success to mean the postponement for a time of the final liquidation, and with unshaken vigor continued preparations for a second struggle, all the while with growing persistence demanding help from the army. By order of the Chief Commander I held three consultations with the Commander of "Drapacz," [5] * Mr. Konar.[6] * Konar agreed to aid the Warsaw ghetto with materials and instructions and spoke of the possibility of our units helping from outside the ghetto. Work was begun immediately under the direction of Chirurg.[7] * Contact was established between Jurek [8] * of the Jewish Fighting Organization and our officers. The Jewish Fighting Organization received 50 revolvers, a large quantity of bullets, about 80 kgs. [170 lbs.] of material for the preparation of "bottles" and a certain number of defensive grenades. A workshop was put into operation in the ghetto for the manufacture of bottles. In addition it was made easier to obtain the arms which the Jewish Fighting Organization was providing for itself. The plan for the struggle in the ghetto was worked out jointly, and took into account help to be given by our unit. On March 6, 1943, Jurek was arrested (in the apartment in Wspolnej Street). This fact stoppped the work process which had been carried out jointly by the Jewish Fighting Organization and "Drapacz." More than ten days after the arrest I had a conversation with Konar. The subject of the conversation was defining the aims of the cooperation between our units and the ghetto fighters. The aim had been supposed to be to get as many Jews as possible away from Warsaw and give them shelter, something that I could do at any time. This plan was not carried out. No units moved out into the designated area. The Jewish Fighting Organization decided that it was to be avoided that their people should have to force their way through a distance of hundreds of kilometers, and the base for materials and shelter established by the order of Edward of "Len" [9] * for "Hreczka" [10] * proved to be insufficient help. It proved to be impossible to take Jews into our military units in the areas of "Drapacz" and "Cegielnia." [11] * Instead, Konar agreed to organize the Jews into units for passive resistance. One such unit was set up in Warsaw. One of the officers was appointed to train this unit. He came to the place where the training was to be carried out, and arranged a meeting, but failed to come to the meeting. As the result of many interventions the above officer did come once more to the training area, but he arrived drunk. Further requests failed to produce results. The Jewish rebel unit received no military training and ceased to exist...

B. Mark, *Powstanie w getcie warszawskim* ("The Warsaw Ghetto Revolt"), Warsaw, 1963, pp. 345-347.

1 * The man in charge of Jewish affairs in the AK was Henryk Wolinski, whose name in the Underground was "Waclaw."

2 * The reference is to funds obtained by the Jewish Fighting Organization in the ghetto for the purchase of arms.

3 * The date is incorrect; it should read January 18. January 18 also was not the date of the final liquidation of the ghetto, which began only on April 19, 1943.

4 * Receipt of this consignment is not confirmed by Jewish sources.

5 * The secret name of the AK in the Warsaw District.

6 * The Underground name of General Antoni Chrusciel, Commander of the AK forces in the Warsaw District.

7 * The AK Chief of Staff in the Warsaw District, Stanislaw Weber.

8 * Arie Wilner, representative of the Jewish Fighting Organization on the Aryan side of Warsaw.

9 * AK, Lublin District.

10 * AK Volhynia District.

11 * A district in the neighborhood of Warsaw.

143

SS GENERAL STROOP ON THE BATTLES IN THE WARSAW GHETTO REVOLT — FINAL REPORT FROM THE GERMAN BATTLE DIARY, APRIL-MAY 1943

...In January 1943, the *Reichsführer* SS, on the occasion of his visit to Warsaw, ordered the SS and Police Leader (*SS-und Polizeiführer*) in the Warsaw District to *transfer to Lublin the armament factories and other enterprises of military value installed within the ghetto, including the labor force and machinery.* It proved to be rather difficult to carry out this order, since both the managers of the enterprises and the Jews resisted this transfer in every conceivable way. The SS and Police Leader therefore decided to carry out the transfer of the enterprises forcibly in the course of a *Grossaktion* (major *Aktion*), which was to have been carried out in the course of three days. The preparations and military orders for this *Grossaktion* had been completed by my predecessor.* I myself arrived in Warsaw on April 17, 1943, and took over command of the *Grossaktion* at 8 o'clock, after the *Aktion* itself had [already] started at 6 o'clock on the same day...

Es gibt keinen jüdischen Wohnbezirk — in Warschau mehr!

"There Is No Longer a Jewish Residential Quarter in Warsaw," the heading on the first page of SS General Stroop's reports on the suppression of the revolt in the Warsaw Ghetto

The number of Jews brought out from the houses and held during the first few days was relatively small. It proved that the Jews were hiding in the sewer canals and in specially constructed bunkers. Where it had been assumed during the first days that there were only isolated bunkers, it proved in the course of the *Grossaktion* that the whole ghetto had been systematically provided with cellars, bunkers and passage ways. The passages and bunkers all had access to the sewers. This enabled the Jews to move underground without interference. The Jews also used this network of sewers to escape underground into the Aryan part of the city of Warsaw. There were constant reports that Jews were attempting to escape through the sewer holes... How far the Jews' precautions had gone was demonstrated by many instances of bunkers skillfully laid out with accommodation for entire families, facilities for washing and bathing, toilets, storage bins for arms and ammunition and large food reserves sufficient for several months. There were different bunkers for poor and for rich Jews. It was extremely difficult for the task forces to discover the individual bunkers owing to camouflage, and in many cases it was made possible only through betrayal on the part of Jews.

After a few days it was already clear that the Jews would under no circumstances consider voluntary resettlement, but were determined to fight back by every means and with the weapons in their possession. Under Polish-Bolshevik leadership so-called fighting units were formed which were armed and paid any price asked for available arms....

...While at first it had been possible to capture the Jews, who are ordinarily cowards, in considerable numbers, the apprehending of the bandits** and Jews became increasingly difficult in the second half of the *Grossaktion*. Again and again, fighting units of 20 to 30 or more Jewish youths, 18 to 25 years old, accompanied by corresponding numbers of females, renewed the resistance. These fighting units were under orders to continue armed resistance to the end and, if necessary, to escape capture by suicide.

311

One such fighting unit succeeded in climbing out of the sewer through a manhole in so-called Prosta [Street] and to get on to a truck and escape with it (about 30 to 35 bandits). . .***

During the armed resistance females belonging to the fighting units were armed in the same way as the men; some were members of the He-Halutz Movement. It was no rarity for these females to fire pistols with both hands. It happened again and again that they kept pistols and hand-grenades (Polish "egg" grenades) hidden in their bloomers up to the last moment, in order to use them against the men of the *Waffen*-SS [military unit of the SS], Police and Wehrmacht.

The resistance offered by the Jews and bandits could be broken only by the energetic, tireless deployment of storm-patrols night and day. *On April 23, 1943, the* Reichsführer SS, *through the Higher SS and Police Führer for the East, in Cracow, issued the order that the Warsaw ghetto be combed out with maximum severity and ruthless determination.* I therefore decided to carry out the total destruction of the Jewish quarter by burning down all residential blocks, including the blocks attached to the armament factories. One by one the factories were systematically cleared and then destroyed by fire. Almost always the Jews then emerged from their hiding places and bunkers. Not rarely, the Jews stayed in the burning houses until the heat and fear of being burned to death caused them to jump from the upper floors after they had thrown mattresses and other upholstered objects from the burning houses to the street. With broken bones they would then try to crawl across the street into buildings which were not yet, or only partially, in flames. Often, too, Jews changed their hiding places during the night, by shifting into the ruins of buildings already burned out and taking refuge there until they were found by one of the shock troop units. . . .

Only as a result of the unceasing and untiring efforts of all forces did we succeed in capturing altogether 56,065 Jews, i.e., definitely destroying them. To this figure should be added

Jews who lost their lives in explosions, fires, etc., the number of which could not be definitely established. . . .

Warsaw, May 16, 1943

The SS and Police Leader
in the Warsaw District
Stroop
SS *Brigadeführer*
and Major General of Police

PS-1061.

* SS and Police Leader in the Warsaw District, *Oberführer* von Sammern-Frankenegg.
** This was the word used by the Germans for partisans and armed underground fighters.
*** The reference is to a group of the Jewish Fighting Organization which escaped through a sewer in Prosta Street on the Aryan side of the city on May 10, 1943.

144

DAILY REPORT FROM THE GERMAN BATTLE DIARY

Telegram

Warsaw, April 20, 1943

From: The SS and Police Leader (SS-*und Polizeiführer*)˙ in the Warsaw District
Ref. No.: I ab/St/Gr-16 07-Journal No. 516/43 Secret
Re: Ghetto Operation
To: The High SS and Police Leader East, Cracow

Progress of the Ghetto *Aktion* on April 19, 1943:

Closing of ghetto commenced at 03.00 hrs. At 06.00 hrs. the *Waffen-SS* was ordered to comb out the remainder of the ghetto at a strength of 16/850.*

313

As soon as the units had entered, strong concerted fire was directed at them by the Jews and bandits. The tank employed in this operation and the two SPW [heavy armored cars] were attacked with Molotov cocktails. The tank was twice set on fire. This attack with fire by the enemy caused the units employed to withdraw in the first stage. Losses in the first attack were 12 men (6 SS men, 6 Trawnicki men**). About 08.00 hrs. the units were sent in again under the command of the undersigned. Although there was again a counter-attack, in lesser strength, this operation made it possible to comb out the blocks of buildings according to plan. We succeeded in causing the enemy to withdraw from the roofs and prepared elevated positions into the cellars, bunkers and sewers. Only about 200 Jews were caught during the combing-out operation. Immediately afterwards shock-troop units were directed to known bunkers. with orders to pull out the occupants and destroy the bunkers. About 380 Jews were caught in this operation. It was discovered that the Jews were in the sewers. The sewers were completely flooded, to make it impossible to remain there. About 17.30 hrs. very strong resistance was met with from one block of buildings, including machine-gun fire. A special battle unit overcame the enemy, and penetrated into the buildings, but without capturing the enemy himself. The Jews and criminals resisted from base to base, and escaped at the last moment through garrets or subterranean passages. About 20.30 hrs. the external closure of the ghetto was reinforced. . . .

PS-1061.

* 16 officers, 850 men.
** The reference is to auxiliary police recruited from Ukrainians and men from the Baltic states.

145

THE LAST LETTER FROM MORDECAI ANIELEWICZ, WARSAW GHETTO REVOLT COMMANDER,* APRIL 23, 1943

It is impossible to put into words what we have been through. One thing is clear, what happened exceeded our boldest dreams. The Germans ran twice from the ghetto. One of our companies held out for 40 minutes and another — for more than 6 hours. The mine set in the "brushmakers" area exploded. Several of our companies attacked the dispersing Germans. Our losses in manpower are minimal. That is also an achievement. Y [Yechiel] fell. He fell a hero, at the machine-gun. *I feel that great things are happening and what we dared do is of great, enormous importance....*

Beginning from today we shall shift over to the partisan tactic. Three battle companies will move out tonight, with two tasks: reconnaissance and obtaining arms. Do you remember, short-range weapons are of no use to us. We use such weapons only rarely. What we need urgently: grenades, rifles, machine-guns and explosives.

It is impossible to describe the conditions under which the Jews of the ghetto are now living. Only a few will be able to hold out. The remainder will die sooner or later. Their fate is decided. In almost all the hiding places in which thousands are concealing themselves it is not possible to light a candle for lack of air.

With the aid of our transmitter we heard a marvelous report on our fighting by the "Shavit" radio station. The fact that we are remembered beyond the ghetto walls encourages us in our struggle. Peace go with you, my friend! Perhaps we may still meet again! *The dream of my life has risen to become fact. Self-defense in the ghetto will have been a reality. Jewish armed resistance and revenge are facts. I have been a witness to the magnificent, heroic fighting of Jewish men of battle.*

M. Anielewicz

Ghetto, April 23, 1943

[M. Kann], *Na oczach swiata* ("In the Eyes of the World"), Zamosc, 1932 [i.e., Warsaw, 1943], pp. 33-34.

* Written to Yitzhak Cukierman.

146

EXTRACT FROM A REPORT BY THE DELEGATURA * TO LONDON ON THE WARSAW GHETTO REVOLT

...The German units that penetrated into this area of the ghetto at dawn on April 19 were met with strong and effective fire by the defenders. A large number of Germans fell, dead or wounded. The resistance was so strong that the Germans brought up more and more additional units for the operation, including even field guns, flame-throwers and tanks. The situation was complicated by daring sallies on the part of the Jewish fighters, who spread out into sections outside the streets they were defending, and also by the systematic fire of the German attackers which poured into the ghetto from neighboring streets on the other side. The Gendarmerie and SS units did not gain control of the situation, and as a result a Wehrmacht unit was brought into the battle against the ghetto. Throughout Monday, April 19, and Tuesday, April 20, attacks continued by the Gendarmerie, the SS units and the Army units on the ghetto, which was defending itself stubbornly, and all these attacks failed. Heavy shelling continued near the ghetto walls night and day without stopping. German columns in battle formation moved out many times for the assault. Hundreds of Germans fell dead or wounded, and the ghetto continued to defend itself. This brought about a change in the German tactics. They stopped making direct attacks on the ghetto and began instead to lay siege to it. Movement was stopped in a number of streets close to the ghetto on the Aryan side and the Jewish stronghold surrounded by a great ring of armed German units. The drainage channels were sealed. German guns began to bombard the ghetto with fire-bombs. Many houses went up in flames. For several days past huge clouds of smoke have been rising up over the ghetto, and at night tremendous flames are seen over the northern part of the city. Special loudspeakers ceaselessly call on the inhabitants of the ghetto to surrender. Some of the Jews obeyed the substance of these appeals. Fewer than 10,000 persons lined up at the concentration points named by the Germans and were taken outside of Warsaw. But these were old people, including many women, the aged and weak among the men. All the rest, mainly young men, numbering more than 20,000, are fighting stubbornly. It is quite clear that in this battle the Jewish side is also suffering heavy losses. But it is a fact that in the six days that have passed since the Germans began the *Aktion* against the Warsaw ghetto, the Jews have not suffered defeat, and they reveal absolute determination to continue their self-defense and the struggle, and it looks as though it may continue for a longer period.

This war between the Jews and the Germans has awakened feelings of sympathy and admiration on the Aryan side of Warsaw, and shame among the Germans, who feel rightly that the situation that has come about in Warsaw is an uncommon blow to German prestige. It now appears that the Gestapo, which knows all and can do all, did not succeed in preventing the excellent preparations made by the Jewish population for the struggle and for its defense, with the result that the com-

317

bined forces of the Gendarmerie, the SS and the Army were unable up to now to overcome this resistance despite the assaults they have been mounting for the past six days. ...

Archiwum Zakladu Historii Partii (Archives of the Institute for the Party's History), 202/I-33, pp. 343-344.

* The reference is to the Polish Underground leadership, which operated under the Polish Government-in-Exile in London.

147

FRANK ON THE WARSAW GHETTO REVOLT *

Today's session of the Administration of the Government-General, held to mark the Führer's birthday, was dominated by developments in the security situation. This has indeed developed in a most dangerous fashion as the result of various circumstances. Since yesterday we have a well-organized uprising in the Warsaw ghetto, which has to be fought with the aid of artillery...

Faschismus — Getto — Massenmord ("Fascism — Ghetto — Mass Murder"), Berlin, 1961², p. 514.

* From a letter written by Frank to the Head of the Chancellor's Bureau, Lammers, dated April 20, 1943.

148

EXTRACT FROM GOEBBELS' DIARY ON THE GHETTO REVOLT

May 1, 1943 (Saturday)

There is nothing sensational in the reports from the Occupied Territories. The only thing noteworthy is exceptionally sharp fighting in Warsaw between our Police, and in part even the Wehrmacht, and the Jewish rebels. The Jews have actually succeeded in putting the ghetto in a condition to defend itself. Some very hard battles are taking place there, which have gone so far that the Jewish top leadership publishes daily military reports. Of course this jest will probably not last long. But it shows what one can expect of the Jews if they have arms. Unfortunately they also have some good German weapons in part, particularly machine-guns. Heaven only knows how they got hold of them.

J. Goebbels, *Goebbels Tagebücher aus den Jahren 1942-1943, mit andern Dokumenten* ("Goebbels' Diaries for the Years 1942-1943, and Other Documents"), Zurich, 1948, p. 318.

149

"THE LAST BATTLE IN THE GREAT TRAGEDY," FROM THE POLISH UNDERGROUND PRESS ON THE WARSAW GHETTO REVOLT *

...A week ago the second stage began in the brutal annihilation of the Polish Jews. The Germans set about expelling the 40,000 Jews who still remained in Warsaw. The ghetto replied with armed struggle. The Jewish Fighting Organization opened a war of the weak against the strong. With scant forces, few arms and little ammunition, without water, blinded by smoke and fire, the Jewish fighters defended streets and individual houses. In the dusk they withdrew step by step, more because of the fire that had taken hold in the close-built houses than because of the enemy who was equipped with modern military arms. They considered it a victory if a part of those imprisoned in the ghetto were able to escape; it was a victory in their eyes if the forces of the enemy were weakened just a little; and finally — it was a victory in their eyes to die while their hands still grasped arms. . . .

Yad Vashem Archives, O-25/25.

* From the Underground AK newspaper *Biuletyn Informacyjny* ("Information Bulletin"), No. 17, April 29, 1943.

150

"THE GREATEST CRIME IN THE WORLD," FROM THE POLISH UNDERGROUND PRESS ON THE GHETTO REVOLT *

. . . Now that Warsaw has witnessed the last act of the bestial German action, we cannot simply pass over the change in attitude of the victims, who, being unable to change their fate, decided to fall with arms in their hands. This stand of theirs, understood by every Pole, changes the picture significantly. From a people without hope, a herd slaughtered by the German murderers, the Jews rose to the heights of a fighting people. And if it could not fight for its existence — a thing made impossible by the overwhelming advantage in numbers of the enemy — it did demonstrate its right to life as a nation.

The Polish public looks upon this happening with great respect, gives it its moral support and hopes that its resistance will continue for as long as is possible...

Yad Vashem Archives, O-25/25.

* From the Underground newspaper *Mysl Panstwowa* ("State Thought"), No. 37, April 30, 1943.

151

"THE HEROIC RESISTANCE OF THE JEWS IN THE WARSAW GHETTO," FROM THE POLISH UNDERGROUND PRESS *

...Warsaw is waiting tensely for an air attack by the Soviets or the British, in retaliation, which would raise the spirits of the Jews fighting in the ghetto. The impression is meanwhile gaining ground that people abroad do not know what is going on in the Warsaw ghetto. Who is responsible for this? Is it the man who occupies the position of Delegate or the ZWZ?** We recall that very minor facts, a hundred times less important than this, were known in London almost immediately and broadcast to every part of the world. On the other hand, after the previous *Aktion* to liquidate the Jews of Poland, in which more than a million and a half Jews were lost, this became known to the world only after the whole *Aktion* had been completed....

Yad Vashem Archives, O-25/46.

* Extract from the Polish Socialist newspaper *Robotnik* ("The Worker"), May 1, 1943.
** *Zwiazek Walki Zbrojnej* — Armed Struggle Association, the name of the organization which preceded the AK.

152

"GHETTO RESISTANCE SEEN CORRECTLY," FROM THE POLISH UNDERGROUND PRESS *

The resistance of the Jews at the time of the final liquidation of the Warsaw ghetto was not, as some of the Underground press reported, collective resistance indicating a certain change in the attitude of the remaining Jews. If the great majority of the Jews of Europe remained entirely passive when they were killed, so the remnant, in their racially based materialism, have remained without any motivation to resist. Only a tiny fraction of some tens of thousands of Jews remaining in Warsaw, about 10 percent, joined the struggle under Communist influence. The Jews who resisted were not those registered in the ghetto, they were the "wild" residents of the ghetto. As against this, the registered Jews, those who report for work, took no part in the operation and surrendered to the Germans in great numbers, and were taken by them according to the old system to the new slaughter center at Majdanek.

The resistance and the supply of arms to a population of tens of thousands in the ghetto was organized and carried out by the Bund and the Communists. These were elements which showed the most hostile attitudes towards the Poles during the period of the occupation, and they prepared themselves within the framework of Communist organizations for a blood-bath directed against the Poles during the crucial transitional period.

According to the Communist plan the ghetto was to have been used as a spur for an uprising at too early a time, which the PPR* is seeking to bring about. There were Communist printing presses for a long time in the ghetto, there were arms depots and Communist staff groups, and from there Soviet officers directed diversionary actions.

In view of this fact we may evaluate the Jewish resistance as a positive element, for it caused the premature liquidation of one of the armed positions of the Communists...

Yad Vashem Archives, O-25/1.

* From the Bulletin of the AK intelligence group, *Ajencja A*, May 15, 1943,
** PPR — *Polska Partia Robotnicza* — Polish Workers' Party (Communist Party).

153

MESSENGER FROM THE POLISH UNDERGROUND ON TALKS WITH JEWISH UNDERGROUND LEADERS IN WARSAW

"Tell the Jewish leaders that this is no case for politics or tactics. Tell them that the earth must be shaken to its foundations, the world must be aroused. Perhaps then it will wake up, understand, perceive. Tell them that they must find the strength and courage to make sacrifices as painful as the fate of my dying people, and as unique. This is what they do not understand. German aims and methods are without precedent in history. The democracies must react in a way that is also without precedent, choose unheard-of methods as an answer. If not, their victory will be only partial, only a military victory. Their methods will not preserve what the enemy includes in his progress of destruction. Their methods will not preserve us..."

"You ask me what plan of action I suggest to the Jewish leaders. Tell them to go to all the important English and American offices and agencies. Tell them not to leave until they have obtained guarantees that a way has been decided upon to save the Jews. Let them accept no food or drink, let them die a slow death while the world is looking on. Let them die. This may shake the conscience of the world...."

"This we did not intend to tell you, but I want you to know it. We do not demand such sacrifices from our leaders abroad out of cruelty. We expect to make them here ourselves. The ghetto is going to go up in flames. We are not going to die in slow torment, but fighting. We will declare war on Germany — the most hopeless declarations of war that has ever been made..."

J. Karsky, *Story of a Secret State,* Boston 1944, pp. 327-328.

154

THE LAST LETTER FROM SZMUL ZYGIELBOJM, THE BUND REPRESENTATIVE WITH THE POLISH NATIONAL COUNCIL IN EXILE *

May 11, 1943

To His Excellency
The President of the Republic of Poland
Wladyslaw Raczkiewicz
Prime Minister
General Wladyslaw Sikorski

Mr. President,
Mr. Prime Minister,

I am taking the liberty of addressing to you, Sirs, these my last words, and through you to the Polish Government and the people of Poland, and to the governments and people of the Allies, and to the conscience of the whole world:

The latest news that has reached us from Poland makes it clear beyond any doubt that the Germans are now murdering the last remnants of the Jews in Poland with unbridled cruelty. Behind the walls of the ghetto the last act of this tragedy is now being played out.

SZMUL M. ZYGIELBOJM
członek Rady Narodowej R.P.

11 maja 1943   12, PORCHESTER SQUARE,
                          LONDON, W.2

Do Pana Prezydenta R.P.
      Władysława RACZKIEWICZA,
Do Pana Prezesa Rady Ministrów
      Generała Władysława SIKORSKIEGO?

Panie Prezydencie,
Panie Premierze.

Pozwalam sobie kierować do Panów ostatnie moje słowa,a przez Panów ●─do Rządu i społeczeństwa polskiego,do Rządów i Narodów państw sprzymierzonych,do sumienia świata:

Z ostatnich wiadomości z Kraju wynika bez żadnych wątpliwości,że Niemcy z całym bezwzględnym okrócieństwem mordują już obecnie resztki Żydów w Polsce.Zamurami ghett odbywa się obecnie ostatni akt niebywałej w dziejach tragedji.

Odpowiedzialność za zbrodnię wymordowania całej narodowości żydowskiej w Polsce spada przedewszystkiem na sprawców,ale pośrednio obciąża ona również ludzkość całą,Narody i Rządy Państw Sprzymierzonych,które do dziś dnia nie zdobyły się na żaden czyn konkretny w celu ukrócenia tej zbrodni.Przez bierne przypatrywanie się temu mordowi miljonów bezbronnych i zmaltretowanych dzieci,kobiet i mężczyzn, stały się jego współwinowajcami.

Muszę też stwierdzić,że,aczkolwiek Rząd Polski w bardzo dużym stopniu przyczynił się do poruszenia opinji świata,jednak nie dostatecznie,jednak nie zdobył się na nic takiego nadzwyczajnego,co by odpowiadało rozmiarom dramatu,dokonywującego-się w Kraju.

Z blisko 3 i pół miljona Żydów polskich i około 700.000 Żydów deportowanych do Polski z innych krajów,żyło jeszcze w kwietniu tego roku,według doniesień oficjalnych kierownictwa podziemnego 'Bundu',przesłanych nam przez Delegata Rządu,około 300,000. A mord trwa nadal bez przerwy.

Milczeć nie mogę i żyć nie mogę gdy giną resztki ludu żydowskiego w Polsce,którego reprezentantem jestem.

Towarzysze moi w ghecie warszawskim zginęli z bronią w ręku, w ostatnim porywie bohaterskim.

Nie było mi dane zginąć tak jak oni,razem z nimi.Ale należę do nich,do ich grobów masowych.

Przez śmierć swą pragnę wyrazić najgłębszy protest przeciwko bezczynności z jaką świat się przypatruje i pozwala lud żydowski wytępić.Wiem jak mało znaczy życie ludzkie,szczególnie dzisiaj.Ale skoro nie potrafiłem tego dokonać za życia,może śmiercią swą przyczynię się do wyrwania z obojętności tych,którzy mogą i powinni działać by teraz jeszcze,w ostatniej bodaj chwili,uratować od niechybnej zagłady te garstkę Żydów Polskich,jaka jeszcze żyje.

Życie moje należy do ludu żydowskiego w Polsce,więc je daję. Pragnę by ta garstka,która ostała się jeszcze z kilkumiljonowego żydowstwa polskiego,dożyła wraz z masami polskimi wyzwolenia,by mogła oddychać w Kraju i w świecie wolności i sprawiedliwości socjalizmu,za wszystkie swe męki i cierpienia nieludzkie.A wierzę, że taka właśnie Polska powstanie i że taki właśnie świat nastąpi.

Ufam,że Pan Prezydent i Pan Premier skierują skierują powyższe moje słowa do wszystkich tych,dla których przeznaczone są,i że Rząd Polski natychmiast rozpocznie odpowiednia akcje na terenie dyplomatycznym i propagandowym,ażeby jednak tę resztkę żyjących jeszcze Żydów polskich uratować przed zagładą.

Żegnam wszystkich i wszystko co
mi było drogie i co kochałem.

[signature]

The last letter sent by Szmul Zygielbojm, the Bund representative with the Polish National Council in Exile, before his suicide, May 11, 1943

The responsibility for the crime of the murder of the whole Jewish nationality in Poland rests first of all on those who are carrying it out, but indirectly it falls also upon the whole of humanity, on the peoples of the Allied nations and on their governments, who up to this day have not taken any real steps to halt this crime. By looking on passively upon this murder of defenseless millions — tortured children, women and men — they have become partners to the responsibility.

I am obliged to state that although the Polish Government contributed largely to the arousing of public opinion in the world, it still did not do enough. It did not do anything that was not routine, that might have been appropriate to the dimensions of the tragedy taking place in Poland.

Of close to 3.5 million Polish Jews and about 700,000 Jews who had been deported to Poland from other countries, there were, according to the official figures of the Bund transmitted by the Representative of the Government,** only 300,000 still alive in April of this year. And the murder continues without end.

I cannot continue to live and to be silent while the remnants of Polish Jewry, whose representative I am, are being murdered. My comrades in the Warsaw Ghetto fell with arms in their hands in the last, heroic battle. I was not permitted to fall like them, together with them, but I belong with them, to their mass grave.

By my death I wish to give expression to my most profound protest against the inaction in which the world watches and permits the destruction of the Jewish people.

I know that there is no great value to the life of a man, especially today. But since I did not succeed in achieving it in my lifetime, perhaps I shall be able by my death to contribute to the arousing from lethargy of those who could and must act in order that even now, perhaps at the last moment, the handful of Polish Jews who are still alive can be saved from certain destruction.

My life belongs to the Jewish people of Poland, and therefore I hand it over to them now. I yearn that the remnant that has

remained of the millions of Polish Jews may live to see liberation
together with the Polish masses, and that it shall be permitted
to breathe freely in Poland and in a world of freedom and
socialist justice, in compensation for the inhuman suffering and
torture inflicted on them. And I believe that such a Poland
will arise and such a world will come about. I am certain that
the President and the Prime Minister will send out these words
of mine to all those to whom they are addressed, and that
the Polish Government will embark immediately on diplomatic
action and explanation of the situation, in order to save the
living remnant of the Polish Jews from destruction.

I take leave of you with greetings,
from everybody, and from everything that was dear to me and that
I loved.

S. Zygielbojm

Yad Vashem Archives, O-55.

* Zygielbojm committed suicide early on the morning of May 12, 1943.
** Authorized representative with full powers in the Polish Underground
on behalf of the Polish Government-in-Exile in London.

155

APPEAL BY THE POLISH UNDERGROUND ASSOCIATION FOR AID TO THE JEWS, ZEGOTA, ASKING FOR HELP IN HIDING JEWS AND FOR THE PUNISHMENT OF TRAITORS

Poles!

The German murderer is trying to tell the world that it was
we who set fire to the Warsaw Ghetto and we who murdered
Jews, and the part played by the German soldiers in this crime
is called "armed intervention."

We and our children, who are suffering all the terror of
bloody occupation and are unable at present to defend ourselves,

could not give the Jews effective aid in their struggle at this time of crisis.

No Pole who is faithful to Christian morality has taken part or will take part in this terrible crime. In the record of glowing deeds of heroism performed by Underground Poland will be engraved, no less than other deeds, deeds of heroism in the saving of people from the Hitlerite beast.

The late Prime Minister of the Polish Republic in London, General Sikorski, in branding the unprecedented German crimes before the world, sent a message of gratitude to the Fatherland for its fine stand and for the help it is giving to the Jews in their terrible situation.

The leadership of the civil struggle and the special courts are already sentencing to death traitors and the extortioners who give away Jews to the German hangmen, and soon the courts of the Free Polish Republic will carry out a full measure of justice against such individuals.

Polish Independence Organizations

Warsaw, September 1943

W. Bartoszewski and Z. Lewinowna, eds., *Ten jest z ojczyzny mojej — Polacy z pomoca Zydom 1939-1945*, Cracow, 1969², p. 951. (English version: *Righteous Among the Nations: How Poles Helped the Jews, 1939-1945*, London, 1969.)

156

EXTRACT FROM A POLISH WOMAN'S * DIARY IN WARSAW

June 7, [1943]

... When they both had left the house, Henryk stole out through the window in order not to have to cross the yard... He returned the same way from the barber's, but a *Volksdeutsche* woman called Podgorska watched Henryk from an upper balcony as he stole in and out. As it turned out later, she had long suspected Teresa of harboring a Jew. She ran at once to the Gendarmerie post and within a few minutes the house was surrounded. The Gendarmes broke open the door and found only Henryk. They beat him but he said nothing. He pretended he was mute. They waited for the owner of the apartment.

The occupants of the house decided to warn Teresa with the help of their children. When she learned what had happened she returned home instead of escaping. It had seemed that she was an ordinary and rather empty-headed person, but she proved to be a courageous girl. It had seemed to her that if she gave evidence that she had known Henryk for a number of years and believed him to be an "Aryan" she would be able to save him. She did not think about herself. When she entered, Henryk, who was bleeding badly, gave her to understand that he had said nothing. An investigation was begun to find out who he was and why he did not speak. She explained: "He must have been frightened." She also explained that she had known him for two years and that he was a Pole. She was asked why he had climbed out through the window, and she replied that they had agreed that he would do so when she was not at home. One of the Germans then gave an order, without hesitating, to examine Henryk in a brutal manner in Teresa's presence. They were both taken away. Henryk was killed. Teresa was saved with great effort by *Volksdeutsche* relations who had connections. She was sent to a concentration camp.

W. Bartoszewski and Z. Lewinowna, eds., *Ten jest z ojczyzny mojej — Polacy z pomoca Zydom 1939-1945*, Cracow, 1969[2], pp. 589-590.

* Sabina Dluzniewski.

157

"SHMALTSOVNIKES" — EXPLOITATION OF JEWS LIVING IN DISGUISE AS POLISH CHRISTIANS *

The name derives from the word *"shmalts"* (chicken fat). These people used to approach their victims with the words "Give me [money] for *shmalts"* — a kind of euphemism for their ugly trade. This was a terrible plague for the Jews who lived on the Aryan side. Apart from the deadly fear of the men of the Gestapo, the SS men and other Angels of Destruction, whom it was possible to recognize from afar, there was another form of inquisition which lay in ambush for these latter-day Marranos. It came in the person of the scum of Polish humanity, who made a business for themselves of Jewish lives. These *"shmaltsovnikes"* [*"shmalts* people"] were organized in whole gangs; hundreds busied themselves with this ugly occupation: to look for, recognize and catch those unfortunates who escaped from the ghetto and lived with Aryan documents, forced to live the life of genuine Catholics. The *"shmaltsovnikes"* sucked the last drops from them, and if they did not [pay] — they handed them over to the bestial Germans. . . .

This scum recruited itself from various strata of the population: former school-mates could usually recognize the Jewish comrades with whom they had studied together at school or university; neighbors recognized Jews who had lived together with them in one courtyard or one house; merchants, traders, shopkeepers recognized those Jews who handed over, "sold" their businesses and apartments to them when they were forced to move away into the ghetto; Polish policemen and officials who knew the Jews well from before [the war] "recognized" them now, armed with all the powers of the new rulers and always at their service; and many others. All of these blackmailed the wretched Jews who were condemned to death, and held the sword of the Angel of Death over their heads at all times.

This was a many-branched organization spread over the whole city section by section. Each group watched the victims in their quarter; they waited at the gates of the ghetto searching with greedy eyes for suspicious [passers-by] in the street, the tramway or the train — they pursued their every step, and ruined and embittered the life of such a one. Once they laid hold on such a victim it was not easy for him to escape from their clutches. . . .

We appealed many times to the organizations of the Polish Underground, and demanded that they take steps against the *"shmaltsovnikes,"* that they should treat them, too, as common agents and Nazi collaborators, whom they punished with death. The Underground Press often published reports from the organizations concerning the trials of persons who worked with the Germans, helping them in one way or another; there were reports of death sentences carried out on such persons. Warnings were printed several times against the actions of the *"shmaltsovnikes"* against Jews; but there was not a single trial of any such person, and they suffered no penalty. The Polish Underground, with its wide network of organizations did not consider it to be its task, it paid no attention to our warnings and demands that they take up the fight against the *"shmaltsovnikes"* as a part of their program. . .

B. Goldstein, *Finf yor in Varshever geto,* New York, 1947, pp. 369-372. (English version: B. Goldstein, *Five Years in the Warsaw Ghetto,* New York, 1961.)

* Extract from a book of reminiscences by Bernard Goldstein, one of the leading activists in the Bund in the Warsaw Underground.

158

SS STATISTICS ON THE "FINAL SOLUTION OF THE JEWISH QUESTION," MARCH 23, 1943 *

V. *Evacuation of the Jews*

...

At least in the area of the Reich the evacuation of the Jews has taken the place of the emigration of the Jews. Following the ban on Jewish emigration from Fall 1941 [the evacuation] was prepared on a large scale and carried out to a far-reaching extent throughout the area of the Reich in 1942. In the balance sheet of Jewry (*Bilanz des Judentums*) it appears as "Emigration."

According to the figures of the Reich Security Main Office (*Reichssicherheitshauptamt*) up to January 1, 1943, the following moves took place:

From the *Altreich*** and Sudetenland	100,516 Jews
From the *Ostmark* [Austria]	47,555 „
From the Protectorate	69,677 „

Total	217,748 Jews

These figures include Jews evacuated to the Old-Age Ghetto in Theresienstadt.

The total of these evacuations from the area of the Reich, including the eastern territories, and beyond them in the area of German control and influence in Europe, from October 1939 or later, and up to December 31, 1942, were as follows:

1. Evacuation of Jews from Baden and the Palatinate (Pfalz) to France ... ...   6,504 Jews
2. Evacuation of Jews from the Reich, including the Protectorate and the District of Bialystok to the *East* ... ...   170,642 „
3. Evacuation of Jews from the Reich and the Protectorate to *Theresienstadt* ... ...   87,193 „

4. Transportation of Jews from the eastern
   provinces to eastern Russia   1,449,692   ,,
   [Numbers] who passed through the camps
   in the Government-General   1,274,166   ,,
   Through the camps in the Warthegau ...   145,301   ,,

5. Evacuation of Jews from other countries:

   France (insofar as it was occupied before
        November 10, 1942) ..   ..   41,911 Jews
   Netherlands   38,571   ,,
   Belgium   16,886   ,,
   Norway   532   ,,
   Slovakia   56,691   ,,
   Croatia   4,927   ,,

Total evacuations (including Theresienstadt and
Special Treatment — *Sonderbehandlung*)   ...   1,873,549   ,,
   Without Theresienstadt   1,786,356   ,,

6. To this must be added, according to the
   figures of the Reich Security Main Office,
   the evacuation of   633,300   ,,
   from the Russian territories, including the
   former Baltic countries, from the start of
   the Eastern Campaign.

These figures do not include the inmates of ghettos and
concentration camps.

The evacuations from Slovakia and Croatia were carried out
by these states themselves.

VI. *The Jews in the Ghettos*

These include:

1. The Old-Age Ghetto *Theresienstadt,* to which were sent
   altogether   ...   .   87,193 Jews
   of these, from the Reich   47,471   ,,
   (*Ostmark* 14,222)
   of these, from the Protectorate   39,722   ,,

The total number of Jewish inmates at the beginning of the
year 1943 was :   49,392
   of these, German subjects   24,313
   Protectorate   25,079

The reduction in numbers was due mainly to deaths. In addition
to *Theresienstadt* there were a number of smaller Jewish old-age
and invalid homes within the area of the Reich, but these were
not considered either ghettos or evacuation centers.

2. At the beginning of 1943 there were 87,180 Jews in the Lodz
Ghetto, of whom 83,133 were former Polish citizens.

3. On December 31, 1942, the great majority of Jews in the
Government-General were housed in the remnants of ghettos.
The figures given or estimated are:

District	*No. of Jews*
Cracow	37,000
Radom	29,400
Lublin	20,000 (estimate)
Warsaw	50,000
Lvov	161,514
Total for Government-General	297,914***

NO—5194.

* Prepared by Richard Korherr, head of the Statistics Department in
Himmler's office.
** Germany before 1938.
*** The total number of Jews in these areas at the beginning of the war
had been about 2 million.

159

FROM THE FINAL REPORT BY KATZMANN, COMMANDER OF THE SS AND POLICE IN THE DISTRICT OF GALICIA, ON "THE SOLUTION OF THE JEWISH PROBLEM" IN GALICIA

Reich Secret Document

The SS and Police Leader (*SS-und Polizeiführer*) in the District
of Galicia   Lvov, June 30, 1943
   Re: Solution of the Jewish Question in Galicia.
   Reference: Attached Report.
   Enclosure: 1 Report (3 copies)
              1 Copy (bound)
To the
Higher SS and Police Leader East
SS *Obergruppenführer* and General of the Police
Krüger
Cracow
Enclosed I forward the first copy of the final report on the
Solution of the Jewish Question in the District of Galicia, and
request that you may acknowledge it.

Katzmann
SS *Gruppenführer*
and *Generalleutnant* of Police

Solution of the Jewish Problem in the District of Galicia

Owing to the phrase "Galician Jew," Galicia was probably
the small corner on earth most widely known and most frequently
mentioned in connection with the Jews. Here they lived in
great, compact multitudes, forming a world of their own, from
which the rest of world Jewry renewed its population continuously.
Jews were to be met with in their hundreds of thousands in
all parts of Galicia.

According to old statistics dating back to 1931, there were then about 502,000 Jews. This number is unlikely to have diminished in the period between 1931 and the summer of 1941. There are no precise figures for the number of Jews present when the German troops marched into Galicia. The figure of 350,000 was given by the Judenräte of Galicia for the end of the year 1941. That this figure was incorrect can be seen from the records concerning evacuation appended to this report. The city of Lvov alone housed about 160,000 Jews in the months of July-August 1941....

Our first measure was to identify every Jew by means of a white armlet with the blue Star of David. In accordance with a decree issued by the Governor General, the Interior Administration was responsible for the identifying and registration of the Jews, as well as setting up the Judenräte.[1] * Our task as police was first of all to fight effectively against the immense black market operated by the Jews all over the District. Energetic measures also had to be taken against idlers loafing around and against do-nothings.

The best means for this was the establishment of Forced Labor Camps by the SS and Police Leader. There was, first of all, work on the urgently needed reconstruction of [highway] Dg. 4., which was extremely important for the entire southern section of the Front and which was in catastrophically bad condition. On October 15, 1941, a start was made on the building of camps along the railroad tracks, and after a few weeks, despite considerable difficulties, 7 camps had been put up, containing 4,000 Jews. More camps soon followed, so that in a very short period of time the completion of 15 such camps could be reported to the Higher SS and Police Leader. About 20,000 Jewish laborers passed through these camps in the course of time. Despite all conceivable difficulties that turned up on this project, about 160 km. have now been completed.

At the same time all other Jews who were fit for work were registered by the Labor Offices and directed to useful work. Both when the Jews were identified with the Star of David and when they were registered by the Labor Offices, the first indications were noted that the Jews were trying to evade the orders issued by the Authorities. The control measures carried out as a result led to thousands of arrests. It became increasingly apparent that the Civil Administration was not in a position to move the Jewish problem to an even reasonably satisfactory solution. Because repeated attempts of the City Administration of Lvov, for instance, to move the Jews into a Jewish quarter, failed, this question, too, was solved by the SS and Police Leader and his organizations. This measure had become all the more urgent because in the winter of 1941 centers of typhus infection had appeared all over the city, endangering not only the local population but, even more, the German troops either stationed in the city or passing through. . . .

Owing to the peculiarity that almost 90 percent of the artisans in Galicia consisted of Jews, the problem to be solved could only be carried out gradually, as an immediate removal of the Jews would not have been in the interest of the war economy. Not that one could observe that those Jews who were working made any special contribution by their work. Their place of work was often only a means to an end for them: firstly, to escape the sharper measures taken against the Jews; and, secondly, to be able to carry out their black-market dealings without interruption. Only continuous police intervention could prevent these activities. Draconic measures had to be introduced by us after it was noted in increasing numbers of cases that the Jews had succeeded in making themselves indispensable to their employers by providing goods in short supply, etc. It is very sad to have to note that the wildest black-market deals with the Jews were made by Germans who were brought here, and in particular those in the so-called "operating firms" (*Einsatszfirmen*) or the "ill-reputed trustees" (*berüchtigte Treuhänder*), both of which operated Jewish firms taken from their owners. Cases were known where Jews seeking to obtain some kind of working certificate not only did not ask for pay from their employers but paid regularly themselves. In addition, Jewish "organizing" [2] * on behalf of their "employers" reached such catastrophic dimensions that energetic action had to be taken in the interest of the reputation of the German people.

As the Administration was not in the position to overcome this chaos, and proved weak, the whole issue of Jewish labor was simply taken over by the SS and Police Leader. The existing Jewish Labor Offices, which were staffed by hundreds of Jews, were dissolved. All work certificates issued by firms and official employers were declared invalid, and the cards given to Jews by the Labor Offices revalidated by the Police.

In the course of this *Aktion* thousands of Jews were again caught in possession of forged certificates or labor certificates obtained fraudulently by means of all kinds of excuses. These Jews were also sent for special treatment (*Sonderbehandlung*). The Wehrmacht authorities in particular aided the Jewish parasites by issuing special certificates without proper control... There were cases where Jews were caught with from 10 to 20 such certificates. When Jews were arrested in the course of further checks, most of the employers felt obliged to attempt to intervene in favor of the Jews. This was often done in a manner that can only be described as deeply shameful. . . .

Despite all these measures for the regulation of Jewish labor, a start was made in April 1942 on the evacuation of Jews [3] * from the District of Galicia, and this was carried out steadily.

When the Higher SS and Police Leader again intervened in the Jewish question in general on November 10, 1942, and a Police Order was issued for the formation of Jewish quarters, 254,989 Jews had already been evacuated or resettled. Since the Higher SS and Police Leader gave further instructions to accelerate the total evacuation of the Jews, further considerable work was necessary in order to catch those Jews who were, for the time being, to be left in the armaments factories. These remaining Jews were declared labor prisoners of the Higher SS and Police Leader and held either in the factories themselves or in camps erected for this purpose. For Lvov itself a large camp [4] * was erected on the outskirts, which holds 8,000 Jewish labor prisoners at the present time. The agreement made with the Wehrmacht concerning employment and treatment of the labor prisoners was set down in writing...

In the meantime further evacuation was carried out vigorously, with the result that by June 23, 1943, all Jewish quarters could be dissolved. Apart from the Jews in camps under the control of the SS and Police Leader, the District of Galicia is thus *free of Jews (judenfrei)*.

Individual Jews occasionally picked up by the Order Police or the Gendarmerie were sent for special treatment. Altogether, *434,329 Jews* had been evacuated up to June 27, 1943... [This is followed by a list of 21 camps in which there were still 21,156 Jews.]

Together with the evacuation *Aktionen* Jewish property was collected. Valuables were secured and handed over to the Special Staff "Reinhard." Apart from furniture and large quantities of textiles, etc., the following were confiscated and delivered to Special Staff "Reinhard":

As of June 30, 1943 :

25.580	kg.	copper coins
53.190	„	nickel coins
97.581	„	gold coins
82.600	„	silver chains
6.640	„	chains, gold
4.326.780	„	broken silver
167.740	„	silver coins
18.490	„	iron coins
20.050	„	brass coins
20.952	„	wedding rings — gold
22.740	„	pearls
11.730	„	gold teeth — bridges
28.200	„	powder compacts — silver or other metal
44.655	„	broken gold
482.900	„	silver flatware
343.100	„	cigarette cases — silver and other metal

339

20.880 kg.	rings, gold, with stones
39.917 „	brooches, earrings, etc.
18.02 „	rings, silver
6.166 „	pocket watches, various
3.133 „	pocket watches, silver
3.425 „	wrist watches — silver
1.256 „	wrist watches — gold
2.892 „	pocket watches — gold
68	cameras
98	binoculars
7	stamp collections — complete
5	travel baskets of loose stamps
100.550 „	3 sacks of rings, jewelry — not genuine
3.290 „	1 box corals
0.460 „	1 case corals
0.280 „	1 case corals
7.495 „	1 suitcase of fountain pens and propelling pencils
	1 travel basket of fountain pens and propelling pencils
	1 suitcase of cigarette lighters
	1 suitcase of pocket knives
	1 trunk of watch-parts
Currency :	Bank Notes and Metal [this is followed by a detailed list of coins and bank notes of various kinds]. . . .

There were also other immense difficulties during the *Aktionen* as the Jews tried to avoid evacuation by all possible means. They not only tried to escape, and concealed themselves in the most improbable places, drainage canals, chimneys, even in sewage pits, etc. They barricaded themselves in catacombs of passages, in cellars made into bunkers, in holes in the earth, in cunningly contrived hiding places, in attics and sheds, inside furniture, etc.

As the number of Jews still remaining decreased, their resistance became the greater. They used weapons of all types for their defense, and in particular those of Italian origin. The Jews bought these Italian weapons from Italian soldiers stationed in the district in exchange for large sums in zlotys....

Subterranean bunkers were discovered which had cleverly concealed entrances, some in the flats, and some out of doors. In most cases the entrance to the bunker was only just large enough for one person to slip through. The entrances to the bunkers were so well hidden that they could not be found if one did not know where to look....

Owing to increasingly grave reports of the growing arming of the Jews, the sharpest possible measures were taken for the elimination of Jewish banditry in all parts of the District of Galicia in the last two weeks of June 1943. Special measures were needed for the breaking up of the Jewish quarter in Lvov, where the bunkers described above had been installed. In order to avoid losses to German forces, brutal measures had to be taken from the outset; several houses were blown up or destroyed by fire. The astonishing result was that in place of the 12,000 Jews registered a total of 20,000 were caught....

L—18.

1 * See Documents 74, 75, 82.
2 * The reference is to the payment of bribes.
3 * They were sent to death camps.
4 * Janowska Camp was a forced-labor and concentration camp, established in October 1941 in Ianowska Street in Lvov, where many Jews were murdered.

160

HITLER BANS PUBLIC REFERENCE TO THE "FINAL SOLUTION OF THE JEWISH QUESTION," JULY 11, 1943

National-Socialist German Workers' Party
Party Secretariat

Head of the Party Secretariat
Führer Headquarters, July 11, 1943

Circular No. 33/43 g.
Re : *Treatment of the Jewish Question*

On instructions from the Führer I make known the following :
Where the Jewish Question is brought up in public, there may be no discussion of a future overall solution (*Gesamtlösung*).
It may, however, be mentioned that the Jews are taken in groups for appropriate labor purposes.

signed M. Bormann

Distribution : *Reichsleiter*
Gauleiter
Group leaders
File Reference : Treatment/Jews

NO—2710.

Nationalsozialistische ☒ Deutsche Arbeiterpartei

Partei-Kanzlei

Der Leiter der Partei-Kanzlei   Führerhauptouartier, den 11.7.1943

R u n d s c h r e i b e n Nr. 33/43 g.
■■■

Betrifft: Behandlung der Judenfrage.

Im Auftrage des Führers teile ich mit:

Bei der öffentlichen Behandlung der Judenfrage muss
jede Erörterung einer künftigen Gesamtlösung unterblei-
ben.

Es kann jedoch davon gesprochen werden, dass die Juden
geschlossen zu zweckentsprechendem Arbeitseinsatz her-
angezogen werden.

                         gez. M. B o r m a n n

F.d.R.:

Verteiler: Reichsleiter,
           Gauleiter,
           Verbändeführer.

Schlagwortkartei: Behandlung / Juden.

Bormann's letter stating Hitler's ban on any public reference to the
"final solution of the Jewish question," July 11, 1943

343

161

FROM A SPEECH BY HIMMLER BEFORE SENIOR SS OFFICERS IN POZNAN, OCTOBER 4, 1943

Evacuation of the Jews

. . .

I also want to speak to you here, in complete frankness, of a really grave chapter. Amongst ourselves, for once, it shall be said quite openly, but all the same we will never speak about it in public. Just as we did not hesitate on June 30, 1934,* to do our duty as we were ordered, and to stand comrades who had erred against the wall and shoot them, and we never spoke about it and we never will speak about it. It was a matter of natural tact that is alive in us, thank God, that we never talked about it amongst ourselves, that we never discussed it. Each of us shuddered and yet each of us knew clearly that the next time he would do it again if it were an order, and if it were necessary.

I am referring here to the evacuation of the Jews, the extermination of the Jewish people. This is one of the things that is easily said: "The Jewish people are going to be exterminated," that's what every Party member says, "sure, it's in our program, elimination of the Jews, extermination — it'll be done." And then they all come along, the 80 million worthy Germans, and each one has his one decent Jew. Of course, the others are swine, but this one, he is a first-rate Jew. Of all those who talk like that, not one has seen it happen, not one has had to go through with it. Most of you men know what it is like to see 100 corpses side by side, or 500 or 1,000. To have stood fast through this and — except for cases of human weakness — to have stayed decent that has made us hard. This is an unwritten and never-to-be-written page of glory in our history, for we know how difficult it would be for us if today — under bombing raids and the hardships and deprivations of war —

if we were still to have the Jews in every city as secret saboteurs, agitators, and inciters. If the Jews were still lodged in the body of the German nation, we would probably by now have reached the stage of 1916-17.

The wealth they possessed we took from them. I gave a strict order, which has been carried out by SS *Obergruppenführer* Pohl, that this wealth will of course be turned over to the Reich in its entirety. We have taken none of it for ourselves. Individuals who have erred will be punished in accordance with the order given by me at the start, threatening that anyone who takes as much as a single Mark of this money is a dead man. A number of SS men — they are not very many — committed this offense, and they shall die. There will be no mercy. We had the moral right, we had the duty towards our people, to destroy this people that wanted to destroy us. But we do not have the right to enrich ourselves by so much as a fur, as a watch, by one Mark or a cigarette or anything else. We do not want, in the end, because we destroyed a bacillus, to be infected by this bacillus and to die. I will never stand by and watch while even a small rotten spot develops or takes hold. Wherever it may form we will together burn it away. All in all, however, we can say that we have carried out this most difficult of tasks in a spirit of love for our people. And we have suffered no harm to our inner being, our soul, our character. . .

PS—1919.

* The reference is to "the night of the long knives" — murder of Röhm. SA leaders and other purges.

162

LETTER FROM GREISER, GAULEITER AND GOVERNOR OF WARTHELAND TO POHL, CONCERNING THE FATE OF LODZ GHETTO, FEBRUARY 14, 1944

On the occasion of the visit of the RFSS [*Reichsführer* SS] in Poznan yesterday and the day before I had an opportunity to discuss and clarify two questions which concern the area of your work.

The first question is as follows :

The ghetto in Lodz will not be converted into a concentration camp, as was emphasized at the discussion on February 5, held at my office, the Reich Governorate in Poznan, by SS *Oberführer* Baier and SS *Hauptsturmführer* Dr. Volk, who had been sent to my *Gau* (province) by your office. The Order of the RFSS of June 11, 1943, will therefore not be carried out. I have agreed the following with the RF :

1.   The population of the ghetto is to be reduced to a minimum, and only those Jews are to remain who are absolutely required in the interests of the armaments industry;

2.   The ghetto thus remains a *Gau* ghetto of the *Reichsgau* Wartheland;

3.   The reduction of the population will be carried out by the *Sonderkommando* of SS *Hauptsturmführer* Bothmann, which operated in the area previously. The RF will issue an Order instructing SS *Hauptsturmführer* Bothmann and his *Sonderkommando* to leave their station in Croatia and be available for service in the Wartheland; *

4.   The disposal and use of the property of the ghetto will remain the responsibility of the *Reichsgau* Wartheland;

5.   After the removal of all the Jews from the ghetto and its demolition, the entire area of the ghetto will become the property of the city of Lodz.

The RF will then give appropriate orders to the Central Trustee's Office for the East (*Haupt-Treuhandstelle Ost*).

May I request you to convey your proposals on this subject to me.

Greiser

NO—519.

* Bothmann and his unit set up and operated the extermination camp at Chelmno in the Wartheland.

163

FROM NOTES MADE BY KURT GERSTEIN, AN ENGINEER WORKING FOR THE SS, ON THE EXTERMINATION CAMP AT BELZEC *

...In Lublin, SS *Gruppenführer* Globocnik was waiting for us. He said : This is one of the most highly secret matters there are, perhaps the most secret. Anybody who speaks about it is shot dead immediately. Two talkative people died yesterday. Then he explained to us that, at the present moment — August 17, 1942 — there were the following installations :

1. Belzec, on the Lublin-Lvov road, in the sector of the Soviet Demarcation Line. Maximum per day : 15,000 persons (I saw it!).
2. Sobibor, I am not familiar with the exact situation, I did not visit it. 20,000 persons per day.
3. Treblinka, 120 km. NNE of Warsaw, 25,000 per day, saw it!
4. Majdanek, near Lublin, which I saw when it was being built.

Globocnik said: You will have very large quantities of clothes to disinfect, 10 or 20 times as much as the "Textiles Collection," which is only being carried out in order to camouflage the origin of the Jewish, Polish, Czech and other items of clothing. Your second job is to convert the gas-chambers, which have up to now been operated with exhaust gases from an old Diesel engine, to a more poisonous and quicker means, cyanide. But the

Führer and Himmler, who were here on August 15, the day before yesterday, that is, gave orders that I am myself to accompany all persons who visit the installations. Professor Pfannenstiel replied "But what does the Führer say?" Then Globocnik, who is now Higher SS and Police Leader in Trieste on the Adriatic Coast, said "The whole *Aktion* must be carried out much faster." Ministerial Director Dr. Herbert Lindner [Linden] of the Ministry of the Interior suggested "Would it not be better to incinerate the bodies instead of burying them? Another generation might perhaps think differently about this?" Then Globocnik, "But, Gentlemen, if we should ever be succeeded by so cowardly and weak a generation that it does not understand our work, which is so good and so necessary, then, Gentlemen, the whole of National Socialism will have been in vain. On the contrary, one should bury bronze plaques [with the bodies], on which is inscribed that it was we, we who had the courage to complete this gigantic task." Hitler said to this, "Well my good Globocnik, you have said it, and that is my opinion, too."

The next day we moved on to Belzec. There is a separate little station with two platforms, at the foot of the hill of yellow standstone, due north cf the Lublin-Lvov road and rail line. To the south of the station, near the main road, there are several office buildings with the inscription "Belzec Office of the *Waffen*-SS" [Military Unit of the SS]. Globocnik introduced me to SS *Hauptsturmführer* Obermeyer from Pirmasens, who showed me the installations very much against his will. There were no dead to be seen that day, but the stench in the whole area, even on the main road, was pestilent. Next to the small station there was a large barrack labelled "Dressing Room," with a window that said "Valuables," and also a hall with 100 "Barbers Chairs." Then there was a passage 150 m. long, in the open, enclosed with barbed wire on either side, and signs inscribed "To the Baths and Inhalation Installations." In front of us there was a house, the bath house, and to the right and left large concrete flower pots with geraniums or other flowers. After climbing a few steps there were three rooms each, on

348

the right and on the left. They looked like garages, 4 by 5 m. and 1.90 m. high. At the back, out of sight, there were doors of wood. On the roof there was a Star of David made of copper. The front of the building bore a notice "Heckenholt Institution." That is all I saw that afternoon.

Next morning, a few minutes before 7 o'clock, I was told that the first train would arrive in 10 minutes. And in fact the first train from Lvov arrived a few minutes later. There were 45 carriages with 6,700 persons, of whom 1,450 were already dead on arrival. Through small openings closed with barbed wire one could see yellow, frightened children, men and women. The train stopped, and 200 Ukrainians, who were forced to perform this service, tore open the doors and chased the people from the carriages with whips. Then instructions were given through a large loud-speaker : The people are to take off all their clothes out of doors — and a few of them in the barracks — including artificial limbs and glasses. Shoes must be tied in pairs with a little piece of string handed out by a small four-year-old Jewish boy. All valuables and money are to be handed in at the window marked "Valuables," without any document or receipt being given. The women and girls must then go to the barber, who cuts off their hair with one or two snips. The hair disappears into large potato sacks, "to make something special for the submarines, to seal them and so on," the duty SS *Unterscharführer* explained to me.

Then the march starts : Barbed wire to the right and left and two dozen Ukrainians with rifles at the rear. They came on, led by an exceptionally pretty girl. I myself was standing with Police Captain Wirth in front of the death chambers. Men, women, children, infants, people with amputated legs, all naked, completely naked, moved past us. In one corner there is a whimsical SS man who tells these poor people in an unctuous voice, "Nothing at all will happen to you. You must just breathe deeply, that strengthens the lungs; this inhalation is necessary because of the infectious diseases, it is good disinfection!" When somebody asks what their fate will be, he explains that the men will of course have to work, building streets and houses. But the women will not have to work. If they want to, they can help in the house or the kitchen. A little glimmer of hope flickers once more in some of these poor people, enough to make them march unresisting into the death chambers. But most of them understand what is happening; the smell reveals their fate! Then they climb up a little staircase and see the truth. Nursing mothers with an infant at the breast, naked; many children of all ages, naked. They hesitate, but they enter the death chambers, most of them silent, forced on by those behind them, who are driven by the whip lashes of the SS men. A Jewish woman of about 40, with flaming eyes, calls down [revenge] for the blood of her children on the head of the murderers. Police Captain Wirth in person strikes her in the face 5 times with his whip, and she disappears into the gas chamber. . . .

PS—1553.

* Gerstein wrote down his evidence on May 26, 1945.

164

EXTRACT FROM WRITTEN EVIDENCE OF RUDOLF HÖSS, COMMANDER OF THE AUSCHWITZ EXTERMINATION CAMP

In the summer of 1941, I cannot remember the exact date, I was suddenly summoned to the *Reichsführer* SS,* directly by his adjutant's office. Contrary to his usual custom, Himmler received me without his adjutant being present and said in effect :

"The Führer has ordered that the Jewish question be solved once and for all and that we, the SS, are to implement that order.

350

The existing extermination centers in the East are not in a position to carry out the large *Aktionen* which are anticipated. I have therefore earmarked Auschwitz for this purpose, both because of its good position as regards communications and because the area can easily be isolated and camouflaged. At first I thought of calling in a senior SS officer for this job, but I changed my mind in order to avoid difficulties concerning the terms of reference. I have now decided to entrust this task to you. It is difficult and onerous and calls for complete devotion notwithstanding the difficulties that may arise. You will learn further details from *Sturmbannführer* Eichmann of the Reich Security Main Office who will call on you in the immediate future.

The departments concerned will be notified by me in due course. You will treat this order as absolutely secret, even from your superiors. After your talk with Eichmann you will immediately forward to me the plans for the projected installations.

The Jews are the sworn enemies of the German people and must be eradicated. Every Jew that we can lay our hands on is to be destroyed now during the war, without exception. If we cannot now obliterate the biological basis of Jewry, the Jews will one day destroy the German people."

On receiving these grave instructions, I returned forthwith to Auschwitz, without reporting to my superior at Oranienburg.

Shortly afterwards Eichmann came to Auschwitz and disclosed to me the plans for the operations as they affected the various countries concerned. I cannot remember the exact order in which they were to take place. First was to come the eastern part of Upper Silesia and the neighboring parts of Polish territory under German rule, then, depending on the situation, simultaneously Jews from Germany and Czechoslovakia, and finally the Jews from the West : France, Belgium and Holland. He also told me the approximate number of transports that might be expected, but I can no longer remember these.

We discussed the ways and means of effecting the extermination. This could only be done by gassing, since it would have been absolutely impossible to dispose by shooting of the large numbers of people that were expected, and it would have placed too heavy a burden on the SS men who had to carry it out, especially because of the women and children among the victims.

Eichmann told me about the method of killing people with exhaust gases in lorries,** which had previously been used in the East. But there was no question of being able to use this for these mass transports that were due to arrive in Auschwitz. Killing with showers of carbon monoxide while bathing, as was done with mental patients in some places in the Reich, would necessitate too many buildings and it was also very doubtful whether the supply of gas for such a vast number of people would be available. We left the matter unresolved. Eichmann decided to try and find a gas which was in ready supply and which would not entail special installations for its use, and to inform me when he had done so. We inspected the area in order to choose a likely spot. We decided that a peasant farmstead situated in the north-west corner of what later became the third building sector at Birkenau would be the most suitable. It was isolated and screened by woods and hedges, and it was also not far from the railway. The bodies could be placed in long, deep pits dug in the nearby meadows. We had not at that time thought of burning the corpses. We calculated that after gas-proofing the premises then available, it would be possible to kill about 800 people simultaneously with a suitable gas. These figures were borne out later in practice.

Eichmann could not then give me the starting date for the operation because everything was still in the preliminary stages and the *Reichsführer* SS had not yet issued the necessary orders.

Eichmann returned to Berlin to report our conversation to the *Reichsführer* SS.

A few days later I sent to the *Reichsführer* SS by courier a detailed location plan and description of the installation. I have never received an acknowledgement or a decision on

my report. Eichmann told me later that the *Reichsführer* SS
was in agreement with my proposals...

R. Höss, *Commandant of Auschwitz — The Autobiography of Rudolf*
Höss, London, 1961, pp. 206-208.

* Heinrich Himmler.
** See Document 191.

165

EXTRACT FROM THE WRITTEN EVIDENCE BY JACOB WIERNIK ON THE EXTERMINATION CAMP AT TREBLINKA *

...I stood in the line opposite my house in Wolynska Street,
and from there we were taken to Zamenhof Street. The Ukrainians
divided up the loot amongst themselves before our eyes. They
fought amongst themselves, valued and sorted everything. Despite
the great number of people there was silence in the street.
A silent and cruel despair fell upon all. Oh what despair it
was! They photographed us as though we were animals from
before the Flood. There were also some who remained calm.
I myself hoped that we would go home again. I thought they
would check our documents. An order was given, and we moved
off from our places. Woe to us! The naked truth was revealed
before our eyes. Railway cars. Cars that were empty. That
day was a fine, hot summer's day. It seemed as though the
sun was protesting against the injustice. What was the guilt
of our wives, our children, our mothers? What was it? The
sun disappeared behind thick clouds. It is beautiful, warms
and shines and does not wish to witness our suffering and
humiliation.

An order is given to get into the cars. Eighty are pushed
into each car. The way back is sealed off. I had on my body

353

only trousers, a shirt and shoes. A back-pack with other things and high boots had stayed at home. I had prepared it because there were rumors that we would be sent to the Ukraine for work. The train was shunted from one siding to another. I knew this rail junction well and realized that we were staying in the same place. Meanwhile we could hear the Ukrainians amusing themselves, the sound of their shouting and cheerful laughter reaching us. It was becoming increasingly suffocating inside the car, and from minute to minute there was less air to breathe; it was all despair, blackness and horror... With indescribable suffering we finally arrived at Malkinia. We stopped there all night. Ukrainians came into the car and demanded valuables. Everybody gave them up in order in preserve their lives a little while longer.

...In the morning the train moved and we reached Treblinka station. I saw a train that passed us and in it people who were hungry, ragged and half naked. They said something to us but we did not understand them. The day was burning hot. The lack of air was terrible. As a result we were very thirsty. I looked out of the window. The peasants brought water and charged 100 zloty for each bottle. I had no money, apart from 10 gold coins. Also a 2, a 5 and a 10 in silver, with a portrait of the Marshal,** that I had kept as a memento. So I was forced to do without the water. Others bought it. They paid 500 zloty for a kilogram of black bread. I was tortured by thirst until mid-day. Then the future *Hauptsturmführer* came in and picked 10 men who brought us water. I assuaged my thirst a little. An order was given to take out the dead, but there were none. At four in the afternoon the train moved off. We arrived at Treblinka in a few minutes. It was only there that the blinkers dropped from our eyes. Ukrainians with rifles and machine-guns stood on the roofs of the huts. The whole area was strewn with bodies, some dressed and some naked. Their faces were distorted with fear and horror. They were black and swollen. Their eyes were frozen wide open. Their tongues hung out, brains were spattered around and the bodies twisted. There was blood everywhere. Our innocent blood. The blood of our children, our brothers and sisters. The blood of our fathers and mothers. And we are without hope, we realize that we will not escape our fate. . . .

There is an order to get out of the cars. Belongings are to be left behind. We are taken to the yard. There were huts on either side. There were two large notice boards with orders to hand over gold, silver, precious stones and all valuables. Failure to do so would bring the death penalty. On the roofs of the huts were Ukrainians with machine-guns. The women and children were ordered off to the left and the men told to sit down in the yard, on the right. Some distance away from us people were working: they were sorting the belongings taken from the train. I managed to steal over among the workers, and began to work; I suffered the first lash from the whip of a German whom we called Frankenstein. The women and children were told to take off their clothes.

. . . When we carried, or more correctly, dragged, the bodies away we were made to run, and were beaten for the least delay. The dead had been lying there for a long time. They had already begun to decompose. There was a stench of death and decomposition in the air. Worms crawled on the wretched bodies. When we tied on the belts, an arm or a leg would frequently drop off. We also labored on graves for ourselves until dusk, without food or drink. The day was hot, and thirst plagued us greatly. When we reached the huts in the evening each one of us began to search for the people he had known the day before — in vain — they were not to be found, they were no longer among the living. . . .

Shana be-Treblinka (Mi-pi Ed Re'iya) ("A Year in Treblinka by an Eye Witness"), Jerusalem, 1945, pp. 5-14.

* Wiernik took part in the uprising at the Treblinka camp. He succeeded in escaping and reached Warsaw in 1944. He recorded his ~vidence there, and it was first published by the Underground in Poland.
** The reference is to Marshal Jozef Pilsudski.

166

THE REVOLT AT THE SOBIBOR
EXTERMINATION CAMP *

... as though in response to an order, several axes that had been hidden under coats appeared and were brought down on his head. At that moment the convoy from the second camp approached. A few women who were frightened by what they saw began to scream, some even fainted. Some began to run crazily, without thinking and without purpose. In that situation there was no question of organizing or maintaining order, and therefore I shouted at the top of my voice : "Forward, comrades !"

"Forward !" someone echoed behind me on the right.
"For the Fatherland, for Stalin, forward !"

The proud cries came like thunder from clear skies in the death camp. In one moment these slogans united the Jews of Russia, Poland, Holland, Czechoslovakia, Germany. Six hundred men who had been abused and exhausted broke into cries of "Hurrah !" for life and freedom.

The assault on the arms store failed. Machine-gun fire barred our way.

Most of the people who were escaping turned in the direction of the main gate. There, after they finished off the guards, under cover of fire from the rifles that a few of them had, they threw stones and scattered sand in the eyes of the Fascists who stood in their way, broke through the gate and hurried in the direction of the forest.

One group of prisoners turned left. I saw how they attacked the barbed-wire fence. But after they had cleared away this obstacle, they still had to cross a mine-field that was about 15 meters wide. Many of them surely fell here. I turned towards the Officer's House with a group of prisoners; we cut the barbed wire there and so made an opening. The assumption that the area near the Officers' House would not be mined proved correct.

356

Three of our comrades fell near the barbed wire, but it was not clear whether they stepped on mines or were wounded by bullets, as salvoes were fired on us from various directions.

We are already on the far side of the fence, and the mine-field is behind us. We have already gone 100 meters, then another 100... fast, still faster... we must cross the bare open area where we are exposed to the bullets of the murderers... fast, still faster, we must get to the forest, get among the trees, get into shelter... and already we are in the shade of the trees.

I stopped for a moment to catch my breath and cast a glance backwards. Exhausted, with their last strength, running bent over, forwards... we were near the forest. Where is Loka? Where is Shlomo?

*　　　*　　　*

...It is difficult to say for certain how many people escaped from the camp. In any case, it is clear that the great majority of the prisoners escaped. Many fell in the open space that was between the camp and the forest. We were agreed that we should not linger in the forest, but divide up into small groups and go in different directions. The Polish Jews escaped in the direction of Chelm. They were drawn there by their knowledge of the language and the area. We, the Soviets, turned east. The Jews who had come from Holland, France and Germany were particularly helpless. In all the wide area that surrounded the camp there was none with whom they had a common language.

The shots from machine-guns and rifles that rattled behind us from time to time helped us to decide on the direction that we needed. We knew that the shooting came from the camp. The telephone line had been cut, and Franz had no way of calling for help. The echo of the shots became more distant and disappeared.

It was already beginning to get dark when we once more heard shots echoing far away. Probably they came from our pursuers...

We began to march.

From time to time, from one side or the other, we were joined by new people. I questioned all of them whether they had seen Loka or Shlomo. Nobody had seen them.

We emerged from the forest. We walked for 3 kilometers over open fields, until we reached an open canal about 5 or 6 meters wide. The canal was very deep, and it was not possible to cross it on foot. When I tried to walk around it, I observed a group of people at a distance of about 50 meters from us. We dropped flat on the ground and sent out Arkadiosh to reconnoiter. At first he crawled on his stomach, but after a minute he got to his feet and ran up to the people. A few minutes later he was back.

"Sasha, they are some of our people. They found tree trunks by the side of the canal and are crossing on them to the other side. Kalimali is there among them."

That is how we crossed the canal. . . .

A. Peczorski (Sasha), *"Ha-Mered be-Sobibor"* ("The Revolt in Sobibor"), *Yalkut Moreshet*, No. 10 (1969), pp. 30-31.

* The author, Alexander Peczorski, a Jewish Soviet prisoner of war, was one of the organizers of the uprising in the Sobibor Camp on October 14, 1943.

167

EXTRACT FROM EVIDENCE GIVEN AT THE NUREMBERG TRIALS ON THE AUSCHWITZ EXTERMINATION CAMP *

M. Dubost : What do you know about the Jewish transport that arrived from Romainville about the same time as you ?

Vaillant-Couturier : When we left Romainville the Jewish women who were together with us remained behind. They were sent to Drancy, and finally arrived in Auschwitz, where we saw them again three weeks later. Of 1,200 who left, only 125 arrived in the camp. The rest were taken to the gas chambers immediately, and of the 125 not a single one was left by the end of a month.

The transports were carried out as follows : at the beginning, when we arrived, when a Jewish transport came there was a "selection." First the old women, the mothers and the children. They were told to get on trucks, together with the sick and people who looked weak. They kept only young girls, young women and young men; the latter were sent to the men's camp.

In general, it was rare for more than 250 out of a transport of 1,000 to 1,500 to reach the camp, and that was the maximum; the others were sent to the gas chambers straight away.

At this "selection" healthy women between 20 and 30 years old were also chosen, and sent to the Experimental Block. Girls and women, who were a little older or not chosen for this purpose, were sent to the camp and, like us, had their heads shaved and they were tattooed.

In the spring of 1944 there was also a block for twins. That was at the time of the immense transport of Hungarian Jews, about 700,000** persons. Dr. Mengele, who was carrying out the experiments, kept back the twin children from all transports, as well as twins of any age, so long as both twins were there. Both children and adults slept on the floor in this block. I don't know what experiments were made apart from blood tests and measurements.

M. Dubost: Did you actually see the "selection" when transports arrived ?

Vaillant-Couturier: Yes, because when we were working in the Sewing Block in 1944, the block in which we lived was situated just opposite the place where the trains arrived. The whole process had been improved : Instead of carrying out the "selection" where the trains arrived, a siding took the carriages practically to the gas chamber, and the train stopped about 100 m. from the gas chamber. That was right in front of our block, but of course there were two rows of barbed wire between.

Then we saw how the seals were taken off the trucks and how women, men and children were pulled out of the trucks by soldiers. We were present at the most terrible scenes when old couples were separated. Mothers had to leave their daughters, because they were taken to the camp, while the mothers and children went to the gas chambers. All these people knew nothing of the fate that awaited them. They were only confused because they were being separated from each other, but they did not know that they were going to their death.

To make the reception pleasanter there was then — in June and July 1944, that is — an orchestra made up of prisoners, girls in white blouses and dark blue skirts, all of them pretty and young, who played gay tunes when the trains arrived, the "Merry Widow," the Barcarolle from the "Tales of Hoffmann," etc. They were told it was a labor camp, and as they never entered the camp they saw nothing but the small platform decorated with greenery, where the orchestra played. They could not know what awaited them.

Those who were taken to the gas chambers — that is, the old people, children and others — were taken to a red brick building.

M. Dubost : Then they were not registered ?

Vaillant-Couturier : No.

Dubost : They were not tattooed ?

Vaillant-Couturier : No, they were not even counted.

Dubost : Were you yourself tattooed ?

Vaillant-Couturier : Yes.

(The witness shows her arm)

They were taken to a red brick building with a sign that said Baths. There they were told to get undressed and given a towel before they were taken to the so-called shower room. Later, at the time of the large transports from Hungary, there was no time left for any degree of concealment. They were 'ndressed brutally. I know of these particulars because I was acquainted with a little Jewess from France, who had lived on the Place de la Republique. . . .

360

Dubost : In Paris ?

Vaillant-Couturier : In Paris; she was known as "little Marie" and was the only survivor of a family of nine. Her mother and her seven sisters and brothers had been taken to the gas chambers as soon as they arrived. When I got to know her she worked on undressing the small children before they were taken into the gas chamber.

After the people were undressed they were taken into a room that looked like a shower room, and the capsules were thrown down into the room through a hole in the ceiling. An SS man observed the effect through a spy-hole. After about 5 to 7 minutes, when the gas had done its job, he gave a signal for the opening of the doors. Men with gas-masks, these were prisoners too, came in and took the bodies out. They told us that the prisoners must have suffered before they died, because they clung together in bunches like grapes so that it was difficult to separate them. . . .

Trial of the Major War Criminals before the International Military Tribunal, Nuremberg 14 November 1945-1 October 1946, VI, Nuremberg, 1947, pp. 214-216.

* From the evidence of a Frenchwoman, Marie-Claude Vaillant-Couturier, who was a prisoner in the Auschwitz concentration camp, where she arrived on January 1, 1943.
** The correct number of Hungarian Jews sent to Auschwitz was about 430,000.

168

"THE FACE OF THE FUTURE," EDITORIAL FROM THE NEWSPAPER OF A JEWISH UNDERGROUND YOUTH ORGANIZATION IN CRACOW *

In view of the tragic existence of the Jews, where the life of the individual depends on chance, and the life of the community as a whole has long been on the brink of cessation, one must, more than ever, see the situation comprehensively. An individual point of view — everyone will surely understand that now — is of no significance today. As individuals, we are all lost. The likelihood of staying alive is minute. Broken and alone — there is not much we can expect of life. Dying together with Polish Jewry we must clearly visualize for ourselves the historic character of this time and tell ourselves with courage that our death does not spell the end of the world. The record of humanity and of the Jewish people will continue at its own speed in the future, even after we are safely under the ground.

The numerical balance-sheet of the Jews will be sad when peace finally comes to the world after the historical blood-bath. This is indeed not the first defeat of a defenseless people scattered over the face of the earth. Slaughter, murders, confiscation of property, and the burning alive of people — all these have been known to us for generations as the essential elements of our martyrology. But there has never been such wholesale extermination. Never did a situation develop like this, where there is no way out. Never before did great numbers of people armed with the most modern technology move against the Jews. Of 16 million Jews in the world, we shall scarcely reach 9 million after the war. And, most important of all, the Jews of Europe will no longer be there, those who up to now made up the healthiest part of the nation...

Nobody held out a helping hand to the Jews who were being destroyed, nobody made any effort to help them to the extent that they could escape from the danger of extermination. They looked on our destruction as on the death of maggots, and not as the loss of a nation with high cultural values. When the question of the Jews came up even the hatred towards the Germans lessened. There was solidarity with the enemy in the joy over the fall of the Jews. Only a few retained any degree of humanity, and even they did not dare to give this public expression. The truth of aloneness was again confirmed.

We shall carry the heavy burden of this isolation until the end of our days, and it points to the fact that the only proper approach is that of self-liberation : We have nobody on whom to depend except ourselves. All other political concepts will lead us astray. We have paid the highest possible price because we were lulled asleep by the prosperity of Europe, or guided by false hopes of rescue that would come from outside. We lost our sense of reality and instead of planning our independence we scattered invaluable forces in alien fields. Who knows what would have been the future of the Jewish people if there were no *Yishuv* (Community) of half a million in Palestine, that built its foundations before the war broke out and which has now reached a million souls ? Only this nucleus of a Jewish State now offers assurance for the survival of the people. It makes us believe that an independent Jewish nation will rise again, a well-spring of profound spiritual values, as always. It is easier to die, therefore, in the knowledge that a genuine Jewish life still throbs there, that in that one small corner of the wide world we were not undesirables, lonely victims. There would be no sense in our death but for the feeling that, after we have gone, they will be the only ones who will think about us with genuine emotion.

Therefore, despite certain death, we join them in their struggle for the future. Every one of our deeds paved the way for freedom, and furthers the building of an independent homeland. Our revolt is a protest against the evil that is engulfing the world. To counter the terror that has crushed our people we shall stand prepared for the struggle for justice and freedom that should light up the life of humanity as a whole. We are willing to die in order that the shame of death in slavery shall not burden the future of the Jews, and that these Jews shall not have to recall the Jews of Europe with shame because they allowed themselves to be led unresisting to slaughter, and they had not the spirit and courage to defend themselves against destruction. As we had not been allowed to make our contribution to the creative work of building, we shall at least fulfill our historic duty here : it is we who must raise up the name of the lost people, to wipe away the mark of shame of slavery, and to place it among the ranks of people free in spirit...

Yad Vashem, O-6/59.

* From the Underground newspaper of the Fighting Organization of the Jewish Pioneer Youth (Akiva) in Cracow, *He-Halutz ha-Lohem* ("Fighting Pioneer"), No. 29, August 13, 1943.

Part Three

Soviet Union

INTRODUCTION

The selection of documents in this section covers the areas of the Soviet Union that were occupied by Nazi Germany. These areas were divided up politically and administratively by the Germans into areas under civilian German rule — including the *Reichskommissariat Ostland* (Lithuania, Latvia, Estonia and part of Byelorussia) and *Reichskommissariat* Ukraine — and an area under military rule, which included the rest of the occupied territory of the Soviet Union. Chronologically these documents cover the period from the preparations for the German invasion of the Soviet Union in March 1941, and continue into the period of Nazi occupation. In the western parts of the occupied territories, German rule continued for about three years, from the summer of 1941 to the summer of 1944; in the eastern areas the occupation was of shorter duration, depending on the advance and changes in the military front lines.

In some areas and localities many documents were preserved (particularly in the *Ostland* areas and in the Vilna and Kovno ghettos); however, in the other areas fewer documents have remained. For a period of two to three years, there were a number of ghettos in *Ostland* where Jewish skilled and unskilled workers were left alive, while the ghettos in the Ukraine were liquidated within a year. In the occupied areas of the Soviet Union (i.e., the borders up to September 1939), all the ghettos were liquidated within a few months after the occupation, except in Minsk. Understtndably, the fate of the Jewish communities, the specific developments in each place, and the length of time that they survived affected the amount of documentation that has come into our possession.

367

The German invasion of the Soviet Union on June 22, 1941, marked the beginning of a new phase in Nazi policy towards the Jews — the stage of total extermination. Mass murder by shooting the victims at the edge of open pits was carried out by the *Einsatzgruppen* and other units of the SS, the Security Police and SD, with the active assistance of local populations, mainly the Lithuanians, Latvians, Estonians and Ukrainians. In *Ostland* and the Ukraine, the civilian German authorities took part in the extermination of the Jews in their areas and were responsible for it — as was the military government elsewhere.

From the documents in our possession we cannot tell whether the total extermination in the occupied areas of the Soviet Union was carried out as the result of the decision and order to liquidate all of European Jewry (the "Final Solution"), or whether the orders to liquidate the Jews of the Soviet Union, and, subsequently, all the Jews of Europe were given separately. Nor do we have documents or information concerning the exact date that the decision was taken for the total destruction of the Jews of the Soviet Union and of the rest of Europe, nor of the forum in which this took place. The documents that do exist — some of which are reproduced in this section — enable us to determine with certainty that the decision to destroy the Jews of the Soviet Union was taken during the preparations for the invasion of the Soviet Union ("Operation Barbarossa"), in the first two or three months of 1941.

The first document that refers to the "special duties of the SS" in the area of the Soviet Union was published in March 1941 (Document 169). As a result of this order and an agreement reached between the Higher Command of the SS and the High Command of the Army, the *Einsatzgruppen* of the SS were activated. They followed closely behind the army's advance units and murdered Jews and Communists activists. The orders for the total destruction of the Jews were delivered verbally and were regarded as top secret. Evidence to this effect was given by commanders of the *Einsatzgruppen* (A. Ohlendorf and others) at their trials after the war. On the other hand, orders were given in writing for the execution of Commissars — "The Commissar's Order" (Document 170) — and "Jews in Party and State employment" in Heydrich's guidelines for Higher SS and Police leaders in the occupied area of the Soviet Union (Document 171). While the order for the total extermination of the Jews was given verbally, many written reports by *Einsatzgruppen* were found on the implementation of the extermination, including figures for the numbers murdered and the dates and locations of the killings (Documents 177, 189).

Regiments of the *Waffen SS* also took part in these murder operations. A report by the second SS Cavalry Regiment specifically records these operations, referring to the attempt of a special form of murder — driving Jewish women and children into the marshes to drown (Document 188). The *Einsatzgruppen* also used gas vans to kill thousands of Jews. This system was used on a large scale mainly in the Eastern Ukraine (Document 191) and in Byelorussia.

In the areas under German military administration, all the Jews were murdered in the first few months after the occupation as a result of the close cooperation between the German military authorities and the Security Police and the SD (Documents 192-194). In many cases the mass killings were carried out openly, in full view of Wehrmacht soldiers, who watched the shocking spectacle. The report from the Inspector for Armaments in the Ukraine to General Thomas records the murder of the Ukrainian Jews, which was carried out with the cooperation of the local population and the participation of German military personnel (Documents 190, 195.)

The milittry administration and army units employed Jews on forced labor at the same time that the extermination process was going on. In order to prevent any close contact or possible aid that might be given by German soldiers to Jews who worked for them, the High Command of the Wehrmacht issued an order forbidding the employment of individual Jews in services for army units, authorizing instead the exploitation of Jews in forced-labor companies used for building and construction work under extremely harsh conditions (Document 175). Both army units and individual German soldiers took part in outbreaks of violence and the murder of Jews. For reasons of military discipline, General von Rundstedt forbade independent actions of this type by soldiers serving in the army, but emphasized the justification of such operations when they were carried out by the *Einsatzgruppen* (Document 176).

The German civilian administration, which was established at the end of July 1941 in the western areas of the occupied Soviet Union territories, was also in charge of Jewish affairs. The various levels of this administration — from the Ministry for Eastern Territories in Berlin down to the *Gebietskommissare* who made up the lowest level of the German civil administration in the East — issued a large number of orders concerning anti-Jewish policy. Two documents are included on this subject: provisional directives by Lohse, *Reichskommissar* for *Ostland* (Document 172), and an order in connection with forced labor for Jews, which was issued by A. Rosenberg, Minister for the Occupied Eastern Territories (Document 173).

Certain areas of the occupied Soviet Union, particularly the district of Minsk in Byelorussia and of Riga in Latvia, served as the site for the destruction of tens of thousands of Jews who had been brought from Germany, Austria and Czechoslovakia at the end of 1941 and during 1942, before the death camps were established (Documents 185 and 186).

The Germans encountered a Soviet Partisan movement in the occupied territories and saw the Jews as one of the main elements in its activities. In various reports the Germans linked the destruction of the Jews with their operations against the partisans (Document 187).

The failure of the German *Blitzkrieg* and the need to prepare for a protracted war, which meant exploiting economic resources and manpower in the occupied areas, brought about a difference of opinion within sections of the German authorities in the *Ostland*. This debate centered around the question of whether all the Jews should be destroyed, or whether the annihilation of

Jewish manpower, some of it skilled, should be postponed for a period, as there was no way of replacing it and as it was essential for the war economy. Some parts of the German civilian administration and maintenance sections of the German army demanded that the liquidation of Jews employed by and of use to them be ceased; the Security Police and SD, who were directly involved with the annihilation process, demanded that the total destruction should continue (Documents 178 and 179).

The Jews of the Soviet Union suddenly found themselves up against the German machinery of destruction. They were left without organizations or leadership of their own, for these had been disbanded under Soviet rule, and they had to organize quickly so as to react to the adverse situation. One of the first steps taken by the Germans was the establishment of Judenräte (Jewish Councils), but they were faced with difficulties in setting them up (Document 174). Jews struggled for survival and escape at the time of the *Aktionen;* thousands of Jews went into hiding and were able to save themselves for a time in this way (Document 181). Problems involving ethical considerations or religious law arose during this struggle for survival. There were cases in which a Judenrat or individual Jews turned to their spiritual leaders, the rabbis in the ghettos, asking how they should act in such cases (Document 182).

In the ghettos that remained after the first wave of mass executions, some of the Judenräte adopted the ideology of "survival through work." This was based on the assumption that the Germans were in need of Jewish manpower and Jewish skilled workers, and if the Jews in the ghetto could prove that they were an efficient and productive work force, they could delay their murder for some time. In effect the Jews hoped to be able to gain time and hold out until the Germans might be defeated (Document 198 and 206).

Life in the ghetto was carried on under the leadership of the Judenräte, which operated the ghetto institutions and internal services, such as social welfare, etc. (Document 201). Many

371

ghettos sponsored lively activities in the fields of education and culture (Documents 202 and 203). Despite the difficult conditions in the ghetto, the Jews tried to organize their lives and to fight hunger and disease. The scant food supplied to them by the German authorities was not sufficient for survival, and the only way to avoid starvation was to smuggle in food. This was done at great risk, for Jews were sentenced to death for smuggling in food (Document 184). In some of the ghettos in the course of the *Aktionen*, the Germans demanded that the Judenrat assist them in removing the "non-essential" Jews. In some places the Judenrat agreed, taking the position that this way they could save the rest of the Jews (Documents 199 and 200).

After the first wave of extermination, Jewish underground organizations sprang up in the ghettos and concentration camps, and these began to store arms and to prepare to fight. In places where conditions permitted this, many went out into the forests and joined the partisans. The first Jewish underground fighting organization that called for armed revolt against the Germans was formed in the Vilna Ghetto. On January 1, 1942, the first proclamation was issued there, declaring "they shall not take us like sheep to slaughter!" (Document 196). One of the main problems for the underground organizations in the ghetto was the timing of an uprising and the question of whether they should remain in the ghetto or go to the forests and join the partisans (Document 197), According to the Judenräte, these underground activities would have endangered the very existence of the ghetto had the Germans discovered them (Document 205). In June 1943 Himmler issued an order (Document 207) for the liquidation of the ghettos in the *Ostland*. (For the execution of Himmler's order in Lithuania, see Document 208.) When the liquidation of the Vilna Ghetto began, the F.P.O. issued an appeal to the Jewish population in which it called for them to take up arms and resist (Document 209). Thousands of Jews, mainly young people, escaped to the forests, set up partisan units or joined existing units, or organized family camps (Documents 210 and 211).

When it became clear that the war was liable to end with their defeat, the Germans decided to obliterate the evidence of the mass murder carried out by the *Einsatzgruppen*. To this end Himmler ordered the establishment of a special unit, Commando 1005, under the command of Paul Blobel, which was to open the enormous mass graves and to burn the bodies of those who were murdered (Document 212). A party of Jews, from among those who were to burn the bodies in the Ninth Fort near Kovno, succeeded in escaping and gave eye-witness reports of this operation (Document 213).

When the occupied territories were liberated by the Soviet army, no single Jewish community had survived. Only small numbers of Jews emerged from the forces or came back from the camps. Over one million Jews had been killed in the occupied territories of the Soviet Union.

Yitzhak Arad

169

SPECIAL DUTIES FOR THE SS IN "OPERATION BARBAROSSA," MARCH 13, 1941

March 13, 1941

Staff Command Secret Document
Chief Only
Only Through Officer
High Command of the Wehrmacht
WFST [Armed Forces Operational Staff] Div. L (IV/Qu)
No. 44125/41 g.K.Chiefs

Orders for Special Areas* in Connection with Directive No. 21
(Operation Barbarossa)

... b) Within the area of Army operations the *Reichsführer SS* will be entrusted, on behalf of the Führer, with *special tasks* for the preparation of the *political administration* — tasks which derive from the decisive struggle that will have to be carried out between the two opposing political systems. *Within the framework of these tasks, the Reichsführer SS will act independently and on his own responsibility.* Apart from this, the executive power vested in the Supreme Commander of the Army and in command levels acting under his orders will not be affected. The *Reichsführer SS* will ensure that operations are not interfered with by the execution of his tasks. Details will be worked out directly between the High Command of the Army and the *Reichsführer SS...*

NOKW-2302.

* Occupied Eastern Territories.

170

EXTRACT FROM THE COMMISSAR'S ORDER FOR "OPERATION BARBAROSSA," JUNE 6, 1941

Staff Command Secret Document
Chief Only
Only Through Officer
High Command of the Wehrmacht
WFST [Armed Forces Operational Staff] Div. L (VI/Qu)
No. 44822/41 g.K Chiefs

June 6, 1941

Guidelines for the Treatment of Political Commissars

In the fight against Bolshevism it is *not* to be expected that the enemy will act in accordance with the principles of humanity or international law. In particular, the *political commissars* of all kinds, who are the real bearers of resistance, can be expected to mete out treatment to our prisoners that is full of hate, cruel and inhuman.

The army must be aware of the following:

1. In this battle it would be mistaken to show mercy or respect for international law towards such elements. They constitute a danger to our own security and to the rapid pacification of the occupied territories.

2. The barbaric, Asiatic fighting methods are originated by the political commissars. Action must therefore be taken against them *immediately*, without further consideration, and with all severity. Therefore, when they are picked up in battle or resistance, they are, as a matter of principle, to be finished immediately with a weapon.

In addition, the following regulations are to be observed:

Operational Areas

1) Political commissars operating *against our armies* are to be dealt with in accordance with the decree on judicial provisions

in the area of "Barbarossa." This applies to commissars of every type and rank, even if they are only suspected of resistance, sabotage or incitement to sabotage...

NOKW-484.

171

EXTRACT FROM GUIDELINES BY HEYDRICH FOR HIGHER SS AND POLICE LEADERS IN THE OCCUPIED TERRITORIES OF THE SOVIET UNION, JULY 2, 1941

Berlin, July 2, 1941

Chief of the Security Police and the SD
B. No. IV - 1100/41 top secret
B. No. g. Rs. 7/41

EK 3

Reich Secret Document

a) To the Higher SS and Police Leader (*Höherer SS- und Polizeiführer*)
SS *Obergruppenführer* Jeckeln...
b) To the Higher SS and Police Leader
SS *Gruppenführer* von dem Bach...
c) To the Higher SS and Police Leader
SS *Gruppenführer* Prützmann...
d) To the Higher SS and Police Leader
SS *Oberführer* Korsemann...

Owing to the fact that the Chief of the Order Police invited to Berlin the Higher SS and Police Leaders and commissioned them to take part in Operation Barbarossa without informing me of this in time, I was unfortunately not in a position also to provide them with basic instructions for the sphere of jurisdiction of the Security Police and SD.

377

In the following I make known briefly the most important instructions given by me to the *Einsatzgruppen* and Kommandos of the Security Police and the SD, with the request to take note of them.

...4) *Executions*

All the following are to be executed:

Officials of the Comintern (together with professional Communist politicians in general)

top and medium-level officials and radical lower-level officials of the Party, Central Committee and district and sub-district committees

People's Commissars

Jews in Party and State employment, and other radical elements (saboteurs, propagandists, snipers, assassins, inciters, etc.)

insofar as they are, in any particular case, required or no longer required, to supply information on political or economic matters which are of special importance for the further operations of the Security Police, or for the economic reconstruction of the Occupied Territories...

Yad Vashem Archives 0-4/53-1.

172

PROVISIONAL DIRECTIVES BY LOHSE, REICHSKOMMISSAR FOR OSTLAND, CONCERNING THE TREATMENT OF JEWS, AUGUST 13, 1941

The *Reichskommissar* for *Ostland*
IIa 4
Secret!

Provisional Directives for the treatment of Jews in the area of the *Reichskommissariat Ostland*.

The final solution of the Jewish question in the area of the

378

Reichskommissariat Ostland will be in accordance with the instructions in my address of July 27, 1941, in Kovno.

Insofar as further measures are taken, particularly by the Security Police, to carry out my verbal instructions, they will not be affected by the following *provisional directives.* It is merely the purpose of these provisional directives to assure that where, and as long as, further measures for the final solution are not possible, minimum measures will be taken by the *General-kommissare* or *Gebietskommissare.*

I. a. For the time being only such Jews who are citizens of the German Reich, the Protectorate of Bohemia and Moravia, of the former Republics of Poland, Lithuania, Latvia, Estonia, of the U.S.S.R. or of its component states, or stateless Jews, will be subject to these directives.

I. b. Other Jews of foreign citizenship, *Mischlinge,* and spouses of Jews who do not wish to share the fate of their Jewish spouses, will be denied permission to leave the area of R.K. [*Reichskommissariat*] *Ostland* as it is a military area. They are to be kept under surveillance. In addition they may be subjected to the following [measures] among others : Obligation to report daily, a ban on moving [from their place of residence], assignment to a specific dwelling, a ban on leaving the city area, limitations on moving about. If necessary they may be taken into police custody until a further decision is made.

II. A Jew is a person descended from at least three grandparents who are fully Jewish by race.

In addition, a Jew is a person descended from one or two grandparents Jewish by race, if he

a) belongs or belonged to the Jewish religious community, or

b) on June 20, 1941, or subsequently, was married to, or living in common-law marriage with, a person who is Jewish within the definition of these directives, or who now or in the future enters into such a relationship.

III. In case of doubt, the *Gebietskommissar* or *Stadtskommissar* will decide who is a Jew in accordance with his best judgment and within the definition of these directives.

IV. The *Generalkommissar* in whose areas a civil administration has been introduced will provide immediately for the following :

a) The Jews are to be registered by means of an order to report by name, sex, age and address. The records of the Jewish Communities can be used as a further basis for the registration, as well as the statements of reliable local residents.

b) It will be decreed that Jews identify themselves by the wearing of constantly visible yellow six-cornered stars, at least 10 cms. across, on the left side of the chest and in the center of the back.

c) The following is forbidden to Jews :

1. to move from their locality or change their place of residence without the permission of the *Gebietskommissar* or *Stadtskommissar*.

2. The use of sidewalks, public transportation ... and. automobiles.

3. The use of recreational facilities and institutions serving the public (resort areas and bathing facilities, parks and open spaces, playgrounds and athletic fields).

4. To attend theaters or movie houses, libraries, or museums.

5. To attend schools of any type.

6. To possess automobiles or radios.

7. [Kosher] slaughtering.

d) Jewish doctors and dentists may treat or advise Jewish patients only. Where ghettos or camps are set up they will be distributed through them for the care of the inmates.

Jewish druggists are permitted to practice their profession only in ghettos and camps, according to need. Drug stores previously managed by Jews are to be transferred, under trusteeship, to Aryan druggists.

Jewish veterinarians are forbidden to practice their profession.

e) Jews are forbidden the exercise of the professions and occupations listed below:

1. Attorney-at-Law...

2. Banking, money-changing and pawnbroking.

3. Middleman and agents.

4. Trade in real estate.

5. Traveling peddlers.

f) The following is decreed for the handling of Jewish property:

1. *General*:

The property of the Jewish population is to be confiscated and placed in safekeeping. . . .

2. *Compulsory Registration*:

All Jewish property is to be registered. . .

3. *Compulsory Surrender*:

Jewish property is to be surrendered on special demand. The demand may be made by general proclamation or by order to certain individuals.

The *Generalkommissare* will order the immediate surrender of the following by proclamation:

a) Local and foreign currency.

b) Securities. . . .

c) Valuables of all kinds (coins and gold and silver bullion, other precious metals, jewelry, precious stones, etc.).

4. For their subsistence, the Jewish population may retain:

a) Household items needed for minimum requirements (furniture, clothing, linens).

b) A daily sum of money amounting to 0.20 RM (2 Rubles) for every Jewish member of the household. The money to be released one month in advance.

V. The following further measures are to be strived for vigorously, with due consideration for local, and particularly economic, conditions.

a) The countryside is to be cleansed of Jews.

b) The Jews are to be removed from all trade, and especially from trade in agricultural products and other foodstuffs.

c) The Jews are to be forbidden residence in localities that are of economic, military or ideological importance, and also in resorts and spas.

d) As far as possible the Jews are to be concentrated in cities or in sections of large cities, where the population is already predominantly Jewish. There, ghettos are to be established, and the Jews are to be prohibited from leaving these ghettos.

In the ghettos the Jews are to receive only as much food as the rest of the population can spare, but not more than is required for their bare subsistence. The same applies to the allocation of otl.er essential goods.

The inmates of the ghettos will regulate their internal affairs by an administration of their own, which will be supervised by the *Gebietskommissar* or *Stadtskommissar* or a person appointed by him. Jews can be assigned as police for internal order. They may be equipped at most with rubber truncheons and sticks, and are to be identified by wearing white armbands with a yellow Jewish star on the right upper arm.

The external hermetic sealing of the ghetto is to be carried out by auxiliary police drawn from the local population.

Permission must be obtained from the *Gebietskommissar* before any person may enter the ghetto.

e) Jews fit for work will be drafted for forced labor as required. The economic interests of deserving members of the local population should not be harmed by the use of Jewish forced labor. Forced labor can be performed by working parties outside the ghettos, or in the ghettos, or, where a ghetto has not yet been established, by single persons outside (for instance, in the workshop of the Jew).

Payment for the work need not be based on performance, but should cover only the bare subsistence of the forced laborer and members of his family not capable of working, taking into account other monies at his disposal.

The private establishments and persons on whose behalf the forced labor is being carried out will pay an appropriate sum into the payments office of the *Gebietskommissar*, which, in turn, will pay the forced laborers. Special orders will be issued regarding the accounting for these monies.

VI. The *Generalkommissare* will decide whether to order the measures under Para. V. for the entire districts at one time, or whether to leave their introduction to be carried out separately by the *Gebietskommissare*. The *Generalkommissare* are also authorized to issue more detailed instructions within the framework of these directives or to instruct their *Gebietskommissare* to do so.

Distribution :
Reichskommissariat
Higher SS and Police Leader (*Höherer SS-und Polizeiführer*)
Generalkommissar : Estonia
                     Lithuania
                     Latvia
                     Byelorussia

PS-1138.

173

ROSENBERG'S ORDER ON FORCED LABOR FOR JEWS IN THE OCCUPIED TERRITORIES, AUGUST 16, 1941

Regulation on the Introduction of Forced Labor for the Jewish Population, August 16, 1941

Pursuant to Article 8 of the Führer's Edict on the Administration of the newly occupied Eastern Territories of July 17, 1941, I order the following:

Article 1

Male and female Jews aged from their completed 14th to completed 60th year, residing in the newly occupied Eastern Territories, are liable for Forced Labor. The Jews will be collected in Forced Labor groups for this purpose.

Article 2

1) Any person evading Forced Labor will be sent to prison with hard labor.

2) In the event of several persons conspiring to avoid Forced Labor, or in other especially grave cases, the death penalty may be imposed.

3) Cases will be judged by the Special Courts.

Article 3

The orders required for the implementation of this regulation will be published by the *Reichskommissare*.

Berlin, August 16, 1941
>   The Reich Minister for the Occupied Eastern Territories

>   signed   Rosenberg

Yad Vashem Archives, 0-4/53-1.

174

THE ELECTION OF ELKES AS HEAD OF THE JUDENRAT IN KOVNO

... In the first days of August, Kaminsky informed the Jewish Committee that the ghetto in Slobodka would be headed by an *Ältestenrat* (Council of Elders) which would be elected by the Jews themselves. But first of all they would have to elect a "Head of the Jews" — that was the demand of *Hauptsturmführer* Jordan, who was responsible for Jewish affairs in Kovno. This created a very grave problem for the Kovno Jews: whom to elect to this position of exceptionally great responsibility, which was at the same time difficult and dangerous. For this purpose the Council called an enlarged meeting of all those who had been active in public affairs of any kind and had remained in the city. The meeting was held on August 5 in the offices of the Council in Daukshos Street, and about 30 persons attended.

This Jewish meeting, the last in the city of Kovno itself before it was left by its Jewish residents, was unusually dramatic. Everybody was deeply aware that a solution must be found for a problem which literally involved their lives. It was not easy to find a suitable candidate for this unusual position. The candidate would have to know how to find a common language with the Germans, and know also how to appear before them as the representative of the ghetto. Even if it was understood from the outset that the man elected would be only "Head of the Jews," that is, the lowly representative of the "accursed Jews" — in the defiled vocabulary of the Germans — nevertheless it was also understood that everything possible must be done that the man elected would, despite everything, have a certain authority in the eyes of the Germans and that they would take into consideration what he said. Everybody understood that the man elected must have qualities that enabled him to influence the Germans to a certain degree. It was also necessary that the man who would stand at the head of the ghetto must have a clean public record, be a good Jew and a good man, discerning and clever, courageous and of strong character, so that he would not be easily discouraged and would not bend his knees when he had to stand before the Germans as the tragic messenger of an unhappy Jewish community, without salvation and surrounded by ravening beasts.

Several candidates were proposed at the meeting. However, none of them could unite those taking part in the meeting around himself. In addition, the candidates proposed all refused to accept this task. A great feeling of depression spread through the meeting. After lengthy discussions Dr. Z. Wolf, the chairman of the meeting, proposed the candidacy of Dr. E. Elkes, a loyal and Zionist Jew, and a famous doctor in the city of Kovno. The proposal was accepted immediately by the whole assembly, and with great enthusiasm. But Dr. Elkes refused to accept this appointment. Again there was great confusion of spirit. Rabbi Schmukler then rose from his place and made a speech that was moving and full of pain, and shook everyone

385

deeply. "How terrible is our position" — he said in a trembling voice — "that we are not offering the revered Dr. Elkes the respected position of head of the Jewish Community of Kovno, but the shameful and humiliating one of 'Head of the Jews,' who is to represent us before the Germans. But please understand, dear and beloved Dr. Elkes, that only to the Nazi murderers will you be 'Head of the Jews,' in our eyes you will be the head of our Community, elected in our most tragic hour, when blood runs from all of us and the murderer's sword is suspended over our heads. It has fallen to your part to accept duties of unequalled difficulty, but at the same time it is also a great privilege and a deed of charity, and you do not have the right to escape from it; stand at our head, defend us, you shall be with us and we will all be with you, until we arrive at the great day of salvation!" When Rabbi Schmukler had finished speaking he wept, and all the assembly wept bitter tears with him. Dr. Elkes stood pale and silent. All could see what was happening in the depth of his soul and all felt that in these tragic moments Dr. Elkes understood that it was his duty to make this great sacrifice that a cruel fate had imposed upon him. A feeling of relief descended on all, and a ray of secret hope shone into the broken hearts of all those present. . .

L. Garfunkel, *Kovna ha-Yehudit be-Hurbana* ("The Destruction of Jewish Kovno"), Jerusalem, 1959, pp. 47-48.

175

ORDER BY KEITEL BANNING WEHRMACHT CONTACTS WITH JEWS IN THE OCCUPIED TERRITORIES IN THE EAST, SEPTEMBER 12, 1941

High Command of the Wehrmacht
WFST [Armed Forces Operational Staff] Div. L (IV/Qu)
No. 02041/41 Secret

Führer Headquarters, September 12, 1941

Re : Jews in the Occupied Eastern Territories

... The struggle against Bolshevism demands ruthless and energetic action, and first of all against the Jews as well, as the main bearers of Bolshevism.

There will, therefore, be no cooperation whatever between the Wehrmacht and the Jewish population, whose attitude is openly or secretly anti-German, and no use is to be made of individual Jews for any preferential auxiliary services for the Wehrmacht. Under no circumstances are papers to be issued by Military Offices to Jews confirming that they are employed for purposes of the Wehrmacht.

The only exception to be made is the use of Jews in specially organized labor columns, which are only to be employed under German supervision.

It is requested to make this order known to the troops.

Chief of the High Command of the Wehrmacht

signed Keitel

NOKW-3292.

176

THE WEHRMACHT AND THE EINSATZGRUPPEN AKTIONEN, SEPTEMBER 1941

High Command
Army Group South
Ic/AO (Abw. III)

H.Q., September 24, 1941

Re : The Struggle Against Elements Hostile to the Reich

The investigation of and struggle against tendencies and elements hostile to the Reich (Communists, Jews, etc.), insofar as they are not a part of a hostile military force is, in the occupied areas, *exclusively* the task of the *Sonderkommando* (Special Unit) of the Security Police and the SD, which will take the necessary measures on their own responsibility and carry them out.

Individual actions by members of the Wehrmacht or participation by members of the Wehrmacht in excesses by the Ukrainian population against the Jews is forbidden; they are also forbidden to watch or take photographs of measures taken by the *Sonderkommando*.

This prohibition is to be made known to the members of all units. [Commanders] in charge of discipline at all levels are responsible for the implementation of this prohibition. In the event of breaches it is to be investigated in every case whether the commander failed to carry out his duty of supervision, and when necessary he is to be severely punished.

signed   von Rundstedt

Distribution :

AOK (Intelligence Command), PzGr (Tank Group)
Bef rückw H (Rear Command)
Befehlsstelle Süd (Southern Command)
Abt. des Stabes u. Wach-Kp. (Staff Dept. and Guard Companies)
Nachr. : Luftflotte (info : Air Force)

NOKW-541.

177

EXTRACTS FROM A REPORT BY EINSATZGRUPPE A IN THE BALTIC COUNTRIES, 1941

Reich Secret Document

Einsatzgruppe A

General Report up to October 15, 1941

... II *Cleansing* [of Jews] *and securing the area of operation.*

1) *Encouragement of Self-cleansing* Aktionen (Selbstreinigungs-aktionen).*

Basing [oneself] on the consideration that the population of the Baltic countries had suffered most severely under the rule of Bolshevism and Jewry while they were incorporated into the U.S.S.R., it was to be expected that after liberation from this foreign rule they would themselves to a large extent eliminate those of the enemy left behind after the retreat of the Red Army. It was the task of the Security Police to set these self-cleansing movements going and to direct them into the right channels in order to achieve the aim of this cleansing as rapidly as possible. It was no less important to establish as unshakable and provable facts for the future that it was the liberated population itself which took the most severe measures, on its own initiative, against the Bolshevik and Jewish enemy, without any German instruction being evident.

In *Lithuania* this was achieved for the first time by activating the partisans** in Kovno. To our surprise it was not easy at first to set any large-scale anti-Jewish pogrom in motion there. Klimatis, the leader of the partisan group referred to above, who was the first to be recruited for this purpose, succeeded in starting a pogrom with the aid of instructions given him by a small advance detachment operating in Kovno, in such a way that no German orders or instructions could be observed by outsiders. In the course of the first pogrom during the night of June 25/26, the Lithuanian partisans eliminated more than 1,500 Jews, set fire to several synagogues or destroyed them by other means, and burned down an area consisting of about sixty houses inhabited by Jews. During the nights that followed, 2,300 Jews were eliminated in the same way. In other parts of Lithuania similar *Aktionen* followed the example set in Kovno, but on a smaller scale, and including some Communists who had been left behind.

These self-cleansing *Aktionen* ran smoothly because the Wehrmacht authorities who had been informed showed understanding for this procedure. At the same time it was obvious from the beginning that only the first days after the Occupation would offer the opportunity for carrying out pogroms. After the disarmament of the partisans the self-cleansing *Aktionen* necessarily ceased.

It proved to be considerably more difficult to set in motion similar cleansing *Aktionen* and pogroms in *Latvia*. The main reason was that the entire national leadership, especially in Riga, had been killed or deported by the Soviets. Even in Riga it proved possible by means of appropriate suggestions to the Latvian auxiliary police to get an anti-Jewish pogrom going, in the course of which all the synagogues were destroyed and about 400 Jews killed. As the population on the whole quietened down very quickly in Riga, it was not possible to arrange further pogroms.

Both in Kovno and in Riga evidence was taken on film and by photographs to establish, as far as possible, that the first spontaneous executions of Jews and Communists were carried out by Lithuanians and Latvians.

In *Estonia* there was no opportunity of instigating pogroms owing to the relatively small number of Jews. The Estonian self-defense units only eliminated some individual Communists, who were particularly hated, but in general limited themselves to carrying out arrests...

3) *The Fight Against Jewry*
It was to be expected from the beginning that the Jewish problem in the *Ostland* could not be solved by pogroms alone. At the same time the Security Police had basic, general orders

for cleansing operations aimed at a maximum elimination of the Jews. Large-scale executions were therefore carried out in the cities and the countryside by *Sonderkommandos* (Special Units), which were assisted by selected units — partisan groups in Lithuania, and parties of the Latvian Auxiliary Police in Latvia. The work of the execution units was carried out smoothly. Where Lithuanian and Latvian forces were attached to the execution units, the first to be chosen were those who had had members of their families and relatives killed or deported by the Russians.

Particularly severe and extensive measures became necessary in *Lithuania*. In some places — especially in Kovno — the Jews had armed themselves and took an active part in sniping and arson. In addition, the Jews of Lithuania cooperated most closely with the Soviets.

The total number of Jews liquidated in Lithuania is 71,105.

During the pogrom 3,800 Jews were eliminated in Kovno and about 1,200 in the smaller cities.

In *Latvia*, too, Jews took part in acts of sabotage and arson after the entry of the German Wehrmacht. In Dünaburg so many fires were started by Jews that a large part of the city was destroyed. The electric power station was burned out completely. Streets inhabited mainly by Jews remained untouched. Up to now 30,000 Jews have been executed in Latvia. The pogrom in Riga eliminated 500.

Most of the 4,500 Jews living in *Estonia* at the start of the Eastern campaign fled with the retreating Red Army. About 2,000 stayed behind. In Reval alone there were about 1,000 Jews.

The arrest of all male Jews over the age of sixteen is almost completed. With the exception of the doctors and the Jewish Elders appointed by the *Sonderkommando* they [the remaining Jews] are being executed by the Estonian Self-defense under the supervision of *Sonderkommando* 1a. Jewesses between the ages of 16 through 60 in Reval and Pernau, who are fit for work, were arrested and used to cut peat and for other work.

391

At present a camp is being built at Harku in which all the Jews in Estonia will be sent, so that in a short time Estonia will be cleared of Jews.

After the carrying out of the first large-scale executions in Lithuania and Latvia it already proved that the total elimination of the Jews is not possible there, at least not at the present time. As a large part of the skilled trades is in Jewish hands in Lithuania and Latvia, and some (glaziers, plumbers, stove-builders, shoemakers) are almost entirely Jewish, a large proportion of the Jewish craftsmen are indispensable at present for the repair of essential installations, for the reconstruction of destroyed cities, and for work of military importance. Although the employers aim at replacing Jewish labor with Lithuanian or Latvian workers, it is not yet possible to replace all the Jews presently employed, particularly in the larger cities. In cooperation with the labor exchange offices, however, Jews who are no longer fit for work are picked up and will be executed shortly in small *Aktionen.*

It must be also noted in this connection that in some places there has been considerable resistance by offices of the Civil Administration against large-scale executions. This [resistance] was confronted in every case by pointing out that it was a matter of carrying out orders [involving] a basic principle.

Apart from organizing and carrying out the executions, preparations were begun from the first days of the operation for the establishment of ghettos in the larger cities. This was particularly urgent in Kovno, where there were 30,000 Jews in a total population of 152,400. At the end of the early pogroms, therefore, a Jewish Committee was summoned and informed that the German authorities had so far seen no reason to interfere in the conflicts between the Lithuanians and the Jews. A condition for the creation of a normal situation would be, first of all, the creation of a Jewish ghetto. When the Jewish Committee remonstrated, it was explained that there was no other possibility of preventing further pogroms. At this the Jews at once declared that they were ready to do everything to transfer their co-racials as quickly as possible to the Viliampole Quarter, where it was planned to establish the Jewish ghetto. This area is situated in the triangle between the River Memel and a branch of the river, and is linked with Kovno by only one bridge, and therefore easily sealed off.

In Riga the so-called "Moscow Suburb" was designated as the ghetto. This is the worst residential quarter of Riga, which is already inhabited mainly by Jews. The transfer of Jews into the ghetto area proved rather difficult because the Latvians living in that district had to be evacuated and residential space in Riga is very crowded. Of about 28,000 Jews remaining in Riga, 24,000 are now housed in the ghetto. The Security Police carried out only police duties in the establishment of the ghetto, while the arrangements and administration of the ghetto, as well as the regulation of the food supply for the inmates of the ghetto, were left to the Civil Administration; the Labor Office was left in charge of Jewish labor.

Ghettos are also being set up in other cities in which there are a large number of Jews...

L-180.

* The reference is to *Aktionen* against Jews carried out by the local population.
** A nationalist organization in Lithuania which rose against Soviet rule on the day the Germans moved in.

178

EXCHANGE OF LETTERS BETWEEN REICHSKOMMISSAR LOHSE AND THE MINISTRY FOR THE EASTERN TERRITORIES, CONCERNING THE "FINAL SOLUTION"

Riga, November 15, 1941

Reichskommissar for *Ostland*

IIa 4 M.219/41g

Secret

To

Reich Minister for the Occupied Eastern Territories

Re: Execution of Jews
in reply to letter I/259141 of October 31, 1941
Report from: Government Counselor Trampedach
I have forbidden the unauthorized ("wild") executions of Jews in Libau because the manner in which they were carried out was irresponsible.

Will you please inform me whether your inquiry of October 31 should be interpreted as a directive to liquidate all the Jews in *Ostland*? Is this to be done regardless of age, sex, and economic requirements (for instance, the Wehrmacht's demand for skilled workers in the armament industry)? Of course the cleansing of *Ostland* of Jews is a most important task; its solution, however, must be in accord with the requirements of war production.

So far I have not been able to find such a directive either in the regulations concerning the Jewish question in the "Brown Portfolio" (*Braune Mappe*) or in any other decree.

L[ohse]

PS-3663.

Berlin, December 18, 1941

Reich Minister for the Occupied Eastern Territories
Nr. I/1/157/41

To
Reichskommissar for *Ostland*
Riga

Re : Jewish question

in reply to your letter of November 15, 1941.

The Jewish question has presumably been clarified meanwhile by means of verbal discussion. In principle, economic considerations are not to be taken into account in the settlement of the problem. It is further requested that any questions that arise be settled directly with the Higher SS and Police Leader (*Höherer SS- und Polizeiführer*).

f/Bräutigam

PS-3666.

179

ORDER BY REICHSKOMMISSAR LOHSE TO HALT THE KILLING OF JEWISH SKILLED WORKERS, DECEMBER 1941

Reichskommissar for *Ostland*   Riga, December [2], 1941
IIa Diary No. 220/41g

To
Reichskommissar for *Ostland*
Higher SS and Police Leader (*Höherer SS- und Polizeiführer*) in *Riga*
Generalkommissare
in *Reval*
  Riga
  Kovno
  Minsk
For info : Commander of the Wehrmacht for *Ostland* in *Riga*
The Chief Quartermaster (*Chefintendant*) of the Wehrmacht Command in *Ostland* has lodged a complaint that armament plants and repair workshops have been deprived of Jewish skilled workers through their liquidation, and that they cannot be replaced there at the present time.

I request most emphatically that the liquidation of Jews employed as skilled workers in armament plants and repair workshops of the Wehrmacht who cannot be replaced at present by local personnel be prevented.

Agreement on which of the Jewish workers are to be considered irreplaceable will be reached with the *Gebietskommissare* (Department of Social Administration).

Provision is to be made as quickly as possible for the training of suitable local personnel as skilled workers.

The same applies to Jewish workers in enterprises which do not serve the purpose of the Wehrmacht directly, but have important tasks to carry out within the framework of the war economy.

PS-3664.

Riga, den   Dezember 1941

An
    den Reichskommissar f.d.Ostland
    - Höherer SS- und Polizeiführer-

        in R i g a

    die Herren Generalkommissare
        in R e v a l
            R i g a
            K a u e n
            M i n s k

    Nachrichtlich an den Wehrmachtbefehlshaber Ostland

        in R i g a

Der Chefintendant beim Wehrmachtbefehlshaber Ostland
beschwert sich darüber, dass der Wehrmacht in Rüstungsbetrieben
und Reparaturwerkstätten jüdische Facharbeiter durch Liquidation entzogen würden, die dort zur Zeit nicht zu ersetzen
sind.

Ich ersuche nachdrücklichst die Liquidation von Juden zu
verhindern, die in Rüstungsbetrieben und Reparaturwerkstätten der Wehrmacht als Fachkräfte tätig und zur Zeit durch
Einheimische nicht zu ersetzen sind. Das Einvernehmen darüber,
wer zu den unersetzlichen jüdischen Arbeitskräften gehört,
ist mit den Gebietskommissaren (Abtlg. Soziale Verwaltung)
zu erzielen.

Für Schulung geeigneten einheimischen Nachwuchses als
Facharbeiter ist beschleunigt Sorge zu tragen.

Das gleiche gilt für jüdische Fachkräfte in Betrieben,
die nicht unmittelbar den Zwecken der Wehrmacht dienen, aber
wichtige Aufgaben im Rahmen der Kriegswirtschaft zu erfüllen
haben.

Order by *Reichskommissar* for *Ostland* to halt the killing of Jewish skilled
workers, December 1941

180

EXTRACT FROM A REPORT BY KARL JÄGER, COMMANDER OF EINSATZKOMMANDO 3, ON THE EXTERMINATION OF LITHUANIAN JEWS, 1941

Commander of the Security Police and the SD
Einsatzkommando 3

Kovno, December 1, 1941

Reich Secret Document

Final Summary of Executions carried out in the operating area of EK [Einsatzkommando] *3 up to December 1, 1941.*
...I can confirm today that *Einsatzkommando* 3 has achieved the goal of solving the Jewish problem in Lithuania. There are no more Jews in Lithuania, apart from working Jews and their families.

These number :
        in Shavli, about 4,500
        in Kovno, about 15,000
        in Vilna, about 15,000

I wanted to eliminate the working Jews and their families as well, but the Civil Administration (*Reichskommissar*) and the Wehrmacht attacked me most sharply and issued a prohibition against having these Jews and their families shot.

The goal of clearing Lithuania of Jews could only be achieved through the establishment of a specially selected Mobile Commando under the command of SS *Obersturmführer* Hamann, who adopted my aims fully and who was able to ensure the cooperation of the Lithuanian Partisans and the Civil Authorities concerned.

The carrying-out of such *Aktionen* is first of all an organizational problem. The decision to clear each sub-district systematically of Jews called for a thorough preparation for each *Aktion* and the study of local conditions. The Jews had to be concentrated in one or more localities and, in accordance with their numbers,

Date	Place	Juden		Jüdinn.		J.-Kind.		Total
12.9.41	Wilna-Stadt	993	Juden,	1670	Jüdinn.	771	J.-Kind.	3 334
17.9.41	" "	337	"	687	"	247	"	1 271
	und 4 lit.Kommunisten							
2o.9.41	Nemencing	128	Juden,	176	Jüdinn.	99	"	4o3
22.9.41	Novo-Wilejka	468	" ,	495	"	196	"	1 159
24.9.41	Riesa	512	"	744	"	511	"	1 767
25.9.41	Jahiunai	215	"	229	"	131	"	575
27.9.41	Eysicky	989	"	1636	"	821	"	3 446
3o.9.41	Trakai	366	"	483	"	597	"	1 446
4.1o.41	Wilna-Stadt	432	"	1115	"	436	"	1 983
6.1o.41	Semiliski	213	"	359	"	390	"	962
9.1o.41	Svenciany	1169	"	184o	"	717	"	3 726
16.1o.41	Wilna-Stadt	382	"	5o7	"	257	"	1 146
21.1o.41	" "	718	"	1o63	"	586	"	2 367
25.1o.41	" "	-	"	1766	"	812	"	2 578
27.1o.41	" "	946	"	184	"	73	"	1 2o3
3o.1o.41	" "	382	"	789	"	362	"	1 533
6.11.41	" "	34o	"	749	"	252	"	1 341
19.11.41	" "	76	"	77	"	18	"	171
19.11.41	" "	6 Kriegsgefangene, 8 Polen						14
2o.11.41	" "	3	"					3
25.11.41	" "	9 Juden, 46 Jüdinnen, 8 J.-Kinder,						64
		1 Pole wegen Waffenbesitz u.Besitz						
		von anderem Kriegsgerät						

Teilkommando des EK.3
    in Minsk
vom 28.9.-17.1o.41:

        Fleechnitza,
        Bicholin,
        Scak,
        Bober,
        Uzda   62o Juden,1285 Jüdinnen,1126 J.-Kind.
                und 19 Kommunisten   3 o5o

                                        133 346

    Vor Übernahme der sicherheitspol.Aufgaben durch das EK.3, 4 ooo
Juden durch Progrome und Exekutionen - ausschliesslich von
Partisanen - liquidiert.

                             Ss.   137 346

From the summary report of Karl Jäger, commander of *Einsatzkommando* 3, on the extermination of the Lithuanian Jews, December 1941 a site had to be selected and pits dug. The marching distance from the concentration points to the pits averaged 4 to 5 kms. The Jews were brought to the place of execution in groups of 500, with at least 2 kms. distance between groups... All the officers and men of my command in Kovno took active part in the *Grossaktionen* in Kovno. Only one official of the intelligence corps was released from participation on account of illness.

I consider the *Aktionen* against the Jews of EK 3 to be virtually completed. The remaining working Jews and Jewesses are urgently needed, and I can imagine that this manpower will continue to be needed urgently after the winter has ended. I am of the opinion that the male working Jews should be sterilized immediately to prevent reproduction. Should any Jewess nevertheless become pregnant, she is to be liquidated...

Jäger
SS *Standartenführer*

Yad Vashem Archives, 0-18/245.

181

FROM THE DIARY OF A JEWISH YOUTH IN HIDING DURING AN AKTION IN THE VILNA GHETTO, 1941

[September 1941]
A troubled evening approaches. The streets are full of people. The owners of the yellow craftsmen certificates* are registering. Whoever can do so, hides. The word*"maline"* has become relevant. To hide, to bury oneself : in a basement, in an attic, to save one's life...

The tenants of the house go into a hide-out. We go with them. Three floors of warehouses in the courtyard of Shavli 4. Stairs lead from one story to the other. The stairs from the first to the second story have been taken down and the opening has been closed up with boards. The hide-out consists of two small warehouses. You enter the hide-out through a hole in the wall of an apartment which borders on the uppermost story of the hide-out. The hole is blocked ingeniously by a kitchen cupboard. One wall of the cupboard serves at the same time as a little gate for the hole. The hole is barricaded by stones. The flat through which you enter the hide-out is located near our apartment. Little groups of people with bundles go in. Soon we also crawl through the hole of the hide-out. Many people have gathered in the two stories of the hide-out. They sneak along like shadows by candlelight around the cold, dank cellar walls. The whole hide-out is filled with a restless murmuring. An imprisoned mass of people. Everyone begins to settle down in the corners, on the stairs...

We are like animals surrounded by the hunter. The hunter on all sides: beneath us, above us, from the sides. Broken locks snap, doors creak, axes, saws. I feel the enemy under the boards on which I am standing. The light of an electric bulb seeps through the cracks. They pound, tear, break. Soon the attack is heard from another side. Suddenly, somewhere upstairs, a child bursts into tears. A desperate groan breaks forth from everyone's lips. We are lost. A desperate attempt to shove sugar into the child's mouth is of no avail. They stop up the child's mouth with pillows. The mother of the child is weeping. People shout in wild terror that the child should be strangled. The child is shouting more loudly, the Lithuanians are pounding more strongly against the walls. However, slowly everything calmed down of itself. We understand that they have left. Later we heard a voice from the other side of the hide-out. You are liberated. My heart beat with such joy! I have remained alive!

Y. Rudashevski, *The Diary of the Vilna Ghetto,* Tel Aviv, 1973, pp. 36-37, 39.

* Certificates that were distributed to Jewish skilled workers employed in places authorized by the Germans.

182

RESPONSA BY RABBI EPHRAIM OSHRY IN THE KOVNO GHETTO

Question : *May it be explained whether it is permissible to save oneself, and thereby cause another to be killed.*

I was asked the following in the Kovno Ghetto, on 23 Elul 5701 (September 15, 1941) : Jordan, accursed be his name, Commander for Ghetto Affairs in Kovno, had given the *Ältestenrat* (Council of Elders) 5,000 white cards ("Jordan permits"), which were to be distributed among the craftsmen and their families, and only those who had cards would remain. At that time there were almost 30,000 Jewish souls in the ghetto, and among them about 10,000 craftsmen and their families. There was a great tumult, and those who were strongest snatched the cards from the *Ältestenrat*.

And now the first question is whether it is permissible for the *Ältestenrat* to take the cards and distribute them among the craftsmen in accordance with the orders of Jordan, accursed be his name? The second question is whether it is permissible for the craftsmen to snatch these cards and to push away their comrades among the craftsmen who will remain over and above the number of 5,000 cards, and what will be with them?

[Answer :] ... it is possible to say that in this case all the craftsmen are in a sense partners in all the cards, for it is conceded that they were given for all of them, and therefore all have a share in them. And if so, then each one may snatch who has a share in them. And later, when I came to write, I was shown by my distinguished friend, our Rabbi and teacher, Israel Gostman, may he live good days, Amen, the head of the Torah School at the Yeshiva of Lubavitch, that the commentary of Rabbi Eliezer Edels (Maharsha) on the Tractate Baba Metzia [of the Talmud] 62 states: "that if a flask of water (which can sustain but one person) belongs to two (men), then Rabbi Akiva accepts the position of Ben Petora, that in this case both should die rather than one drink and witness the death of his friend. This, therefore, represents a position opposite to the one we proposed, for if we consider them partners then they may not snatch [the permits], for that would make them as one who takes a thing from his fellow and saves himself by means of a thing that belongs to the other.

But while all this must be considered, it may be said that in this case the ruling does not apply, for it is not a matter of a specific person; it had been the intention of the evil ones, may they be accursed, to destroy all, but now there is a way to save a few by means of the permits that have been issued, and thus acceptance of the cards and their distribution becomes a matter of saving [persons]. Later I heard from the revered and learned Rabbi A. D. Schapira, may he be remembered as a just man and blessed, the head of the Rabbinical Court of Kovno, that when the order went out on 6 Heshvan 5702 from the evil ones, accursed be their names, to the *Ältestenrat* that it should post a notice on 8 Heshvan 5702 (October 26, 1941) that all the occupants of the ghetto — men, women and children — be assembled at the *Demokraten Platz,* the *Ältestenrat* came to ask the head of the Rabbinical Court what they should do in accordance with the laws of the Torah, for it was known that a great part of those who assembled would be doomed to die. After he had considered the matter the head of the Rabbinical Court ruled as follows : if the order was made that a community in Israel be destroyed, and if by some means it was possible to save a small part of the people, then the heads of the community must gather up courage in their souls, and it is their responsibility to act and to save who may be saved. And therefore in this case it appears that taking and distributing the permits is also a matter of rescue and it is not appropriate to rule in this case according to the law for an individual and therefore the *Ältestenrat* is required to accept the permits and to distribute them.

*   *   *

Question : *Are infants subject to the commandment to sanctify the Name of God by martyrdom?*

I was asked on 3 and 4 Nisan 5704 [March 27-28, 1944] in the Kovno Ghetto, in the days of the killing and loss and terrible fate for the glory of our offspring, concerning our children and infants, the children of Israel.

In their desire to save their children, the parents devised a way: they bought birth certificates from the unbelievers and abandoned the children at the orphanage of the unbelievers in order that the unbelievers might think that the abandoned child was also an unbeliever. The parents also gave the children to priests and wrote to the priests that the children had been converted from their faith. Is this permissible?

2. Is it permissible to give the children to the unbelievers to hide until after the war and the fall of Hitler, may his name be accursed, where there is doubt that the parents will remain alive and therefore the children will be bound to remain among the unbelievers and live in their faith and their ways?

[Answer :] ... if the child is not given to the unbelievers it is certain that it will die, and if they are among the unbelievers they will live, and it is possible that the parents may remain alive and take the child back and return it to Judaism, and it is possible that the unbelievers themselves may return the child to a Jewish institution, and there are many possibilities in favor. And the Almighty in His goodness will have mercy on the remnants of His oppressed people and not add further to their suffering, and we shall witness the consolation of Zion and of Jerusalem.

E. Oshry, *Sefer Divre Ephraim* ("The Sayings of Ephraim"), New York, 1949, pp. 95-96, 101-102.

183

FROM THE DIARY OF A LITHUANIAN WOMAN DOCTOR ON THE JEWS IN THE KOVNO GHETTO, 1941

October 15 [1941]

Announcement in the Lithuanian language :

"Although sensible people, and they include the very great majority of the Lithuanian people, avoid contact with Jews, it can be observed that the Jews who leave the ghetto daily for work and return there succeed in establishing contacts with individual Lithuanian citizens. Therefore:

1. It is hereby forbidden to non-Jewish residents to maintain any form of relations whatsoever with Jews, *even any simple conversation between a non-Jew and a Jew*. It is forbidden to sell, exchange, or make a gift of any foodstuffs or any goods; it is forbidden altogether to trade with Jews.

2. The German Police and the Lithuanian Auxiliary Police have ordered that all contact between non-Jews and Jews be cut off. Any person contravening this Order will be *severely punished*."

A threat to think about. Thousands of people humiliated, without any protection, worse than animals, and all that because they have "other blood."...

October 30

Again (10.28) 10,000 people have been taken out of the ghetto to die. They selected the old people, mothers with their children, those not capable of working. There were many tragedies : there were cases where a husband had been in town and on his return he no longer found either his wife or his four children ! And there were cases where they left the wife and took away the husband. Eye-witnesses tell the tale : On the previous day there was an announcement that everybody must come at six in the morning to the big square in the ghetto and line up in rows, except workers with the documents which were recently distributed to specialists and foremen. In the first row were the members of the Council of Elders and their families, behind them the Jewish Police, after that the administration officials of the ghetto, after that the various work-brigades and all the others. Some of them were directed to the right — that meant death — and some were directed to the left. The square was surrounded by guards with machine guns. It was freezing. The people stood on their feet all through that long day, hungry and with empty hands. Small children cried in their mothers' arms. Nobody suspected that a bitter fate awaited them. They thought that they were being moved to other apartments (the previous evening there had been arguments and even quarrels about the apartments). At dawn there was a rumor that at the Ninth Fort* (the death Fort) prisoners had been digging deep ditches, and when the people were taken there, it was already clear to everybody that this was death. They broke out crying, wailed, screamed. Some tried to escape on the way there but they were shot dead. Many bodies remained in the fields. At the Fort the condemned were stripped of their clothes, and in groups of 300 they were forced into the ditches. First they threw in the children. The women were shot at the edge of the ditch, after that it was the turn of the men... Many were covered [with earth] while they were still alive... All the men doing the shooting were drunk. I was told all this by an acquaintance who heard it from a German soldier, an eyewitness, who wrote to his Catholic wife: "Yesterday I became convinced that there is no God. If there were, He would not allow such things to happen"...

Y. Kutorgene, *"Kaunaski dnievnik* (Kovno Diary) 1941-1942," *Druzhba Narodov* ("Amity of Nations"), VIII, 1968, pp. 210-211.

* The Ninth Fort — the place where the Jews of Kovno were killed.

184

DEATH PENALTY FOR TRADE IN A CONCENTRATION CAMP

Report of the Commander of the Jewish Concentration Camp of Daugavpils

To the Commander of Section No. 1 of the Police at Daugavpils
Daugavpils
February 19, 1942

On February 19th of this year the Jewess Chaya Mayerova, born 1893, was arrested in the Jewish Camp for exchanging a piece of material against approximately 2 kgs. of flour, with a maintenance laborer* in the concentration camp. In accordance with the instructions of the German Security Police, the Jewess Mayerova was executed by shooting at ten o'clock today in the yard of the camp, in the presence of the other Jews of the camp. The laborer who exchanged the flour for the material was not found. Attached : the bag with the flour.

***

My Obviniayem ("We Accuse"), Riga, 1967, p. 184.

* The reference is to a non-Jew.

185

APPLICATION BY KUBE, GENERALKOMMISSAR OF BYELORUSSIA, TO LOHSE CONCERNING THE CONDITION OF GERMAN JEWS IN MINSK, DECEMBER 16, 1941

Minsk, December 16, 1941

Generalkommissar for Byelorussia
to *Reichskommissar* for *Ostland*
Gauleiter Hinrich Lohse
Riga

Reich Secret Document

My Dear Hinrich,

I wish to ask you personally for an official directive for the conduct of the civilian administration towards the Jews deported from Germany to Byelorussia. Among these Jews are men who fought at the Front and have the Iron Cross, First and Second Class, war invalids, half-Aryans, even three-quarter Aryans. Up to now only 6,000 to 7,000 Jews have arrived, of the 25,000 who were expected. I am not aware what has become of the others. In the course of several official visits to the Ghetto I noted that these Jews, who also differ from the Russian Jews in their personal cleanliness, there are also skilled workers capable of doing five times as much in a day as the Russian Jews.

These Jews will probably freeze or starve to death in the coming weeks. They present a terrible threat of disease for us, as they are naturally just as much exposed to the 22 epidemics prevalent in Byelorussia as we Reich-Germans (*Reichsdeutsche*). Serum is not available for them.

On my own responsibility I will not give the SD any instructions with regard to the treatment of these people, although certain units of the Wehrmacht and the police already have an eye on the possessions of the Jews from the Reich. Without asking, the SD has already simply taken away 400 mattresses from the

Jews from the Reich, and has also confiscated various other things. I am certainly a hard [man] and willing to help solve the Jewish question, but people who come from our own cultural sphere just are not the same as the brutish hordes in this place. Is the slaughter to be carried out by the Lithuanians and Letts, who are themselves rejected by the population here? I couldn't do it. I beg you to give clear directives [in this matter,] with due consideration for the good name of our Reich and our Party, in order that the necessary action can be taken in the most humane manner.

With heartfelt greetings
Heil Hitler!
Your
Wilhelm Kube

PS-3665.

186

NOTES BY A JEW FROM VIENNA DEPORTED TO A CAMP IN THE MINSK DISTRICT

On May 6, 1942, we left the collection camp (in Vienna)... (at the) railway station we learned... that we were being taken to Minsk. We traveled by passenger coach as far as Wolkowisk, where we had to... change over into cattle vans... We arrived in Minsk on May 11 (at the) station we were met by SS and Police... For the transport of the sick, of persons who went out of their mind during the journey, the aged and infirm (about 200 in number in our transport) box-cars stood waiting — great, grey, closed motor-vans — into which the people were thrown one on top of the other in confusion... 81 persons fit for work were picked from among the arrivals and taken to the camp of the Security Police and SD in Mali-Trostinez (12 kms. from Minsk). The camp consisted of a few rotting old barns and stables. That is where we were housed... When new people arrived, others who were not 100 percent fit for work were taken out. We were told that some of these were sent to hospital and others to other estates to work there. (Only) the best workers were to stay on our estate, Mali-Trostinez, so that our camp would be an example to others... The highest complement in the camp was about 600 Jews and 300 Russian prisoners... On July 28, 1942, the news reached us in the camp of a *"Grossaktion in the Ghetto."* It involved at that time about 8,000 Russian and 5,000 German, Austrian and Czech Jews, who had been in the Minsk Ghetto from November 1941... The transports ceased at the end of 1942... (in the meantime) we learned that there were no "other estates" in the vicinity of Minsk and that it was to "Estate 16" that all the people were taken... "Estate 16" is about 4–5 kms. from Mali-Trostinez on the main road to Mogilev, (it contains mass graves) of thousands of persons who were shot or (murdered) in the gas vans...*

J. Moser, *Die Judenverfolgung in Österreich 1938-1945* ("Persecution of the Jews in Austria, 1938-1945"), Vienna, 1966, pp. 35-36.

* See document 191.

187

REPORT BY KUBE ON THE EXTERMINATION OF JEWS AND THE FIGHT AGAINST THE PARTISANS IN BYELORUSSIA

The *Generalkommissar* for Byelorussia   Minsk, July 31, 1942
Gauleiter /G 507/42 g

To
Reichkommissar for *Ostland*
Gauleiter Hinrich Lohse
Riga

Secret

Re: *Combating Partisans and* Aktion *Against Jews in the*
Generalbezirk *of Byelorussia*

In all the clashes with the partisans in Byelorussia it has proved that Jewry, both in the formerly Polish, as well as in the formerly Soviet parts of the District General, is the main bearer of the partisan movement, together with the Polish resistance movement in the East and the Red Army from Moscow. In consequence, the treatment of Jewry in Byelorussia is a matter of political importance owing to the danger to the entire economy. It must therefore be solved in accordance with political considerations and not merely economic needs. Following exhaustive discussions with the SS *Brigadeführer* Zenner and the exceedingly capable Leader of the SD, SS *Obersturmbannführer* Dr. jur. Strauch, we have liquidated about 55,000 Jews in Byelorussia in the past 10 weeks. In the area of Minsk county Jewry has been completely eliminated without any danger to the manpower requirements. In the predominantly Polish area of Lida, 16,000 Jews were liquidated, in Slonim, 8,000, etc.

Owing to encroachment by the Army Rear Zone (Command), which has already been reported, there was interference with the preparations we had made for the liquidation of the Jews in Glebokie. Without contacting me, the Army Rear Zone Command liquidated 10,000 Jews, whose systematic elimination had in any case been planned by us. In the city of Minsk about 10,000 Jews were liquidated on July 28 and 29. Of these 6,500 were Russian Jews — mainly old men, women and children — and the rest Jews incapable of work, who were sent to Minsk in November of last year by order of the Führer, mainly from Vienna, Brünn, Bremen and Berlin.

The District of Sluzk has also been relieved of several thousand Jews. The same applies to Nowogrodek and Wilejka. Radical measures are planned for Baranowitschi and Hanzewitschi. In Baranowitschi there are still another 10,000 Jews in the city itself, of whom 9,000 will be liquidated next month.

In the city of Minsk about 2,600 Jews from Germany have remained. In addition all of the 6,000 Russian Jews and Jewesses remained alive who were employed during the *Aktion* by various units [of the Wehrmacht]. In future, too, Minsk will remain the largest Jewish element owing to the concentration of armament industries in the area and as the requirements of the railroad make this necessary for the time being. In all other areas the number of Jews used for work will be reduced by the SD and myself to a maximum of 800, and, if possible, 500, so that when the remaining planned *Aktionen* have been completed there will be 8,600 in Minsk and about 7,000 Jews in the 10 other districts, including the Jew-free Minsk District. There will then be no further danger that the partisans can still rely to any real extent on Jewry. Naturally I and the SD would like it best if Jewry in the *Generalbezirk* of Byelorussia was finally eliminated after their labor is no longer required by the Wehrmacht. For the time being the essential requirements of the Wehrmacht, the main employer of Jewry, are being taken into consideration.

In addition to this unambiguous attitude towards Jewry, the SD in Byelorussia also has the onerous task of continually transferring new transports of Jews from the Reich to their destination. This causes excessive strain on the physical and spiritual capacities of the personnel of the SD, and withdraws them from duties within the area of Byelorussia itself.

I should therefore be grateful if the Reichskommissar *could see his way to stopping further deportations of Jews to Minsk at least until the danger from the partisans has been finally overcome.* I need 100 percent of the SD manpower against the Partisans and the Polish Resistance Movement, which together occupy the entire strength of the not overwhelmingly strong SD units.

After completion of the *Aktion* against the Jews in Minsk, SS *Obersturmbannführer* Dr. Strauch reported to me this night, with justified indignation, that suddenly, without instructions from the *Reichsführer,* and without notification to the *Generalkommissar, a transport of 1,000 Jews from Warsaw* has arrived for the local *Luftwaffe* Command.

I beg the *Reichskommissar (already warned by telegram)* to prevent the dispatch of such transports, in his capacity as supreme authority in *Ostland.* The Polish Jew, exactly like the Russian Jew, is an enemy of the German nation. He represents a politically dangerous element, a danger which far exceeds his value as a skilled worker. Under no circumstances should the army or the *Luftwaffe* import Jews into an area under civil administration, either from the Government-General or from elsewhere, without the approval of the *Reichskommissar,* as this endangers the entire political task here and the security of the *Generalbezirk.* I am in full agreement with the Commander of the SD in Byelorussia that we should liquidate every transport of Jews not arranged, or announced to us, by our superior officers, to prevent further disturbances in Byelorussia.

The *Generalkommissar*
for Byelorussia
signed Kube

PS-3428.

188

REPORT BY WAFFEN SS ON KILLING OF JEWS IN THE PRIPET MARSHES

2nd SS-Cavalry Regiment   Regt. st. Qtrs., Aug. 12, 1941
Mounted Unit

Report
On the Course of the *Aktion*
in the Pripet [Marshes] from
July 27 to August 11, 1941.

Impressions of the battle : None

Population: Mainly Ukrainian; Byelorussians in second place; in third place Poles and Russians; only a very few of the latter. The Jews are mainly in the larger places, where they make up a high percentage of the population, in some cases from 50-80 percent, but in others as little as 25 percent...

In many cases when the troops moved in we found that, according to a Ukrainian practice, a table with a white cloth had been prepared with bread and salt that was offered to the commanders. In one case there was even a small band of musicians to welcome the troops...

Type of land : The whole area consists of large marshes interspersed with patches of sand, so that the ground is not very fertile. There are some better places, but others were all the poorer...

...Jewish doctors were preferred. In the towns and villages it was also noticeable that only Jewish artisans were found. There was a large number of Jewish émigrés from the *Altreich* [Germany before 1938] and the *Ostmark* [Austria]...

Pacification: Pacification was carried out through the commanders of units or companies who contacted the local mayors and discussed all matters concerning the population. On these occasions the numbers and composition of the population, i.e., Ukrainians, Byelorussians, etc., were checked. Further, whether there were still Communists in the locality or secret members of the Red Army, or others who had been active Bolsheviks. In most cases local residents also reported that they had seen gangs or other suspicious persons. Where such individuals were still in the locality, they were detained and, after a brief inter-rogation, they were either released or shot...

Jewish looters were shot. Only a few skilled workers employed in the Wehrmacht repair workshops were permitted to remain.

The driving of women and children into the marshes did not have the expected success, because the marshes were not so deep that one could sink. After a depth of about a meter there was in most cases solid ground (probably sand) preventing complete sinking...

...The Ukrainian clergy were very cooperative and made themselves available for every *Aktion.*

It was also conspicuous that in general the population was on good terms with the Jewish sector of the population. Never-theless they helped energetically in rounding up the Jews. The locally recruited guards, who consisted in part of Polish police and former Polish soldiers, made a good impression. They operated energetically and took part in the fight against looters...

The total number of looters, etc., shot by the Mounted Units was 6,526...

signed Magill
SS *Sturmbannführer*

Kriegstagebuch des Kommandostabes Reichsführer SS ("War Diary of the Kommandostaff *Reichsführer* SS"), Vienna, 1965, pp. 217-220.

189

FROM A REPORT BY EINSATZGRUPPEN ON THE EXTERMINATION OF THE JEWS IN THE UKRAINE, OCTOBER 1941

Operations and Situation Report No. 6 by the Einsatzgruppen of the Security Police and SD in the U.S.S.R. (for the period October 1-31, 1941)

... c) *Jews*

The bitter hostility of the Ukrainian population against the Jews is extremely great, because it is thought that they were responsible for the explosions in Kiev. They are also seen as NKVD informers and agents, who unleashed the terror against the Ukrainian people. All Jews were arrested in retaliation for the arson in Kiev, and altogether 33,771 Jews were executed on September 29th and 30th. Gold, valuables and clothing were collected and put at the disposal of the National-Socialist Welfare Association (NSV), for the equipment of the *Volksdeutsche,* and part given to the appointed city administration for distribution to the needy population.

Schitomir

In Schitomir 3,145 Jews had to be shot, because experience showed they must be considered as bearers of Bolshevist propaganda and saboteurs.

Cherson

In Cherson 410 Jews were executed in retaliation for acts of sabotage.

The solution of the Jewish question in the area east of the Dnjepr in particular has been firmly attacked by the *Einsatzgruppen* of the Security Police and the SD. The areas newly occupied by the commandos were cleared of Jews. In the course of this action 4,891 Jews were liquidated. In other localities the *Jews were marked and registered*. This made it possible to put at the disposal of Wehrmacht offices Jewish *worker groups of up to 1,000 persons* for urgent work...

———————

R-102.

190

FROM A WEHRMACHT REPORT ON THE EXTERMINATION OF THE JEWS IN THE UKRAINE

Armament in the Ukraine   December 2, 1941
Inspector

                                                          Secret

To
The Office of Wi Rü [Industrial Armament Department]
O K W [High Command of the Wehrmacht]
General of the Infantry Thomas
Berlin

... c. The Jewish Question
The settling of the Jewish Question in the Ukraine has been made more difficult because in the cities the Jews constituted a major part of the population. What we have here is therefore — just as in the Government-General — a massive population policy problem. Many cities had more than 50 percent Jews. Only the rich Jews fled before the German troops. The great majority of the Jewish masses remained under the German Administration. The entire situation was complicated by the fact that *these Jews carried out almost all the work in the skilled trades and even provided part of the labor for small- and medium-sized industries;* apart from trade, some of which had become superfluous as the result of the direct or indirect effects of the war. [*Their*] *elimination was therefore bound to have profound economic consequences,* including even direct effects on the military economy (supplies for troops).

417

From the outset the attitude of the Jewish population was anxious-willing. They tried to avoid anything that might displease the German Administration. That they hated the German Administration and the Army in their hearts is obvious and not surprising. However, there is no evidence that the Jews, either as a body, or even in any considerable numbers, have taken part in sabotage, etc. Without doubt there have been some terrorists or saboteurs among them, just as there have been among the Ukrainians. But it cannot be claimed that the Jews as such present any kind of danger for the German Wehrmacht. The troops and the German Administration have been satisfied with the work output of the Jews, who are of course motivated by no emotion except fear.

Immediately following the military operations, the Jewish population remained undisturbed at first. It was only weeks, in some cases months, later that systematic shooting of the Jews was carried out by units of the Order Police specially set up for this purpose. This *Aktion* moved in the main from east to west. It was carried out entirely in public, with the assistance of Ukrainian militia; in many cases, regrettably, also with the voluntary participation of members of the Wehrmacht. These *Aktionen* included aged men, women, and children of all ages, and the manner in which they were carried out was appalling. The gigantic number of executions involved in this *Aktion* is far greater than any similar measure undertaken in the Soviet Union up to now. Altogether about 150,000 to 200,000 Jews may have been executed in the section of the Ukraine belonging to the RK [*Reichskommissariat*]; up to now no consideration was given to the interests of the economy.

To sum up it could be said that the solution of the Jewish Question as carried out in the Ukraine, evidently motivated by ideological principles, has had the following consequences:

a) Elimination of some, in part superfluous, eaters in the cities.
b) Elimination of a part of the population which undoubtedly hated us.

418

c) Elimination of urgently needed craftsmen, who were in many cases indispensable for the requirements of the Wehrmacht.

d) Consequences in connection with foreign propaganda that are obvious.

e) Adverse effects on troops which in any case have indirect contact with executions.

f) Brutalizing effects on the units (Order Police) which carry out the executions...

PS-3257.

191

EXTERMINATION IN GAS VANS IN THE UKRAINE, 1942

Kiev, May 16, 1942

Field Post Office No. 32704
B. Nr 40/42

Reich Secret Document

To SS-*Obersturmbannführer* Rauff
Berlin

The overhauling of the vans of [*Einsatz*] *Gruppe* D and C has been completed...

I have had the vans of [*Einsatz*] *Gruppe* D disguised as house-trailers, by having a single window shutter fixed to each side of the small vans, and on the large ones, two shutters, such as one often sees on farm houses in the country. The vans had become so well known that not only the authorities but the civilian population referred to them as the "Death Vans" as soon as one appeared. In my opinion the vans cannot be kept secret for any length of time even if they are camouflaged.

The brakes of the Saurer van which I took from Taganrog to Simferopol were damaged on the way... When I reached Stalino and Gorlovka a few days later the drivers of the vans there complained of the same trouble...

I also gave instructions that all personnel should stay as far away as possible from the vans when the gassing is in progress to prevent damage to their health in the event of gas leaking out. I would like to take this opportunity to call attention to the following: several of the special units let their own men do the unloading after gassing.

I pointed out to the commanders of the *Sonderkommando* (Special Unit) concerned the enormous psychological and physical harm this may cause the men, possibly later even if not immediately. The men complained to me of headaches that recur after each such unloading. Nevertheless there is reluctance to change the orders because it is feared that if prisoners are used for this work they might make use of a favorable moment to escape. I request appropriate instructions in order to save the men from suffering harm.

The gassing is generally not carried out correctly. In order to get the *Aktion* finished as quickly as possible the driver presses down on the accelerator as far as it will go. As a result the persons to be executed die of suffocation and do not doze off as was planned. It has proved that if my instructions are followed and the levers are properly adjusted death comes faster and the prisoners fall asleep peacefully. Distorted faces and excretions, such as were observed before, no longer occur.

Today I shall continue my journey to [*Einsatz*] *Gruppe* B, where I may be reached for further instructions.

Dr. Becker
SS *Untersturmführer*

PS-501.

192

EVIDENCE ON THE KILLING OF JEWS IN KHARKOV

On the Mass Shooting of Jews by the German Murderers in the Drobitzki Valley Protocol

Kharkov, September 5, 1943

We, the undersigned, members of the Commission constituted as follows: Ilya Ivanovich Profatilov — Chairman of the District Commission for the determination and investigation of the crimes of the German-Fascist invaders and their collaborators; and the following members: Aleksander Ignatyevich Selivanov — Chairman of the Executive Committee of the City Council of Kharkov; Major General Nikolai Ivanovich Trufanov — the Military Commander of the city of Kharkov; the Representatives of the Extraordinary Government Committee—Konstantin Alekseyevich Lebedev and Dmitri Ivanovich Kudryavtzev; Protoyerey (Senior Priest) of the Church of Pokrov — Ivan Yakovlevich Kamyshan; Representative of the Executive Committee of the City Council of Kharkov— Valentina Vasilyevna Karpenko; the professors — Aleksei Ivanovich Shevtzov, and Yevgeni Sevastyanovich Katkov, Ivan Vasilyevich Kudintzev, and Ivan Ivanovich Makletzov, compiled the present protocol, and these are its contents:

During the occupation of the city of Kharkov by the German-Fascist invaders the peaceful population was destroyed systematically, and the Jewish population was totally destroyed one by one. According to incomplete records, upwards of 15,000 Jewish residents of the city of Kharkov were shot during the months of December 1941 and January 1942 alone near the village of Rogan, 8 kms. from the city of Kharkov in the so-called valley of Drobitzki. This barbarity inflicted on innocent citizens was confirmed by evidence obtained from witnesses, from protocols by medical experts and from other reliable documents, and these barbarous acts were also confirmed at the place where they

421

were committed by a member of the State Commission, Academy Member A. N. Tolstoy.

The German Military Commander of the city of Kharkov on December 14, 1941, issued an order according to which all the Jewish population of the city were required, within two days, to move to the huts of the Lathe Factory on the outskirts of the city. It was stated in the order that those failing to comply with these instructions would be shot.

In the huts into which all the Jews of the city were herded the doors and windows were broken, the water system and stoves destroyed. Hundreds of people were pushed into these huts, which had been intended to house 60 to 70 persons. The Germans starved the population in the ghetto that was set up, and forbade them to go out to fetch water or find food. At night they were even forbidden to leave the huts to relieve themselves. Anyone who infringed the regime in the least way was shot immediately. Many of the people fell sick and died. The corpses of the dead were left lying in the huts, and it was forbidden to take them out from there. The citizen Anna Yosifovna Chernenko-Nazvich, who succeeded in escaping from the camp, related the following:

"On December 28, 1941, in the evening, the Nazis burst into the huts, took out 60 persons and shot them on the spot. Shootings of this kind were a common occurrence."

According to the evidence of F. I. Kersten and A. F. Grigorova, the Germans continued to plunder the property of the occupants of the camp. Every day the Germans made demands that they be given warm clothing, watches and other valuables. If their demands were not fulfilled because the goods were not available, then the soldiers used to take out some tens of persons from the huts and shoot them. There were many who could not endure the systematic brutality and humiliation and lost their minds or committed suicide. One who lost her mind was Dr. Belyayevskaya, the wife of Prof. Mamutov, and others. Within the area of the ghetto there was a so-called "living grave," from which, after the killings, groans were heard coming from people who had been buried alive there. On December 26, 1941, the Germans announced that a list would be made of persons wishing to travel to Poltava, Romny and Kremenchug, noting that those who went would not be permitted to take any baggage at all with them. On the following day automobiles arrived outside the huts. The people understood this *provokatzia* and refused to get into the automobiles. The soldiers pushed them in by force and they were taken out of the camp. In the course of a few days the inmates of the ghetto were taken to the valley of Drobitzki by car or on foot, and there they were all shot. An eye-witness to the slaughter, from the village of Rogan, Anastasya Zakharovna Osmachko, said the following:

"When I learned of the murder of Soviet citizens by Germans in the valley of Drobitzki, on the morning of January 7, 1942, I went to see what was happening there together with my son Vladimir, aged 12, and another 11 people from the village. In the valley we discovered a pit several tens of meters long, ten meters wide and several meters deep. Many bodies of those who had been shot were piled up in the pit. When we had looked at the bodies we decided to go home. But we had not yet had time to leave the valley when three trucks arrived carrying German soldiers. The soldiers stopped us. They took us to the pit and one of them began to shoot at us with a machine-gun. When my son fell I fainted and fell into the pit. When I recovered I found myself lying on dead bodies. Later I heard the cries of women and children whom the Germans were bringing to the pit and shooting. The bodies of those who were shot fell into the pit where I lay.

I was in the pit from the morning until 4:00 or 5:00 in the afternoon and saw how, throughout the whole day, the Germans kept bringing groups of people to the pit and killing them. Before my eyes several thousand people were shot. They were Jews — men and children. When the Germans had finished the slaughter they left the place. From among the corpses groans and cries went up from the living wounded. About half an hour after the German soldiers had left the place

I crawled out of the pit and ran home. My son and the other people who had come with me from the village had been shot."

The witnesses Chernenko-Nazvich, Anna Yosifovna, Daniil Aleksandrovich Serikov and Fyodor Lukyanovich Kovrizhko gave evidence that together with the shooting the German-Fascist invaders killed people, mainly children, by means of poison, and afterwards burned the bodies inside the camp huts. The witnesses F. I. Kersten and A. F. Grigorova and others gave evidence that in December 1941 the Germans put into the building of the synagogue on Meshchansky Street elderly Jews, the disabled and children, who remained in Kharkov and were unable to reach their new destination on foot; a large number of them froze to death and others died of hunger. Altogether 400 persons died in the synagogue building.

The Commission opened up two pits near the village of Rogan in the valley of Drobitzki, one of them 100 meters long and 18 to 20 meters wide, and the second 60 meters long and 20 meters wide. According to the findings of the Expert Medical Commission, upward of 15,000 bodies were buried in these pits (attached: the report of the Medico-Legal Commission). Five hundred bodies were removed from the pits, of which 215 were submitted to medico-legal examination. They included the bodies of 83 men, 117 women and 60 children and infants. It was established that the cause of death of almost all these persons whose bodies had been examined was a wound and hole in the back of the skull caused by the passage of a bullet. This indicated that the shooting was carried out from behind the person to be killed and from a short distance away.

The Commission considers the following responsible for the crimes committed against the peaceful population of the city of Kharkov: the former Commander of the Special Unit SK4 (*Sonderkommando*) of the Gestapo Hellenbruch, the Commander of Special Unit SK4 of the Gestapo *Sturmbannführer* Willi Neumann, Deputy Commander Major Radetzki, Major Miller, who worked with the Gestapo, Under-officer Schneider, Gestapo interrogator Under-officer Falker, Gestapo assistant Under-officer

Ostermann, Gestapo member Captain Beuthen and Under-officer Franz Lovichko.

All these must suffer severe punishment for horrendous crimes committed against the Soviet people.

signed:

Chairman of the Commission, Ilya Ivanovich Profatilov

Members of the Commission: Chairman of the Executive Committee of the City Council of Kharkov, A. I. Selivanov

Major General N. I. Trufanov

Representatives of the Extraordinary State Committee A. K. Lebedev, D. I. Kudryavtzev

Arch-Priest of the Church of Pokrov I. Y. Kamyshan

Representative of the Executive Committee of the City Council of Kharkov, V. V. Karpenko

The professors: A. I. Shevtzov, I. V. Kudintzev, I. I. Makletzov, and Y. S. Katkov.

Dokumenty Obviniayut ("Documents Accuse"), II, Moscow, 1945, pp. 307-309.

193

ORDER TO THE JEWS BY THE GERMAN COMMAND IN THE CITY OF KISLOVODSK

To All the Jews

With the aim of populating areas of the Ukraine which are sparsely populated, all the Jews living in the city of Kislovodsk and also all Jews who have no permanent place of residence are required to be at the railway station (freight platform) of the city of Kislovodsk on Wednesday, September 9, 1942, at 5:00 in the morning Berlin time (6:00 o'clock Moscow time).

Each Jew can take baggage weighing no more than 20 kgs.

(including food for at least two days). Subsequent food requirements will be supplied by the German authorities at the railway stations.

It is suggested that only the most important items be taken, such as: valuables, money, clothing and blankets. Every Jewish family must lock the door of its apartment and affix a note to the key, on which are inscribed the name of the family, first names, occupations and the address of the family; the key with the note must be handed in to the German commanders of the railway station. Owing to transport difficulties it is not possible to take more than 20 kgs. of baggage and no furniture.

With regard to the preparation and dispatch of property remaining behind, each family must pack and mark their goods, linens, etc., and note down exactly to whom they belong. [Military City] Command No. 12 is responsible for the storage and protection of this property.

Any person who tries to put his hands on Jewish property or to break into Jewish apartments will be shot on the spot.

The transfer applies also to Jews who have been baptized. The transfer does not apply to families in which one of the parents is a Jew and the second a Russian, Ukrainian or member of another nationality. Nor does the transfer apply to persons of mixed origins.

Voluntary transfers by mixed families [*Mischlinge*] of type 1 or 2 may possibly be carried out later.

All the Jews are ordered to line up at the station in groups of 45 to 50 persons; they should pay attention that all members of a family stand together. The line-up must be completed by 5:45 Berlin time (6:45 Moscow time).

The Jewish Committee is responsible for carrying out the order according to plan. Jews who try to interfere with the execution of this order will be punished most severely.

Kislovodsk, September 7, 1942
Command Post No. 12

Dokumenty Obviniayut ("Documents Accuse"), II, Moscow, 1945, pp. 142-144.

194

EVIDENCE OF WITNESSES ON THE DEPORTATION AND KILLING OF THE JEWS OF KISLOVODSK

Destruction of the Jewish Population of Kislovodsk
Protocol

Kislovodsk, July 5, 1943

We, the undersigned, citizens of the city of Kislovodsk: Pyotr Aleksandrovich Ostankov, Professor of Leningrad Medical Institute No. 1, distinguished scientist, living at Clara Zetkin Street 4; Timofei Yefremovich Gnilorybov, professor, Head Surgeon at the convalescent home of Kislovodsk, living at Paris Commune Street No. 9; Mikhail Yefimovich Gontaryov, assistant at the Medical Institute in Leningrad, living at Paris Commune Street No. 9; Mikhail Zakharovich Fingerut, living at Ch'kalov 42a; Naum Mikhaylovich Gorelik, living at Ch'kalov No. 45; Yevgenya Terentyevna Kovnatnaya, living at Volodarskaya No. 3; and Boris Yakovlevich Khshive, living at Terski Square No. 1/4, have compiled this protocol on the crimes committed by the German invaders against citizens of the Jewish nationality, residents of the city of Kislovodsk, in the region of Stavropol.

On August 16, 1942, the German Command and its representatives, the military commander of the city of Kislovodsk, Pohl, and the head of the Gestapo, Welben, set up a Jewish Committee in the city of Kislovodsk, under the chairmanship of Moisey Samoylovich Beninson, born 1878 (dentist, who lived at Stalin Street 22). He was told by the German Command to collect from the Jewish population and hand over immediately such valuables as gold, diamonds, silver, carpets, clothing, linens and shoes.

In the hope of saving Jewish lives by handing over the above valuables to the Germans, the Jewish Committee collected and delivered to the German Commander, Pohl, 100,000 rubles in cash, 530 articles made of gold or silver, rings, watches,

427

cigarette cases, 105 dozen silver spoons, 230 pairs of shoes, men's suits, coats, and carpets. According to market prices this contribution [forced levy] was worth about 5,000,000 rubles.

On August 18, 1942, the military commander of the City of Kislovodsk, Pohl, ordered a register to be made of the Jewish population without regard to sex or age. After the registration all persons of Jewish nationality were ordered to wear an identifying mark on the right side of the chest — a six-cornered star — which they call the "Star of David."

The Jewish population between the ages of 16 through 60 was rounded up by the German Command for various forms of forced labor: for the building of the airfield, and the paving of roads. The doctors and professors were made to sweep and clean the streets. The work was done without any payment.

On September 7, 1942, the German Command No. 12 issued an order requiring the Jews to report to the railway station (at the freight station) on September 9, to take with them baggage not exceeding 20 kgs. in weight, valuables, and food for two days, in order, it was indicated, to travel from there to "sparsely populated" places in the Ukraine. They were ordered to hand in to Command No. 12 the keys of their apartments, each key to be marked with a label with the address.

On September 9, 1942, 2,000 Jews assembled at the freight station in Kislovodsk, including aged people, women and children. The Nazis took the hand baggage and also the food from the Jews, who were loaded onto 18 open freight cars and two covered cars, which stood ready for this purpose. The train then pulled out with a reinforced German guard in the direction of the railway station of Mineralnya Vody, where, according to eye-witnesses, the Jews were shot.

Among those deported and shot by the Germans were many medical workers including: Professor Baumholtz, Dr. Chatzki and his family, Dr. Schwarzman, the physician Sokolski, Dr. Mereynes, Dr. Drivinski and the Jewish writer Bregman. Altogether 117 medical workers perished.

Many of the Jews committed suicide because of the danger of

brutality by the German Command against the Jews; these included Dr. Wilenski and his wife; Dr. Bugayevskaya and the nurse Pokrovskaya.

Dr. Feinberg, his wife and daughter tried to commit suicide by taking morphine and cutting their arteries, but the vile Germans did not let them die; they moved them to the clinic, cured them and shot them afterwards.

Among the Jews deported from Kislovodsk and shot in Mineralnya Vody were 9 Jewish children from the Children's Home No. 18, aged 4-6 years. These were Olya Nimerovskaya, aged 6, Rosa Steinberg, aged 6, Grisha Shops, aged 7, Vova Shops, aged 5, Lyusik Shmaroner, aged 5, Ella Uritzkaya, aged 6, Yasha Uritzki, aged 4, Pavel Uritzki, aged 4, and Kolya Klunger, aged 5.

The citizen Fingerut, who escaped the shooting of the Jews, gave detailed evidence on the course of the shooting.

The train with the deported Jews arrived at the glass factory. The Germans who accompanied the transport ordered the Jews to get down from the freight cars, hand over their money and valuables, and then ordered them to undress.

With heart-rending cries the women, children and old people took off their clothing and stood dressed only in their underwear. Afterwards this mass of people, almost out of its mind with fear, was taken away to the anti-tank ditches, surrounded by German guards carrying submachine-guns. Anyone who tried to escape was shot dead.

At the ditches the Germans shot the Jews with submachine-guns and machine-guns.

The Germans took out 40 persons — men — and forced them to collect and load on the freight cars all the possessions of those who had been shot and afterwards took them, too, to the ditch and shot them.

As a result it has been established that the Military Commander of the city of Kislovodsk, Pohl, the head of the Gestapo Welben, and his assistant Weber, on September 9, 1942, carried out a cruel slaughter of the Jews of the city of Kislovodsk, 2,000 in number, including old people, women and children.

The facts stated above are confirmed by the following:

1. The printed decree of German Command No. 12 of September 2, 1942, given in the city of Kislovodsk, concerning the deportation of the Jews,

2. The official list of valuables handed over to the German Command,

3. The printed announcement by the German Supreme Commander "to the Civilian Population of the Caucasus" in Russian and German,

4. The evidence of M. Z. Fingerut, Y. T. Kovnatnaya, B. Y. Khshive, L. R. Lipman, Ch. R. Gertzber, E. I. Parkhomenko, L. I. Pavlova, A. M. Mirzoyan, Z. I. Kovina,

5. The document of Hospital No. 5404,

6. The document of Children's Home No. 18,

7. The list of Jews killed, numbering 894 persons.

Signed :

P. A. Ostankov, T. Y. Gnilorybov, M. Y. Gontaryov, M. Z. Fingerut, N. M. Gorelik, Y. T. Kovnatnaya, B. Y. Khshive.

Dokumenty Obviniayut ("Documents Accuse"), II, Moscow, 1945, pp. 140-142.

195

REPORT BY WEHRMACHT OFFICER ON MASSACRE IN THE UKRAINE

Roesler, Major   presently Kassel, January 3, 1942

Report

The notification from the Infantry Reserve Regiment 52 concerning "Conduct with regard to the Civilian Population in the East" causes me to submit the following report :

Towards the end of July 1941, I. R. [Infantry Regiment] 528, of which I was in command, was on its way from the West to Schitomir, where it was to move into a rest camp. On the day of our arrival, in the afternoon, when I had moved into the Staff Quarters together with my Staff, we heard salvoes of rifle fire at regular intervals, fired at no great distance, and followed by pistol shots after a little while. I decided to investigate this matter and with my Adjutant and Ordnance Officer (First Lieutenant v. Bassewitz and Lt. Müller-Brodmann) set out in the direction of the rifle fire. We soon received the impression that some cruel show must be taking place here because after a while we saw numerous soldiers and civilians streaming towards a railway embankment in front of us; we were informed that executions were being carried out continuously behind it. Throughout this time we were unable to see across the railway embankment to the other side, but at regular intervals we heard the sound of a trilling whistle and then a salvo of about 10 rifle shots, followed after a certain interval by pistol shots. When we finally climbed up the railway embankment a sight was revealed to us on the other side of a horrible cruelty that was bound to shake and disgust anyone who came face to face with it unprepared. A pit had been cut in the ground, about 4 m. wide and 7–8 m. long, and the excavated earth had been piled up on one side. This mound and the side of the pit beneath it was stained all over with streams of blood. The pit itself was filled with human corpses of all kinds and both sexes in such numbers that it was difficult to estimate them; it was not possible to judge the depth of the pit. Behind the mound of excavated earth a Police Commando was lined up with a Police Officer in command. The uniforms of the commandos were stained with blood. In a wide circle stood countless soldiers of troop units already stationed there, some as spectators, dressed in swimming trunks, as well as many civilians with women and children. I stepped right up to the pit to obtain a picture that I have not been able to forget until this day. Among others there was an old man with a long white beard lying in the grave, with a little walking stick still hooked over his left arm. As this man still gave signs of life by his stertorous breathing, I requested one of the policemen to kill him off, but he answered with a laugh: "I fired seven shots into his belly, he'll croak on his own." The persons who had been shot were not placed in the grave in any order, but stayed there lying as they had fallen from the wall of the pit after they were shot. All these persons had been killed by shots in the back of the neck and then finished off with pistol shots from the top. I did not acquire any excessive sensitivity of the emotions during my service in the World War and in the French and Russian campaigns of this war; and experienced much that was more than unpleasant when I was active in the volunteer units in 1919, but I cannot recall ever having witnessed a scene such as that I have described here. I am not concerned here with whatever court decisions may have formed the basis for the executions I have described, I felt it was not reconcilable with our concepts of custom and decency up to the present time that a mass slaughter of human beings should be carried out quite publicly, as on an outdoor stage. I wish to add that according to statements by soldiers who frequently watch these executions, several hundreds of persons were said to be shot every day.

Prestupnye tseli-Prestupnye sredstva. Dokumenty ob okkupatsionnoy politike fashistskoy Germanii na territorii SSSR, 1941-1944 ("Criminal Aims — Criminal Means — Documents on Occupational Policy of Fascist Germany in the Territory of the USSR, 1941-1944"), Moscow, 1968, pp. 110-111.

196

PROCLAMATION BY JEWISH PIONEER YOUTH GROUP IN VILNA, CALLING FOR RESISTANCE, JANUARY 1, 1942

They Shall Not Take Us Like Sheep to the Slaughter !

Jewish youth, do not be led astray. Of the 80,000 Jews in the "Jerusalem of Lithuania" [Vilna] only 20,000 have remained. Before our eyes they tore from us our parents, our brothers and sisters. Where are the hundreds of men who were taken away for work by the Lithuanian "snatchers"? Where are the naked women and children who were taken from us in the night of terror of the *provokatzia*?
Where are the Jews [who were taken away on] the Day of Atonement?
Where are our brothers from the second ghetto?
All those who were taken away from the ghetto never came back.
All the roads of the Gestapo lead to Ponary.
And Ponary is death!
Doubters! Cast off all illusions. Your children, your husbands and your wives are no longer alive.
Ponary is not a camp — all are shot there.
Hitler aims to destroy all the Jews of Europe. The Jews of Lithuania are fated to be the first in line.
Let us not go as sheep to slaughter!
It is true that we are weak and defenseless, but resistance is the only reply to the enemy!
Brothers! It is better to fall as free fighters than to live by the grace of the murderers.
Resist! To the last breath.

January 1, 1942, Vilna Ghetto.

Moreshet Archives, D. 1.4630.

433

A proclamation calling for resistance, read at a meeting of Jewish pioneer
youth in Vilna on January 1, 1942

COMMENTS ON THE PROGRAM OF THE F.P.O.* IN VILNA **

Comments to the Program

During the study of the program [for fighting], which was on the whole well received by the organization and taken seriously, questions of fundamental importance were raised by some groups. Some of these questions were based on doubts, and derived from weakness and *inadequate* preparation for the *realities* of the *direct* struggle.

Without reference to the question of which groups had posed these questions, the Command Staff considered it necessary to answer these questions as follows:

A. *How will the F.P.O. react in the event of a partial destruction of the ghetto?*

B. *What should a single fighter do if he remains alone in a battle without any possibility of carrying on the battle alone?*

C. *Should we not go to the forest immediately?*

D. *What is the aim of the battle (the ultimate goal)?*

E. *Is there a necessity to hide in a* maline?

Answers

A. *How will the F.P.O. react in the event of a partial destruction?*

1) The F.P.O. *will move out into battle when the existence of the ghetto as a whole is threatened.*

2) It may be that there will be various kinds of murder-*Aktionen* of a local character or reprisals by the Gestapo for "crimes," that may cost the lives of individuals, or of tens or hundreds of Jews.

3) It is our view that the life of every single Jew is worthy of defense and must not be abandoned to the murderers without resistance.

435

4) The F.P.O., however, is not a large military force which can enter into a battle of equals with the enemy, and it cannot and *will not come out* in defense of each, *single* Jewish life.

5) The F.P.O., which is the spearhead of the remainder of the Jewish Community (not only in Vilna) could, *by premature* action bring about its own premature destruction, leaving the ghetto without any defense at all, without the F.P.O., the only organization capable of fighting.

6) This kind of action would be quixotic, a suicidal tactic. Furthermore, Jews might condemn us as provocateurs, and this might cause us to fight against our own brethren.

7) But just as premature action would be irresponsible so action *delayed too long* would be criminal.

8) The F.P.O. will move out in such an *Aktion* when it is estimated that the *beginning of the end* has come; at that point it will no longer be a question of the numbers involved in the *Aktion*.

9) The *Command Staff* will decide when the time has come to move into battle. It will judge the situation on the basis of sources of information which are available and open to it.

10) Our inadequate supply of arms justifies the fact that the F.P.O. cannot go into action *at all times*. But our inadequate arms cannot justify under any circumstances the avoiding of fighting when the whole existence of the ghetto is threatened.

When total destruction threatens us we must come out to fight whatever the position regarding weapons; we must come out even if we have no arms and must fight with our bare hands.

B. *What shall a single fighter do if he remains alone in the battle, after he has used up all his fighting possibilities, without contact or prospects of continuing to fight against overwhelming enemy forces?*

436

11) Where such a situation *is the result of battle* the single fighter can and must *retreat.*

12) In the event of there still being other fighting groups, the individual must at all costs reach them and join them.

13) If no other groups have survived, the individual should save himself by whatever means possible at that time.

14) Although prepared to fall in battle — *it is not the F.P.O.'s aim to fall fighting for the last positions in the ghetto.*

15) The aim of the F.P.O. is *resistance as such,* and not the defense of the ghetto to the end.

16) The aim of the F.P.O. is *resistance, struggle and rescue.*

17) The above does not mean that anyone who observes the unequal forces and the inadequate arms in his possession should give up the battle *from the beginning.*

18) *Avoidance of the battle while fighting is in progress, for whatever reason (inadequate arms, lack of favorable prospects, etc.) is treason.*

C. *Should we not go to the forest immediately?*

19) No. The wish to go to the forests now is evidence of failure to understand the idea of the F.P.O.

20) The principle of the *Jewish Partisans Organization is social and national,* to organize the struggle of the Jews and to defend our lives and our honor.

21) To go to the forests at this time would mean the search for *individual security,* individual escape, just as hiding in a *maline* means search for *individual security.*

22) We will go to the forests, but as the *result of battle.* When we have carried out our purpose here, we will take with us as great a number of Jews as possible, and continue our struggle against the murdering occupier as part of the partisan movement.

23) It is only through battle, and as a result of our resistance, that we shall be able to save large numbers of Jews.

This is also a reply to Question D.

E. *Is there a necessity to hide in the* maline?

24) No. This question receives the same vigorous treatment as in the orders: *It is treason under all circumstances to go to a* maline.

The Commander

April 4, 1943, Vilna Ghetto

Moreshet Archives, D. 1.360.

* *Fareinikte Partizaner Organizatsie* — United Partisans Organization.
** See Document 209.

198

ADDRESS BY GENS AFTER HIS APPOINTMENT AS GHETTO LEADER, JULY 1942

Announcement

By Order of the *Gebietskommissar* of Vilna of July 12, 1942, I have assumed full responsibility for the ghetto as Representative of the Ghetto and Chief of Police.

The basis of existence in the ghetto is *work, discipline and order*. Every resident of the ghetto who is capable of work is a pillar on which our existence rests.

There is no room among us for those who hate work and in devious ways engage in crime. In the belief that all the inmates of the ghetto will understand me, I have given orders to free all persons now under arrest in the ghetto. I hereby proclaim a general amnesty, in this way permitting the criminals of yesterday to return to better ways, in the understanding that this is in their own interest. But let no one doubt that in time of need I will not hesitate to use stringent methods in the struggle against criminal elements wherever they may appear.

I believe that all inmates of the ghetto without exception will support this declaration and have given the following orders:

1. All charges of administrative character will be cancelled and crimes committed within the ghetto by occupants of the ghetto up to 7 p.m. on July 13, 1942, will be pardoned.

2. All investigations and court procedures will be closed with regard to offenses referred to under Para. 1, regardless of the stage reached in the investigation.

3. Persons serving prison sentences with respect to offenses under Para. 1 will be released on the basis of my decision.

4. Fines imposed, but not yet collected, with respect to offenses under Para. 1 are herewith cancelled.

5. The order set out under Paras. 1-4 do not apply to persons who committed the following offenses:

    a) Murder;
    b) Grievous or serious personal injury;
    c) Insulting or physically attacking a policeman carrying out his official duties, or in connection with these duties;
    d) Offenses against the authorities;
    e) Disciplinary offenses (on the part of officials of the ghetto management or ghetto police).

6. Persons in illegal possession of permits or Bread Cards will benefit from the amnesty if they return the illegal permits or Bread Cards voluntarily by 7 p.m. on July 28, 1942. They should be returned to the appropriate Police Station in the Registration Office or to the Housing Office.

7. The closing of investigation or court procedures and the remission of sentences already imposed, on the basis of this amnesty, do not release a person from an order to pay compensation either to individuals or to the ghetto management.

8. The prison sentences or fines cancelled by this amnesty can be reactivated by a court order or other appropriate authority in the event of the offender committing any other offense, or failing to obey instructions, or showing lack of discipline at his

place of work or when he is sent to work, within three months of the date of publication of this amnesty.

Vilna Ghetto, July 15, 1942

Representative of the Ghetto and Chief of Police

Gens

Moreshet Archives, D. 1.352.

199

GENS REPORTS TO THE JEWISH LEADERSHIP IN VILNA ON THE AKTION IN OSZMIANA, OCTOBER 1942

Protocol of the Meeting on the Aktion in Oszmiana

October 27, 1942

Present: The head of the ghetto, Mr. J. Gens; Commissar Dessler; the head of the Health Department, Milkonovicki; the deputy head of the ghetto, Fried; Mr. Fishman; Mr. Braude, liaison; Rabbi Jakobson; Z. Kalmanovitch; the Commander of the Gate Guards, Levas; the Commander of the Work Police, Toubin; the Commander of Police District No. 1, Ring; P. Natanson; and M. Ganionska.

Gens: Gentlemen, I asked you to come here today in order to relate to you one of the most terrible tragedies in the life of Jews — when Jews led Jews to their death. Once more I have to speak openly to you.

A week ago Weiss of the SD came to us in the name of the SD with an order that we were to travel to Oszmiana. There were about 4,000 Jews in the Oszmiana ghetto and it was not possible to keep so many persons there. For that reason the ghetto would have to be made smaller — by picking out the people who did not suit the Germans, to take them away and shoot

440

פּראָטאָקאָל

פֿון דער פֿאַרזאַמלונג, געהיימסטע דער פֿראַגע

אַקציע אין אָשמענע

27 אָקטאָבער 1942

-:-

אָנװעזנד: געמ״פֿאַרשטײער ה׳ י. י. געגס קאָמ. דעסלער לײמער פֿון דער געזונדהײטס
אָפּטײלונג מילקאָנאַחיצקי שטעלפֿאָרהרדמער פֿון געמ״פֿאַרשטײער פֿריר
ח׳ פּישמאַן, פֿאַרב״גדונגסמאַן בראָווע חרב ראַקאָװסקי ח׳ קאַלמאַנאָװי־
לײמער פֿון פּאָריעראַמאַן ה׳ לעוואַ לײמער פֿון דער אַרבעטספֿאַרצ״מאָרגין
לײמער פֿון 1-טן פּאָליצײ־רעװאָ״יר׳רינג, נאַמאַנזאָן פ. און גאַני־אָנסקא מ.

ה׳ י. י. געגס: מרנע הערן אירהאַפֿ איך ה־גס אײנגעלאַדן כדי צו ערצ״לן א׳־גע פֿון־
סוים. איך האָב דאָם עולם אין אַנדער מאַל צו רידן אָמ.

ס.ד. א האַן צורוק אין געקומען פֿון ס.ד. און ד״מ און בעגעגענוג אין אָן געמוך פֿון
ד׳רן און אזױ־פֿיל קען מען אין אַשמענער געמם ז״נען פֿאָראָן צירקאַ 4000
פֿאַרקלענערן – אױמקלװ־אַן די מענטשן האָם פֿאָן גיט פֿאַר די ד״שן, אָדו־יּספּערן
און ס״ס ז״. אין דער ערשטער ר״ אַלויספּירן פֿרייען מיט קינדער ״מענטנס מענער
ס״ד״־נען פֿאַראַראַן צוגענומען געראַרן פֿון כאַװענעמ״. אינדער צח״מער ר״ פֿרוייען
און פֿאַמילײעס האָם האַבן א זֿך קינדער. האָן מיר האָבן עראַהאַלסן דעם באַפֿעל האַבן מיר
געענטספֿערם: צום בסּפֿעל.

ח׳ דעסלער און ״דישע פֿאָליצ״ ז׳נען אַחענגענומארן ק״ן אַשמענע. אין 2־3 מענ
אַרום האָב ה׳ ״דישע פֿאָליצ״ פּעספּנגעטשטאַלם און ערקלערם אין ״געבסּט״קאָמ״סאַ־רים
אין הילנע, אַז ערטשפּאָן זינען די פֿרויען די מענמען אַרויספּירן אַן פֿאַראַ״ן
צונעוומען נעחען ״אַשעמפּסימקאַ און מען קען ז׳ גיט־גים אַרויספּירן און צח־סנס
מעם 2 קינדער. מים ה קינדער ז״נען נאָר עסליכע. אַלדאַ דאָם קען מען אױך גים
איך האָב פֿאַרנגעמ צו זאָגן אַז האָם א אַז האָם צאַל ״פֿאַרארום ארויספּירן גים ד־ני־קער ח־
1500 פֿערזאָן/. מיר האָבן געזאַגגם אַז אזא צאַל פֿסּסּסּסּ קענגעמ מיר גים שטעלן.
מיר האָבן זיך אָנגעהיבן צו דינגען. דער ה׳ דעסלער אין געקומען מים דער מע״־
דונג פֿון אַשמענע, אַז די ר״ צאַל געפֿאַל בּיז 800. װען איך בּין אַנגעגעמּפֿאָרן מים
ח״מ אין אַשמענע׳ אין דער ר״ דער געפֿאַל אױף 600. אין דער ר״קעלעכ־מ
איך די לאַנע געװ״ן אָנדערש. מיר האָבן זיך גערונגען ״ד״ 600 אין א אין דער צ״ם
איך דערח״ל געװאָלם די פֿראַנע פֿון פֿראַנע מים קינדער און ס״א״ן געבליבן
די פֿראַנע פֿון אַלטע מענטשן. די אַלטע מענטשן ז׳נען א אין א״ אַשמענע צוזאַמען־
געקל״בן געװאָרן 406 אַלטע מענטש. די אַלטע מענטשן ז״נען געװאָרן ארויסגענומען.

װען ח״מ איך געקומען צום ערשטן מאָל און געערדעם העג געל פֿרוי״ען אַן קינדער
האַב איך אים געגעבן מ״ן געװאָל א די גענעג אַלטע מענטשן. עד האָם פֿ־געספֿערם: ד״ אַלטע
העל דורכ״ ח״נסער אַלך א״רגס אױ־מטשאַ־ן און ה״גס דאַרף מיר פֿאַרקלענערן דעם
געמאַ.

די ״דישע פֿאָליצ״ האָם געראַטעװעט דאָס װאָם מװ מוז לעבן. די חעלכע פֿאַאַ ס׳א״ן
געבּליבן פֿאָליצ״ ח״ג־ק צוm לעבּן ז״נען אָנעק, און זאָלן די אַלמע רדן אַנג מוחל ז״נ.
ז׳ ז׳נען געמ״ן א קרבן פֿאַר אונזערע ״רדן־ פֿאַר אונזער צוקונסם.

איך חיל ג״ס רירן העגן דעם װאָם ס׳האָבן אב״בערלעבּם אונזערע ׳דן פֿון הילנע
אין אַשמענע, ה־גס באַדוער איך ׳נאַר האָם אין ק״מעל׳שעם און א״ן צ״סספּריג
גען ג׳ דער אַקצ״ע גים געגמען ק״גינע ׳דן. פֿאַרקיק מאָך האָם מען דאַרם אויסגעש
גען א ע ד׳רן – אַ אוומערלחד. הר־גס ז״נען ג׳ מיר געג״ן 2 ד׳ן שױנעצ״אַניס
/אַלס־סמאַנצ׳אַן/ און האָבן געסראַגם ז׳ צ צו ראַ׳עחון. דארטן ז׳נען ראַ ד׳ן פֿון
ס׳פֿראַנציאַן, תבד און אָנדערע ארומ־מע שמעמלעך. און ה־גס שמעל ך זינד־דהסער
ד׳ פֿראַנע האָם חעמ ז׳ן װען מיר חעלן דארפֿ נאַכאַמאד דורכפֿרן ד׳ סעגעראַנאַ״ע
ס׳ן פֿליכם א״ך זי צו זאָ׳ד׳׳ גופֿ ד׳ ח״ך זיך גים געמוצן ס״מ
חעגס און ש׳ק מרנע פֿאָליצ״סמן מאָן ד׳ שמוציקע אַרבעם. הר־גס זאָ איך סּמּ
מ׳ן פֿליכּ אַ׳ך דעל מרדנע חענגמ ח״ל אַ״ם לעבן אי־בער דאָם ״ד״שע פֿאָלק
ש־ערקלעכם צ״מ. הען 5 מיל׳אָן מעננטשן ז״נען שױן אוג־טעל אונ׳כמ ס״לכ־
ראָשעהעט שמאַרקע און ׳ונגע – גים נסָר אין ד׳ ׳ארן, נאָר אױך אין ג׳סם. און
 גים פֿ׳לן א״ן פֿענגשכ אוג־ם. חען מען ה־ם אין אַשמעגו נעצ־אַנס דעם רב ׳אָ׳ אָ וא עס
האָ־עד געזאַגגס מען זאָל עסענגען ד׳ מאליגע. דאָס אי אַ סענשט מים א מענטש־אָ
׳ונגן ׳גיסם.

From the protocol of October 27, 1942, on the discussion about the *Aktion*
in Oszmiana

From the protocol of October 27, 1942, on the discussion about the *Aktion*
in Oszmiana

them. The first to go should be children and women whose husbands were taken away last year by the "snatchers." The next to be taken would be women and families with a large number of children. When we received this order we replied: "At your command."

Mr. Dessler and Jewish Police went to Oszmiana. After two or three days the Jewish Police observed and reported to the *Gebietskommissariat* (in Vilna) that, first of all, the women whose men had been taken away last year were now working and could not be taken away, and, secondly, that there were no families with 4 or 5 children. The largest were families with two children. There were only a few [families] with three children. So that would also not work. (I forgot to say that no fewer than 1,500 persons had to be taken away.) We said that we could not provide such a number. We started to bargain. When Mr. Dessler arrived with the report from Oszmiana, the number dropped to 800. When I went to Oszmiana with Weiss, the number dropped again to 600. In reality the situation was different. We argued about the 600 and during this time the question of the removal of women and children was dropped. There remained the question of old people. In reality, 406 old people were collected in Oszmiana. These old people were handed over.

When Weiss came the first time and spoke about the women and children, I told him that old people should be taken. He answered: "The old people would die off in any case during the winter and the ghetto has to be reduced in size now."

The Jewish Police saved those who must live. Those who had little time left to live were taken away, and may the aged among the Jews forgive us. They were a sacrifice for our Jews and for our future.

I don't want to talk about what our Jews from Vilna have gone through in Oszmiana. Today I only regret that there were no Jews [i.e., Jewish Police] when the *Aktion* was carried out in Kiemieliszki and in Bystrzyca. Last week all the Jews were shot there, without any distinction. Today two Jews from

Swieciany (Old-Swieciany) came to me and asked me to save them. The Jews from Swieciany, Widze and other small places in the neighborhood were [collected] there. And today I ask myself what is to happen if we have once more to carry out a selection. It is my duty to tell them: my good Jews, away with you; it is not my wish to soil my hands and send my Police to do the dirty work. Today I will say that it is my duty to soil my hands, because terrible times have come over the Jewish people. If five million people have already gone it is our duty to save the strong and the young, not in years only, but in spirit, and not to indulge in sentimentality. When the Rabbi in Oszmiana was told that the number of persons required was not complete and that five elderly Jews were hiding in a *maline* (hiding place), he said that the *maline* should be opened. That is a man with a young and unshaken spirit.

I don't know whether everybody will understand this and defend it, and whether they will defend it after we have left the ghetto, but the attitude of our police is this — rescue what you can, do not consider your own good name or what you must live through.

All these things that I have told you do not sound sweetly to our souls nor yet for our lives. These are things one should not have to know. I have told you a shocking secret which must remain locked in our hearts. I want to tell you what the policemen did who carried out the terrible task, who segregated people and ordered "left" or "right"... This is no court of law. I want men of public affairs, men of *Gemara* [Talmud] to know what is a ghetto, and, on the other hand, what is police and what were the roads that other Jews had to tread.

From you, gentlemen, I want moral support. We all want to live to leave the ghetto. Today, as we work, it may be that not many of the Jews fully comprehend the danger in which we operate. None of us can know how many times every day he could get to Ponary... I myself, as it happens, was on the battlefield. I was not afraid then, only later when I

443

remembered it. It is the same for us now. We will think about it well later, after the ghetto. Today we must just be strong. Those who have faith will say: the Almighty will aid us. Those who have no faith must ask the aid of the spirit of Jewish patriotism and public feeling. To survive it all and to remain, after the ghetto, a human being fit for the great Jewish future. Rosenberg said recently that it is the task of the Germans to exterminate the Jewish people in Europe. I don't know what he means. If he were to come here to us in the ghetto he might well be frightened by us: people who have been driven into *maline*, to Ponary, torn from their families — and in the course of a year we have built up a new life, we have built up much more than the Aryans — that is the Jewish people: a strong spirit and faith that we shall live. So that Rosenberg's words do not come true, we must fight today. In every fight the aim justifies the means, and sometimes the means are terrible. Unfortunately we must use all means in order to fight our enemy.

The Jewish people saw no blood in the whole of the 2,000 years. They saw fire, but blood they did not see. But now the ghetto has seen it. Jews have come from Ponary with bullets through their feet and hands. Once there were five women and a child in the hospital, all returned from Ponary. The Jewish people has become familiar with blood, and then one loses one's sentimentality.

I want to draw you into today's life a little and to let you understand the naked facts of this life, the naked fight. That is why I called you here, you, who are people far from police [affairs]. . . .

Moreshet Archives, D. 1.357.

444

200

FROM A DIARY BY ZELIG KALMANOVITCH FOLLOWING THE REPORT BY GENS

October 27 [1942]

This evening at the Commander's the men were relating things that had happened to them. The scroll of agony. How they handed over 400 souls to the murderers. An order came together with a threat. They went there and a thousand and more were demanded. They demanded women and large families. Till they agreed on 600, and gave 400. Ring saved women who were already on the carts. They were assembled in the square. The children were left in the houses. It was not known in advance what their task would be. They only guessed in their hearts. Slowly, it became clear. The Jews themselves agreed when they realized that it was possible to save the rest. The rabbi ruled that the old ones should be handed over. Old ones who asked that they should be taken. There was one woman who was a hundred. They asked for police, sons of servants, soldiers of the Mistress [Germany]. They paid no heed. They offered their lives in ransom, it was not accepted. The possessions remained. The food remained. If outsiders had done the job — there would have been more victims and all the property would have been stolen. In the synagogue some read Psalms. The women wept in front of the Holy Ark.

Sunday, November [1942]

Hard and bitter days once more. The [Jewish] Police has again been called on to "fix"' affairs in the city of Swieciany. They were afraid that it would be done without them, and then the number of victims would have been greater. But apparently their fear was unnecessary. But it is here that the difficulty starts. The Commander began to demand that he and his assistants should not be the only ones employed on this operation; he does not want others to say "our hands are clean." At first sight he seemed to express the view that all the responsibility was his and that he alone would have to be judged by his Maker. But in fact he is not willing to be satisfied with spiritual cooperation, and he demands practical cooperation. The man who was his former assistant* was arrested yesterday because he refused to obey the order to go out to S[wieciany] with a group of policemen for this operation. The Ghetto is boiling; gatherings, meetings, consultations. Apparently he demands that others take part. In truth we are in any case not innocent in [among the people of] Israel; we have bought our lives and our future with the death of tens of thousands. If we have decided that we must continue with this life despite everything, then we must go on to the end. May the merciful Lord .forgive us. The old rabbi can show us the way. One must have what one can. That is the situation and it is not in our hands to change it. Of course delicate souls cannot bear such acts, but the protest of the soul has no more than psychological value, and there is no moral value to it. Everybody is guilty or, more correctly, all are innocent and holy, and most of all those who take real action, who must overcome their spirit, who must overcome the torture of the soul, who free the others of this task, and save their souls from pain....

Z. Kalmanovitch, *Yoman be-Getto Vilna u-Ketavim me-ha-Izavon she-Nimze'u ba-Harisot* ("A Diary from the Ghetto in Nazi Vilna"), Tel Aviv, 1977, pp. 85-87.

* The reference is to Josef Glazman, Deputy Commander of the Ghetto Police and member of the F.P.O. staff in Vilna.

201

INCOME AND EXPENDITURE OF THE ADMINISTRATION OF THE VILNA GHETTO IN THE FIRST HALF OF THE YEAR 1942

Income of the Ghetto Management for the First Half of 1942
Income (in thousands of Marks)

Month	Food Dept.	Work Tax	Inter. Tax	Housing Dept.	Health Dept.	Industr. Works	Ceme- tery	Various	Total
January	16.7	10.5	—	13.3	4.2	1.0	1.5	10.4	57.6
February	30.4	11.8	—	13.7	4.7	2.2	2.1	8.2	73.1
March	48.8	19.2	1.3	17.0	8.4	1.9	1.9	6.1	104.6
April	48.8	20.1	2.0	22.0	12.5	2.5	1.1	5.0	114.0
May	61.7	20.8	6.5	21.4	19.7	2.1	0.8	5.4	138.4
June	86.0	26.3	6.2	23.0	19.6	2.1	0.6	7.1	170.9
Total	292.4	108.7	16.0	110.4	69.1	11.8	8.0	42.2	658.6

Expenses of the Ghetto Administration During the First Half of 1942
Expenses (in thousands of Marks)

Month	Salaries	Social Welfare	Technical Stores	Various	Total
January	32.5	7.8	—	7.6	47.9
February	46.4	15.5	6.1	11.2	79.2
March	59.4	23.2	2.8	4.5	89.9
April	52.0	23.8	11.6	2.7	90.1
May	71.1	34.2	10.2	1.0	116.5
June	74.1	38.0	7.0	1.2	120.3
Total	335.5	142.5	37.7	28.2	543.9

R. Korczak, *Lehavot ba-Efer* ("Flames in Ash"), Merhavia, 1965[3], p. 362.

202

FROM THE DIARY OF A JEWISH YOUTH ON EDUCATION AND CULTURE IN THE VILNA GHETTO, 1942

Thursday the 22nd [October 1942]

The days pass quickly. Having finished my few lessons, I began to do a little housework. I read a book, wrote the diary, and off to class...

Our youth works and does not perish. Our history group works. We listen to lectures about the great French Revolution, about its periods. The second section of the history group, ghetto history, is also busy. We are investigating the history of Courtyard Shavli 4. For this purpose questionnaires have been distributed among the members, with questions that have to be asked of the courtyard residents. We have already begun the work. I go with a friend. The questions are divided into four parts: questions relating to the period of Polish, Soviet and German rule (up until the ghetto), and in the ghetto. The residents answer in different ways. Everywhere, however, the same sad ghetto song: property, certificates, hide-outs, the loss of things, the loss of relatives. I got a taste of a historian's task. I sit at the table and ask questions and record the greatest sufferings with cold objectivity. I write, I probe into details, and I do not realize at all that I am probing into wounds, and the one who answers me — indifferent to it: two sons and a husband taken away — the sons Monday, the husband Thursday... And this horror, this tragedy is formulated by me in three words, coldly and dryly. I become absorbed in thought, and the words stare out of the paper crimson with blood...

Sunday the 13th [December 1942] ...

Today the ghetto celebrated the circulation of the 100,000th book in the ghetto library. The festival was held in the auditorium of the theater. We came from our lessons. Various speeches were made and there was also an artistic program. The speakers analyzed the ghetto reader. Hundreds of people read in the ghetto. The reading of books in the ghetto is the greatest pleasure for me. The book unites us with the future, the book unites us with the world. The circulation of the 100,000th book is a great achievement for the ghetto, and the ghetto has the right to be proud of it.

Y. Rudashevski, *The Diary of the Vilna Ghetto*, Tel-Aviv, 1973, אָ). 72-73, 106.

203

ADDRESS BY GENS ON THE FIRST ANNIVERSARY OF THE ESTABLISHMENT OF THE JEWISH THEATER IN THE VILNA GHETTO, JANUARY 15, 1943

J. Gens

Last year they said that the theater was just a fad of mine. "Gens is amusing himself." A year has passed and what do we see? It was not just a fad of Gens. It was a vital necessity. The little theater, the first concert, the first mourning assembly, the second concert, a light performance by the second Commissariat and another performance and after that — big performances followed by — the big schools in Vilna. For the first time in the history of Vilna we were able to get a curriculum of studies that was all Jewish. A big Jewish Writers' association, big children's homes, a big Day Home, a wide Jewish life. Our care for children has reached a level never seen before in the Jewish life of Vilna. Our spiritual life reaches high, and we have already held a literary competition. A musical competition will be held in another few weeks. All this was achieved by artists who mounted the stage.

How did the idea come up? Simply to give people the opportunity to escape from the reality of the ghetto for a few hours. This we achieved. These are dark and hard days. Our body is in the ghetto but our spirit has not been enslaved. Our body knows work and discipline today because this maintains the body. The spirit knows of tasks that are harder.

Before the first concert they said that a concert must not be held in a graveyard. That is true, but the whole of life is now a graveyard. Heaven forbid that we should let our spirit collapse. We must be strong in spirit and in body.

The singer Lyuba Levicka is not with us today,* but we must not despair. I am certain that we shall still hear her. I am convinced that the Jewish [life] that is developing here and the Jewish [faith] that burns in our hearts will be our reward. I am certain that the day of the phrase "Why hast Thou deserted us?" will pass and that we shall still live to see better days. I would like to hope that those days will come soon and in our lifetime.

Moreshet Archives, D.1. 363.

* She had been arrested about this time on a charge of smuggling food and was executed.

204

THE BAN ON BIRTHS IN SHAVLI GHETTO, FROM THE DIARY OF E. YERUSHALMI, 1942-1943

July 4, 1942

... Dr. Charny drew the attention of the Jewish delegation to the Order concerning births. The Order was first issued on March 5, 1942. The latest date for authorized births was August 5, 1942. He would extend the date to August 15, 1942. In the event of a birth taking place in a Jewish family after this date the whole Jewish family would be "removed"* and the responsibility would rest with the Jewish delegates...

July 13, 1942
Re: Security Police Order
In accordance with the Order of the Security Police, births are permitted in the ghetto only up to August 15, 1942. After this date it is forbidden to give birth to Jewish children either in the hospitals or in the homes of the pregnant women. It is pointed out, at the same time, that it is permitted to interrupt pregnancies by means of abortions. A great responsibility rests on the pregnant women. If they do not comply with this order, there is a danger that they will be executed, together with their families. The delegates** are making this matter widely known. In warning the women of the possible consequences, they believe that the women concerned will remember it well... and will take the necessary measures during the registration of pregnant women which will take place during the next few days, and subsequently.

The Delegation

Protocol of the meeting of the Shavli Judenrat on March 24, 1943

Those present: M. Lejbowicz, B. Karton, A. Heller and A. Katz of the Delegation; the doctors: Burstein, Blecher, Goldberg, Dyrektorowicz, L. Pesachowicz and others. The Agenda: *How should births be prevented in the ghetto?* M. Lejbowicz: We will go back to the question of the births. The ban on giving birth to children which has been imposed on the Jews applies with the utmost severity to all the ghettos. There was a birth recently in Kovno and all members of the family were shot and killed. But no attention is being paid to this and people are behaving most irresponsibly here. There are already several cases of pregnancy and no measures have been taken against them. Dr. Blecher asks: Can the pregnant women be forced to

451

have abortions performed? Are there statistics on the women who are pregnant? Dr. L. reports: We have had three births since August 15 of last year; he did not know how they took place because he did not treat the cases. At the present time there are about 20 pregnant women in the ghetto, most of them in the first few months, but some who are already in the fourth or fifth month and one even in the eighth month. Only two of the pregnant women refuse to have an abortion; for one of them this would be a third abortion and she is threatened by the danger of subsequent childlessness, and the other is the one who has reached the eighth month. Dr. P.: They must be persuaded to agree to have an abortion. They must be told what happened in Kovno and Riga. If necessary one must make use of a white lie in this emergency and tell them that the Security Police is already looking for these cases. Dr. Burstein proposes that the whole medical team, including the midwives, should be forbidden to attend to births. Dr. Bl. proposes that all cases of pregnancy should be registered and the pregnant women persuaded to have abortions. M.L.: We must not make propaganda against births in public! The matter could reach ears that should not hear it. We must discuss the matter only with those concerned. He proposes that the pregnant women be summoned to the clinic, that they be warned in the presence of the doctor and a representative of the Delegation, and the full danger that awaits them be explained. Dr. L.: How can one perform an abortion on a woman who has already reached the eighth month of her pregnancy? Surely we must understand the feelings of the mother. It will surely be impossible to convince her. And what will happen to the infant if we cause a premature birth? We cannot carry out an operation like that in a private home, and it is forbidden to leave the child at the hospital. And what will happen if despite everything the child is born alive? Shall we kill it? I cannot accept such a responsibility on my conscience. Dr. Bl. adds that the position is really very difficult in a case like this for no doctor will take upon himself the responsibility of killing a live child, for that would be murder. Dr. P. asks: Perhaps we should let the child be born and give it to a Christian? M.L.: We cannot allow the child to be born because we are required to report every case of a birth. We have been asked three times whether there were any births and each time we answered in the negative. B.K.: What can we do when the ghetto is in such danger? If the danger were only to the family of the infant we could leave the matter to the responsibility of the person concerned, but it endangers the whole ghetto. The consequences are liable to be most terrible....

E. Yerushalmi, *Pinkas Shavli* ("Records of Shavli"), Jerusalem, 1958, pp. 88, 188-189.

* The reference is to physical extermination.
** The Shavli Judenrat.

205

ADDRESS BY GENS ON THE DANGER OF BRINGING ARMS INTO THE VILNA GHETTO, MAY 15, 1943

Address by Gens, Head of the Ghetto at the Meeting of Brigadiers,* Supervisors and Policemen, May 15, 1943

Ladies and Gentlemen! Today I have called you here because there is something I have to tell you:

A few days ago I went to the Gestapo and spoke to the Commander of the SD there about the revolvers. I may tell you that he is not at all stupid. He said to me: "From an economic point of view the ghetto is very valuable, but if you are going to take foolish risks and if there is any question of security, then I will wipe you out. And even if you get 30, 40 or 50 revolvers, you will not be able to save yourselves and will only bring on your misfortune faster."

Why did I call you together? Because today another Jew has been arrested for buying a revolver. I don't yet know how this case will end. The last case ended fortunately for the ghetto. But I can tell you that if it happens again we shall be very severely punished. Perhaps they will take away those people over 60, or children... Now consider whether that is worth-while ! ! ! There can be only one answer for those who think soundly and maturely : It is not worth-while ! ! !

It is not worth-while having anything to do with the Poles. I have said it from the first day, and today I say it more than ever. You would do better to take a good look at what goes on among the Poles, how they sell each other out, and how many Jews have gone to Ponary because of the Poles — and then consider whether it is worth while.

As long as the ghetto remains a ghetto those of us who have the responsibility will do everything we can so that nothing shall happen to the ghetto. Nowadays a Jew's whole family is responsible for him. If that is not enough, then I will make the whole room responsible for him, and if even that is not enough — the apartment and even the building.

You will have to watch each other, and if there are any hot-heads then it is your duty to report it to the Police. That is not informing. It would be informing if you were to keep silent and the people were to suffer.

I am saying this for the brigadiers who are responsible for their brigades. I demand of the brigadiers that they should know their people. In an army an officer must know his men well. And the brigadiers do not know their people. They just have their passes, sit in offices and carry in [smuggle foodstuffs] through the gate. Yesterday for the first time I punished brigadiers because the badges** were not worn properly by their brigades. By nature I am a very lazy man. I give an order and then I pay no further attention. I gave an order that the badges were to be worn on all garments. Yesterday I remembered this order — and straightaway 35 brigadiers were sitting in the lock-up. Starting tomorrow the brigades will be checked by Levas, and if there is anything that is not in order, then the brigadier will be punished. It is enough that the Police have to act as nursemaids. If the workers do not go to work then the brigadier is trash, he is no use!

Don't cause trouble yourselves. If they do not provoke us, then we must not do it ourselves. Because it is we alone who pay! Look, think, and see where we stand!!!

[I wish you] A good night.

Moreshet Archives, D. 1.355.

* Leaders of labor units.
** The yellow badge.

206

FROM AN ARTICLE IN GHETTO NEWS * ON THE IMPORTANCE OF INDUSTRY AND WORK IN THE VILNA GHETTO

[June 1943]

... The most remarkable new development in the life of the ghetto is the growth of the ghetto industry.

Our industry was still on a very small scale last year and today it has become the main source of employment in the ghetto. About 3,000 persons now work in ghetto industries and efforts are being made to increase this number to 4,000 and even 5,000.

Both in the ghetto industries and in the work in small units we have been obliged to prove that, contrary to the accepted view that we will not succeed in any craft, we have in fact proved very efficient and they cannot find a replacement for us. Under the present war conditions the work in general and the work for the Wehrmacht in particular are absolutely the need of the hour.

It is a fact, the Head of the Ghetto said, among other things, that the clouds of recent days have begun to be scattered, and economic factors alone influence this issue. Because of this we are obliged, and in the future as well, not to drop away from the working plan. The number of persons working in the ghetto at present is 14,000, and we must take steps to reach 16,000 persons employed in the ghetto and outside it. . .

R. Korczak, *Lehavot ba-Efer* ("Flames in Ash"), Merhavia, 1965³, p. 355.

* A newspaper published in the Vilna Ghetto by Gens.

207

ORDER BY HIMMLER FOR THE LIQUIDATION OF THE GHETTOS OF OSTLAND, JUNE 21, 1943

Field Command, June 21, 1943

Reichsführer SS

Secret

To:
1. The Higher SS and Police Leader (*Höherer SS- und Polizei-führer*) *Ostland*
2. Chief of the SS Economic and Administrative Main Office (*Chef des SS-Wirtschafts-Verwaltungshauptamtes*)

1) I order that all Jews still remaining in ghettos in the *Ostland* area be collected in concentration camps.
2) I prohibit the withdrawal of Jews from concentration camps for [outside] work from August 1, 1943.
3) A concentration camp is to be built near Riga to which will be transferred the entire manufacture of clothing and equipment now operated by the Wehrmacht outside. All private firms will be eliminated. The workshops are to be solely

concentration camp workshops. The Chief of the SS Economic and Administrative Main Office is requested to see to it that there will be no shortfall in the production required by the Wehrmacht as the result of this reorganization.

4) Inmates of the Jewish ghettos who are not required are to be evacuated to the East.

5) As many male Jews as possible are to be taken to the concentration camp in the oil-shale area for the mining of oil-shale.

6) The date set for the reorganization of the concentration camps is August 1, 1943.

Signed   H. Himmler

NO-2403.

208

REPORT BY THE COMMANDER OF THE SECURITY POLICE AND SD ON THE FUTURE OF THE VILNA GHETTO, JULY 1943

Situation Report by the Commander of the Security Police and SD for Lithuania for the Month of July 1943

July 31, 1943

...*Jews*

In the month under consideration enemy propaganda dealt with the Jews to an increased degree. Rumors were spread in the various ghettos that *Grossaktionen* would take place within a short period in which not only children, old people and the unfit would be shot by the Security Police, but all the inmates of the ghettos without exception. It went so far that Moscow radio named those responsible for carrying out the alleged *Aktionen,* SS *Standartenführer Jäger* and SS *Obersturmführer Neugebauer.* As a result there was something like panic in the various ghettos, particularly in the Vilna Ghetto. In two

457

peat-cutting camps near Vilna the Jews tried to escape and to join a group of bandits.* In a third peat camp an atonement measure** was carried out, and the rest of the camp, together with the entire fourth Jewish peat camp were transferred to the Vilna Ghetto. This measure bécame necessary because the *Gebietskommissar* for the Vilna area was unable, despite repeated requests, to provide a permanent, satisfactory guard. The Commander of the Security Police and SD for Lithuania had agreed to the housing of the Jews in four peat camps for the sake of the energy supply. In addition to the four Jewish peat camps that have now been dismantled there are still, outside the Vilna Ghetto, two Jewish camps of the OT [Organization Todt], which must complete the important connecting road between Vilna and Kovno by September 1, 1943. As soon as this work is finished these Jewish camps will also be dismantled and [the occupants] moved to the central ghetto in Vilna.

The exposed situation of the Vilna area, with respect to the neighboring area of partisans and the activities of the PW,*** necessitate the withdrawal of the Jews from the Vilna area and their continued placement in concentration camps elsewhere. An incident that took place on July 25, 1943, near Vilna demonstrates that such measures are essential: On this day a group of about 30 Jews succeeded for the first time in leaving the city and acquiring arms in order to join the bandits. The group was stopped by a Commando of an anti-Partisan unit of the German and Lithuanian Sipo (Security Police) and the Lithuanian Order Police, and most of them were shot....

YIVO Archives, OccE3bα-96.

* This was the word used by the Germans for partisans and armed underground fighters.
** Murder.
*** The reference is apparently to the *Polnische Widerstandsbewegung* — Polish Resistance Movement, units of the AK which operated in the neighborhood of Vilna.

209

PROCLAMATION BY THE F.P.O. CALLING FOR REVOLT IN VILNA, SEPTEMBER 1, 1943 *

Jews, Prepare for Armed Resistance!

The German and Lithuanian hangmen have reached the gates of the ghetto. They will murder us all. They will take us, group by group, through the gates.

That is how they took them in their hundreds on the Day of Atonement.

That is how they took them at the time of the White, the Yellow and the Pink papers.**

That is how they took our brothers, sisters, fathers, mothers, our children.

That is how they took tens of thousands away to their death.

But we will not go!

We will not let them take us like animals to slaughter.

Jews, prepare for armed resistance!

Do not believe the false assurances of the murderers, do not believe the words of the traitors. Whoever is taken through the gate of the ghetto has only one road ahead — Ponary. *And Ponary is death.*

Jews, we have nothing to lose.

Death is certain. Who can still believe that he will survive when the murderers kill systematically? The hand of the hangman will reach out to each of us. Neither hiding nor cowardice will save lives.

Only armed resistance can save our lives and honor.

Brothers, it is better to fall in battle in the ghetto than to be led like sheep to Ponary.

Know that in the ghetto there is an organized Jewish force which will rise up with arms in its hands.

Rise up for the armed resistance!

Dont hide in the *malines*. You will fall there like mice in the hands of the murderers.

Jewish masses

Out into the streets!

Those who have no arms get hold of an axe.

Those who haven't an axe take hold of an iron bar or a cudgel!

— *For our murdered children,*

— *For our parents,*

— *For Ponary.*

Strike the murderers!

In every street, in every yard, in every room, within the ghetto and outside the ghetto.

Strike the dogs!

Jews, we have nothing to lose. *We can save our lives only if we kill the murderers.*

Long live liberty! Long live armed resistance!

Death to the murderers!

Command Staff

United Partisans Organization — F.P.O. (*Fareinikte Partizaner Organizatsie*)

Vilna Ghetto

September 1, 1943

Moreshet Archives, D. 1.382.

* See Document 197.

** Documents of various types that were distributed in the ghetto.

210

LIFE OF JEWISH PARTISANS AND JEWISH FAMILY CAMPS IN THE FOREST, FROM A DIARY BY A JEWISH PARTISAN, 1942-1943

August 12, 1942

... The idea of the forest returned and came to life. After the second mass-murder all of us were certain that the Germans made no difference between one Jew and another... They deceived the Judenrat and the Jewish Police when they promised them that they would stay alive if they helped to carry out the slaughter, and in the end they killed them too. Once more we began to search for ways of escape outside the ghetto...

The first to escape were Jews from the neighborhood Naliboki Forest. They disappeared and nothing more was heard of them. The people from Zhetl also went, to Lipiczanka Forest, and they were joined by some from Nowogrodek, who returned after a while to take with them their relatives and friends. From them we heard details of life in the forest. They have arms, they carry out attacks on Germans traveling on the roads; the peasants are afraid of them and supply them with food. There are Russian partisans in the forest who live on good terms with the Jews and carry out joint attacks on the Germans with them.

Young boys of 15 to 17 snatch arms from the Germans and fix stocks to pistols and rifles. A small group got together and moved out to the Belskis. Two of them came back to the ghetto. They would have nothing to do with anyone there, and refused to speak to their former friends — weren't they partisans? They went back to the forest and took with them their relatives, wives and acquaintances.

[1943]

As a result of our many attacks on the Germans in the area of our camp, a German assault was to be expected any day.

461

Information reached us that the Germans knew where we were. The Staff decided to dissolve the separate groups and to re-establish the Brigade.

At the beginning of April all the groups were ordered to leave their valleys and move within 24 hours to Brozova Forest, in Stara-Huta.

We packed our belongings, filled our knapsacks, and fastened our blankets on top of them. The cooking gear and other things were loaded on carts and we moved out. The night was cloudy and the sky full of rain. The damp penetrated into the very marrow of our bones. The dry, bare branches of the young trees waved and bent hither and thither. Our thoughts were black too. Many of us had been lost in our wanderings from forest to forest, from base camp to base camp. They had fallen, and who knew what awaited us at the next base?

By day the snow began to melt. Long pools of water stretched along the sandy paths. We had many kilometers to go. Our feet sink in the mud as though it were soft dough. You want to rest and there is no place to sit. Everything is wet and damp. Now we have found a kind of hillock from which the water has run off. The people sit down, rest, eat their fill and then continue on their way. In this way we crossed forests, fields, and roads until we reached Brozova Forest, in Stara-Huta.

There we found groups that had arrived before us — the group of Yudel Belski, who had lost 10 of his best men; he had few fighting men and their arms were poor: the group could no longer survive on its own. Also the Dworecki group, which had arrived early at the new base. The cold was not yet over and they had built huts for themselves.

After a brief consultation we decided not to build huts. We found a dry hill, stretched out on our knapsacks, rested and set about putting up a shelter of branches.

In the course of a few days all the groups gathered in one place. We began to live according to the plan that had applied before the winter. Every evening the whole unit assembled. One platoon was selected for guard duty for the next 24 hours;

several groups were sent out to get food; the people were divided up according to kitchens, each group doing its own cooking. The groups received their supplies from a central store, in accordance with the number of its members.

At the beginning of April a group of Jews and their families were sent to us from the *Iskra* (spark) group. Their arms were taken from them and they were told to join the Jewish company. These were the first Jewish refugees from Lida Ghetto. The young and single people stayed with the Russians...

J. Jaffe, *Partizanim* ("Partisans"), Tel-Aviv, 1951, pp. 24-25, 70-72,

211

OPERATIONS DIARY OF A JEWISH PARTISAN UNIT IN RUDNIKI FOREST, 1943-1944

Serial No.	Date	Operation	Number of Fighters	Name of Commander
1	10/7/43	Destruction of telegraph link along the Grodno-Vilna road in the section between Pirciupie and Tetiance. More than 50 telegraph poles were sawn through, the wires were cut and the insulators broken. Three units took part in the operation: "Avenger," "To Victory" and "Death to Fascism."	35	I. Czuzoj & Aron Aronowicz

Serial No.	Date	Operation	Number of Fighters	Name of Commander
2	10/11/43	Destruction of telegraph link along the Vilna-Lida road, in the section near Krzyzowka. More than 70 poles were sawn through, the wires were cut and the insulators broken. Three units took part in the operation: "Avenger," "To Victory" and "Death to Fascism."	25	[Name erased in original document]
3	10/23/43	The telephone and telegraph were destroyed along the railroad from Lida to Vilna, in the Jaszuny-Stasily section, not far from Gudelki. Three units took part in the operation: "Avenger," "Death to Fascism" and "To Victory."	25	Ch. Magid and Brand
4	10/43	Three road barriers [were destroyed] at the approaches to Rudniki; two on the main road and one on the road through the forest. The action was carried out simultaneously by three groups. Three units took part in the action: "Avenger," "To Victory," and "Death to Fascism."	55	Chaim Lazar, N. Ring, and Aronowicz
5	10/29/43	Sabotage operation in the city of Vilna: Four transformers and a mechanical water conveyor were destroyed with the aid of English mines. Carried out by a sabotage party consisting of four partisans: Witka Kempner, Matys Lewin, Rozow and Chajele [Szapiro]	4	

Serial No.	Date	Operation	Number of Fighters	Name of Commander
6	11/2/43	Sixty people were brought to the partisans from Vilna. The group was brought by Witka Kempner and Chajele. It arrived safely.	2	
7	10/17/43	Destruction of two bridges in the village of Zagarino and blowing up of two engines on the narrow-gauge railroad line. There was a small force of Germans stationed in the village at the time. Fighters from three units took part in the operation: "Avengers," "To Victory" and "Death to Fascism."	40	Aba Kovner and ...[name erased]
8	11/3/43	The fighter Dobka [Debeltov Doba] brought three armed fighters to the partisans from Vilna: Druc, Mostowicz and Anglenik.		
9	11/43	Purpose: To take arms from the village of Kursze. Four rifles were captured from the Shaulists:* Wiersocki and the forester. The fighters of the "Avenger" units took part in the action.	7	Aba Kovner
10	12/14/43	Purpose: To take the arms from the armed village of Posol. During the operation [German] troops stationed at Rakliszki were summoned from the armed villages in the neighborhood. A two-hour battle ensued and as a result several Fascists were killed or wounded.	40	Kaplinski Szmulka

Serial No.	Date	Operation	Number of Fighters	Name of Commander
11	12/43	In the town Olkieniki, where a force of two hundred enemy troops was stationed, 300 kgs. of turpentine were confiscated from the turpentine factory.	5	Jacob Prener
12	12/43	A bridge was burned in the village of Darguze. The bridge had been built on the new road from Vilna to Orany, in the section between Olkieniki and Pirciupie. The operation was carried out under fire from the troops stationed in Olkieniki. There were no losses. Fighters from two units took part: "Avenger" and "To Victory."	40	Aba Kovner Chanan Magid
13	12/27/43	A train was blown up on the railroad from Vilna to Grodno. An engine and ten cars were derailed: [the train] had carried men and supplies.	6	Didalis [Isar Shmit]
14	12/31/43	A train was blown up on the railroad from Vilna to Grodno, near Landwarow station. The engine and twenty-one cars carrying troops and supplies were derailed. The train had been on its way from Warsaw to Vilna.	6	Aba Kovner
15	12/31/43	Discovery and capture of Gestapo agent Uczkurolis from Dajnowa village near Ejszyszki.	7	Chaim Lazar

Serial No.	Date	Operation	Number of Fighters	Name of Commander
16	12/31/43	Discovery and capture of Gestapo agent Andriuszkiewicz from Dajnowa village. Those who took part: Lipenholc and Witka Kempner.	2	Lipenholc
17	1/44	Blowing up of a boiler and 100-horse-power steam engine at the cardboard factory at Olkieniki. The factory, that is, the machinery and the steam engine were to have been transferred to Germany.	6	Misza Lipenholc & Jacob Prener
18	1/44	Blowing up of a train on the railroad from Vilna to Grodno, in the section between Matuzy and Szarkiszki. It was not established how many cars were derailed. About two hundred Italian soldiers returning from the front were killed.	6	Szmulka Kaplinski
19	1/44	In the operation to destroy the armed village of Koniuchy, 30 fighters took part, of the units "Avenger" and "To Victory."	30	Jacob Prener
20	3/44	Obstruction and mining of the Grodno-Vilna road in the section near Nowe Macele. Fighters from two units took part, "Avenger" and "To Victory."	30	Abrasza Resel
21	3/13/44	In the course of an operational patrol near the village of Skorbuciany the following were captured: a Dutchman Henk Dekker, a	12	Lipenholc Brand Szlomo

467

Serial No.	Date	Operation	Number of Fighters	Name of Commander
		Pole, Gestapo agent Rysiek Luksza, and two Turkomans.		
22	3/44	As part of the general plans of the "Lithuanian Brigade" two units of "Avenger" and "To Victory" destroyed 120 poles along the railroad line Vilna-Lida, in the section near Merecz.	38	Ch. Magid Lipenholc
23	3/18/44	The Vilna units were ordered to carry out the destruction of telephone and telegraph links between the town Ejszyszki and other centers. The two units, "Avengers" and "To Victory" sawed off 75 poles on the road from Grodno to Orany. In the operation wires were cut and insulators broken.	36	Chaim Lazar Ch. Magid
24	3/44	During a patrol near Cieciorka four men were caught who had escaped from a concentration camp for prisoners of war near Suwalki. All four were accepted by partisan units.	3	A. Resel
25	4/16/44	On "Railroad" day** and as part of the general operations which the Vilna units had been ordered to carry out, 300 rails were blown up by our units on the Vilna-Lida line, in the section between Stasily and Jaszuny.	40	[erased]
26	4/44	Barricade on the road from Zygmunciszki to Niewojniance.	20	Ch. Magid

Serial No.	Date	Operation	Number of Fighters	Name of Commander
27	4/44	The building of the "White Poles"*** was burned down in the village of Niewojniance.	40	I. Czuzoj & ...[erased]
28	5/10/44	Ambush on the Grodno road in the section between Pirciupie and Zygmunciszki. Two units, "Avenger" and "To Victory" took part. Eleven Germans were killed. Booty captured: 6 rifles, 4 hand-grenades, 4 grenade throwers, and 2 "Degtyarov" machine-guns.	70	Pietrujtis Ch. Magid Brand
29	5/23/44	At the turpentine factory in Olkieniki 360 kgs. of turpentine were confiscated and 2,000 kgs. were destroyed.	3	Ch. Magid
30	5/27/28/44	Capture of arms from the village of Jurkiance. Twelve rifles of different types were confiscated, with ammunition. At the same time an arms search was carried out in a number of houses in the village of Krumince. Two rifles, a pistol and a hand-grenade were taken. On the way back two "White Poles" were taken prisoner and the following arms in their possession were confiscated: one semi-automatic rifle, one rifle, one revolver, two hand-grenades and ammunition.	35	
31	6/3/44	At Melachowicze protection was given to the arrival of a group of survivors from Vilna, who are about	15	Natan Celnik

Serial No.	Date	Operation	Number of Fighters	Name of Commander
		to join the partisans. Eight persons arrived, four of whom were accepted by our unit: Nisanelowicz, Basia Nisanelowicz, Bielic, Rundbaken; four were accepted by the unit "To Victory."		
32		Near Rudniki a patrol found a group of some tens of persons engaged on building a short railroad line. Working tools were taken from the group and they were ordered not to continue with the work. Eighteen spades were taken back to the base.	4	[erased]
33	6/7/44	In the town of Olkieniki the turpentine and tar factory was blown up.	8	Jacob Prener
34	6/22/44	An engine and two railroad cars were derailed on the Vilna-Lida road.		Szlomo Brand
35	6/25/44	In the town of Zagarino one German was killed and one wounded.		Benia Lewin
36		On the Vilna-Lida railroad line the rails were blown up for a distance of one kilometer. There were 40 explosions.		Szlomo Brand
37	7/3/44	Burning of bridges used by troops stationed in the town of Rudniki.		Jefremow

Serial No.	Date	Operation	Number of Fighters	Name of Commander
38	7/4/44	Train blown up on the Vilna-Lida railroad line. One engine and cars carrying men and supplies were derailed.	30	Szlomo Brand
39	7/8/44	Vilna-Lida railroad line blown up for a distance of two kilometers. Three units took part.		Szlomo Brand

---

Moreshet Archives, D. 1.4650.

* Members of a Lithuanian nationalist organization that collaborated with the Germans. Armed members of this organization took part in Jewish extermination *Aktionen*.

** "H-hour" for a widespread operation that was to strike simultaneously against the railroad network and behind the lines of the German front-line army.

*** A.K. Command.

212

EVIDENCE BY BLOBEL ON THE BURNING OF BODIES AND OBLITERATING THE TRACES OF BODIES OF JEWS KILLED BY THE EINSATZGRUPPEN

Affidavit

I, Paul *Blobel*, swear, declare and state in evidence:

1. I was born in *Potsdam* on August 13, 1894. From June 1941 to January 1942 I was the Commander of *Sonderkommando* 4 A.

471

2. After I had been released from this command, I was to report in *Berlin* to SS *Obergruppenführer* Heydrich and *Gruppenführer Müller*, and in June 1942 I was entrusted by *Gruppenführer* Müller with the task of obliterating the traces of executions carried out by the *Einsatzgruppen* in the East. My orders were that I should' report in person to the commanders of the Security Police and SD, pass on Müller's orders verbally, and supervise their implementation. This order was top secret and *Gruppenführer Müller* had given orders that owing to the need for strictest secrecy there was to be no correspondence in connection with this task. In September 1942 I reported to Dr. *Thomas* in *Kiev* and passed the order on to him. The order could not be carried out immediately, partly because Dr. *Thomas* was disinclined to carry it out, and also because the materials required for the burning of the bodies was not available. In May and June 1943 I made additional trips to *Kiev* in this matter and then, after conversations with Dr. *Thomas* and with SS and Police Leader *Hennecke*, the order was carried out.

3. During my visit in August I myself observed the burning of bodies in a mass grave near *Kiev*. This grave was about 55 m. long, 3 m. wide and 2½ m. deep. After the top had been removed the bodies were covered with inflammable material and ignited. It took about two days until the grave burned down to the bottom. I myself observed that the fire had glowed down to the bottom. After that the grave was filled in and the traces were now practically obliterated.

4. Owing to the moving up of the front-line it was not possible to destroy the mass graves further south and east which had resulted from executions by the *Einsatzgruppen*. I traveled to Berlin in this connection to report, and was then sent to Estonia by *Gruppenführer Müller*. I passed on the same orders to *Oberführer Achammer-Pierader* in *Riga*, and also to *Obergruppenführer Jeckeln*. I returned to *Berlin* in order to obtain fuel. The burning of the bodies began only in May or June 1944. I remember that incinerations took place in the area of *Riga* and *Reval*. I was present at such incinerations

near *Reval*, but the graves were smaller here and contained only about 20 to 30 bodies. The graves in the area of *Reval* were about 20 or 30 kms. east of the city in a marshy district and I think that 4 or 5 such graves were opened and the bodies burned.

5. According to my orders I should have extended my duties over the entire area occupied by the *Einsatzgruppen*, but owing to the retreat from Russia I could not carry out my orders completely. . . .

I have made this deposition of my own free will, without any kind of promise of reward, and I was not subjected to any form of compulsion or threat.

Nuremberg, June 18, 1947

signed Paul Blobel

NO-3947.

213

EVIDENCE OF JEWISH ESCAPEES FROM THE NINTH FORT IN KOVNO ON THE BURNING OF THE BODIES

Protocol, Kovno, December 26, 1943

We, the undersigned, a group of prisoners from the Ninth Fort, who escaped from there during the night from the 25th to the 26th of December of this year, consisting of: J. L. Vaslenitzki [Vasilenko], A. Diskant, A. Faitelson, M. Gelbtrunk, P. Krakinowski, M. Daitz, A. Wilenczuk, T. Pilownik, Gempel, Sh. Idelson, and A. Menaiski have put together this protocol regarding the following:

1. In the period of the years 1941-42, the area of the Ninth Fort was used by the German Command to carry out mass shootings.

473

2. In order to conceal this crime, the German Command, in the person of the Commander of the Kovno Gestapo, arranged for the re-opening of all the graves where the victims of the executions had been buried and set about burning the bodies.
3. In order to carry out this work the Gestapo collected 72 persons at the Ninth Fort at the end of October and beginning of November of this year. These were 34 Soviet prisoners of war, 14 Jewish partisans, 3 local Russians, caught while carrying out sabotage, 4 women — 3 of them Jewish, one Polish — and 17 Jews from the Kovno ghetto.
4. The work was organized in such a fashion that the surrounding population should not find out anything about it, and in fact that nobody should know what was being done in the area of the Ninth Fort. Notices were put up everywhere at a distance of 2 kms. forbidding closer approach under threat of execution. The working area of 2-3 acres was surrounded with a canvas (screen). None of the people who carried out the work were intended ever to leave the Fort alive. This is supported by the fact that one of the Jews from the ghetto, who was taken ill with appendicitis, was shot on November 5, and 7 of the prisoners of war — older men and invalids — were shot on November 13 of this year. There then remained 64 persons for the work.
5. During the period of the work, i.e., from November 1 until December 25 (the day of the escape) 4½ graves were opened, each of them 100-120 meters long, 3 meters wide and 1½ meters deep. More than 12,000 bodies were taken out — men, women, children. These bodies were piled up together, 300 at a time, to be burned. What was left after the burning (charcoal and bones) was ground down to powder in pits. This powder was then mixed with earth so that no trace of it should remain.
6. In order to prevent any escapes during work, the workers were linked together with chains. There were towers for machine-guns. The guards were armed with sub-machine-guns and pistols.
7. Among the 12,000 bodies burned there were about 7,000 Jews from Kovno...

8. The position of the bodies was proof that groups of people were driven into the graves and shot afterwards. The result was that many were buried when they were only wounded or even had not been wounded at all by the bullets.

9. On the day of escape there were many graves still unopened. The Gestapo Commanders had figured that they would finish the work by April 1, 1944. . . .

Eleven signatures

Z. A. Brown and D. Levin, *Toldoteha shel Mahteret* ("History of an Underground"), Jerusalem, 1962, pp. 172-173.

LIST OF ABBREVIATIONS

A. Books and Publications

Blumental — N. Blumental, *Darko shel Judenrat — Te'udot mi-Getto Bialystok* ("Conduct and Actions of a Judenrat — Documents from the Bialystok Ghetto"), Jerusalem, 1962.

Eksterminacja — *Eksterminacja Zydow na ziemiach polskich w okresie okupacji hitlerowskiej — zbior dokumentow* ("Extermination of Jews in the Polish Territories During the Period of the Nazi Occupation — Collections of Documents"), T. Berenstein, A. Eisenbach, A. Rutkowski, eds., Warsaw, 1957.

Ringelblum — E. Ringelblum, *Ksovim fun geto* ("Notes from the Ghetto"), I-II, Warsaw, 1961-1963.

VBlGG — *Verordnungsblatt für das Generalgouvernement* ("Official Gazette of the Government-General"), Cracow.

B. Nuremberg Documents

L   NG   NO   NOKW   PS   R

SELECTED BIBLIOGRAPHY

GENERAL BOOKS AND ARTICLES

Ainsztein, Reuben, *Jewish Resistance in Nazi-Occupied Eastern Europe, with a Historical Survey of the Jew as Fighter and Soldier in the Diaspora,* London, 1974.

Bauer, Yehuda, *The Holocaust in Historical Perspective,* Seattle, 1978.

———, *The Jewish Emergence from Powerlessness,* Toronto, 1979.

Bracher, Karl Dietrich, *The German Dictatorship — The Origins, Structure, and Effects of National Socialism,* London, 1971.

Browning, Christopher R., *The Final Solution and the German Foreign Office,* New York, 1980.

Dawidowicz, Lucy S., *The War Against the Jews 1933-1945,* New York, 1975.

Donat, Alexander, *The Holocaust Kingdom — A Memoir,* New York, 1965.

Friedman, Philip, *Roads to Extinction — Essays on the Holocaust,* New York, 1980.

Gilbert, Martin, *Auschwitz and the Allies — How the Allies Responded to the News of Hitler's Final Solution,* London, 1981.

Gutman, Yisrael and Rothkirchen, Livia, eds., *The Catastrophe of European Jewry — Antecedents – History – Reflections,* Jerusalem, 1976.

Hilberg, Raul, *The Destruction of European Jews,* Chicago, 1967.

Höhne, Heinz, *The Order of the Death's Head — The Story of Hitler's S.S.,* London, 1969.

Höss, Rudolf, *Commandant of Auschwitz — The Autobiography of Rudolf Höss,* London, 1961.

Jäckel, Eberhard, *Hitler's Weltanschauung — A Blueprint for Power,* Middletown, Conn., 1972.

Kogon, Eugen, *The Theory and Practice of Hell — The German Concentration Camps and the System Behind Them,* London, 1950.

Krausnick, Helmut, et al., *Anatomy of the SS State,* London, 1968.

Laqueur, Walter, *The Terrible Secret — An Investigation into the Suppression of Information About Hitler's 'Final Solution',* London, 1980.

Mosse, George L., *The Crisis of German Ideology — Intellectual Origins of the Third Reich,* New York, 1964.

Schleunes, Karl A., *The Twisted Road to Auschwitz — Nazi Policy Toward German Jews 1933-39*, London, 1972.

Sereny, Gitta, *Into That Darkness — From Mercy Killing to Mass Murder*, London, 1974.

Suhl, Yuri, ed., *They Fought Back — The Story of the Jewish Resistance in Nazi Europe*, New York, 1967.

Trunk, Isaiah, *Judenrat — The Jewish Councils in Eastern Europe Under Nazi Occupation*, New York, 1972.

Tushnet, Leonard, *The Pavement of Hell*, New York, 1972.

Bar-On, Zvi A., "Jewish Leadership — Policy and Responsibility," *Jewish Resistance During the Holocaust. Proceedings of the Conference on Manifestations of Jewish Resistance, Jerusalem, April 7-11, 1968*, Jerusalem, 1971, pp. 227-244.

Bein, Alex, "The Jewish Parasite; notes on the Semantics of the Jewish Problem, with Special Reference to Germany," *Leo Baeck Yearbook*, IX, 1964, pp. 3-40.

Broszat, Martin, "Hitler and the Genesis of the 'Final Solution' — An Assessment of David Irving's Theses," *Yad Vashem Studies*, XIII, 1979, pp. 73-125.

Dworzecki, Meir, "The Day-To-Day Stand of the Jews," *Jewish Resistance During the Holocaust. Proceedings of the Conference on Manifestations of Jewish Resistance, Jerusalem, April 7-11, 1968*, Jerusalem, 1971, pp. 152-181.

GERMANY AND AUSTRIA

Esh, Shaul, "Between Discrimination and Extermination," *Yad Vashem Studies*, II, 1958, pp. 79-93.

———, "The Establishment of the 'Reichsvereinigung der Juden in Deutschland' and Its Main Activities," *Yad Vashem Studies*, VII, 1968, pp. 19--38.

Gruenwald, Max, "The Beginning of the Reichsvertretung," *Leo Baeck Yearbook*, I, 1956, pp. 57-67.

Kulka, Otto D., "The Reichsvereinigung of the Jews in Germany (1938/9-1943)." *Patterns of Jewish Leadership in Nazi Europe, 1933-1945. Proceedings of the Third Yad Vashem International Historical Conference — April 1977*, Jerusalem, 1979, pp. 45-58.

Margaliot, Abraham, "The Problem of the Rescue of German Jewry During the Years 1933-1939; The Reasons for the Delay in their Emigration from the Third Reich," *Rescue Attempts During the Holocaust. Proceedings of the Second Yad Vashem International*

Historical Conference, Jerusalem, April 8-11, 1974, Jerusalem, 1977, pp. 247-265.

Margaliot, Abraham, "The Reaction of the Jewish Public in Germany to the Nuremberg Laws," *Yad Vashem Studies,* XII, 1977, pp. 75-107.

———, "The Struggle for Survival of the Jewish Community in Germany in the Face of Oppression," *Jewish Resistance During the Holocaust. Proceedings of the Conference on Manifestations of Jewish Resistance, Jerusalem, April 7-11, 1968,* Jerusalem, 1971, pp. 100-111.

Rosenkranz, Herbert, "The Anschluss and the Tragedy of Austrian Jewry 1938-1945," Fraenkel Josef, ed., *The Jews of Austria — Essays on their Life, History and Destruction,* London, 1967, pp. 479-545.

———, "Austrian Jewry — Between Forced Emigration and Deportation," *Patterns of Jewish Leadership in Nazi Europe, 1933-1945. Proceedings of the Third Yad Vashem International Historical Conference — April 1977,* Jerusalem, 1979, pp. 65-90.

Rosenstock, Werner, "Exodus 1933-1939; A Survey of Jewish Emigration from Germany," *Leo Baeck Yearbook,* I, 1956, pp. 373-390.

Simon, Ernst, "Jewish Adult Education in Nazi Germany as Spiritual Resistance," *ibid.,* pp. 68-104.

Walk, Joseph, "Jewish Education Under the Nazis — An Example of Resistance to the Totalitarian Regime," *Jewish Resistance During the Holocaust. Proceedings of the Conference on Manifestations of Jewish Resistance, Jerusalem, April 7-11, 1968,* Jerusalem, 1971, pp. 123-131.

POLAND

Bartoszewski, Wladyslaw and Lewin, Zofia, eds., *Righteous Among the Nations — How Poles Helped the Jews, 1939-1945,* London, 1969.

Czerniakow, Adam, *The Warsaw Diary of Adam Czerniakow,* ed. by Raul Hilberg, Stanislaw Staron, Joseph Kermish, New York, 1979.

Goldstein, Bernard, *Five Years in the Warsaw Ghetto,* New York, 1961.

Gutman, Yisrael, *The Jews of Warsaw 1939-1943 — Ghetto, Underground, Revolt* (English edition soon to be published).

Kaplan, Chaim A., *The Warsaw Diary of Chaim A. Kaplan,* New York, 1973.

Meed, Vladka, *On Both Sides of the Wall — Memoirs from the Warsaw Ghetto,* Tel Aviv, 1972.

Ringelblum, Emmanuel, *Notes from the Warsaw Ghetto,* New York, 1958.

———, *Polish-Jewish Relations During the Second World War,* ed. by Joseph Kermish and Shmuel Krakowski, Jerusalem, 1976.

Gutman, Yisrael, "The Genesis of the Resistance in the Warsaw Ghetto," *Yad Vashem Studies,* IX, 1973, pp. 29-70.

————, "Youth Movements in the Underground and the Ghetto Revolts," *Jewish Resistance During the Holocaust. Proceedings of the Conference on Manifestations of Jewish Resistance, Jerusalem, April 7-11, 1968,* Jerusalem, 1971, pp. 260-284.

Kermish, Joseph, "On the Underground Press in the Warsaw Ghetto," *Yad Vashem Studies,* I, 1957, pp. 85-123.

Weiss, Aharon, "Jewish Leadership in Occupied Poland — Postures and Attitudes," *Yad Vashem Studies,* XII, pp. 335-365.

————, "The Relations Between the Judenrat and the Jewish Police," *Patterns of Jewish Leadership in Nazi Europe, 1933-1945. Proceedings of the Third Yad Vashem International Historical Conference, April 1977,* Jerusalem, 1979, pp. 201-217.

SOVIET UNION

Arad, Yitzhak, *Ghetto in Flames — The Struggle and Destruction of the Jews in Vilna in the Holocaust,* Jerusalem, 1980.

Dallin, Alexander, *German Rule in Russia 1941-1945 — A Study of Occupation Policies,* London, 1957.

Rudashevski, Yitzhak, *The Diary of the Vilna Ghetto, June 1941-April 1943,* Tel Aviv, 1973.

Arad, Yitzhak, "The 'Final Solution' in Lithuania in the Light of German Documentation," *Yad Vashem Studies,* XI, 1976, pp. 234-272.

————, "Jewish Family Camps in the Forests — An Original Means of Rescue," *Rescue Attempts During the Holocaust. Proceedings of the Second Yad Vashem International Historical Conference, April 1974,* Jerusalem, 1977, pp. 333-353.

Cholavsky, Shalom, "Jewish Partisans — Objective and Subjective Difficulties," *Jewish Resistance During the Holocaust. Proceedings of the Conference on Manifestations of Jewish Resistance, Jerusalem, April 7-11, 1968,* Jerusalem, 1971, pp. 323-334.

UPDATED SELECTED BIBLIOGRAPHY

SOVIET UNION

Arad, Yitzhak. "The Holocaust of Soviet Jewry in Occupied Territories of the Soviet Union," *Yad Vashem Studies XXI*. Jerusalem, 1991.

The Black Book. New York, 1981.

Davies, Norman, and Antony Polonsky. *Jews of Eastern Poland and the USSR, 1939-1946*. New York, 1991.

Dobroszycki, Lucjan and Jeffrey Gurock, eds. *The Holocaust in the Soviet Union*. Armonk, NY, 1993.

Garrard, John. "The Nazi Holocaust in the Soviet Union: Interpreting Newly Opened Russian Archives," *East European Jewish Affairs* 25, no. 2 (1995): 8.

Gross, Jan. *Revolution from Abroad: The Soviet Conquest of Poland's Western Ukraine and Western Belorussia*. Princeton NJ, 1988.

Hunczak, Taras. "Ukrainian-Jewish Relations during the Soviet and Nazi Occupations." In *Ukraine during World War II: History and Aftermath*, edited by Yuri Boshyk, 39-57. Edmonton, Alberta, 1986.

Kupovetsky, Mark. "Estimation of Jewish losses in the USSR during World War II," *Jews in Eastern Europe* 28 (summer 1997): 25-37.

Levin, Dov. *Baltic Jews under the Soviets, 1940-1946*. Jerusalem, 1994.

—————. *Fighting Back: Lithuanian Jewry's Armed Resistance to the Nazis, 1941-1945*. New York, 1985.

—————. *The Lesser of Two Evils: Eastern European Jewry under Soviet Rule, 1939-1941*. Philadelphia, 1995.

Potichnyj, Peter and Howard Aster, eds. *Ukrainian-Jewish Relations in Historical Perspective*. Edmonton, 1988.

Redlich, Shimon, ed. *War, Holocaust and Stalinism*. New York, 1995.

Sabrin, B. F., ed. *Alliance for Murder*. New York, 1991.

For additional information regarding this topic, please refer to the *Encyclopedia of the Holocaust*, 4 volumes (New York, 1990), edited by Yisrael Gutman.

GERMANY

Arad, Yitzhak. *Belzec, Sobibor, Treblinka: The Operation Reinhard Death Camps*. Bloomington, 1987.

483

Bezwínska, Jadwiga. *Amidst a Nightmare of Crime: Manuscripts of Members of Sonderkommando*. Oswiecim [Auschwitz], 1973.

Browning, Christopher. *The Path to Genocide: Essays on Launching the Final Solutions*. New York, 1992.

———. *Fateful Months: Essays on the Emergence of the Final Solution*. New York, 1985.

———. *The Final Solution and the German Foreign Office: a Study of Referat D III of Abteilung Deutschland, 1940-43*. New York, 1978.

Fleming, Gerald. *Hitler and the Final Solution*. Berkeley, 1984.

Friedlander, Henry. *The Origins of Nazi Genocide: From Euthanasia to the Final Solution*. Chapel Hill, 1995.

Friedlander, Saul. "From Anti-Semitism to Extermination: A Historiographical Study of Nazi Policies toward the Jews," *Yad Vashem Studies* 16 (1984): 1-50.

———. *Nazi Germany and the Jews*. New York, 1997.

Goldhagen, Daniel J. *Hitler's Willing Executioners: Ordinary Germans and the Holocaust*. New York, 1996.

Hilberg, Raul. *Perpetrators, Victims, Bystanders and the Jewish Catastrophe 1933-1945*. New York, 1992.

Hirschfeld, Gerhard, ed. *The Policies of Genocide: Jews and Soviet Prisoners of War in Nazi Germany*. London, 1972.

Jackel, Eberhard. *Hitler in History*. Hanover NH, 1984.

Kershaw, Ian. *The Nazi Dictatorship: Problems and Perspectives of Interpretation*. London, 1985; revised and expanded edition, 1989.

Kulka, Otto Duv. "Major Trends and Tendencies of German Historiography on National Socialism and the 'Jewish Question' (1924-1984)," *Yearbook of the Leo Baeck Institute* 30 (1985): 215-42.

Kulka, Otto Duv. "Singularity and Its Relativization: Changing Views in German Historiography on National Socialism and the 'Final Solution,'" *Yad Vashem Studies* 19 (1988): 151-86.

Lifton, Robert Jay. *The Nazi Doctors: Medical Killing and the Psychology of Genocide*. New York, 1986.

Marrus, Michael R. *The Holocaust in History*. New York, 1987.

POLAND

Browning, Christopher. *Ordinary men: Reserve Police Battalion 101 and the final solution in Poland*. New York, 1992.

Dobroszycki, Lucjan, ed. *The Chronicle of the Lods Ghetto, 1941-1944*. Trans. Richard Lourie et al. New Haven, 1984.

Gutman, Yisrael. *The Jews of Warsaw, 1939-1943: Ghetto, Underground, Revolt*. Trans. Ina Friedman. Bloomington IN, 1983.

484

————, and S. Krakowski. *Unequal Victims: Poles and Jews During World War II.* New York, 1986.

————, and Michael Berenbaum, eds. *Anatomy of the Auschwitz Death Camp.* Bloomington, 1994.

————, and Avital Saf, eds. *The Nazi Concentration Camps: Structure and Aims. The Image of the Prisoner. The Jews in the Camps. Proceedings of the Fourth Yad Vashem International Historical Conference, Jerusalem, January 1980.* Jerusalem, 1984.

Hilberg, Raul, Stanislaw Staron, and Josef Kermisz, eds. *The Warsaw Diary of Adam Czerniakow: Prelude to Doom.* Trans. Stanislaw Staron et al. New York, 1979.

Krakowski, Shmuel. *The War of the Doomed: Jewish Armed Resistance in Poland, 1942-1944.* Trans. Ora Blaustein. New York, 1984.

Trunk, Isaiah. *Jewish Responses to Nazi Persecution: Collective and Individual Behavior in Extremis.* New York, 1982.

AUSTRIA

Bassett, Richard. *Waldheim and Austria.* New York, 1989.

Berkeley, George E. *Vienna and Its Jews: The Tragedy of Success, 1880-1980s.* Maryland, 1988.

Botz, Gerhard. "The Dynamics of Persecution in Austria, 1938-45." In *Austrians and Jews in the Twentieth Century: From Franz Joseph to Waldheim,* edited by Robert S. Wistrich. London, 1992.

Ganglmair, Siegwald. *Resistance and Persecution in Austria, 1938-1945.* Vienna, 1988.

Parkinson, Fred, ed. *Conquering the Past: Austrian Nazism Yesterday and Today.* Detroit, 1989.

Pauley, Bruce. *From Prejudice to Destruction: A History of Austrian Antisemitism.* Chapel Hill: London, 1992.

————. "Political Antisemitism in the Interwar Period." In *Jews, Antisemitism and Culture in Vienna,* edited by I. Oxaal, M. Pollak, and G. Botz. London, New York, 1987.

Pulzer, P. G. J. *The Rise of Political Anti-Semitism in Germany and Austria.* Rev. ed. Cambridge, 1988.

Schneider, Gertrude. *Exile and Destruction: The Fate of Austrian Jews, 1938-1945.* Westport, 1995.

INDEX OF NAMES

INDEX OF PLACES

INDEX OF ORGANIZATIONS AND INSTITUTIONS

The following is a selective index of major organizations and institutions.